Advice and Support:

The Early Years of the United States Army in Vietnam 1941-1960

by

Ronald H. Spector

THE FREE PRESS
A Division of Macmillan, Inc.
New York

Collier Macmillan Publishers
London

Preface to The Free Press Edition
Copyright © 1985 by The Free Press
                    A Division of Macmillan, Inc.

The Free Press
A Division of Macmillan, Inc.
866 Third Avenue, New York, N.Y. 10022

Collier Macmillan Canada, Inc.

First Free Press Paperback Edition 1985

First published by the Center of Military History,
United States Army, Washington, D.C., in 1983.

Printed in the United States of America

printing number

1 2 3 4 5 6 7 8 9 10

Library of Congress Cataloging in Publication Data

United States Army in Vietnam
  Advice and support.

  Reprint. Originally published: United States Army in
Vietnam. Washington, D.C. : Center for Military History :
For sale by the Supt of Docs., 1983.
  Bibliography: p.
  Includes index.
  Contents: [1] 1941-1960.
  1. Vietnam—History, Military. 2. Vietnam—History—
20th century. 3. United States. Army—History.
4. United States—Foreign relations—Vietnam. 5. Vietnam
—Foreign relations—United States. I. Spector,
Ronald H.   II. Title.
[DS556.8.U55 1985]   959.704   84-25971
ISBN 0-02-930370-2

United States Army in Vietnam

David F. Trask, General Editor

Advisory Committee

(As of 1 January 1982)

U.S. Army Center of Military History

iii

. . . **to Those Who Served**

Foreword

With the publication of this volume the United States Army Center of Military History inaugurates the United States Army in Vietnam series. This comprehensive new collection of historical studies continues the Army's attempt to record its role in major conflicts, an effort begun in the earlier United States Army in World War II and United States Army in the Korean War series. *Advice and Support: The Early Years, 1941–1960* is the first of three volumes that will treat the Army's effort to advise the South Vietnamese. Other titles in the series will describe combat operations; the Army's role in pacification, logistics, communications, engineer operations, medical support, and training; relations with the media; and activities at the Department of the Army level.

The present volume describes the activities of the U.S. Army in Vietnam during World War II, military advice and assistance to the French government during the immediate postwar years, and the advisory program that developed after the Geneva Agreements of 1954. Its scope ranges from high-level policy decisions to low-echelon advisory operations in the field, presented against a background of relevant military and political developments. The author enjoyed access to the official records of the period and examined personal papers, interviews, other documentary sources, and miscellaneous published materials. Useful not only as a study of military assistance but as a view of the Army as an agent of national policy, this volume is a fitting introduction to the overall study of the conflict in Vietnam.

Washington, D.C.

JAMES L. COLLINS, JR.
Brigadier General, USA
Chief of Military History

The Author

Ronald H. Spector is a graduate of Johns Hopkins University and received his M.A. and Ph.D. degrees from Yale University. He served as a field historian with the U.S. Marine Corps in Vietnam during 1968 and 1969 and is a major in the Marine Corps Reserve. He was assistant professor of history at Louisiana State University from 1969 until 1971, when he joined the U.S. Army Center of Military History. During 1977–78 he was a Fulbright senior lecturer in India. He is presently associate professor of history at the University of Alabama.

Dr. Spector is the author of *Eagle Against the Sun: The American War with Japan* (The Free Press, 1985), *Admiral of the New Empire: The Life and Career of George Dewey* and *Professors of War: The Naval War College and the Development of the Naval Profession.*

Preface to the Free Press Edition

The preliminary work for this book was begun in the fall of 1971, at a time when the My Lai incident was still being discussed in the media and the Vietnam War was good for a heated argument at any party or office rap session. At that time the possibility that the Army really wished to have a comprehensive, multi-volume history of the war, or that such a work would meet with any degree of interest or even credibility on the part of the public, seemed remote indeed. Fortunately, individuals more farsighted than I had already set the work in motion. Mr. Charles B. MacDonald, then Chief of the U.S. Army Center's Current History Branch, had established a close working relationship with Army Chief of Staff General William C. Westmoreland. General Westmoreland encouraged his former subordinate commanders to write short monographs on their professional experiences in the war and to deposit their official files with the Center of Military History. General Westmoreland's own extensive papers were deposited there. With the help of Mr. Vincent Demma and Mr. Charles V.P. von Luttichau, who had been with the Vietnam project since its inception, papers of other key figures, such as Lt. General Samuel T. Williams and Lt. General John W. O'Daniel, were acquired and a series of oral history interviews begun. Thomas Scoville, who had served with the Civil Operations and Revolutionary Development Support (CORDS) organization during military service in Vietnam, joined the Center in 1969 and was instrumental in obtaining important records of former CORDS leaders.

Although the Center of Military History had established an enviable reputation for high quality, accuracy, and objectivity with its *U.S. Army in World War II* series, many historians believed that the Vietnam War was too complex and controversial, the Army's role too unusual, for the Center to be able to produce anything similar for the Vietnam period. Writing in 1972, Peter Paret declared that though the official histories of World War II had been a success, "it is questionable whether they provide satisfactory models for interpreting more recent war."[1] Actually, though the operations and records of the Vietnam War were considerably different from those of World War II, the techniques, standards, and procedures established by the Center through many years of compiling the World War II histories proved extremely valuable in preparing the Vietnam series.

Since the time that this book was begun, there have been significant changes in the public's attitude toward and interest in the Vietnam conflict and in the nature of research on the war. During the 1960s most of the research and writing

---

[1]Peter Paret, "The History of War," in Felix Gilbert and Stephen R. Graubard, *Historical Studies Today* (New York: Norton 1972), p. 379.

concerning the war was done by opponents of American involvement in Southeast Asia. By the end of the 1970s, however, most serious research on the war was being carried out by former participants in the conflict, such as Douglas Blaufarb, Douglas Kinnard, Robert Komer, Herbert Schandler, and Harry Summers, or former journalists such as Peter Braestrup, Arnold Isaacs, and Don Oberdorfer. Many, although by no means all, of these authors tended to suggest that the war might have been won, or at least brought to a more satisfactory conclusion, if certain decisions or courses of action had been taken; if air power had been properly applied, if pacification had received more attention and support, if the press and the public had been better informed about the real nature of the war, if political and military leaders had better understood the type of war and enemy they were fighting.

While many of the writers on the war in the 1960s and early 70s believed that the Communists had, in effect, won the war by 1950 or certainly by 1960, many of the later writers tended to ignore the period prior to 1963, or treat it as irrelevant. They argued that whatever mistakes the U.S. and South Vietnamese governments may have made before 1965, whatever the degree of Communist success in the South, the massive application of American power and technology after that date fundamentally transformed the situation, and, in effect, cancelled out what had gone before. The idea that the appropriate use of American power will provide a satisfactory outcome to even the most intractable problem in the Third World is a far from novel one. It was succinctly, if inelegantly, expressed in the slogan which one saw everywhere in Vietnam, "Once we have them by the balls, their hearts and minds will follow." The work presented here suggests a fundamentally different conclusion, but one which was also embodied in an expression commonly heard in Vietnam, "You can't make somethin' out of nothin'."

From the beginning of its continuing involvement in Vietnam in 1950, until 1975 the United States was continually placed in the position of supporting regimes with no popular following and consequently little chance of remaining in power. As Jeffrey Race observed in the 1960s, "... the fact that the Saigon government which the U.S. supports is corrupt and perpetuates an oppressive social order is not an inconvenient handicap but the heart of the problem."[2]

In the first IndoChina War the French, with their puppet Vietnamese regimes, could hope to win only through granting genuine independence to Vietnam. Yet since the French were fighting in IndoChina primarily to perpetuate their rule, they could never hope to gain popular support. From the beginning, American leaders recognized the contradiction between their aim of keeping France in the war and pressing her to move closer to real independence for Vietnam. But the alternative of a Communist-dominated Vietnam was so unacceptable that Americans focused only upon the absolute necessity of saving the French from defeat.

The tendency to see the consequences of Communist victory in Vietnam as so dire as to justify any scheme to avoid it, no matter how costly or uncertain, was a common thread running through all American efforts in Vietnam. Indeed an echo may be heard today in the U.S. government's justifications of its programs

[2]Jeffrey Race, "Unlearned Lessons of Vietnam," *Yale Review* LXVI, Dec. 1976, p. 165.

in the Middle East and Latin America. These programs are usually discussed in terms of the urgent need to prevent the spread of Communist influence in those regions and the unfavorable consequences for the U.S. should the Communists succeed. The possible unfavorable consequences of the programs themselves and, more important, their chances of success, are seldom noted. On the one occasion when the costs and benefits of U.S. involvement in Vietnam were carefully weighed, thanks to the skillful advocacy of General Ridgway and his staff during the Dien Bien Phu crisis, the U.S. drew back from taking the plunge.

Following the defeat and gradual withdrawal of the French, the U.S. once again found itself backing a weak and unpopular anti-communist regime led by Ngo Dinh Diem. The Joint Chiefs of Staff recognized that the Diem regime lacked a competent leader and popular support. They doubted that such a government could build a viable military force to face the Communists. Secretary of State Dulles, however, in a neat inversion of the problem, bludgeoned the military into approving a military assistance program on the assumption that a strong army would somehow produce a strong government and society.

Dulles' idea that massive aid, technical assistance, money, and American determination would somehow produce a South Vietnam able to deal with the Communist threat was to become a continuing theme in the next two decades. As one former American advisor recalled, "The illusion was that somehow better management by the Americans would substitute for bad government by the South Vietnamese."[3] Every evidence of failure, every breakdown, every shortcoming of the Vietnamese government was met with added infusions of American advisors, organization charts, money, and weapons.

Added to this propensity to try to make something out of nothing was an American ignorance of Vietnamese history and society so massive and all-encompassing that two decades of federally-funded fellowships, crash language programs, television specials, and campus teach-ins made hardly a dent. In chapter 1 of the present work I attempt to show how infrequent and tenuous were American contacts with Vietnam before 1945 and what little knowledge of IndoChina there was in the U.S. even among specialists. U.S. contacts with Japan and China, however distorted by mutual suspicion, ignorance and prejudice, were rich and varied in comparison to those with Southeast Asia. As late as 1960, fewer than a dozen of the hundreds of Americans in Vietnam could carry on a conversation in Vietnamese. (By contrast, hundreds of Vietnamese had been force-fed English.)

If there is any lesson to be drawn from the unhappy tale of American involvement in Vietnam in the 1940s and 50s, it is that before the United States sets out to make something out of nothing in some other corner of the globe, American leaders might consider the historical and social factors involved and the likelihood of winning, instead of simply pondering the awful consequences of losing.

October, 1984

---

[3]William F. Long, "Counter-Insurgency: Corrupting Concept," *U.S. Naval Institute Proceedings*, April 1979, p. 60.

Preface

This book traces the origins of the Army's long, and frequently unhappy, involvement in Indochina from World War II to the end of the Eisenhower administration. In order to place that involvement in context, I have frequently found it necessary to describe at some length the evolution of overall U.S. policy toward Indochina as well. The focus of the work, however, is American military involvement. Those readers seeking a comprehensive history of U.S.-Vietnam relations, the political development of North and South Vietnam, or the international and legal ramifications of the wars in Indochina may refer to the many excellent works on those subjects cited in the footnotes and the Bibliographical Note.

While this book does not cover all aspects of American policy toward Vietnam, I believe the reader will find that this examination of the activities of Americans on the scene sheds considerable light on that policy. He will also agree, I think, that frequently U.S. actions in Vietnam were shaped far more by the beliefs and decisions of Americans in Saigon than by those in Washington.

The Vietnam War has left a legacy of controversy concerning most major American actions and decisions as well as those of our enemies and allies. I have no expectation that the conclusions reached in this account will meet with universal agreement on the part of former participants in, and students of, the conflict. Nevertheless, I hope they will agree that the events and decisions have been described fairly, accurately, and without bias toward any particular organization or individual.

In the course of research and writing of this book I have received the generous support of a large number of people. Brig. Gen. James L. Collins, Jr., Chief of Military History, was a constant source of support throughout, as were Col. John E. Jessup, Jr., and Col. James W. Ransone, successively chiefs of the center's Histories Division. I owe a special debt of gratitude to Col. James W. Dunn, the present Histories Division chief, who overcame many obstacles in the process of preparing the book for publication. Charles V. P. von Luttichau and Vincent H. Demma began this project as a monograph in the early 1960s. Mr. Demma also generously shared with me many of the documents he has gathered in connection with research for the successor volume, now in preparation. Maj. Arthur Chapa, USAR, performed much of the basic research upon which Chapter 18 is based during his tour of active duty at the center in 1978. Charles B. MacDonald, former chief of the Current History Branch (now Southeast Asia Branch), guided the first draft to completion, while his successor, Stanley L. Falk, aided and supported me in the many tasks connected with readying the book for publication.

I have also benefited greatly from the advice of the official review panel, under the chairmanship of Maurice Matloff, then chief historian, which included Vincent Demma, William J. Duiker, Col. James Dunn, Maj. Gen. Edward G. Lansdale, Charles B. MacDonald, and Robert Ross Smith.

In addition to the panel members, many other individuals generously read and commented on the manuscript. They include Emily Brown, Edmund Gullion, Robert H. Ferrell, Gerald C. Hickey, Col. James I. Muir, Lt. Gen. Samuel L. Myers, Col. Ernest P. Lasche, Jeffrey Race, Anna Rubino Schneider, General Matthew B. Ridgway, Reginald Ungern, Lt. Gen. Samuel T. Williams, Lt. Gen. Robert C. Taber, Col. Nathaniel P. Ward, and Brig. Gen. Charles A. Symroski. Lt. Gen. James M. Gavin and Lt. Gen. Thomas J. H. Trapnell also read the manuscript and remained constant sources of information and encouragement throughout the period of the book's preparation.

Like all researchers in the voluminous yet elusive records of the Vietnam conflict, I have depended heavily on the knowledge and perseverance of many capable archivists, records managers, and fellow historians in the federal government. I am especially grateful to William H. Cunliffe, John Taylor, and Edward Reese of the Military Archives Division, National Archives and Records Service, Sandra Rangel, Cathy Nicastro, Pat Dowling, and Sally Marks of the Diplomatic Branch, and Mary M. Wolfskill of the Library of Congress. Dean C. Allard of the Naval Historical Center was as usual a source of ideas and information as well as a sure guide to Navy records. Benis M. Frank of the Marine Corps Historical Center facilitated my research in the Marine Corps oral history collection. Paul L. Taborn and John H. Hatcher of the Adjutant General's Office and Theresa Farrell of the State Department took time from their many other duties as records managers to aid me in my search for relevant material. My former colleagues Robert J. Watson and Willard J. Webb of the Historical Division of the Joint Chiefs of Staff helped greatly in my research in the records of that organization.

I am also grateful to George H. Curtis and Sue Jackson of the Dwight D. Eisenhower Library, George Chalou and Michael Miller of the Suitland Federal Records Center, and Nancy Bressler of the Princeton University Library and to General J. Lawton Collins for permission to review portions of his personal files relating to Vietnam. Ann P. Crumpler of the U.S. Army Corps of Engineers Library and Carol I. Anderson of the center's library patiently bore with my many requests for assistance and always found the sometimes arcane material I required. Special thanks are due to Edward L. Morse, former special assistant to the under secretary of state, for his timely assistance at a critical moment in the preparation of the volume.

Finally, I am grateful to fellow players in the Giant Vietnam Jigsaw Puzzle Game—Robert Blum, Lt. Col. John D. Bergen, Sam Adams, Richard A. Hunt, Jeffrey J. Clarke, Neal Petersen, Oscar P. Fitzgerald, Trumbull Higgins, Joel D. Meyerson, Gary R. Hess, Jack Shulimson, George L. MacGarrigle, and William M. Hammond—for advice and criticism. My editors, Catherine A. Heerin, Barbara H. Gilbert, and Joycelyn M. Bobo, ably led by John Elsberg, Editor in Chief, displayed remarkable fortitude in coping with the idiosyncrasies of the author. Arthur S. Hardyman, Chief, Graphic Arts Branch, and Howell C. Brewer, Jr., respectively, planned and prepared the artwork and attempted, with little success, to improve the author's knowledge of geography. Mr. Hardyman worked with me in selecting the illustrations.

This first volume in the U.S. Army's history of the Vietnam War is dedicated to all who served in that conflict. In this connection the author wishes to recall friends and members of his unit who died in Vietnam: Christopher Bell, Kurt C. Hussmann, Timothy John O'Keefe, Thomas Rainy, and Morton Singer.

The author alone is responsible for interpretations and conclusions, as well as for any errors that may appear.

Washington, D.C., 1983   RONALD H. SPECTOR

Contents

PART ONE

The American Discovery of Vietnam

PART TWO

The Franco – Viet Minh War

PART THREE

Going It Alone

Table

Charts

Maps

Illustrations

    Illustrations courtesy of the following sources: pp. 8, 9, 86, 130, 163, 165, 173, 183, and 205, *Indochine;* pp. 74, 276, and 323, Department of State; pp. 39, 78, 82, 91, 113, 226, and 245, National Archives; p. 132, Library of Congress; pp. 53 and 62, Brig. Gen. Philip E. Gallagher Papers; pp. 366 and 369, Lt. Gen. Lionel C. McGarr; pp. 283, 284, 287 (top), 294, 306, and 341, Lt. Gen. Samuel L. Myers; pp. 216, 252, and 265, Lt. Gen. John W. O'Daniel Papers; pp. 234 and 246, James H. Tate; p. 156, Lt. Gen. Thomas J. H. Trapnell; pp. 287 (bottom) and 377, Col. Nathaniel P. Ward; p. 54, Lt. Col. Joseph W. A. Whitehorne; and pp. 256, 257, 258, and 292, Lt. Gen. Samuel T. Williams; p. 16, United Press International; p. 81, Douglas Pike; and p. 244, Maj. Gen. Edward G. Lansdale. All other illustrations from the files of Department of Defense and U.S. Army Center of Military History.

1. Grand Chancelier du Royaume 6. 7. Mandarins de Lettres
2. 3. 4. Mandarins ou Officiers de Guerre ou Officiers de Judicature
5. Chancelier Chef de toutes les Jurisdictions. 8. Premier Huissier

Royal Officials of Tonkin

PART ONE

The American Discovery of Vietnam

1

Conquest and Revolt

The author of a widely read history of the Vietnam conflict observed that "in a sense we discovered Vietnam in 1954."[1] This American discovery came about as a result of the imminent collapse of French power in Indochina. The factors involved in the French collapse went back many years, and in some respects centuries, before the 1950s. These factors, while clear enough to present-day historians, were not at all obvious to the American leaders of the 1950s, who for the most part lacked a knowledge of Vietnamese culture and history. Like the European discoverers of America who believed that the local inhabitants were citizens of China and painted them dressed in European clothing, the American discoverers of Vietnam viewed that country from the vantage point of their own preconceptions.

Nine Centuries of War

The recorded history of Vietnam begins in 208 B.C., and many historians trace the origins of the Vietnamese to an even earlier period.[2] For over a thousand years, from 111 B.C. until A.D. 939, Vietnam was ruled as a part of the Chinese Empire. Although the Vietnamese were heavily influenced by Chinese culture, they never willingly accepted Chinese rule. Sporadic revolts against the Chinese overlords occurred throughout the thousand years, notably in A.D. 39 under the semilegendary Trung sisters, in 248 under Trieu Au, and in 542 under Ly Bon. Independence was finally attained in the tenth century under the leadership of the Ly, Vietnam's first ruling dynasty.[3]

[1]Chester L. Cooper, *The Lost Crusade: America in Vietnam* (New York: Dodd Mead, 1970), p. 16.
[2]Joseph Buttinger, *Vietnam: A Political History* (New York: Praeger, 1968), pp. 3–21; D. G. E. Hall, *History of South-East Asia* (New York: St. Martin's, 1955), pp. 169–70.
[3]Le Thanh Kho, *Le Viet Nam: Histoire et Civilisation* (Paris: Éditions de Minuit, 1955), pp. 98–134.

The Vietnam which emerged from Chinese rule comprised the Red River valley and a narrow coastal strip stretching from the present-day city of Thanh Hoa south to the vicinity of the modern town of Vinh. To the north was China and to the south were other powerful neighbors. In the southwest was the great Khmer Empire of Cambodia, then at the height of its power, and to the immediate south was the kingdom of Champa. The Chams were a people of Indian cultural traditions who were more or less constantly at war with the Sinicized Vietnamese.

The Vietnamese were more than able to hold their own against those formidable neighbors. The Chams were defeated in the eleventh century and again in the fourteenth. Each time a further portion of their kingdom passed under Vietnamese rule. Finally, in 1471, the last remnants of Champa, in what is now central Vietnam, became part of the expanding Vietnamese state. In the interim, the Vietnamese had succeeded in repulsing an invasion by the Mongols in the fourteenth century and a Chinese attempt at reconquest in the fifteenth.[4]

By the mid-eighteenth century the Vietnamese reached the Gulf of Siam (Thailand), occupying new territories and wresting others from the Khmers. By that time, however, the traditional machinery of government, patterned after, but far less effective than, the government of imperial China, had broken down. At the imperial capital of Hue in the central part of the country, the emperors still reigned as the religious and symbolic head of the nation, but actual power since the early seventeenth century had been held by two rival families, the Trinh, who controlled the north, and the Nguyen, who ruled the south.[5]

In 1774 three brothers, called the Tay Son after the name of their native village, led a successful revolt in the south against the Nguyen. They then turned on the Trinh, driving them from Hue and capturing Hanoi. In 1787 one of the Tay Son brothers deposed the moribund imperial dynasty and declared himself emperor under the name Quang Trung. One year later he successfully defeated a Chinese expeditionary force sent to restore the old dynasty, but his reign was short. In a long and bitter war, the last survivor of the Nguyen family, Nguyen Anh, with the aid of French military advisers and technicians, destroyed the Tay Son and in 1802 ascended the throne of a united Vietnam as the Emperor Gia Long.

By any standard, the long history of Vietnam presents an impressive picture of martial prowess, of victory against odds, of violent and often successful resistance to domestic oppression and foreign conquest. Yet on the eve of Vietnam's emergence on the international scene, few Americans appeared to appreciate that history. In 1945, for example, President Franklin

---

[4]A brief account, based on Vietnamese sources, is in David G. Marr, *Vietnamese Anticolonialism, 1885−1925* (Berkeley: University of California Press, 1971), pp. 11−17.

[5]Truong Buu Lam, "Intervention vs. Tribute in Sino-Vietnamese Relations," in John K. Fairbank, ed., *The Chinese World Order: Traditional China's Foreign Relations*, East Asian Series no. 32 (Cambridge: Harvard University Press, 1968), pp. 165−72; Buttinger, *Vietnam: A Political History*, pp. 49−53.

4

The Imperial Palace in Hue

D. Roosevelt casually remarked to Josef Stalin that "the Indochinese were people of small stature . . . and were not war-like."[6] Roosevelt and the handful of Americans who concerned themselves in any way with Vietnam during the 1930s and 1940s viewed it primarily through the eyes of the French.

French Indochina

The French conquest of Vietnam and the rest of what became known as French Indochina had occurred in two stages. Cambodia and the southern areas of Vietnam were occupied during the 1850s and 1860s, and central Vietnam and the Red River valley, in the north, in the early 1880s. Although the Vietnamese fiercely resisted, they suffered from a lack of knowledge of modern military techniques, from a paucity of modern weapons, and from poor coordination and leadership by the moribund and increasingly unpopular imperial government at Hue. The Vietnamese were forced to submit, but

[6]Department of State, *Foreign Relations of the United States: The Conferences at Malta and Yalta, 1945* (Washington, 1955), p. 770.

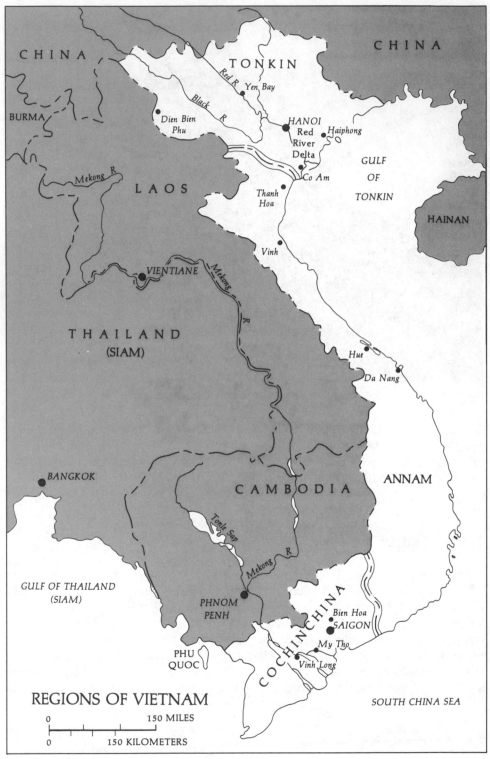

REGIONS OF VIETNAM

0   150 MILES

0   150 KILOMETERS

MAP 1

sporadic movements of resistance by Nghia Quan ("righteous armies") or guerrillas continued to the end of the century.[7]

The French divided Indochina into five parts. They ruled the southern part, Cochinchina, where the local officials had refused to cooperate, directly as a colony of France; central Vietnam, called Annam, and northern Vietnam, called Tonkin, along with Cambodia and Laos (parts of the latter were wrested from Siam in 1893), became protectorates. (*Map 1*) In Annam, the emperor and his traditional officials continued to conduct the ordinary business of government under the watchful eye of a French "resident superior." Both protectorates and the colony of Cochinchina were subject to the authority of the French governor-general of Indochina with headquarters in Hanoi.

To American observers, before World War II, this French Indochina appeared unexciting, uninteresting, and unimportant. The United States had no tradition of cultural and commercial relations with Indochina as she had long maintained with China and Japan.[8] A young American journalist who visited Haiphong in 1923, Gertrude Emerson, found a total of six Americans in that fourth largest city of Vietnam. "An American consul was non-existent, there was not even a tourist bureau to offer expensive tours. . . . three weeks before, I myself had never heard of Haiphong."[9] In the 1920s there were less than a hundred Americans living in Vietnam. Many were Protestant missionaries of the Christian and Missionary Alliance Church who operated modest missions in Saigon, Da Nang, My Tho, Hanoi, Vinh Long, and Bien Hoa.[10]

Until 1940 when a consular office was opened in Hanoi, American interests in Indochina were looked after by a single consul in Saigon. In 1923, the same year Emerson visited Haiphong, that American consul described Indochina as "almost cut off, commercially, from the United States." Opportunities for American business improved somewhat in the late 1920s with the inauguration of a direct Saigon–San Francisco steamship line. American exports of petroleum products, canned goods, and machinery to Indochina grew steadily throughout the interwar period, even after the steamship line became a casualty of the Great Depression in 1937. But American trade with

[7]On the French conquest of Indochina and the Vietnamese response, see John F. Cady, *Roots of French Imperialism in Eastern Asia* (Ithaca: Cornell University Press, 1954); Truong Buu Lam, *Patterns of Vietnamese Response to Foreign Intervention, 1858–1900*, Southeast Asia Studies no. 11 (New Haven: Yale University Press, 1967); Milton E. Osborne, *French Presence in Cochinchina and Cambodia: Rule and Response, 1859–1905* (Ithaca: Cornell University Press, 1969); and Marr, *Vietnamese Anticolonialism*.

[8]For a fuller discussion of American views of Southeast Asia in the interwar period, see Ronald H. Spector, "European Colonialism and American Attitudes Toward Southeast Asia: The Case of Indochina, 1919–1941," vol. 1, *Proceedings of the Seventh International Association of Historians of Asia Conference* (Bangkok, 1978), pp. 269–89.

[9]Gertrude Emerson, "Backwaters of Empire in French Indo-China," *Asia* 23 (September 1923): 672.

[10]Am Consul, Saigon (Harris M. Cookingham), to Dept of State, 23 Nov 27, 851G.0014, Saigon Post records, Record Group (RG) 84, National Archives, Washington, D.C. Although few in number, these missionaries were looked on with great suspicion by the French. In 1940 an article in *Le Courrier d'Haiphong* alleged that their efforts to combat opium addiction among the Vietnamese were actually a plot to encourage the use of American cigarettes instead and that the American missionary effort was being funded by the tobacco industry. Am Consul, Saigon (Peter Flood), to Dept of State, 3 Mar 40, 851G.00/12, RG 84.

Military Mandarin *in traditional uniform.*

Indochina was never a significant item in the total of American exports. American consular officers pointed out that such factors as discriminatory import duties and transit dues tended to discourage American businessmen from trading in Indochina.[11] Indochina did export large amounts of rubber to the United States, but this trade was entirely in the hands of the French.

If French Indochina was of some minor concern to businessmen, American popular interest in the region was almost nil. Articles about Indochina in the *New York Times* averaged less than six per year from 1919 until 1940. In popular magazines, articles on Indochina were even less frequent, averaging about two per year in such journals as *Asia* and the *National Geographic* that specialized in stories about exotic areas.[12] John Gunther's *Inside Asia*, one of the most widely read American books about Asia published between the wars, devoted less than 2 of its 659 pages to Indochina, about the same amount of space that was devoted to the maharaja of Mysore and somewhat less than that given to the rajah of Sarawak.[13]

[11]Am Consul, Saigon, to Dept of State, 26 Jul 23; ibid., 7 Jul 38. Both in RG 59.
[12]*New York Times Index, 1919–1940; Reader's Guide to Periodical Literature, 1919–1940.* Popular magazines are defined rather arbitrarily here to mean magazines intended for the general public and indexed in the *Reader's Guide to Periodical Literature.*
[13]See John Gunther, *Inside Asia* (London: Hamish Hamilton, 1939).

Commander of the Imperial Guard *at Hue, early nineteenth century.*

The image of Indochina which Americans on the scene conveyed to Washington was of a rather somnolent, backward corner of the French Empire. The French were always trying to "develop" it, and the "natives" were contented but lazy. "Indochina is one of the quietest portions of Asia," reported the American consul in 1924. "The Annamites as a race are very lazy and not prone to be ambitious. As for the Laotians and Cambodians [they] have hardly been touched by civilization and are even lazier than the Annamites."[14] Another American diplomat, Henry I. Waterman, gave a similar but more colorful description of Laos. "Laos . . . is still in a state of savagery with most of the inhabitants roaming the jungles without clothing and still killing their meat with poisoned arrows."[15] The veteran Far East news correspondent Frank Warren described the Vietamese as "without any keen desires, disdaining money and clothes, living their low grade existence in perpetual melancholy."[16] In 1927 the American consul suggested that the State Department excuse him from the requirement to submit monthly political reports because "there were almost no political developments to report."[17]

[14]Am Consul, Saigon (Leland L. Smith), to State Dept, 28 Aug 24, 851G.001, RG 84.
[15]Ibid. (Henry Waterman) to State Dept, 16 May 30, Saigon Post records, RG 84.
[16]Frank Warren, "On the Mandarin Road to Hue," *Asia* 39 (October 1939):563.
[17]Under Secy of State (Nelson T. Johnson) to Am Consul, Saigon (Harris M. Cookingham), 29 Nov 27, 851G.0016, RG 59.

Virginia Thompson, who visited Indochina and published a highly regarded study in 1937, echoed these reports. She emphasized the apathy, insensitivity, and placidity of the Vietnamese, which she attributed to their inadequate diet and the intense tropical heat. The Vietnamese lacked "the driving power given by strong desires." Their intelligence was "keen" but their character "weak." So convincing was Thompson's picture of the backwardness of the Vietnamese that her work was cited by the British Foreign Office during World War II to buttress its argument that Indochina should be returned to France.[18]

In contrast to this portrait of a backward and changeless society (as late as 1963 Ambassador Henry Cabot Lodge would describe Vietnam as "a medieval country"), Vietnam actually was undergoing a number of significant transformations which had been precipitated, if not understood, by the French. One immediate consequence of the French conquest of Vietnam had been the destruction or drastic modification of traditional social groupings within Vietnamese society. In central and northern Vietnam, the traditional elite of Confucian-trained scholar-bureaucrats disappeared or survived with greatly reduced power and prerogatives simply as an appendage to the French colonial bureaucracy. The decay of this leadership group greatly weakened the whole fabric of traditional Vietnamese society and removed one of the strongest conservative elements in the country.[19]

The rural village, the most important institution in Vietnam, also drastically changed. The traditional Vietnamese village was autonomous, self-contained, and largely self-supporting. The villagers paid their taxes as a group and were collectively responsible to the imperial or regional government in all matters of law and ritual.[20] This village structure was profoundly shaken when the French introduced such "modern" measures as individual taxation, money, private property, elections, and a census.[21]

By weakening the traditional Vietnamese leadership group and promoting the legal autonomy of individual villagers without establishing new forms of political organization to encompass these changes, "the French were inviting the disintegration of the Vietnamese social system."[22] By the beginning of the twentieth century that disintegration was already well advanced. What American and other observers saw as a traditional and unchanging Vietnam was in fact a society in the midst of transition.

French rule furthered this transition also by contributing to the creation of new social groupings. As the French encouraged production, a small but growing working class emerged in the coal mines and on the rubber plantations. In the south, the French sold land seized during their conquest of

[18]F478 166/61, 26 Jan 44, sub: Record of French in Indochina, FO 371 41723 Foreign Office records, Public Records Office, London.

[19]Quote from Alexander B. Woodside, *Community and Revolution in Modern Vietnam* (Boston: Houghton Mifflin, 1976), p. 248; see also pp. 26–27.

[20]Ibid., pp. 8–9, 27, 130–31.

[21]Paul Mus, "Vietnam: A Nation Off Balance," *Yale Review* 41 (Summer 1952):526–29.

[22]Woodside, *Community and Revolution*, p. 119; see also John T. McAlister, Jr., *Vietnam: The Origins of Revolution* (Garden City: Doubleday, 1971), p. 45.

Cochinchina to French colonists and wealthy Vietnamese in large lots. By 1930, 45 percent of the arable land in the Mekong Delta was owned by the wealthiest 2 percent of the population.[23] With landholding so highly concentrated, most of the population in the south was reduced to the status of small tenants or agricultural laborers.

The wealthy landowners, together with the Vietnamese in urban areas who held administrative posts in the French colonial bureaucracy and law courts or who owned businesses, constituted a new elite. Many were absentee landlords. Educated in Western-style schools, often in France, and living mainly in the larger urban areas, these bureaucrats, large landowners, professionals, and businessmen were almost as far removed from the outlook and life-style of the mass of rural Vietnamese as were the French. Yet to Americans and most Frenchmen this small clique constituted "the Vietnamese." It was the only portion of the local population which Westerners could easily communicate with and understand. For many years, both before and after World War II, Americans equated the opinions of this small elite with the views and desires of the Vietnamese people as a whole.

Neither French nor American observers of Indochina before World War II appear to have had any inkling that these social and political developments could someday coalesce to produce a movement that would drive the French from Vietnam. On the contrary, European colonialism in Asia, particularly in Vietnam, appeared stronger and more vigorous than ever. Even Ho Chi Minh in the early 1930s saw France not as a declining power but as one bent on new imperialist ventures.[24]

Developments since the turn of the century seemed to confirm the assumption of observers that colonialism was here to stay. The last scattered anti-French revolts led by scholar-bureaucrats in the name of the old monarchy had been easily snuffed out by the end of the 1890s.[25] During World War I the French had kept Vietnam peaceful and quiet with less than 10,000 troops and about 15,000 Vietnamese auxiliaries, while sending more than 43,000 Vietnamese to Europe to serve on the Western Front.[26] The indifferent showing of these Vietnamese troops on European battlefields only reinforced the idea that the Vietnamese could never seriously challenge a Western power. During the interwar period American observers generally saw no evidence that the Vietnamese had either the desire or the capacity for self-government. Most tended to accept the view of the conservative French colonials that "the natives" were too backward to be entrusted with Western-style political rights and civil liberties.[27]

At the end of the 1920s a wave of violent anti-French incidents swept Vietnam. The moving force behind them was the Vietnamese Nationalist

[23]McAlister, *Vietnam: Origins of Revolution*, pp. 64–65.
[24]Woodside, *Community and Revolution*, p. 171; Spector, "European Colonialism and American Attitudes Toward Southeast Asia," p. 272.
[25]Marr, *Vietnam Anticolonialism*, pp. 47–76.
[26]McAlister, *Vietnam: Origins of Revolution*, p. 62.
[27]Am Consul, Saigon (Leland L. Smith), to Dept of State, 28 Aug 24, RG 59; ibid. (Cookingham) to Dept of State, 24 Oct 27 and 5 Jun 28, both in RG 84.

French Colonial Troops *in Saigon between the World Wars.*

Party, the Viet Nam Quoc Dan Dang. Known by its initials, VNQDD, the party was a clandestine organization of civil servants, teachers, small shopkeepers, and militiamen, loosely modeled on the Chinese Kuomintang. Its aim was nothing less than the expulsion of the French.[28]

On 9 February 1929, members of the VNQDD murdered a Frenchman named Bazin, the director of the French labor bureau which recruited workers for French plantations in southern Vietnam and on the islands of New Caledonia in the Pacific. The contract labor system which Bazin represented was notorious as little more than "a scandalous slave trade" that sent hundreds of Vietnamese for long years of labor on the French Pacific islands, from which many never returned alive.[29] By their act the young Nationalists of the VNQDD hoped to increase their prestige and widen their support among the population.

One year after the murder of Bazin, two companies of Vietnamese militiamen, subverted by the VNQDD, mutinied at Yen Bay and killed five of their French officers and noncommissioned officers as well as six Vietnamese who

[28]Joseph Buttinger, *Vietnam: A Dragon Embattled*, vol. 1, *From Colonialism to the Vietminh* (New York: Praeger, 1967), pp. 207–09; Woodside, *Community and Revolution*, pp. 59–61; McAlister, *Vietnam: Origins of Revolution*, pp. 79–81.
[29]Virginia Thompson, *French Indochina* (New York: Macmillan, 1937), p. 164.

refused to join them. After French and loyal Vietnamese troops quickly suppressed the mutiny, the colonial authorities began a roundup of VNQDD members. French aircraft bombed the village of Co Am, the reputed head-quarters of the rebels in the Red River Delta, and killed two hundred villagers.[30] Most of the members of the VNQDD were quickly captured, and the leaders were executed.

Although these measures effectively removed the immediate threat to colonial rule represented by the VNQDD, the long-term consequences would prove disastrous to the French in later years. For into the vacuum created by the destruction of the VNQDD stepped the Communists. Ironically, in searching for a nationalistic alternative to the Vietnamese Communist movement during the late 1940s, the French would discover that in crushing the VNQDD they had destroyed the very roots of the alternative they sought.[31]

The Communist movement in Vietnam dated from the mid-1920s when the Tonkinese Ho Chi Minh had formed the Vietnam Revolutionary Youth League among a group of Vietnamese exiles living in Canton, China. Although then only about thirty-five, Ho had already established himself as a veteran revolutionary.[32] He had participated in the creation of the French Communist Party in 1920 and had spent a year in Moscow. Many graduates of a training school for cadres that Ho established at Canton returned to Vietnam to organize cells in their home districts, mainly in Tonkin.

When a wave of strikes, riots, and demonstrations swept Vietnam early in 1930 in the wake of the Yen Bay rebellion, the Communists moved to organize the peasants and industrial laborers against the French. For a while they enjoyed a limited success. In the provinces of Nghe An and Ha Tinh, the colonial authorities fled or went into hiding and were replaced by village peasant soviets under Communist leadership.[33]

By the fall of 1930, the French colonial authorities had recovered from their surprise. They brought in foreign legionnaires, other troops, and a horde of security police and suppressed the soviets with extreme brutality. An estimated 10,000 Vietnamese, many of whom had taken no part in the rebellion, were killed and another 50,000 were deported.[34] Many others suffered assault, rape, robbery, and unjust imprisonment. The conduct of the legionnaires was especially reprehensible. A French court determined, for

[30]For details of these events, see the following: McAlister, *Vietnam: Origins of Revolution*, pp. 80–91; R. B. Smith, "The Development of Opposition to French Rule in Southern Vietnam, 1880–1940," *Past and Present* 54 (February 1972): 117–21; Buttinger, *Vietnam: A Dragon Embattled*, 1:214–20; and Thompson, *French Indochina*, pp. 487–89. The bombing of Co Am is in Louis Roubaud, *Vietnam: La Tragedie Indochinoise* (Paris: Valois, 1931), p. 116.

[31]McAlister, *Vietnam: Origins of Revolution*, p. 83; see also Woodside, *Community and Revolution*, p. 62.

[32]Ho's original name, so far as can be determined, was Nguyen Sinh Cung, later changed to Nguyen Tat Thanh, and by the mid-1920s to Nguyen Ai Quoc. Because there are few family names in Vietnam, most Vietnamese are addressed by their given name, which comes last; but there are exceptions among public figures or people, such as Ho, who take a new name.

[33]William J. Duiker, "The Red Soviets of Nghe-Tinh: An Early Communist Rebellion in Vietnam," *Journal of Southeast Asian Studies* 4 (2 September 1973): 186–98.

[34]Buttinger, *Vietnam: A Dragon Embattled*, 1:213.

example, that a group of legionnaires had murdered an entire truckload of prisoners whom they were transporting to trial.[35]

It would have seemed incredible in 1930 that other legionnaires less than twenty-five years later would be outfought, outgunned, outwitted, and forced to surrender to the sons and grandsons of those same terrorized peasants and laborers at a place called Dien Bien Phu. Yet the uprisings of 1930, though effectively crushed, could be seen later as another step along a road leading inexorably to the French defeat in 1954. The Communists, though their ranks were seriously depleted, had learned valuable lessons and techniques, lessons that would serve them well in their war against the French in the 1940s.[36]

American perceptions of these developments were casual, unconcerned, and distorted, as evidenced by a long report on "communistic activities" in Indochina filed in 1930 by Henry I. Waterman, the American consul general in Saigon. Waterman's sources of information were mainly French officials and journalists, among whom a principal informant was Henri Chavigny, whose pen name was Henri de la Chevrotier. A former draft dodger and police informer who had served time for bribery and blackmail, Chavigny published *L'Impartial*, a newspaper heavily subsidized by the French colonial administration.[37] Not surprisingly, Waterman's dispatches inevitably reflected the views of the more reactionary French colonials. He attributed the outbreaks of violence to "the influence of revolutionary ideas imported from communistic China" and believed that "the agitation was primarily directed against the graft and extortion of the Vietnamese mandarin officials rather than the French."[38]

Not only Ho Chi Minh's Revolutionary Youth League, wrote Waterman, but also the VNQDD was "communistic." He described the VNQDD as led by "young men of education but without experience who became the leaders of the organization for purposes of personal aggrandizement." The VNQDD "gradually became nationalist in the sense that it became ambitious to use its communistic principles against the French. They formed their cells among the poorest and most ignorant . . . making the most absurd promises to them that they would be generals or mandarins or judges."[39]

Waterman generally accepted the official French explanation of revolutionary outbreaks as the work of a few agitators in the protectorates of Annam and Tonkin. The people of Cochinchina, under the direct rule of France, he reported, were "happy to let other people run the affairs of government since they have better living conditions than they ever had before the coming of the French."[40] Only in Annam was there fertile ground for revolution—generated by overpopulation, frequent famines, poor communications, and

---

[35]Andree Viollis, *Indochina S.O.S.* (Paris: Gallimard, 1935), p. 88; Thompson, *French Indochina*, pp. 192–93.
[36]Duiker, "The Red Soviets of Nghe-Tinh," pp. 195–97.
[37]On Chavigny, see Walter Langlois, *Andre Malraux: The Indochina Adventure* (New York: Praeger, 1966), pp. 42, 46, 86, 91.
[38]Am Consul, Saigon, to Dept of State, 16 May 30, 851G.001B/3, RG 59.
[39]Ibid.
[40]Ibid.

ignorance—but even in Annam, Waterman believed, most of the discontent was caused by the graft and extortion of Vietnamese mandarins.

In other reports Waterman tended to emphasize the terrorism and brutality of the revolutionaries and to approve the repressive measures of the French as "necessary to counter the communist policy of terrorism and extortion."[41] He quoted with approval Henri Chavigny's prediction that "the day when we place in these provinces sufficient troops, communism will disappear rapidly because the people, no longer fearing reprisals, will themselves deliver up all the communists to the authorities."[42]

One of the few American scholars of the time to deal with the events of 1930, Thomas E. Ennis, was even more inaccurate than Waterman. In writing *French Policy and Developments in Indochina*, Ennis, a West Virginia history professor, relied upon official French sources. He described the uprisings of 1930 as "controlled from Moscow" and explained the Yen Bay rebellion as the result of the machinations of Soviet agent Michael Borodin, who had, in fact, left Asia in 1927. Like Waterman, Ennis emphasized "the numerous acts of terror committed by the communists."[43]

The American press, in general, paid little attention to the events of 1930–31 in Vietnam. Ennis expressed surprise that "the French government is the only one which has experienced serious trouble in a colony and has been able to suppress detailed news of the many revolts from reaching the foreign press."[44] The Far East correspondent of the *Christian Science Monitor*, Marc T. Greene, was one of the few Americans to cover the revolt. He placed much of the blame for the uprisings upon the French. "The 'iron heel' policy of France," he wrote, "has certainly added fuel to the latent discontent of the Annamese population. . . . A heavy burden of taxation lies upon them, which holds them in an economic state not far from servitude and often casts them into jail. There is no doubt however that the high object of France—to make her possessions pay—is to be achieved if at all possible, and at whatever cost in terms of everything but money."[45] Writing four years later in the *New Republic*, British Socialist Raymond Postgate also blamed the French authorities and described instances of their brutality.[46] The *New York Times*, however, appeared to accept the explanation offered by many French officials that the Vietnamese had been "contaminated" by the spread of nationalist impulses similar to those which the "permissive" policies of the Americans and Dutch had encouraged in the Philippines and Indonesia.[47] The paper focused mainly on the effect that the unrest might have on France's posture at an upcoming disarmament conference in London.

[41]Ibid., 21 May 31, 851G.00.00B/7, RG 59.
[42]Ibid., 30 Jul 31, 851G.00B/19, RG 59.
[43]Thomas E. Ennis, *French Policy and Developments in Indochina* (Chicago: University of Chicago Press, 1936), pp. 185, 190.
[44]Ibid., p. 187.
[45]Marc T. Greene, "Shadows Over Indochina," *Asia*, December 1930, p. 678.
[46]Raymond Postate, "Echoes of a Revolt," *New Republic*, 22 May 1935.
[47]*New York Times*, 15 Feb 30.

Japanese Troops *approach Haiphong, fall 1940.*

In the mid-1930s Waterman's successor as consul in Saigon, Quincy Roberts, had begun to question the rhetoric and methods of French rule. " 'Communism' out in these parts of the world," he told the *Providence Journal*, "very often is the term used by the governing authorities to cover up a nationalistic movement."[48] Later, he reiterated that a key point "in any survey of the communist danger in French Indochina is that government officials and local press are prone to label any criticism or expression of dissatisfaction with Indochinese institutions or existing conditions as communist activity. Certainly any movement or party advocating a Commonwealth of Indochina similar to the Commonwealth of the Philippines would be called communist at once."[49] In his reports Roberts emphasized the large nationalistic ingredient in Vietnamese communism and explained that in Vietnam "the communists have abandoned strict adherence to their principles and now are ready to recruit any enemy of French imperialism regardless of whether he believes in private property, religion, etc."[50] "Repression," he wrote, "drives [both] communist and nationalist agitators under cover," and in the harsh and repressive environment of Vietnam only the Communists could provide such agi-

[48]Roberts to Marc T. Greene, 18 Feb 35, State Dept Central files, RG 59.
[49]Am Consul, Saigon, to Dept of State, 25 May 37, 851G.00, RG 59.
[50]Roberts to Dept of State, 31 Jan 36, 851G.008/22, RG 84.

tators with the type of highly disciplined clandestine organization necessary
for survival.[51]

In her *French Indochina* Virginia Thompson also acknowledged the nationalistic element in Vietnamese communism, even while emphasizing the latter's subordination to Moscow. "The orientation Nguyen Ai Quoc [Ho Chi Minh] gave to its program was nationalistic rather than communistic, which he regards as a subsequent stage. . . . Recognizing the Annamite love of property and their patriarchal family system as well as the numerical and intellectual weakness of the proletariat, he planned first to assure Annam's independence under a democratic bourgeois regime and then by a second step to integrate it into the Soviet Union."[52] Yet few Americans before World War II other than Roberts and Thompson displayed anything approaching a sophisticated understanding of the nature of nationalist opposition in Vietnam.

The Impact of War

Despite the widespread discontent of the 1930s, serious opposition to French rule probably would have been slow in developing had it not been for events during World War II. France's defeat and partial occupation by Germany in the spring of 1940 had a profound influence upon developments in Indochina. Having been at war with China since 1937, the Japanese moved swiftly to take advantage of France's distress. They demanded that the French cease to allow war materials to be sent to China from Tonkin, grant Japan free access to the raw materials of Indochina, and allow the Japanese to use Indochina as a staging area for operations against China.

Washington viewed this development with alarm. As a strong supporter of China and the only remaining power strong enough to challenge Japan in the Pacific, the United States felt obliged to try to prevent what appeared to be but a first step in new Japanese aggressive moves against Southeast Asia.[53] America, however, had few options. It urged the French to resist the Japanese demands but had to admit that it could not offer military or naval aid for the defense of Indochina.[54]

By September 1940 the French had been intimidated into allowing the Japanese transit rights and airfields in northern Indochina and the right to station troops at the port of Haiphong. The United States responded by

[51]Am Consul, Saigon, to Dept of State, 16 Jan 37, 851G.00/01, RG 59.

[52]Thompson, *French Indochina*, pp. 489–90.

[53]Memorandum for Record (MFR), Cecil W. Gray, Asst to Secy of State, 24 Jul 42, *United States–Vietnam Relations, 1945–1967: A Study Prepared by the Department of Defense*, 12 vols. (Washington, 1971), 1:A-11–A-12. A thorough discussion of American policy toward Indochina during 1940–41 may be found in William L. Langer and S. Everett Gleason, *Undeclared War, 1940–1941* (New York: Harper & Row, 1953), pp. 9–16, 641–44.

[54]Memo, Adviser on Political Relations (James C. Dunn) for Under Secy of State (Sumner Welles), 6 Aug 40, Department of State, *Foreign Relations of the United States, 1940*, vol. 4, *The Far East* (Washington, 1955), pp. 64–65.

placing an embargo on sales of high-grade fuels and scrap iron to Japan. In July 1941 the Japanese occupied the southern half of Vietnam without resistance. The French flag still flew over Vietnam and French officials still governed, but 50,000 Japanese garrisoned the country. The Japanese used airfields in the south and naval bases at Cam Ranh Bay.

The Japanese move into southern Vietnam triggered the final crisis in Japanese-American relations which precipitated the Pearl Harbor attack. It also left a legacy of anger and bad feeling on the part of both the French and the Americans. American officials saw France's actions as a supine capitulation to Japanese imperialism that opened the door for a Japanese attack on the Philippines and the British and Dutch colonies in Southeast Asia. "Indochina," wrote Admiral Harold R. Stark, chief of naval operations in 1940 and 1941, "is one of those . . . points that I have always been sore over. . . . I somehow or other always had more or less a grudge with Vichy for this particular action down there in that vital region. . . . Kamranh Bay became a very important assembly and jumping off point for the Japs in their penetration to the South."[55] The French, on the other hand, believed that the negative response by the United States to their repeated calls for aid had left them no choice but to make the best deal possible with the Japanese.[56]

Within Vietnam, France's defeat and the capitulation of the colonial authorities to Japan encouraged anticolonialist groups to launch new revolts in 1940. In the northeast leaders of the Phuc Quoc, a traditionalist and monarchical movement with close ties to Japan, took advantage of the Japanese movement into Tonkin to launch a series of uprisings in mountain regions near the Chinese border around Bac Son, while in November a more serious revolt broke out in Cochinchina where rebels cut major highways and seized public buildings in the Mekong Delta region.[57] The French quickly suppressed the rebellions with troops, artillery, and planes. The American consul in Saigon reported that "thousands of natives have been killed and more are in prison awaiting execution."[58] The vice-consul in Saigon, Peter Flood, described "the promiscuous machine-gunning" of towns by French troops passing through in trucks and the "burning of entire villages" in reprisal for acts of defiance against the French. In the town of My Tho, he reported, the jail was "crowded with 2500 prisoners and many others are reported to have been executed."[59]

In a world preoccupied with the European war and with other Japanese moves in the Far East, the bloody events of 1940 in Vietnam received even less attention than had the uprisings of 1930–31. Most Americans who wrote

[55]Ltr, Stark to Adm Ernest J. King, 3 Mar 43, King Papers, Double O files, Naval Historical Center, Washington, D.C.

[56]See, for example, Telg, Ambassador in France (Admiral William Leahy) to Secy of State, 1 Aug 41, Department of State, *Foreign Relations of the United States, 1941*, vol. 5, *The Far East* (Washington, 1956), pp. 246–47.

[57]McAlister, *Vietnam: Origins of Revolution*, pp. 109–11; Buttinger, *Vietnam: A Dragon Embattled*, 1:243–45.

[58]Am Consul, Saigon (George D. Lamont), to State Dept, 23 Dec 40, 851G.00/67, RG 59; McAlister, *Vietnam: Origins of Revolution*, pp. 121–24.

[59]Vice-Consul, Saigon (Peter H. A. Flood), to Dept of State, 10 Dec 40, 851G.00/63, RG 59.

on the Far East still doubted the existence of any widespread nationalistic feeling in Vietnam. After a visit to Annam, for example, a writer for the popular magazine *Asia* stressed the apathy and misery of the people. "The number of those who discuss political policy is very small," he wrote, "and even in Hue it is hard to find people who are interested in international affairs."[60] The former Tokyo correspondent of the *Christian Science Monitor*, William H. Chamberlain, also writing in *Asia*, observed that "the peoples of Indochina are too passive and backward and lacking in political consciousness and training for modern warfare to play any great part in determining their own destiny."[61] The veteran Far East correspondent Robert Aura Smith concluded in a volume published in 1940 that "the actual threat to the French colonial structure [in Vietnam] has been lessened by the fact that no unified nationalist movement exists. Grievances for the most part have been localized and in most cases might just as well have been directed against the native rulers as against the French overlords. . . . The French administrators have known how to command respect and loyalty."[62]

On the eve of Pearl Harbor, American interest in Indochina was primarily confined to the region's strategic position in the path of a southward Japanese advance. The question of the political future of Vietnam, Laos, and Cambodia was recognized as a problem only by a handful of experts. Almost no one was aware of the political forces within Vietnam that would in the end play the decisive role in settling the question.

---

[60]Warren, "On the Mandarin Road to Hue," p. 563.
[61]William H. Chamberlain, "Derelict Empire in Indochina," *Asia* 40 (December 1940): 626.
[62]Robert Aura Smith, *Our Future in Asia* (New York: Viking Press, 1940), pp. 71–72.

2

From Pearl Harbor to the Japanese Coup

From Pearl Harbor until V–J Day, Indochina was of comparatively little political or military interest to the United States. For most of the war American strategists viewed it as a minor part of the China-Burma-India theater, which itself remained a minor theater in the global war against the Axis. For a time, in early 1943, Allied planners considered the possibility that Indochina, or at least a deep water anchorage known as Cam Ranh Bay along the central coast of Vietnam, might be seized by British forces for use as an alternate route into China.[1] But as the war progressed and as the Central Pacific and South Pacific emerged as the most promising approaches to victory, American interest in an offensive from Southeast Asia or China gradually faded. Probably for that reason the United States never developed a coherent political policy toward Indochina during the war years.

Conflicting Policies

Official American policy regarding Indochina appeared at times to favor continued recognition of French sovereignty. In April 1941, Acting Secretary of State Sumner Welles stated that the United States "recognizes the sovereign jurisdiction of the people of France . . . over French possessions overseas."[2] Somewhat more effusively, Ambassador Robert Murphy assured the American-sponsored governor-general of French North Africa, General Henri Giraud, that "the restoration of France, in all her grandeur, and in all the area which she possessed before the war in Europe as well as overseas, is

---

[1] Memo, Brig Gen J. E. Hull for CofS, 8 Apr 43, sub: Indochina in Relation to Future Operations in the Pacific, OPD 381 CTO (3–2–43), RG 165; Grace P. Hayes, The History of the Joint Chiefs of Staff in World War II: The War Against Japan, vol. 2, Advance to Victory, Hist Sec, JCS, 1954, pp. 61–66, National Archives; Louis Morton, *Strategy and Command: The First Two Years*, United States Army in World War II (Washington, 1962), pp. 447–52.

[2] Department of State *Bulletin*, 18 April 1942.

one of the war aims of the United Nations. . . . French sovereignty should be re-established as soon as possible over all territories, Metropolitan as well as colonial."[3]

Yet American policy was not nearly as clear-cut and unequivocal as those statements suggest. President Franklin D. Roosevelt possessed strong, if somewhat vague, views about the future of Indochina. The president firmly believed that Indochina should not be returned to France at the end of the war but should be given trusteeship status, with China or perhaps Britain as the trustee.[4] In conversations with advisers and foreign diplomats and at wartime conferences, Roosevelt made his position clear. "I saw Halifax [the British ambassador to the United States] last week," he wrote to Secretary of State Cordell Hull in January 1944, "and told him . . . that it was perfectly true that I had, for over a year, expressed the opinion that Indo-China should not go back to France. . . . it should be administered by an international trusteeship. France has had the country . . . one hundred years, and the people are worse off than they were at the beginning."[5]

The president's views on Indochina may have been strongly influenced by his attitude toward France. To Roosevelt the swift French defeat at the hands of the Germans in 1940 was proof that France was no longer worthy of being considered a great power. He was convinced that only the complete collapse of French nerve, society, and government could have accounted for that debacle.[6] In his view the French acquiescence to the Japanese occupation of Indochina was only of a piece with France's earlier collapse before the German assault.[7]

Given Roosevelt's views, it might appear surprising that the United States at first opted to maintain friendly—or at least correct—ties with the quasi-independent French government of Marshal Henri Philippe Petain, established at Vichy after the French surrender. The French Fleet and the French Colonial Empire, however, were under Vichy control, and American leaders believed that diplomatic ties with the Vichy government were essential for the time being. At the same time, General Charles de Gaulle, who headed the Free French movement in London, was viewed with suspicion and dislike by both the president and Secretary of State Hull, who considered him arrogant, untrustworthy, and authoritarian. They doubted that de Gaulle spoke for the

---

[3]William L. Langer, *Our Vichy Gamble* (New York: Harper, 1966), p. 33. Roosevelt later told the Joint Chiefs of Staff that Murphy "had exceeded his authority" in promising that French sovereignty would be restored over *all* French possessions. Min, JCS Mtg, 7 Jan 43, Department of State, *Foreign Relations of the United States: The Conferences at Washington, 1941 – 1942, and Casablanca, 1943* (Washington, 1968), p. 514.

[4]Elliott Roosevelt, *As He Saw It* (New York: Duell, Sloan and Pearce, 1946), p. 115. For a discussion of Roosevelt's views on Indochina, see Gary R. Hess, "Franklin D. Roosevelt and Indochina," *Journal of American History* 59 (September 1972): 353 – 68.

[5]Memo, President Roosevelt for Secy of State, 24 Jan 44, Department of State, *Foreign Relations of the United States: The Conferences at Cairo and Tehran, 1943* (Washington, 1961), pp. 872 – 73.

[6]Marvin R. Zahniser, *Uncertain Friendship: American-French Relations Through the Cold War* (New York: John Wiley Sons, 1975), p. 244.

[7]Hess, "Franklin D. Roosevelt and Indochina," p. 354.

majority of Frenchmen, as he claimed, and they only reluctantly consented in late 1944 to recognize his government.[8]

The president and some of his advisers also felt a commitment to the cause of anti-imperialism and self-determination in general. They were resolved not to sacrifice American lives in the war with Japan simply to restore the old European colonial empires in Asia. Until 1944 American interest in Asia centered on the use of China as a base for aerial bombardment and perhaps invasion of Japan. For that purpose they favored the early reopening of supply routes to China by recapturing northern Burma from the Japanese.[9] The British seemed to American leaders to be more interested in efforts to liberate their Asian possessions, especially Singapore and Hong Kong. Maj. Gen. Raymond A. Wheeler, the chief of the American Services of Supply in the China-India theater, observed, "American interest points north to Japan, British interest south to Singapore."[10]

Despite such views, the United States in August 1943 agreed with Britain to establish a new Anglo-American command to control operations in Southeast Asia, specifically in Burma, Ceylon, Sumatra, and Malaya. Many Americans viewed this new Southeast Asia Command, under Vice-Adm. Lord Louis Mountbatten, with considerable suspicion. Some facetiously suggested that the command's acronym—SEAC—stood for "Save England's Asiatic Colonies." The fact that the precise boundaries between the Southeast Asia Command and the neighboring China theater, under Generalissimo Chiang Kai-shek, were never clearly defined later proved a source of considerable controversy.

Although the president approved establishing the Southeast Asia Command, the United States was careful to dissociate itself politically from the colonial concerns of its Allies. The United States refused to assign any diplomatic representatives to the command, and when the Free French sent a military mission to the headquarters of the Southeast Asia Command to plan for the liberation of Indochina, the president directed the State Department to inform "our British friends that Mr. Churchill and I did not officially recognize" the French presence at Mountbatten's headquarters.[11]

Roosevelt similarly opposed any plans to use French troops in liberating Indochina. With the concurrence of the Joint Chiefs of Staff, he refused to authorize the allocation of shipping to the French to transport an expedition-

---

[8]Zahniser, *Uncertain Friendship*, pp. 245−50, 256−58; James MacGregor Burns, *Roosevelt: The Soldier of Freedom* (New York: Harcourt Brace, 1970), pp. 320−21 and passim; Milton Viorst, *Hostile Allies: FDR and De Gaulle* (New York: Macmillan, 1965); Cordell Hull, *The Memoirs of Cordell Hull*, vol. 2 (New York: Macmillan, 1948), pp. 961−62.

[9]Christopher Thorne, "Indochina and Anglo-American Relations, 1942−1945," *Pacific Historical Review* 45 (February 1976): 79.

[10]Charles F. Romanus and Riley Sunderland, *Stilwell's Mission to China*, United States Army in World War II (Washington, 1953), pp. 357−60; Thorne, "Indochina and Anglo-American Relations," pp. 75−76; Raymond A. Wheeler to George C. Marshall, 24 Mar 45, OPD files; Lt Col Henry G. Morgan, Planning the Defeat of Japan: A Study of Total War Strategy, pp. 109−10, Ms in CMH.

[11]Hess, "Franklin D. Roosevelt and Indochina," pp. 360−61; see also Memo, Roosevelt for Under Secy of State (Edward R. Stettinius, Jr.), 3 Nov 44, Department of State, *Foreign Relations of the United States, 1944*, vol. 3, *The British Commonwealth and Europe* (Washington, 1965), p. 780.

ary corps to Southeast Asia.[12] The president even refused to sanction low-level intelligence and commando-type operations in Indochina involving French participation. In October 1944 Roosevelt told Hull that "we should do nothing in regard to resistance groups, or in any other way in relation to Indochina."[13]

Nevertheless, by 1944 a good deal had already been done, particularly in the area of intelligence. The French in Southeast Asia were in a good position to provide information for Allied bombers on likely Japanese targets in Indochina, on air defenses, on weather, and on Japanese troop movements. Information on troop movements was of special significance because the shifting of Japanese forces in or out of Indochina could affect the military situation in southern China.[14] The French also could help in rescuing pilots shot down over Indochina. In addition, it was widely believed that the Vietnamese—if not the Laotians and Cambodians—were restive under their Japanese masters and that their services might also be enlisted for various types of espionage and fifth-column activities.

Although American commanders in China and India made no deliberate effort to contravene or circumvent American policy toward Indochina, that policy was sufficiently vague and ambiguous to allow for a wide variety of interpretations, and local commanders were seldom kept abreast of its latest twists and modifications. The need for tactical intelligence was sometimes urgent; the instructions from Washington were few and uncertain. From 1943 on, American commanders in the Far East frequently violated the spirit, if not the letter, of Roosevelt's dictum that the United States should "do nothing in regard to Indochina."

America and Indochina

Among the first to take an active interest in Indochina—specifically Vietnam—was Commo. Milton E. Miles. As commander of Navy Group, China, and director in the Far East of the Office of Strategic Services (OSS), the organization responsible under the Joint Chiefs of Staff for unconventional warfare, Miles in 1943 presided over a kaleidoscopic organization with responsibility for liaison, training, espionage, guerrilla warfare, and support of naval operations.[15] He also served as deputy director of a joint Chinese-American espionage group known as the Sino-American Co-operative Organization, led by a Chinese master spy, General Tai Li. One of the principal missions given Miles by the Navy Department was to prepare for an Allied

---

[12]Edward R. Drachman, *United States Policy Toward Vietnam* (Madison, N.J.: Fairleigh Dickinson Press, 1970), p. 71.

[13]Memo, Roosevelt for Secy of State, 16 Oct 44, Dept of State, *Foreign Relations, 1944: British Commonwealth and Europe*, 3:777.

[14]McAlister, *Vietnam: Origins of Revolution*, p. 136.

[15]For a discussion of the activities of Navy Group, China, see Milton E. Miles, *A Different Kind of War* (New York: Macmillan, 1966), and Oscar P. Fitzgerald, "Naval Group China: A Study of Guerrilla Warfare During World War II" (M.A. thesis, Georgetown University, 1968).

landing on the coast of China, a possibility that still seemed likely in 1942 and 1943. Since that landing might also involve operations in Indochina, Miles attempted to extend his intelligence network to Vietnam.

The man he chose to head the operation was a French naval officer, Comdr. Robert Meynier, a supporter of General Giraud. Like Giraud, Meynier was a war hero; he was also anti-German, anti-British, and strongly pro-American. More important, he was married to a woman with important connections among the Vietnamese mandarin class. His wife's uncle, Hoang Trong Phu, was a member of the Privy Council and a former governor of Tonkin. Members of Meynier's espionage group had extensive contacts also with French officers and officials in Vietnam.

Commodore Miles

Almost from the start the Meynier group found its operations hampered and circumscribed by the French Military Mission in Chungking, China, which was Gaullist in its loyalties. Ironically, the Vichyite French in Indochina were also suspicious of the Meynier group because it was associated with the Gaullists in Chungking. By mid-1944 Meynier's position had become untenable, and he returned to Europe.

Despite these handicaps, Meynier enjoyed some success in his efforts. Before his departure, he succeeded in establishing a network of agents in Indochina. Many of them operated inside French government agencies and even inside the French intelligence office, the Deuxieme Bureau. They sent back to Miles a steady stream of information on field fortifications, troop movements, bombing targets, and local political developments.[16]

To complement Meynier's activities among the French in Indochina, Commodore Miles also prepared a plan to utilize the mountain tribesmen of Vietnam for guerrilla warfare and espionage against the Japanese. The mountain peoples, who included the Meo, the Jarai, and the Rhade, were ethnically and culturally distinct from each other and from the lowland Vietnamese. Miles' plan to enlist the support of the tribesmen, labeled the "Special Military Plan for Indochina," had been suggested by U.S. Navy Lt. (jg.) George Devereux, a psychological warfare expert attached to Miles' staff. As a civilian Devereux had done anthropological research among the Meo and was familiar with their dialects and social customs.[17]

[16]Miles, Report on the Activities of SACO Directed Toward Indochina, pp. 1 – 22 and passim, Milton E. Miles Papers, Office of Naval History.
[17]Memo, Miles for Gen William J. Donovan, 7 May 43, Miles Papers.

Montagnard Village *near Ban Me Thuot.*

Devereux's plan called for a group of twenty specially trained agents to be parachuted into the Central Highlands of Vietnam near the town of Kontum. The group would establish friendly relations with the mountain tribesmen—whose long-standing hatred of the French, the Japanese, and the Vietnamese was well known—and would organize them into guerrilla bands. Arms, ammunition, and medicines would be supplied by air. Devereux hoped to begin operations within four or five months after entering Indochina. The guerrilla bands would supply intelligence, "tie up enemy forces, offer a rallying ground for French patriots and native opponents of the Japanese," and pose a threat to the enemy rear during the projected Allied invasion of Burma. Devereux confidently predicted that "a minimum of 20,000" tribal guerrillas could eventually be recruited and trained.[18] The plan was approved by the Office of Strategic Services and by Miles' superiors in the Navy Department, and it was enthusiastically endorsed by the commander of the China-based Fourteenth Air Force, Maj. Gen. Claire L. Chennault, who promised to launch diversionary air raids to cover the parachute drop.[19]

By the end of May 1943, Miles and Devereux had succeeded in assembling a group of eighteen Army, Navy, and Marine Corps personnel, most of

[18]A Program for Guerrilla Warfare in French Indochina, Apr 43, Miles Papers.
[19]Memo, Chennault for Capt Miles, 3 Aug 43, Miles Papers.

whom spoke French and some of whom had civilian backgrounds in anthropology or psychology. For political reasons, two French officers, also former anthropologists, were attached to the mission. In June the group assembled at Fort Benning, Georgia, for special parachute training, but political arguments with the French in Chungking, squabbles between the Office of Strategic Services and Navy Group, China, and a constant "kidnapping" of Devereux's personnel for more urgent assignments delayed and eventually forced cancellation of the project.[20]

Aside from Miles' efforts, the most reliable and widely used source of American intelligence in regard to Indochina was an organization known as the "GBT group," an acronym of the last names of the three leaders of the group: Laurence Gordon, a Canadian citizen who had worked in Vietnam as an employee of the Cal-Texaco Oil Company; Harry Bernard, a British tobacco merchant; and Frank Tan, a Chinese-American businessman. Formed at first to look after Allied business property in Vietnam, the GBT group soon expanded into espionage. From an outpost at Lungching near the Chinese-Vietnamese border, it directed a network of couriers and clandestine radio operators throughout Vietnam that provided "consistently outstanding intelligence on transporters, industry, shipping and airfields." As time passed the group also developed strong contacts within the French government and armed forces in Vietnam, and it encouraged the formation of an anti-Japanese underground among the French colonials.[21] The group was originally sponsored by the director of intelligence of the Chinese Military Operations Board, Admiral Yang Hsuan Chen, with funds and equipment supplied by the British, but as the value of its work came to be appreciated, it received increasing support from the Fourteenth Air Force. By late 1944 the latter was supplying most of the group's operating funds as well as more modern and powerful transmitters for its radio net in Vietnam.[22]

Although the Fourteenth Air Force supported the GBT group primarily to obtain military intelligence, the relationship nevertheless brought the United States into collaboration with a colonial power. Strong anticolonialists such as Maj. Gen. Patrick J. Hurley, appointed ambassador to China in December 1944, were suspicious of all British and French clandestine activities in Southeast Asia, viewing them as part of an effort to reestablish prewar empires. "I indicated to Hurley that I had given you permission to issue some equipment to certain forces in Indochina as requested by Colonel Gordon," wrote Lt. Gen. Albert C. Wedemeyer, commander of United States Forces in the China Theater and chief of staff to Generalissimo Chiang Kai-shek, in late 1944. "He was not pleased by my action, although I mentioned the intelligence contribu-

[20]Interv, author with Professor Weston La Barre (former member of Devereux group), 9 Jan 73, Historians files, CMH. Professor La Barre expressed the opinion that the operation "might very well have succeeded" had it been put into effect.

[21]Wedemeyer's Data Book, sec. 20, RG 332; quote from Organizational Report, 5329th Air Ground Forces Resources Technical Staff, Aug – Sep 44, pp. 13 – 15, 14th Air Force records, 30 Sep 44, Albert F. Simpson Historical Research Center, Maxwell Air Force Base; Charles Fenn, *Ho Chi Minh* (London: Studio Vista, 1973), pp. 75 – 76.

[22]5329th Air Ground Forces Resources Tech Staff Rpt, Aug–Sep 44, pp. 13 – 15.

tion which you desire very much and which caused me to approve the request. . . . However, General Hurley has had increasing evidence that the British, French, and Dutch are working . . . for the attainment of imperialistic policies and he felt we should do nothing to assist them in their endeavors which run counter to U.S. policy."[23]

Hurley's position faithfully reflected President Roosevelt's own views, as expressed again in December 1944 when the British government protested that "it would be difficult to deny French participation in the liberation of Indochina." Roosevelt responded by informing Secretary of State Edward R. Stettinius, Jr., that "I still do not want to get mixed up in any Indochina decision.

General Chennault *talks with Ambassador Hurley.*

It is a matter for post-war. By the same token, I do not want to get mixed up in any military effort toward the liberation of Indochina."[24] The Army Air Forces and other American units in China nevertheless continued to cooperate to a limited extent with the French in Indochina in order to obtain intelligence and aid in rescuing downed pilots.[25] When General Wedemeyer assumed command of the China theater in October 1944 he found relations between the Free French in Kunming and the Fourteenth Air Force to be "very co-operative and friendly." He believed that "an arrangement had been made" between the two without the cognizance of his predecessor, Lt. Gen. Joseph W. Stilwell.[26]

Despite the concern occasionally voiced by Ambassador Hurley and others, American clandestine contacts and activities in Indochina before the spring of 1945 had little or no effect on the internal situation in Indochina or on Allied policy. Their importance lay in the fact that through them American commanders in the China theater came to depend upon intelligence gathered from Indochina. This dependence would lead some commanders to cooperate in 1945 with forces hostile to French colonialism after the Japanese forcibly repressed the French colonial regime in Vietnam.

[23]Ltr, Wedemeyer to Maj Gen Claire L. Chennault, 27 Dec 44, Wedemeyer files, RG 332.

[24]Memo, Roosevelt for Secy of State (Stettinius), 1 Jan 45, Department of State, *Foreign Relations of the United States, 1945*, vol. 6, *The British Commonwealth and the Far East* (Washington, 1969), p. 293.

[25]In late January 1945, a group described as "the Free French under-ground" provided the Navy and the Fourteenth Air Force with "pinpoint targets in the Saigon area," see records of G–2, 14th AF Indochina file, 14th AF records.

[26]Interv, author with Gen Albert C. Wedemeyer, Washington, D.C., 2 Feb 72, Historians files, CMH.

The Japanese Takeover

With the liberation of France and American victories in the Pacific, the French in Indochina underwent a dramatic change of attitude in the latter part of 1944 toward the Japanese occupation. Old feuds between Vichyites and Gaullists were put aside, and attempts were made to establish contact with the new French government of General Charles de Gaulle in Paris.[27] French officers and colonial administrators made preparations to organize an underground resistance movement similar to the Maquis in metropolitan France.

Mountbatten's Southeast Asia Command headquarters in Ceylon parachuted specially trained French officers and agents into Indochina, along with arms, communications equipment, and demolition gear, and brought out resistance leaders for discussions. Eleven wireless stations provided a new communications network throughout the country.[28] Local French leaders told the OSS that following a planned uprising they might be able to hold parts of northern Vietnam for up to three or four months with help from Allied air power.[29]

These French plans and preparations were a poorly kept secret. Japanese intelligence was well aware of the local preparations for resistance, and the Japanese moved energetically to counter them.[30] Japanese Army officials in Indochina wished to place the colony under direct military administration as in Manchukuo. However, officials in Tokyo decided in favor of a grant of "independence" to Vietnam. Such a move, they hoped, would win the cooperation of the Vietnamese and make the takeover look less aggressive.[31]

Mountbatten and his political adviser, Esler Denning, cautioned the de Gaulle government to discourage any premature action in Indochina, but to no avail.[32] As early as September 1944, a State Department expert on Southeast Asia advised President Roosevelt in a draft memorandum that "it is thought the Japanese may shortly disarm the French and take over the country."[33] At the same time, the Office of War Information's Air Liaison representative in Chungking, William Powell, reported that "all of us out here anticipate quite an upheaval in Indochina."[34]

As the likelihood of a Japanese takeover increased, French officials in

[27]Conditions in French Indochina, OSS R&A Unit Kunming, Rpt 0016, 15 Oct 44, copy in G – 2 ID files, RG 319.
[28]Force 136, Future Plans, 16 Nov 44; ibid., Future Plans for French Indochina, 28 Dec 44. Both in WO 203/4331, SEAC records, Public Records Office (PRO). U.S. Military Intelligence Div, Rpt R3 – 45, 11 Apr 45, sub: Indochina Question, G – 2 ID files, RG 319.
[29]OSS Rpt YH/KM-1, 15 Nov 44, sub: Conditions in Northern Tonkin, 15 Nov 44, G – 2 ID files, RG 319.
[30]Lt Col Sakai Tateki, "French Indo-China Operations Record," Japanese Monograph no. 25, p. 22, copy in CMH.
[31]Recent Political Developments in French Indo-China, 6 Apr 45, SRH – 095, records of National Security Agency, RG 457.
[32]Political Adviser, SEAC, to Foreign Office, 24 Jan 45, WO 203/5561A, SEAC records, PRO.
[33]Draft memo, Chief, Southwest Pacific Div, State Dept, for President, 8 Sep 44, RG 59.
[34]Powell to Clarence Gauss, 6 Sep 44, Incl to Gauss to Secy of State, 9 Sep 44, 851G.00/9 – 0944, RG 59.

Kunming "made strenuous efforts to determine the possible lines of action the United States might take."[35] On 2 February 1945 the French military attache in Chungking approached General Wedemeyer to express his anxiety. If the Japanese assumed control of the government the French forces in Indochina, the attache believed, would retreat to the mountains to carry on guerrilla warfare. The attache asked whether, under those circumstances, the United States would be prepared to provide assistance. Wedemeyer was noncommittal, merely indicating that the matter was one for decision at a higher level. Aware that the question of American cooperation with the French in Indochina was delicate and that the president himself held strong views on the subject, Wedemeyer cabled Washington for guidance. The State and War Departments responded that they could only reiterate the president's policy of noninvolvement in Indochina matters.

Roosevelt's position, however, already had begun to change. At the Yalta Conference in February 1945 he told the U.S. Joint Chiefs of Staff that he was "in favor of anything that is against the Japanese in Indochina provided that we do not align ourselves with the French."[36] Accordingly, the acting chief of staff of the China theater, Brig. Gen. Melvin E. Gross, instructed subordinate commanders on 20 February that "appropriate and feasible help," such as medical supplies, might be given to Free French guerrillas who made their way to the Chinese border. The matter of allowing the guerrillas to enter China, however, "should be settled directly between the Chinese and the French."[37] On 7 March, China theater headquarters further cautioned commanders that "any help or aid given to the French by us shall be in such a way that it cannot possibly be construed as furthering the political aims of the French. . . . The governing factor is that the action be in furtherance of *our* military objectives and not a matter of convenience to the French or to any other nation."[38]

Two days later, at eight o'clock on the evening of 9 March, the Japanese ambassador to French Indochina presented Governor-General Admiral Jean Decoux with an ultimatum demanding that direct control of the government, police, and armed forces of the colony be turned over to the Japanese. Two hours later Japanese forces moved against French forts and garrisons all over Indochina. Most were quickly disarmed, but a few offered fierce, although brief, resistance, and a sizable body of troops stationed in the north fell back to the mountainous jungle areas of western Tonkin and Laos, from where they began a fighting retreat to the Chinese border.[39]

The Japanese coup of March 1945 marked a turning point in the history of Indochina. It signaled the end of the painful French pretense to sovereignty and provided new opportunities for Vietnamese opponents of the French to

[35]History of U.S. Forces in the China Theater, p. 24, Ms in CMH.
[36]Memo, Gen Gross, 20 Feb 45, Wedemeyer FIC (French Indochina) Book 2, RG 332; Dept of State, *Foreign Relations, 1945: British Commonwealth and Far East,* 6:297.
[37]History of U.S. Forces, China Theater, p. 30.
[38]Msg, Chennault to Gross, 9 Mar 45, Wedemeyer files, RG 332.
[39]The Aftermath of Japanese Occupation of French Indo-China, SRH–100, 31 May 45, RG 457.

Gia Lam Rail Center *under attack by Fourteenth Air Force bombers.*

expand their activities and add to their following. At the same time, it created acute difficulties for the Free French government of General de Gaulle, newly installed in Paris, which was at pains to obtain Allied recognition of its claim to continued sovereignty in Indochina.

The first news of the Japanese coup received by Americans in the China theater was a radio message from the French garrison at Lang Son in north-eastern Vietnam, transmitted about midnight on 9 March. The message reported a heavy Japanese assault on the garrison and speculated that an attack on all French units in Indochina was probably under way. The defenders requested American air strikes on designated targets in their area.

The commander of the Fourteenth Air Force, General Chennault, requested permission to provide the air assistance that the French had asked for and, more generally, "to co-operate directly with the French authorities in Kunming" to conduct other attacks in Indochina. A few hours later the theater headquarters, apparently on the authority of Maj. Gen. Robert B. McClure, acting commander in the absence of General Wedemeyer, replied, "Go ahead. Co-operate completely with the French. You can use Poseh airfield. Give them hell."[40] A second message sent later that day added that the authorization "pertains entirely to the present emergency."[41]

[40]Msg, Gross to Chennault, CFBX 34041, 10 Mar 45, Wedemeyer files, RG 332.
[41]Ibid., CFBX 34064, 10 Mar 45, Wedemeyer files, RG 332.

31

Indochinese Colonial Troops *retreat to China, March 1945.*

At the same time, General Wedemeyer, in Washington to confer with the Joint Chiefs, was receiving contrary instructions in a private conference with the president himself. According to Wedemeyer, Roosevelt said that he wanted "to discontinue colonization in the Southeast Asia area" and that he was "determined that there would be no military assistance to the French in Indochina."[42] Wedemeyer undoubtedly would not have granted General Chennault such sweeping authority to aid the French.[43] Yet the authority had been given, and it set in motion a chain of events which was to involve American forces in Indochina from that day until the Japanese surrender.

While American planes were preparing to aid the French, General Chennault on 10 March also persuaded Chiang Kai-shek to allow French troops fleeing the Japanese to take refuge in China. Chinese authorities further agreed that "if stiff resistance is put up by the French against the Japanese, military assistance may be rendered."[44]

McClure's authorization of assistance to the French applied only to the Fourteenth Air Force, but on 11 March an event occurred that officials of the

[42]Interv, author with Wedemeyer, 2 Feb 72.
[43]Ibid.
[44]Min, Meeting of National Military Council, 10 Mar 45, Incl to Gen Hsu Yung to Gen Gross, 16 Mar 45, Wedemeyer files, RG 332.

Office of Strategic Services seized upon as a means to obtain permission for themselves to operate in Indochina. On that date a force of about a thousand Vietnamese colonial troops with twenty French officers, slowly fighting their way toward the Chinese border, appealed for American air support. Since the commander, a Colonel LeCog, had been operating an underground radio station that had provided "valuable information" to the Fourteenth Air Force, OSS officials saw "an excellent opportunity to organize this group into an effective guerrilla force and thereby maintain a fruitful source of information."[45] When the OSS proposed to drop arms, equipment, and guerrilla training teams in Vietnam, General McClure and General Chennault resolved to seek "a clear-cut statement" from Washington regarding increased support to the French.[46]

Meanwhile, in Washington, on 12 March, French Ambassador Henri Bonnet met with the secretary of state to request "all possible support" in Indochina. Apparently unaware that the Fourteenth Air Force was already flying tactical air support missions for the French, Bonnet asked for "immediate tactical and material assistance in every field: direct support of operations and the parachuting of arms, medical supplies, quinine and food."[47] The following evening in Paris, General de Gaulle expressed concern to American Ambassador Jefferson Caffery about reports that the Americans and British had failed to come to the aid of the French in Vietnam.[48]

Bonnet's and de Gaulle's remarks and McClure's and Chennault's request for a policy statement were before Secretary of State Stettinius on 16 March when he discussed the question of American aid for Indochina in a memorandum for the president. He assumed that the French were attempting to make the United States "appear responsible for the weakness of their resistance to the Japanese," and suggested that "we combat this trend by making public our desire to render such assistance as may be warranted by the circumstances."[49]

Although the president sanctioned no public statement, he did give his consent to continued support for the French. On the evening of 18 March the U.S. Army's deputy chief of staff, General Thomas C. Handy, telephoned General Wedemeyer's home just outside Washington to report that the president's personal chief of staff, Fleet Admiral William D. Leahy, had "said it was all right to help the Frogs, providing such help does not interfere with our operations."[50] In Wedemeyer's absence, his chief of staff, Col. Paul W. Caraway, took General Handy's call. After trying unsuccessfully to contact General Wedemeyer, Caraway himself drafted and sent a priority message to General Chennault. "The U.S. Government's present attitude," he wrote, "is to aid the French providing such assistance does not interfere with operations

[45]Ibid.; Col Willis H. Bird to HQ OSS, Washington, D.C., 11 Mar 45, records of the OSS.
[46]Msg, Chennault to Marshall for Hull, Mar 45, Wedemeyer FIC Book 2, RG 332.
[47]Dept of State, *Foreign Relations, 1945: British Commonwealth and Far East*, 6:297 – 99.
[48]Telg, Caffery to Secy of State, 13 Mar 45, Dept of State, *Foreign Relations, 1945: British Commonwealth and Far East*, 6:300.
[49]Memo, Stettinius for President, 16 Mar 45, *U.S.-Vietnam Relations*, 7:66.
[50]Memo, Col Paul Caraway for Wedemeyer, 19 Mar 45, Wedemeyer files, RG 332.

now planned. . . . operations against the Japanese to aid the French may be under-taken by the Fourteenth Air Force."[51]

Although the United States was now definitely committed to aiding the French in Indochina, the French government continued to express dissatisfaction about the kind and extent of American support. On 24 March General de Gaulle told Ambassador Caffery that no supplies had been dropped to the French. He could only assume, he said, that, as a matter of policy, the American government did not want to help the French.[52] De Gaulle's complaint was partially justified, for only small quantities of blankets and medicines had been supplied. The problem was an extreme scarcity in the China theater, which had to obtain almost all of its supplies by hazardous flights over the "hump" of the Himalaya Mountains or by truck over the still uncompleted Ledo Road from India.

Yet the Fourteenth Air Force had been helping the French. Between 12 and 28 March it flew a total of 34 missions over Indochina, involving 43 bombing, 24 offensive reconnaissance, and 31 regular reconnaissance sorties. Twenty-eight of these 98 sorties were "in reponse to direct request by the French." General Chennault reported on 14 April that "bad weather, non-availability of surplus equipment, and the fluidity of the situation" had prevented an even larger number of sorties.[53]

Concerned over French complaints, the head of the State Department's European Division, H. Freeman Matthews, suggested informally to the War Department that "even a token drop of supplies would assist in refuting the allegations and accusations" that the United States had no wish to help the French. The War Department in turn, on 7 April, instructed General Wedemeyer, who had returned to China, to honor French requests for supplies "providing they represent only a negligible diversion from Theater's planned operations and entail no additional commitments."[54]

General Wedemeyer, who was hard put to supply his own forces, was in no position to supply much material, particularly a scarce item such as gasoline, which the French had specifically requested. Although a limited number of items were dropped to the French during April, General Wedemeyer was still obliged to turn down most requests except for medicines.[55] Unaware of the War Department's instructions to Wedemeyer, the French were again quick to attribute the failure to provide supplies to a deliberate American policy.

The view that the United States deliberately limited and delayed its help to the French during the Japanese takeover is thus incorrect.[56] Yet that belief

[51]Ibid., 20 Mar 45, Wedemeyer files, RG 332.
[52]Telg, Caffery to Secy of State, 24 Mar 45, Dept of State, *Foreign Relations, 1945: British Commonwealth and Far East*, 6:302.
[53]Msg, Chennault to War Dept, 14 Apr 45, Wedemeyer files, RG 332.
[54]Msg, Hull to Wedemeyer, 7 Apr 45, Wedemeyer files, RG 332.
[55]Msg, Wedemeyer to Sabattier, 21 Apr 45, Wedemeyer files, RG 332.
[56]A typically distorted version is in Bernard Fall, *The Two Vietnams: A Political and Military Analysis*, 2d ed. rev. (New York: Praeger, 1967). Fall states (page 55) that the American posture toward Indochina "meant an automatic death sentence for any French attempt at organized resistance in case of Japanese attack." See also pages 56 – 57.

came to be accepted by many Frenchmen and not a few Americans. The memory of America's supposedly tardy and callous response while Frenchmen died at the hands of the Japanese in the spring of 1945 would endure to poison later Franco-American efforts at cooperation in Indochina, but it was only the first of a series of events during 1945 which would complicate relations. Another disagreement, even more disturbing than the first, soon arose over American contact with the Viet Minh.

3

From the Japanese Coup to V−J Day

In a cave near the village of Pac Bo in a remote part of northeastern Vietnam, Ho Chi Minh in May 1941 convened the eighth meeting of the Central Committee of the Indochinese Communist Party. The meeting produced a decision to found a new anticolonial coalition, the Vietnamese Independence League (Viet Nam Doc Lap Dong Minh Hoi), or Viet Minh, designed to appeal to all opponents of the French and Japanese.[1] The Viet Minh then began an ambitious propaganda program to recruit peasants in the nearby provinces as well as members of the Tho, the mountain tribe least hostile to the Vietnamese. Remnants of the rebel bands that had fought the French in the 1940 uprisings formed the core of the first Viet Minh guerrilla units. During 1943 and 1944 those units occasionally skirmished with elements of the French colonial militia, but they concentrated on developing their strength through a network of training and supply bases in the mountainous regions near the Chinese border.[2]

Ho Chi Minh also sought assistance from China and attempted to organize groups of Vietnamese exiles living in southern China into supporters of the Viet Minh, but Chinese warlords who controlled Kwangsi and Yunnan Provinces had their own plans for Vietnam. On a visit to China in August 1942, Ho was arrested and spent over a year in a Chinese prison; meanwhile, the Chinese organized their own Vietnamese independence movement among the expatriate remnants of the Vietnamese Nationalist Party, the Phuc Quoc monarchists, and old anti-French mandarins. Known as the Dong Minh Hoi, the Chinese-backed organization lacked able leadership or any real following and faced stiff opposition from the Viet Minh.[3]

In September 1943 the Chinese warlord Chang Fa Kwei, who controlled

---

[1] *Days With Ho Chi Minh* (Hanoi: Foreign Language Publishing House, 1965), pp. 191−93; Woodside, *Community and Revolution*, pp. 218−19; McAlister, *Vietnam: Origins of Revolution*, pp. 112−13; William J. Duiker, *The Rise of Nationalism in Vietnam: 1900−1941* (Ithaca: Cornell University Press, 1976), pp. 274−75.

[2] McAlister, *Vietnam: Origins of Revolution*, pp. 110−12, 140−43, and passim.

[3] Ibid., pp. 134−40; King C. Chen, *Vietnam and China, 1938−1954* (Princeton: Princeton University Press, 1969), pp. 56−71.

the region adjacent to the Vietnamese border, decided to try a different approach. He arranged for Ho to be released from prison and put him in charge of organizing the Vietnamese exiles with a subsidy of 100,000 Chinese dollars a month. Although Ho ostensibly made the Viet Minh a part of the Dong Minh Hoi, the Viet Minh soon were in control. With the Chinese subsidy and the cooperation of Tho mountain tribesmen, the Viet Minh established an impressive underground network throughout Tonkin.

American diplomats and consular officials in south China were dimly aware of the activities of the Viet Minh but generally discounted them as of little significance. In December 1942, for example, when Secretary of State Hull queried the American embassy in Chungking concerning reports that "a pro-allied Provisional Government of Indo-China" had been established by an organization known as the "All Indo-China Anti-Imperialist League" (a Viet Minh front organization), Ambassador Clarence E. Gauss replied that the league and other Vietnamese exile groups in China only represented an unimportant "attempt by the Chinese to show their friendly feelings for subject peoples."[4]

State Department observers tended to confuse the lethargic Chinese-dominated Dong Minh Hoi with the dynamic and relatively independent Viet Minh. Their "merger" in 1943 further confused American diplomats. In May 1943 the embassy in Chungking reported that the Vietnamese revolutionary groups were of "no particular importance" and added that the Dong Minh Hoi at Liuchow was "composed entirely of overseas Chinese" from northern Indochina.[5]

In July 1943, when Washington requested a more detailed report on Vietnamese organizations in China, the embassy reported that "all our sources concur in the belief that the organization and support of this group by the Kuomintang is with a view to having a nucleus of pro-Chinese Annamites." The embassy reiterated its belief that the organization was "of little importance." The "sources" cited in the embassy's memorandum included a Korean exile group, members of the French Military Mission in Chungking, and some Chinese Communists, but no Vietnamese.[6]

With the Japanese takeover in March 1945, the casual American attitude toward the Viet Minh abruptly changed to one of serious interest. The whole intelligence network in Vietnam, carefully built upon sources within the French administration and military, at that point became inoperable. As the director of the Office of Strategic Services detachment in China, Col. Paul E. Helliwell, noted at the end of March, "the GBT Group is knocked out, the French system has been destroyed, and General Tai Li's setup has been knocked out lock, stock, and barrel."[7] The Viet Minh appeared to be the one

---

[4]Gauss to Secy of State, 23 Dec 42, 851G.00/12–2342, RG 59.
[5]Charge d'Affaires, Chungking, to State, 31 May 43, 851G.00/5–3143, RG 59. See also Ronald H. Spector, " 'What the Local Annamites Are Thinking': American Views of Vietnamese in South China, 1942–1945," *Southeast Asia International Quarterly* 3 (Spring 1974): 741–52.
[6]Charge d'Affaires, Chungking, to State, 1 Jul 43, 851G.00/6–143, RG 59.
[7]Ltr, Helliwell to Strategic Services Officer, China Theater, 29 Mar 45, records of the OSS.

organization in Vietnam still able to supply information and help in the rescue of Allied pilots.

In March 1945 officers of the U.S. Army Air Forces Air Ground Aid Service contacted Ho Chi Minh in Kunming and agreed to supply him with communications equipment, medical supplies, and small arms in return for intelligence and assistance in rescuing Allied pilots.[8] During the next few months the Air Ground Aid Service supplied Ho's forces with rations, small arms, and medicines by airdrop, while a radio operator stationed with the Viet Minh transmitted intelligence reports to the China theater.

The OSS organization in China, known as the Special Intelligence

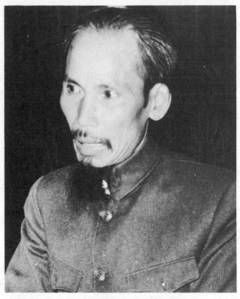

Ho Chi Minh

Branch, or Detachment 202, had been at work for some time on a project to penetrate Indochina for intelligence purposes. The goal was to obtain information on the transportation system, on the Japanese order of battle, and on the attitudes of "internal movements in regard to Chinese, French, and British policies." The Office of Strategic Services expected to receive cooperation from French officials and colonial troops along the China-Indochina border and from "numerous revolutionary groups which have been used successfully in the past." These groups were expected to provide the OSS with both practical aid and a means of "obtaining a clear picture of French Indo-China Politics."[9]

Although Detachment 202 on 1 March 1945 forwarded a plan for penetrating Indochina to OSS headquarters in Washington, two days later the G – 5 section of the China theater staff instructed the detachment to hold the plan in abeyance pending a final decision on extending operations into Indochina. The Japanese takeover six days later and the resultant reduction in the flow of intelligence, together with the increased demand for measures to aid the French, led to a revival of interest in the possibility of OSS operations in Indochina. On 18 March, when General Wedemeyer was in Washington, his chief of staff, Colonel Caraway, met there with OSS officials, including the director, Maj. Gen. William J. Donovan. Caraway observed that there were

[8]Fenn, *Ho Chi Minh*, pp. 74 – 83. Fenn recalls (page 78) that "We asked GHQ Chungking [China Theater] for clearance, in view of Ho's reputed communist background. The instructions came back to 'get that net regardless.' " See also Lloyd Shearer, "When Ho Chi Minh Was an Intelligence Agent for the U.S.," *Parade*, 18 March 1973, p. 8.

[9]Ltr, Col Willis H. Bird (Dep Chief OSS) to Gen Gross, 9 Apr 45, FIC Book 2, China Theater records.

three possible ways to proceed: utilize what was left of the GBT network, create an independent Vietnamese network, or cooperate with the French through the French Military Mission in Chungking. He requested that the Office of Strategic Services prepare plans for the first two types of operations so that they could be implemented as soon as General Wedemeyer returned to the China theater. Mindful of Wedemeyer's recent conversation with the president, in which Roosevelt had opposed military assistance to the French in Indochina, Caraway suggested avoiding the third alternative until the political situation was clarified.[10]

While plans were being developed in Washington, General Gross, acting chief of staff in China, had decided to proceed with clandestine operations forthwith. On 20 March he issued two new directives to the OSS. The first provided for establishing an intelligence network in Indochina as proposed by Detachment 202 in February. The second directive authorized the OSS to render military aid "in the form of supplies and/or U.S.-controlled military personnel to any and all groups opposing the Japanese forces." This directive provided that all resistance groups were to be treated impartially, "irrespective of any particular governmental or political affiliations," since all "resistance to the Japanese accrues to the advantage of United States and China military operations."[11] Groups would receive aid not because of their resistance to or sympathy for French colonialism but solely on the basis of their performance in combat or their usefulness as sources of information. As the deputy chief of the OSS detachment, Col. Willis H. Bird, put it, "If our men deal only with the French, the French will see we never meet any other groups. If we stay away from the French entirely, we will never have a true picture of the situation. . . . we should help the French when they are directly fighting the Japs but also find some other groups fighting the Japs and help them too."[12]

The first OSS team to enter Indochina parachuted into Vietnam soon after the Japanese coup and joined a retreating French column under Generals Marcel Alessandri and Gabriel Sabattier. After a grueling retreat lasting almost two months, scattered groups and units entered southern China, where OSS representatives met with General Alessandri and worked out an agreement to conduct joint intelligence missions in Indochina. In early June twenty-five French officers and about a hundred Vietnamese colonial troops from General Alessandri's force were assigned to the Office of Strategic Services for joint operations in northern Vietnam. The OSS was to equip, transport, and supply the teams. They were to report to the OSS in code; the OSS was to keep the French informed through General Sabattier.[13]

[10]Msg, OSS, Washington, to Heppner, 18 Mar 45, records of the OSS.

[11]ACofS to OSS, China Theater, 20 Mar 45, sub: Intelligence Activities and Aid to Resistance Groups in French Indochina, PSYWAR 091 Indochina, RG 319.

[12]Msg, Bird to Myeland, 23 Mar 45, records of the OSS.

[13]Text of Agreement, 9 Jun 45, in FIC Book 2, Wedemeyer files; Msg, Col Paul Helliwell to Gen Gross, 23 Jun 45, pp. 35, 40, CHP K5053, China Theater records; R. Harris Smith, *OSS: The Secret History of America's First Central Intelligence Agency* (Berkeley: University of California Press, 1973), pp. 328–29.

Viet Minh Guerrillas, *instructed by OSS team, fire U.S. carbines.*

The joint Franco-American operations carried out under that agreement were mostly unsuccessful, primarily because the Vietnamese refused to help the French. In July 1945, for example, Vietnamese guides deliberately led a Franco-American force conducting a raid against Japanese positions at the town of Lang Son in northeastern Vietnam into an ambush set by the Viet Minh. The Viet Minh, reported an American officer, held "the entire area from Langson to the China Frontier."[14] Another American officer observed, "I don't think the French will ever do a hell of a lot of good in Indochina because Annamite hatred makes it a more dangerous place for them than for us."[15]

That the Viet Minh were well organized, efficient, and extremely helpful for intelligence purposes was made clear by an OSS operation known as the "Deer mission" under Maj. Allison K. Thomas. Major Thomas, another American officer, and five American enlisted men formed a team to operate with about a hundred French and Vietnamese colonial troops against the Hanoi – Lang Son railroad, but while the force was training during June 1945

[14]Lt Lucien Conein to Capt A. L. Patti, 26 Jul 45, Records of Mission "Comore," 21 Aug 45, records of the OSS.
[15]Lt James W. Jordan, USNR, to Capt A. L. Patti, 10 Jul 45, Records of Mission "Pakhoi," records of the OSS.

at Tsingsi in south China, Chinese and Vietnamese agents advised Thomas that if he entered Vietnam with the French, he would "find the whole population against him, . . . would be sniped at . . . and would get no food as the natives hate the French."[16] Major Thomas decided to parachute with only part of his American team and a single French officer in American uniform as an advance party to see if the reports were true.

On 16 July, Thomas and his party parachuted into northern Tonkin near the city of Thai Nguyen, a little over fifty kilometers north of Hanoi. The Viet Minh welcomed them warmly, displaying a large sign reading "Welcome to Our American Friends." Thomas had a long conference with Ho Chi Minh— whom Thomas called "Mr. Hoo"—who informed him that French troops would not be welcome. Thomas remained with the Viet Minh for over two months, training them for operations against Japanese communications. He was joined at the end of July by an additional team of four men under Capt. Charles M. Holland. The Viet Minh provided Thomas with useful information on the Japanese order of battle and on Japanese troop movements within the country, and Thomas reported that the Viet Minh had "the sympathy of 85% of the people of Tonkin." He saw no evidence that the Viet Minh were communistic and thought that their "sole purpose was independence."[17]

The limited and almost accidental cooperation between the OSS and the Viet Minh later became the subject of considerable controversy. Frenchmen would protest in the 1950s that without American-supplied arms and ammunition the Viet Minh would have been unable to seize control of much of Vietnam after the Japanese surrender, while some American critics of U.S. involvement in Vietnam during the 1960s would argue that OSS contacts with the Viet Minh should have led, if they had been better exploited, to a clearer understanding of political opinion in Vietnam and to a firm basis for cooperation between the United States and future leaders of the country.

As to the French charge, arms received during World War II accounted for only about 12 percent of the estimated 36,000 small arms in Viet Minh hands in March 1946 and only about 5 percent of the weapons available to them at the start of the war against the French in December 1946, according to one estimate based on French records.[18] Not all of these arms, moreover, had come from American sources. French intelligence agents also had "retained liaison with Viet Minh elements and [had] supplied them with arms." The principal source of Viet Minh armaments was neither the Americans nor the French but the Japanese. Even before the Japanese surrender, Viet Minh units had been able to acquire arms and ammunition from the puppet Vietnamese militia forces of the Emperor Bao Dai set up by the Japanese after the March takeover.[19]

---

[16]Report of Mission "Deer," 16 Sep 45, records of the OSS.
[17]Ibid.
[18]McAlister, *Vietnam: Origins of Revolution*, pp. 229–30.
[19]Jean Sainteny, *Histoire d'une Paix Manquee* (Paris: Fayard, 1967), pp. 104–05; see also McAlister, *Vietnam: Origins of Revolution*, pp. 147–48; French Indochina (Political Situation), 11 Oct 45, SRH–094, RG 457.

It is true that little information from the OSS on the strength and intentions of the Viet Minh ever reached the policy level in Washington. In July 1945, Under Secretary of State Joseph C. Grew complained that "the State Department lacks accurate information from OSS and the military on conditions in Indo-China and as to the temper of the native peoples."[20] Even General Wedemeyer's headquarters received only brief reports on OSS operations in Indochina, and those were wholly tactical in nature.[21] Yet a considerable amount of information about the Viet Minh was forwarded to Washington from American diplomats in southern China, who had frequent contact with Vietnamese Nationalists there, but that information had little discernible influence on American policy.[22]

The principal effect of the brief American collaboration with the Viet Minh during the last months of the war was probably psychological. It aroused annoyance and suspicion on the part of the French, and it enhanced the prestige of the Viet Minh, who could claim to be the associates, and by inference, the representatives, of the victorious Americans. Ho Chi Minh himself reportedly used an autographed picture presented to him by General Chennault for rescuing a Fourteenth Air Force pilot and six pistols given him by the Air Ground Aid Service to demonstrate to his rivals that he was the special representative of the American military.[23]

A Reassessment of Policy

The period after the Japanese takeover in March 1945 thus witnessed a shift to more direct and active involvement by American forces in Indochina. Yet the basic American policy toward Indochina, particularly in regard to the question of the region's postwar fate, remained indefinite. This indecision left U.S. Army and Army Air Forces commanders on the scene without any firm sense of direction.

The need for a more definite Indochina policy was appreciated by most leaders in Washington. There was a general feeling, at least in State and War Department circles, that the matter could be postponed no longer—that certain basic decisions would have to be made well before the end of the war. The State, War, and Navy Coordinating Committee on 13 March 1945 feared that "inaction by the United States [would have] the practical effect of indicating lack of American interest in this area and giving greater influence to the British and the French."[24] The committee recommended that the secretary of state attempt to obtain a "clarification" of U.S. policy from the president. Before any action could be taken, however, President Roosevelt died.

[20]Grew to Director OSS, 19 Jul 45, records of the OSS, RG 59.
[21]Cf., OSS Weekly Op Rpt, 6 – 14 Jul 45, China Theater records.
[22]Spector, "'What the Local Annamites Are Thinking,'" pp. 744 – 52; Thorne, "Indochina and Anglo-American Relations," pp. 82 – 83.
[23]Fenn, *Ho Chi Minh*, p. 76.
[24]Min, Meeting of the State, War, and Navy Coordinating Committee, 13 Mar 45, records of State, War, and Navy Coordinating Committee, RG 165, National Archives.

See footnote p. 38

43

On 13 April 1945, the day after the president's death, Under Secretary of the Army Robert A. Lovett told the State, War, and Navy Coordinating Committee that it was essential to reconsider Roosevelt's prohibition on formulating a definite Indochina policy before the end of the war. The lack of a definite policy was "a source of serious embarrassment to the military," and the head of the French Military Mission in Washington, Admiral Fenard, had taken advantage of the situation. Fenard, Lovett explained, had submitted questions to various agencies of the U.S. government, and "by obtaining negative or even non-committal answers" he had been, "in effect, writing American policy in Indochina."[25]

The State Department's representative on the Coordinating Committee observed that his department's subcommittee on the Far East had been unable to formulate a firm Indochina policy "due to a divergence of views."[26] That divergence in the subcommittee reflected in microcosm differences in the entire State Department. Support for Roosevelt's anticolonialist policy came mainly from a few Far Eastern specialists, such as John Carter Vincent, head of the Office of Far Eastern Affairs, and Abbot Low Moffat, chief of a newly created Southwest Pacific Affairs Division (later the Southeast Asian Affairs Division), who were convinced that the United States had to come to terms with "the mounting groundswell of nationalism . . . engulfing all Southeast Asia."[27]

Most other officials were more concerned about Europe and were anxious to avoid any policy that would tend to complicate America's already strained relations with France. French cooperation would be needed, they pointed out, in helping check Soviet expansionism in Europe and in making the United Nations work.[28] A study prepared by the Office of Strategic Services warned against "schemes of international trusteeships which may provoke unrest and result in colonial disintegration and may at the same time alienate us from the European states whose help we need to balance Soviet power."[29] The State Department's Southeast Asia desk officer, Kenneth P. Landon, recalled that "There was virtually no sympathy . . . for Roosevelt's Indochina policy" outside the Far East Division.[30]

The State, War, and Navy Coordinating Committee's request for a policy statement on Indochina inevitably touched off a debate in the State Department. After two weeks of discussion, the department adopted a policy paper recommending that the United States not oppose restoration of French sovereignty in Indochina but seek assurances of French intentions to establish

---

[25]Ibid., 13 Apr 45, records of State, War, and Navy Coordinating Committee, RG 165.
[26]Ibid.
[27]Testimony of Abbot Low Moffat, in U.S. Congress, Senate, *Hearings Before the Committee on Foreign Relations: Causes, Origins, and Lessons of the Vietnam War*, 92d Cong., 2d sess., 1972 (hereafter cited as Moffat Testimony), p. 163.
[28]George C. Herring, "The Truman Administration and the Restoration of French Sovereignty in Indochina," *Diplomatic History* 1 (Spring 1977): 100 – 101, 116.
[29]OSS Rpt, Problems and Objectives of U.S. Policy, 2 Apr 45, cited in Herring, "Truman Administration and Restoration of French Sovereignty in Indochina," p. 107.
[30]Interv, author with Kenneth P. Landon, 29 Nov 71, Historians files, CMH.

self-government and local autonomy.[31] While labeled a compromise, the recommendation was a long step away from Roosevelt's unwavering insistence on creating a trusteeship.

Over the next few months the United States moved even further away from Roosevelt's position. At the San Francisco Conference, which convened on 26 April 1945 to discuss the postwar structure of the United Nations, the United States did not raise the question of a trusteeship for Indochina. Indeed, a member of the U.S. delegation, Harold E. Stassen, told fellow delegates that independence was "not as important as interdependence" and compared colonial empires to the American federal system.[32] Two weeks later, on 8 May, Secretary of State Stettinius told French Foreign Minister Georges Bidault that "the record is entirely innocent of any official statement of the U.S. government questioning, even by implication, French sovereignty over Indochina."[33] Meanwhile, the State, War, and Navy Coordinating Committee had finally agreed upon a policy for Indochina. It was incorporated into a long report, "Politico-Military Problems in the Far East and Initial Post-Defeat Policy Relating to Japan," which the secretary of state sent to President Harry S. Truman on 2 June 1945. While conceding that "independence sentiment in the area is believed to be increasingly strong," the report declared that "the United States recognizes French sovereignty over Indochina."[34]

Policy at the Field Level

President Roosevelt's death marked the end of any real opposition in Washington to a French return to Indochina, but that fact did not become immediately apparent to American leaders in the Far East. Even as Indochina policy was being carefully reassessed, General Wedemeyer was engaged in a heated dispute with Admiral Mountbatten, commander of the Southeast Asia Command, over theater boundaries in Southeast Asia. At the root of the dispute was the Roosevelt policy.

Since the beginning of 1944 the Southeast Asia Command had been conducting intelligence and paramilitary operations in Siam and Indochina in anticipation of the day when Allied military operations would be extended to those countries. Operations into Indochina, carried out in cooperation with officers of the French Military Mission at the command's headquarters, were intended to establish contact with French leaders in Indochina loyal to de Gaulle and to lay the foundation for underground operations against the Japanese.[35]

[31]Draft Memo for French Government, 30 Apr 45, 851G.00/4 – 2845, RG 59; Moffat Testimony, pp. 176 – 77.
[32]Department of State, *Foreign Relations of the United States, 1945*, vol. 1, *General: The United Nations* (Washington, 1967), pp. 790ff.
[33]Dept of State, *Foreign Relations, 1945: British Commonwealth and Far East*, 6:307.
[34]Ibid., 6:557 – 68.
[35]Force 136, Future Plans for French Indochina, 28 Dec 44.

Although Indochina lay within the boundaries of the China theater, Admiral Mountbatten felt justified in conducting those operations, for Siam and Indochina were of direct importance to his planned future military operations. "With the passage of time," he wrote, those areas would "become of ever increasing importance to the strategy of SEAC."[36] In addition, Mountbatten considered that he had obtained Generalissimo Chiang Kai-shek's approval for the operations at Chungking in October 1943; that meeting had resulted in an informal gentlemen's agreement: Siam and Indochina were to remain in the China theater but since, "as the war develops, the scope of operations . . . of the Southeast Asia theatre . . . may involve Thailand and Indochina, . . . the boundaries between the two theatres are to be decided . . . in accordance with the progress of advances the respective forces make."[37] Mountbatten also claimed to have obtained additional approval to carry out clandestine operations in Indochina when Chiang had visited India in November 1944.

Mountbatten could further claim to have received President Roosevelt's tacit approval for his actions. Only a few weeks after Roosevelt, in October 1944, had bluntly declared that "we should do nothing in regard to resistance groups . . . in relation to Indochina," the British ambassador, Lord Halifax, had told the president that it was essential that "Mountbatten should be free without delay to get some parties of French into Indochina to do sabotage." According to Halifax, the president had replied "that if we felt it was important that we had better tell Mountbatten to do it and ask no questions" but that "he did not want to appear to be committed to anything to prejudice a political decision."[38]

General Wedemeyer, for his part, with little or no knowledge of those informal understandings, was concerned that military operations over which he had no control and about which he had scant information were being conducted in the theater for which he was responsible. To the British he expressed himself as "diametrically opposed to [Mountbatten's] conception of his 'gentlemen's agreement' "with Chiang Kai-shek.[39] Wedemeyer and Ambassador Hurley believed that the British operations in Indochina were designed to aid the French to reestablish their hegemony. Mountbatten's chief political adviser, on the other hand, complained that it was "militarily indefensible that this command, which at present is alone in a position to organize effective clandestine operations in these areas, should be hampered . . . by American obstruction which we know to be based on purely political considerations."[40]

When the French refused to tell Wedemeyer details of their part in the

---

[36]Political Adviser, SEAC, to Foreign Office, 8 Feb 45, WO 203/5561, SEAC records, PRO.

[37]Christopher Thorne, *Allies of a Kind: The United States, Britain, and the War Against Japan, 1942 – 1945* (London: Hamish Hamilton, 1978), p. 301.

[38]Msg, AMSSO to Argonaut, 12 Feb 45, F986/11/G, FO 371, Foreign Office records, PRO.

[39]Chief Political Adviser, SEAC, to Foreign Office, 10 Feb 45, WO 203/5561, SEAC records, PRO.

[40]Ibid., also 8 Feb 45, WO 203/5561; extract from Rpt, Lt Col Carver, WO 203/5210. All in SEAC records, PRO. Charles F. Romanus and Riley Sunderland, *Time Runs Out in CBI*, United States Army in World War II (Washington, 1959), pp. 259 – 60.

Admiral Mountbatten *on inspection tour, 1944.*

operations, Wedemeyer closed Kunming Airport to planes of the Southeast Asia Command flying in support of the clandestine efforts. The British continued to carry out operations from Jessore, near Calcutta in eastern India, and on the night of 23 January 1945 fighters of the Fourteenth Air Force mistook three British bombers, on an intelligence mission into Indochina, for Japanese planes and shot them down. The Royal Air Force liaison officer with the Fourteenth Air Force had not been informed of the mission "owing to the political situation."[41]

Both Mountbatten and Wedemeyer appealed to their respective governments, whereupon President Roosevelt suggested to Prime Minister Churchill in February "the best solution at present is for you and me to agree that all Anglo-American-Chinese military operations in Indo-China, regardless of their nature, be coordinated by General Wedemeyer as Chief of Staff to the Generalissimo."[42] In the Far East itself, General Wedemeyer visited Mountbatten's headquarters at Kandy, Ceylon, in March, and left believing firmly that Mountbatten had agreed not to conduct further operations in Indochina unless approved in advance by the China theater.[43]

[41]Note on Loss of 3 Liberator Aircraft of No. 358 Squadron, Night of 22 – 23 Jan 45, WO 203/4331, SEAC records, PRO.
[42]Memo, Asst to President's Naval Aide, sub: Indochina, Department of State, *Foreign Relations of the United States*, vol. 1, *The Conference of Berlin, 1945* (Washington, 1960), p. 918.
[43]Ibid.

General Wedemeyer (left) with Ambassador Hurley

Admiral Mountbatten, to the contrary, understood only that he had agreed to inform Wedemeyer about his operations, not to submit them for approval.[44] When he informed Wedemeyer in May that he intended to fly twenty-six sorties into Indochina, Wedemeyer asked for more information and suggested that the equipment being furnished to French forces within Indochina might be used to better advantage reequipping the French who had retreated into China following the Japanese takeover. He also wanted to be sure that "equipment furnished guerrilla units will be employed against the Japanese." When Mountbatten responded with only general information, Wedemeyer pronounced it incomplete and asked for more details. After a further fruitless exchange of messages, Mountbatten announced that, because of weather, he could delay no longer and that "the operations are now being carried out."[45]

Wedemeyer was furious. "It had never occurred to me," he radioed Admiral Mountbatten on 25 May, "that you would presume that you have authority to operate in an area contiguous to your own without cognizance and full authority of the commander of that area. . . . Your decision . . . is a

[44]Ibid.; Msg, SACSEA to Chungking, 8 Apr 45, WO 203/5561A, SEAC records.
[45]Memo, Asst to President's Naval Aide, p. 919. The exchange of messages is in WO 203/5210, SEAC records.

direct violation of the intent of our respective directives."[46] Wedemeyer was being true to his charge from President Roosevelt to "watch carefully to prevent any British and French political activities in Indochina," for control of clandestine activities in Indochina might enable the British to influence political developments and alignments there.[47] Wedemeyer was concerned also that the French guerrillas might employ their arms not against the Japanese but against indigenous forces that opposed them.[48]

To the U.S. Army's chief of staff, General George C. Marshall, Wedemeyer noted that the British refusal to recognize Indochina as being in the China theater, the increased activities of the British in Indochina, and the large French military staff at the headquarters of the Southeast Asia Command pointed to the existence of "a British and French plan to reestablish their pre-war political and economic positions in Southeast Asia."[49] Ambassador Hurley supported the general with an even stronger letter to President Truman. The ambassador asserted that Lord Mountbatten "is using the American lend-lease supplies and other American resources to invade Indo-China to defeat what we believe to be the American policy, and to reestablish French imperialism."[50]

Washington's reply undoubtedly came as a surprise to Wedemeyer and Hurley. While declaring that "there has been no basic change in [United States] policy," the State Department added that decisions reached at the conferences at Yalta and San Francisco "would preclude the establishment of a trusteeship for Indochina except under the French government. The latter seems unlikely." The United States, the message stated, "welcomes French participation in the Pacific war to the extent practical," and French offers of assistance should "be considered on their military merits." American forces in China were free to cooperate with French resistance groups in Indochina "provided such assistance does not interfere with requirements of other planned operations." In a similar message General Marshall informed Wedemeyer that "the State Department's [new] position eliminates the political necessity of curtailing Lord Mountbatten's operations in Indo-China."[51] Those operations should in the future "be judged strictly on their military merits and in relation to the stand of the Generalissimo."[52]

So ended the last American attempts at the field command level to restrict French and British activities in Indochina. Yet the true nature of the changes in American policy toward Indochina during the spring of 1945 were never fully perceived in the China theater. General Wedemeyer, for example, saw the Marshall message as signifying no fundamental change in American policy but as merely another concession to French pressure for a role in the

[46]Msg, Wedemeyer to Mountbatten, 25 May 45, FIC Book 1, China Theater records.
[47]Msg, Wedemeyer to Marshall, 28 May 45, FIC Book 2.
[48]Memo, Asst to President's Naval Aide, p. 919.
[49]Msg, Wedemeyer to Marshall, 28 May 45.
[50]Msg, Hurley to Harry S. Truman, 28 May 45, Dept of State, *Foreign Relations: Conference of Berlin, 1945*, 1: 920.
[51]Secy of State to Hurley, 7 Jun 45, RG 165.
[52]Msg, Marshall to Wedemeyer, 4 Jun 45, FIC Book 2.

Pacific war. In regard to Indochina he still considered himself bound by the instructions he had received from the president. Both Wedemeyer and Hurley would continue to try to implement Roosevelt's policy long after Washington had abandoned it.[53]

[53]In interviewing Americans concerned with Indochina near the end of the war, the author asked, "What did you believe American policy on the postwar political disposition of Indochina would be?" Answers ranged from "return to the French" to trusteeship under the United Nations, France, China, or the United States. See intervs, author with Maj Gen Philip E. Gallagher, 13 Jan 72; Maj Gen Robert B. McClure, 26 May 72; Archimedes L. Patti, 26 Jan 73; Col John H. Stodter, 19 May 72; Frank White, 18 Feb 72; and James R. Withrow, Jr., 9 Mar 72. All in Historians files, CMH.

4

The Chinese Occupation of North Vietnam August – October 1945

When the heads of the Allied governments and the Soviet Union met at Potsdam in July 1945, the dispute between Mountbatten and Wedemeyer over theater boundaries was still fresh in the minds of the British and American Chiefs of Staff. The British had decided that the only solution was to transfer the whole of Indochina to Mountbatten's Southeast Asia Command.[1] When they proposed that arrangement at Potsdam, the American Joint Chiefs of Staff countered with a suggestion that Indochina be divided between the two theaters. In the end it was agreed, despite General Wedemeyer's objections, to divide Indochina along the 16th Parallel with the Southeast Asia Command responsible for the south and the China theater for the north.

That command arrangement was in effect on 14 August 1945 when Japan accepted the Allied surrender terms. Thus it followed that the Chinese would accept the surrender of the Japanese north of the 16th Parallel and the British the surrender south of it. In the process each would temporarily occupy its respective zone. Since there were few Japanese in Laos and Cambodia, occupation would be confined largely to Vietnam.

Since Americans in the China theater were advisers to the Chinese armies that would enter the northern part of Vietnam, General Wedemeyer's Theater Planning Section at Chungking began work in early August on a joint American-Chinese plan for the occupation of the northern part of Vietnam.[2] By 7 September Chiang Kai-shek and General Wedemeyer had approved a plan based on the assumption that no American ground forces would be committed but that American "liaison and advisory personnel would accompany the occupation troops to assist the Chinese commanders."[3] The plan provided that the number of occupation forces "should be held to an absolute minimum," partly because only 50,000 Japanese troops were involved but primarily because of food shortages in Vietnam. Tonkin was suffering from a

---

[1] Thorne, *Allies of a Kind*, p. 627.
[2] Msg, CSM 113, 23 Aug 45, China Theater files, RG 407.
[3] History of U.S. Forces, China Theater, p. 28.

severe food shortage caused by flooding of the Red River and wartime disruption of the transportation system, and famine in various parts of the country had recently claimed about two million lives. A large body of occupying troops would only serve to aggravate those conditions.

In his guidance for the American liaison teams, which were to accompany the Chinese forces, Wedemeyer added his long-held belief that "the ultimate political fate of Indo-China remains to be decided."[4] At the same time, he and the theater planners regarded the occupation of Indochina as a rather unimportant sideshow compared to the problems likely to be encountered in the occupation of north China, Manchuria, and Korea.[5] Wedemeyer's directive gave first priority to the occupation of those areas of China proper that had been held by the Japanese, second priority to Korea, Manchuria, and Formosa, and third priority to Indochina.[6] Three of the four Chinese armies assigned to enter Vietnam—the 52d, the 62d, and the 93d—were scheduled for early redeployment to Formosa and Manchuria once they had completed the preliminary task of disarming the Japanese in northern Vietnam. Only the fourth Chinese army, the 60th, with a strength of about 38,000 men and a "very good" rating from its American advisers, was to remain in northern Vietnam as the occupation force.

Events, however, followed a different course. The plan called for a minimum force, but some 125,000 to 150,000 Chinese troops came to be stationed in, or passed through, northern Vietnam between October 1945 and the spring of 1946. The 93d Chinese Army, assigned to "secure the length of the Red River and relieve the 52d Army at Hanoi," instead "took up positions in the highlands of Laos, where no Japanese had ever been, in order to control the opium poppy harvest. The 93d Army refused to leave Indo-China until September, 1946 . . . when a second crop became available."[7]

The reason for the wide divergence between the plan and what happened lay in the different conceptions of the occupation held by the Chinese and the Americans. The Americans saw the occupation as an unimportant but necessary bit of postwar housekeeping until the future of Indochina was decided. General Wedemeyer, for example, instructed his commanders that there was to be "no intimation that U.S. personnel are in French Indo-China for any mission other than a humanitarian one."[8] To the Chinese, on the other hand, the occupation was "a projection of the warlord politics of south China onto the revolutionary scene of northern Viet Nam."[9] Of the troops chosen for the occupation, more than 60 percent were Yunnanese soldiers of the warlord Lung Yun. This was a premeditated step on the part of the Chinese Nationalist government in Chungking to weaken General Lung Yun's military strength

---

[4]Ibid.

[5]Intervs, author with Gallagher, 13 Jan 72; McClure, 26 May 72; and Reginald Ungern, 18 Nov 71, Historians files, CMH.

[6]Op Directive 25, HQ USFCT, 28 Aug 45, China Theater files.

[7]History of U.S. Forces, China Theater, p. 31; McAlister, *Vietnam: Origins of Revolution*, p. 211.

[8]Radiogram on Censorship, Wedemeyer, 31 Aug 45, China Theater files.

[9]McAlister, *Vietnam: Origins of Revolution*, p. 209.

Generals Gallagher and Lu Han

by sending the bulk of his troops outside China. Early in the occupation the Nationalist government would take advantage of the situation to depose him.

The Occupation and the Viet Minh

Lung Yun's cousin, Lt. Gen. Lu Han, commanded the occupation troops. Lu Han neither trusted, nor was trusted by, the central government of China and pursued his own policies, which were sometimes at variance with those of Chungking. Basically, Lu Han intended to enrich himself and his supporters at the expense of the Vietnamese, to settle old scores with the French, and to manipulate volatile political forces unleashed by the Japanese surrender. That Lu Han was conducting the occupation for his own ends was apparently never fully understood by either the Americans or the French.

American liaison teams accompanied each of the major components of Lu Han's forces. General Wedemeyer drew these teams from the Chinese Training Combat Command, an advisory command that for just under a year had been working with newly formed units in south China. All the teams were under the command of Brig. Gen. Philip E. Gallagher, Lu Han's adviser. The primary task of the liaison teams was to advise and assist the Chinese in

The Completeness of the August Revolution *extended even to postage stamps. Left, the Vichy government stamp depicting Marshal Petain. Right, Ho Chi Minh replaces Petain.*

implementing the Japanese surrender and conducting the occupation. The teams were charged specifically with rendering all possible assistance to recovered Allied prisoners and reporting on the "effectiveness and spirit of the Chinese enforcement of the terms of surrender."[10] Instructions to the teams said nothing about political matters. For Gallagher and his men, the occupation was basically a logistical problem involving the prompt disarming of the Japanese and the repatriation of Allied prisoners. As for the political future of Vietnam, some believed the country would be returned to French control, others expected it would attain independence or be accorded a trusteeship status, and others had no opinion. All agreed that it was not their concern.[11]

Hindered by the floods in the Red River valley, the Chinese armies and their American advisers advanced slowly into Tonkin, and not until nearly a

[10]Maj Gen Robert B. McClure, Instructions to CCC Liaison Teams, 4 Sep 45, China Theater files.

[11]Ltr, Gallagher to Bernard B. Fall, 30 Mar 56, Gallagher Papers; Intervs, author with Gallagher, 13 Jan 72, Col John H. Stodter and Ungern, 18 Nov 71, and E. S. Waddell, 13 Jan 72, Historians files. All in CMH.

month after Japan's surrender did they reach Hanoi, the capital, in force. In the interval Vietnam had undergone one of the most momentous events in its history, the assumption of power and declaration of independence by the Viet Minh, generally referred to as "the August Revolution."

The August Revolution had its immediate origins in the months following the Japanese coup in March 1945 that destroyed the French colonial regime.[12] Senior colonial officials, except for a few who escaped to China, were imprisoned. After establishing a puppet regime under Nguyen Emperor Bao Dai, the Japanese proclaimed that Vietnam was "independent" and brought a longtime collaborator, Tran Trong Kim, from Singapore to head the new cabinet.

Tran Trong Kim's government was one in name only. Although the Japanese were too preoccupied with immediate military needs to pay much attention to civil government or internal political developments, the Japanese Army continued to exercise all real power in Vietnam. The Japanese grant of independence, spurious as it was, nevertheless inspired a great increase in patriotic and nationalistic activities among the Vietnamese people. "Once they were assured of Japanese indifference to political activities which were not overtly anti-Japanese, political participation became increasingly varied, enthusiastic, and better organized."[13]

As the best organized and most experienced political group in Vietnam, the Communists, who controlled the Viet Minh, were able to take advantage of the upsurge of nationalistic feeling. Membership in Viet Minh—sponsored organizations swelled. At the same time, the Viet Minh stepped up guerrilla activities against the Japanese, utilizing weapons and ammunition left behind by the French forces that had withdrawn to China and recruiting former members of the French-trained Vietnamese militia into their own military units.[14] In more remote rural areas the Viet Minh established shadow governments called People's Revolutionary Committees which were soon in effective control of their districts. They also capitalized on the widespread hardship and starvation caused by the famine in much of northern Vietnam by organizing tax boycotts and raiding granaries. By V−J Day, 15 August 1945, the Viet Minh controlled large areas of north and north central Vietnam.

With news of the Japanese acceptance of surrender terms, the Viet Minh stepped easily into the power vacuum created by Japan's collapse and the tardy arrival of Allied occupation forces. Everywhere in northern Vietnam local People's Revolutionary Committees took control of the governmental machinery. In Hanoi the Viet Minh expelled the Tran Trong Kim government, while in Hue on 30 August the Emperor Bao Dai, last descendant of the Nguyen lords of Vietnam, abdicated in favor of what would be known as the

---

[12]Unless otherwise noted this account is based on Huynh Kim Khanh, "The Vietnamese August Revolution Reinterpreted," *Journal of Asian Studies* 30 (1971): 761−82, and Ellen J. Hammer, *The Struggle for Indochina, 1940−1955* (Stanford: Stanford University Press, 1966), pp. 95−105.

[13]Khanh, "The Vietnamese August Revolution Reinterpreted," p. 767.

[14]French Indochina (Political Situation), 11 Oct 45, pp. 4−7.

Democratic Republic of Vietnam. Three days later, in an impressive ceremony carefully stage-managed by the Viet Minh, Ho Chi Minh proclaimed the independence of Vietnam before a crowd of some 500,000 in Hanoi.[15]

It was in the midst of those rapid and far-reaching political events that the first Americans entered Hanoi on 22 August 1945, almost a month in advance of the Chinese troops. The first U.S. unit to arrive was a joint OSS – Air Ground Aid Service team of about a dozen men under an OSS officer who had organized and directed some of the wartime OSS missions into Vietnam, Maj. Archimedes L. A. Patti. With Patti's team came five French officers commanded by the head of the French intelligence mission in Kunming, Maj. Jean Sainteny. Patti established a headquarters in the Hotel Metropole, while the Japanese temporarily interned the French officers in the palace of the former governor-general "as a protective measure."[16] Two days later, on 24 August, eight more men arrived to join Patti's team, and at the end of the month a small U.S. Army Civil Affairs and Military Government detachment under Col. Stephen Nordlinger also reached Hanoi.

Although clear on paper, the missions and command relationship of the American groups soon became a source of confusion. Reporting to the G – 5 (Civil Affairs) Division of the China theater, Nordlinger was to locate and aid prisoners of war and "to do everything possible to secure humanitarian treatment of all elements of the civil community."[17] Although Patti's team was under Nordlinger's operational control in regard to matters having to do with prisoners of war, Nordlinger had no authority over Patti's OSS intelligence work. For the latter, Patti was responsible both to the Strategic Services Officer, China theater, and directly to the chief, Secret Intelligence Branch, OSS, in Washington. The men of the Air Ground Aid Service, although also concerned with prisoners of war, reported to the Fourteenth Air Force. Sainteny claimed to be the official representative in Indochina of the French government, but by his own admission French authorities in Kunming and Calcutta had not confirmed his status.[18]

The fact that the Americans in Hanoi also lacked a true knowledge of current U.S. policy regarding Indochina also contributed to the confusion. That lack was attributable, at least in part, to General Wedemeyer's continuing failure to understand that the United States had come to recognize French sovereignty in Indochina. Orders from the China theater specified the U.S. personnel in Indochina were "*not* to become involved . . . in French-Chinese relations or in any way become associated with either side in possible conflicts."[19] As Major Patti reported during his first week in Hanoi, "our policy

[15]Ibid., p. 12.

[16]Rpt of G – 5 to Shanghai Base Command, 2 Jan 46, China Theater files; Drachman, *United States Policy Toward Vietnam*, pp. 140 – 41.

[17]Drachman, *United States Policy Toward Vietnam*, pp. 140 – 41.

[18]OSS Msg, Mayer and Helliwell to Nordlinger and Bernigue, No. 55, 7 Sep 45; Patti, Project No. 1 [Rpt], pt. B, p. 6. Both in PSYWAR 091 (1957) Indochina, RG 319. See also, Sainteny, *Histoire d'une Paix Manquee*, pp. 105 – 09.

[19]Rpt of G – 5 to Shanghai Base Command; OSS Msg, Indiv to Patti, No. 22, 28 Aug 45, PSYWAR 091 (1957) Indochina, RG 319.

Major Patti, *left, with OSS team members and Viet Minh leaders. Giap is third from right.*

here has been one of strict neutrality." The Americans had made "it quite clear . . . that our interests here at the moment are strictly a military mission and have no political implications."[20]

Such a stance was certainly not appreciated by the French. Indeed, Sainteny was later to accuse Patti of having deliberately delayed the departure of his French mission to Hanoi for more than a week after the Japanese surrender and of having engaged in anti-French and pro–Viet Minh activities. Other French writers have charged Patti's men with siding openly with the Viet Minh and with prospecting for American business interests.[21]

Patti had always been willing to work with the French during the war, but it took only a day or two in Hanoi to convince him that any attempt by the French to reoccupy Vietnam would precipitate civil war. "Political situation critical," he signaled to Kunming. "Viet Minh strong and belligerent and definitely anti-French. Suggest no more French be permitted to enter French Indo-China and especially not armed."[22] Patti later asserted that only the

[20]OSS Msg, Patti to Indiv, No. 19, 27 Aug 45, PSYWAR 091 (1957) Indochina, RG 319.
[21]See Sainteny, *Histoire d'une Paix Manquee,* pp. 62–87, 95–125, passim; Gabriel Sabattier, *Le Destin de l'Indochine* (Paris: Plon, 1952), pp. 334–40; and Pierre Maurice Dessinges, "Les Intrigues Internationales en Indochine," *Le Monde,* 13 April 1947.
[22]OSS Msg, Patti to Indiv, No. 2, 23 Aug 45, PSYWAR 091 (1957) Indochina, RG 319.

French Prisoners of War *in the Citadel, Hanoi.*

presence of armed Americans had prevented a Vietnamese massacre of French civilians during the turbulent days of the August Revolution.[23] French civilians in Hanoi, observed another American officer, were "terrified of the Annamese." Their homes were being looted by armed bands of Annamese, and Frenchmen found on the streets at night were frequently jailed for short periods.[24]

Particularly serious was the plight of some 4,500 Frenchmen, mainly foreign legionnaires, who had been imprisoned in the old Citadel in Hanoi during the Japanese takeover in March.[25] One of Patti's men described health and sanitary conditions in the Citadel as "incredibly bad." A prison hospital designed to accommodate 150 had 350 patients, half of them critically ill. Six or seven people were dying daily.[26] The prisoners were the special concern of Colonel Nordlinger's Civil Affairs detachment. One of Nordlinger's first tasks, accomplished by late September with the help of the Air Ground Aid Service, was to provide a new hospital with 400 beds.[27] He was able to obtain a

[23]Drachman, *United States Policy Toward Vietnam*, pp. 141–42; Abbot Low Moffat, Memo of Conversation With Major A. L. Patti, 5 Dec 46, 851G.00/12–546, RG 59.
[24]Ltr, Lt Col John C. Bane to Gallagher, 15 Sep 45, FIC file, China Theater files.
[25]Rpt, Col Stephen Nordlinger to Lt Col John C. Bane, Sep 45, FIC file, China Theater files.
[26]Ibid.; Rpt of G–5 to Shanghai Base Command, 2 Jan 46; OSS Msg, Patti to Indiv, No. 62, 1 Sep 45 PSYWAR 091 (1957) Indochina, RG 319.
[27]Ltr, Bane to Gallagher, 15 Sep 45.

considerable quantity of medical supplies and such emergency food items as powdered milk from American headquarters in Kunming and from the Red Cross.[28] Nordlinger also persuaded the Viet Minh to return control of all the hospitals in Hanoi to French medical personnel.

Although French officials pressed for release of able-bodied prisoners from the Citadel to "serve as a protective force against Annamites' attacks on French civilians," both Nordlinger and Patti categorically refused to consider the proposal in the belief that release of the prisoners might set off a civil war.[29] Patti pointed out that arms and ammunition were stored in the houses of many Frenchmen and that the healthy prisoners in the Citadel were waiting for the moment of liberation to take up arms.[30] This decision not to release the French prisoners earned for the United States the lasting enmity of many Frenchmen, but it may well have forestalled fighting.[31] When the commander of the British occupation forces in southern Vietnam, Maj. Gen. Douglas D. Gracey, released French prisoners in Saigon, the result was precisely the kind of civil strife that Patti and Nordlinger had feared.

While endeavoring to remain neutral, the Americans in Hanoi agreed to arrange meetings between the Sainteny mission and the Viet Minh, but at the end of August the China theater ordered them to stop.[32] During that brief period Patti had ample opportunity to observe the Viet Minh government in action. His initial impressions were negative. "The Provisional Government is groping in the dark," he reported to Kunming. "I am convinced they are not politically mature and being misled by Japanese agent provocateurs and Red elements."[33] Yet a few days later, on 1 September, he was advising Kunming that "Ho Chi Minh . . . impresses me as a sensible, well balanced, politically minded individual. . . . From what I have seen these people mean business and I am afraid the French will have to deal with them. For that matter we will all have to deal with them."[34]

Gallagher's Mission

Such was the situation in mid-September 1945 when the Chinese occupation armies entered Hanoi: the Viet Minh remained in control, the French

---

[28]Drachman, *United States Policy Toward Vietnam*, pp. 142–43.
[29]OSS Msg, Nordlinger Thru Patti to Indiv for G–5, No. 54, 31 Aug 45, PSYWAR 091 (1957) Indochina, RG 319.
[30]Ibid., also OSS Msg, Patti to Indiv, Relay to Gallagher, No. 63, 2 Sep 45, PSYWAR 091 (1957) Indochina, RG 319.
[31]As Bernard Fall observed in 1962, "Many of the French officials who were involved in Indo-China then are still in high posts in the French government today . . . and hundreds of present day French majors and colonels were lieutenants interned in Japanese concentration camps and to this day they term American actions of that period as rank 'betrayal' of a loyal ally." See Fall, *The Two Vietnams*, pp. 69–70.
[32]OSS Msg, Indiv to Patti, No. 22, 28 Aug 45.
[33]OSS Msg, Patti to Indiv, No. 36, 28 Aug 45, PSYWAR 091 (1957) Indochina, RG 319.
[34]Ibid., No. 61, 1 Sep 45, PSYWAR 091 (1957) Indochina, RG 319.

were helpless to oust them, and the Japanese were passive but ready to obey any orders put to them by the OSS and Civil Affairs detachment. The Americans, however, had refused to make any change in the status quo. Arriving with the Chinese troops, General Gallagher and his staff now brought the total number of Americans in Hanoi to about sixty.[35]

The small group of Americans who had preceded Gallagher—the men of the OSS, Air Ground Aid Service, and Civil Affairs detachment—had already become the focus of extravagant hopes and fears on the part of both the Vietnamese and the French. The Vietnamese saw the Americans "as a symbol of liberation, not from the Japanese, but from decades of French colonial rule."[36] Fastening on the example of the Philippines (which was about to receive independence) and the high-sounding declarations of the Atlantic Charter, many Vietnamese expected that the United States would champion their revolution.[37] The French, on the other hand, greeted the Americans as allies. "The French are extremely friendly and look to us for protection," reported one of Gallagher's officers.[38] Both groups were to be sorely disappointed.

For the moment, it was not the handful of Americans in Hanoi but the Chinese who controlled the fate of northern Vietnam. Specifically, it was the Yunnan warlord Lu Han, and he apparently had no intention of helping the French to regain control. When Colonel Nordlinger recommended that Viet Minh forces in Hanoi be disarmed, General Lu Han flatly refused, and he promptly expelled the small French mission under Sainteny from the palace of the former governor-general.[39] The Chinese also made no move to release the French soldiers still held in the Citadel or to interfere in any way with the day-to-day functioning of the Viet Minh government. Having received no clear guidance about what the political future of Vietnam was to be, General Gallagher generally approved Lu Han's hands-off approach but supported Colonel Nordlinger's efforts to alleviate conditions for the French prisoners.[40]

For General Gallagher it was difficult to come to a conclusion about the revolution he was witnessing. Upon arrival in Hanoi he was presented with confused and often contradictory reports on the Viet Minh by the American officers who had preceded him. Colonel Nordlinger and his intelligence officer, Lt. Col. John C. Bane, for example, believed that the Viet Minh were sponsored by the Japanese, had "a menacing attitude," and constituted a threat to good order. In urging General Lu Han to disarm the Viet Minh

---

[35]History of U.S. Forces, China Theater, p. 32; Ltr, Bane to Gallagher, 15 Sep 45; Alert Plan for American Personnel in Hanoi, 24 Sep 45, FIC file, China Theater files.

[36]Report of Arthur Hale, USIS (U.S. Information Service), Nov 45, copy in Gallagher Papers, CMH.

[37]That was the impression received by nearly all Americans in Vietnam at the time. See Hale Rpt. See also Gallagher to McClure, 20 Sep 45, Gallagher Papers; Interv, author with Gallagher, 13 Jan 72, and Ungern, 18 Nov 71; Ltr, Maj F. M. Mullins to Gallagher, 26 Sep 45, FIC file, China Theater files.

[38]Ltr, Bane to Gallagher, 15 Sep 45.

[39]Ibid.

[40]Interv, author with Gallagher, 13 Jan 72.

troops, Nordlinger hoped that once Ho Chi Minh's government had lost its coercive power, "a more democratic organization would probably evolve under new leadership to take its place."[41] Another officer, Maj. F. M. Mullins, reported that Ho, although "a disciple of communism," was "pro-American" and "sincere in his political motives and anxious to co-operate with the Americans."[42] While recognizing that Ho was "an old revolutionist" and "a product of Moscow," General Gallagher finally decided that "the Prime Minister and his party represented the real aspirations of the Vietnamese people for independence."[43]

In conversations with Ho, Gallagher quickly learned that the Vietnamese leader looked to the United States for support. "He looks upon America as the savior of all small nations," Gallagher reported to the China theater, "and is basing all his actions on the statement in the Atlantic Charter that the independence of the smaller nations would be assured by the major powers. . . . I pointed out frankly that my job was not as a representative of the State Department nor was I interested in the political situation . . . that I was merely working with Lu Han. Confidentially I wish the Annamites could be given their independence, but, of course we have no voice in this matter."[44]

The French saw General Gallagher's attitude not as neutral but as consciously anti-French. How else, they asked, could they explain the fact that French soldiers were still languishing in the Citadel, or Gallagher's refusal to do anything to help restore France's rightful position in Vietnam? Indeed, the French read political significance into almost everything said or done by the small body of Americans in Hanoi. Many Frenchmen saw American actions as part of a propaganda campaign to impress the Vietnamese with the wealth and power of America and to discredit the French.[45]

General Gallagher unwittingly exacerbated relations with the French on 18 September when he observed in a casual conversation with a Chinese general, Gaston Wang, that the Viet Minh's opposition to return of the French was so strong that entrance of French troops into northern Vietnam would probably initiate armed conflict or disturbances which would make it difficult for Lu Han to maintain peace and order.[46] General Wang, who had many friends and associates among the French colonials, promptly reported this conversation to Sainteny, who in turn reported it to Paris.[47] When the State Department received a protest from the French Foreign Office, the conversation had become a "secret conference" between Gallagher, Wang, and Alessandri. General Gallagher was alleged to have said that the Allies had not yet recognized French sovereignty, that premature participation by the French in

[41]Ltr, Bane to Gallagher, 15 Sep 45.
[42]Ltr, Mullins to Gallagher, 26 Sep 45.
[43]Ltr, Gallagher to McClure, 20 Sep 45.
[44]Ibid.
[45]See Dessinges, "Les Intrigues Internationales en Indochine," Sabattier, *Le Destin de l'Indochine,* and Sainteny, *Histoire d'une Paix Manquee.*
[46]Msg, Gallagher to HQ, CCC, 21 Sep 45, China Theater files.
[47]Interv, author with Gallagher, 13 Jan 72.

Japanese Surrender Ceremony *in Hanoi, September 1945.*

the occupation might precipitate a conflict, and that there could be no question of the restoration of French sovereignty to Indochina.[48]

When General Gallagher learned of the protest, he rushed to General Wang's apartment with a demand that the Chinese officer report the true version of their conversation and its circumstances.[49] Wang eventually provided a written statement, which Gallagher enclosed in a letter to Maj. Gen. Robert B. McClure, commander of the Chinese Combat Command. Gallagher denied that he had ever held a secret meeting with Wang and Alessandri and gave his version of his conversation with Wang.[50] Although General Wedemeyer cautioned Gallagher to be more circumspect in future conversations, both he and General McClure accepted the explanation.[51] The Chinese government, added McClure, recognized French sovereignty in Indochina and desired that its own commanders in Indochina facilitate the resumption of French administration. As for American policy, "it remains hands off."[52]

Although General Gallagher passed that information to the Chinese com-

---

[48]Msg, HQ, CCC, to Gallagher, 21 Sep 45, FIC files.
[49]Interv, author with Gallagher, 13 Jan 72.
[50]Ltr, Gallagher to McClure, 21 Sep 45, FIC files.
[51]Msg, CG, China Theater, to Gallagher, 30 Sep 45, FIC radio msg, China Theater files.
[52]Msg, McClure to Gallagher, Sep 45, Gallagher Papers.

mand, General Lu Han discounted it. He had received no orders from his superiors to assist the French, he said, and added that to help the French might turn the Vietnamese against the ethnic Chinese living in Hanoi.[53] At a meeting with French representatives on 21 September, Lu Han emphasized that he was in command in north Indochina and that he would show no partiality to either French or Vietnamese.[54]

When General Alessandri arrived in Hanoi to attend the formal Japanese surrender ceremony, General Gallagher on 26 September met with him, passed on the Chinese government's view in regard to French sovereignty in Vietnam as he had learned it from General McClure, and indicated his willingness to be of assistance. "Overjoyed," Alessandri presented Gallagher with a long list of measures he wanted the Chinese to implement. They included releasing all prisoners from the Citadel, rearming the French police and military, and returning control of the radio station and the public utilities to the French.[55]

Although General Lu Han promised Gallagher that he would meet the French demands where possible, the attitude he displayed at the formal Japanese surrender was hardly conducive to French optimism.[56] Even though General Alessandri had flown to Hanoi specifically to attend the ceremony, Lu Han refused to allow him to participate in an official capacity because of his "unclear position."[57] Lu Han refused also to allow the French flag to be flown at the ceremony alongside the flags of the other Allied nations.[58] When both Gallagher and Alessandri asked him to reconsider, Lu Han informed Gallagher that he would raise the flag only if specifically ordered to do so by his superiors.[59] Two days later the China theater confidentially advised Gallagher that the Chinese high command would instruct Lu Han to display the French flag at the surrender. Whether he received such an order or not, the flag was conspicuously absent on the day of the ceremony. Displaying it, Lu Han said, might incite the Vietnamese to riot.[60] After Alessandri departed Hanoi in a rage, Lu Han issued a public proclamation warning "the enemy of Vietnam" that if he "dared to stir up any bloody tragedy," he would be severely punished.[61] Few doubted that the proclamation was aimed at the French.

Despite Lu Han's promise to try to meet French demands, the Chinese gave the French, in Gallagher's words, "damn little." At Gallagher's urging, Lu Han grudgingly agreed to release all French captives from the Citadel and also to provide a small amount of gasoline to the French Military Mission.

[53]Ltr, Gallagher to McClure, 27 Sep 45, Gallagher Papers.

[54]MFR, Gallagher, 21 Sep 45, Gallagher Papers.

[55]Memo, Lt Reginald Ungern, ADC, to Gen Gallagher, 26 Sep 45, Gallagher Papers.

[56]Ltr, Gallagher to McClure, 27 Sep 45.

[57]Chen, *Vietnam and China, 1938–1954*, p. 125. Alessandri was placed 115th among those attending as guests, see McAlister, *Vietnam: Origins of Revolution*, p. 212.

[58]Msg, Gallagher to CG, USFCT, 27 Sep 45, FIC radio msg, China Theater files.

[59]Msg, CG, USFCT, to Gallagher, 29 Sep 45, FIC radio msg, China Theater files.

[60]Ibid.

[61]Ltr, Gallagher to McClure, 27 Sep 45.

Anything more he would not do. His reasons were familiar: he had received no clear instructions from his headquarters, and he feared reprisals against the ethnic Chinese if his army appeared to be aiding the French.[62] When Gallagher suggested to the China theater that Lu Han be given firm and unequivocal instructions from the Chinese government, General Wedemeyer replied that the matter was for the Chinese to decide and that he was unwilling to initiate any action which might be interpreted as meddling by China theater in the Indochina political situation.[63]

Chinese and American help to the French, small and ineffective as it was, was still sufficient to alarm the Viet Minh. General Gallagher reported on 4 October "a noticeable change in the attitude of the Annamites toward the Americans here . . . since they became aware of the fact that we were not going to interfere and would probably help the French."[64] In a meeting with Gallagher and Major Patti, Ho Chi Minh had "expressed the fear that the Allies considered Indochina a conquered country and that the Chinese came as conquerers." Gallagher and Patti attempted to reassure him and also urged him to continue to negotiate with the French.[65]

Americans in Southern Vietnam

The situation in Hanoi was also undoubtedly influenced by events in Vietnam south of the 16th Parallel where the British, unlike the Chinese, were doing nothing to interfere with France's resuming control and in many ways were actually facilitating a French return to power.[66] The occupation plan for Indochina prepared by the Southeast Asia Command at the end of August had provided that "eventual reoccupation of French Indochina is a matter for the French" and that "as far as possible all matters affecting the civil population should be dealt with through the French."[67] In addition, an Anglo-French civil affairs agreement signed at the same time had specified that among the reasons for stationing Allied troops in Indochina was restoration of French authority in the country.[68] Given that understanding, it was probably unavoidable that the British forces came into conflict with Vietnamese Nationalists, but relations were further strained by the actions of Maj. Gen. Douglas Gracey, the commander of the occupation force.

The British had arrived in Saigon around the middle of September to find that city, like Hanoi, in the hands of a Nationalist Revolutionary government,

[62]Memo of Conference, 5 Sep 45, Gallagher Papers; Ltr, Gallagher to McClure, 27 Sep 45.
[63]Msg, CG, China Theater, to Gallagher, 4 Oct 45, FIC radio msg, China Theater files.
[64]Ibid.
[65]Ltr, Gallagher to McClure, 27 Sep 45.
[66]For a discussion of the evolution of British policy toward Indochina during World War II, see Thorne, *Allies of a Kind*, pp. 501, 619–22, 678, passim.
[67]SEAC Force Plan No. 1, Occupation of French Indochina, 31 Aug 45, WO 203/5444, SEAC records.
[68]Msg, War Office to SACSEA, 31 Aug 45, WO 203/4117, SEAC records.

but there were important differences. In the north, the Viet Minh had few serious rivals for the leadership of the independence movement; in the south, they competed for leadership with the Trotskyite Dai Viet Party, the old pro-Japanese Phuc Quoc Party, and two part-religious, part-political sects known as the Cao Dai and the Hoa Hao. Out of a total of thirteen members of a Provisional Executive Committee for the South, which was governing when the occupation troops arrived, only four were Viet Minh.[69]

From the outset, General Gracey made it clear that, unlike Lu Han and Gallagher in the north, he was unwilling to work with and through the existing nationalist government. He demanded instead that all Vietnamese be disarmed, and he informed the local Japanese commander, Field Marshal Terauchi Hisaichi, that the Japanese were responsible for maintaining order. In protest against that action the nationalists on 17 September staged a general strike. Gracey responded with a proclamation of martial law, suspension of all Vietnamese newspapers, and a ban on all public meetings and demonstrations. He also released and rearmed about 1,400 French soldiers who had been interned in the Saigon area since the Japanese takeover in March 1945.

The French, described by a member of Mountbatten's staff as "ill-disciplined and excited," promptly reoccupied all public buildings and evicted the Vietnamese from the post offices and police stations. There were "wild shootings and Annamites were openly dragged through the streets to be locked up in prisons. Generally speaking there was complete chaos."[70]

The Provisional Executive Committee for the South answered with a crippling general strike and widespread acts of sabotage. On the evening of 24 September members of the Binh Xuyen, a gangster-type political sect, entered a French residential section of Saigon called the Cite Herault and massacred more than 150 French colonials, mostly women and children. From that point civil war was general throughout the south, with British and even Japanese troops supporting the French against the Viet Minh and other nationalists.

The American role in the south was more conspicuous although much less important than in the north. As early as 10 August, OSS Detachment 404 based in Ceylon had begun plans for an intelligence and observer group to accompany British troops to Saigon. Known by the code name Embankment, the project had a number of widely divergent objectives. A primary purpose was to locate and assist Allied prisoners of war, particularly Americans, and to identify and track down Japanese war criminals. Members of the mission were also to locate and inventory all property of the United States government and American citizens and confiscate or microfilm all Japanese documents and code books. Other objectives were to report on political trends and to keep track of the activities of any anti-Allied or pro-Japanese political groups.[71] The OSS group was instructed to reveal only as much of its mission

[69]Buttinger, *Vietnam: A Political History*, p. 324.
[70]Memo for Adm Mountbatten, 3 Oct 45, sub: FIC Political and Internal Situation, WO 203/5562, SEAC records.
[71]Maj Amos D. Moscrip, A Plan to Penetrate Saigon, 10 Aug 45, records of the OSS.

objectives to the French authorities "as will not offend their sensibilities."[72]

The man selected to command Embankment was Maj. A. Peter Dewey. Dewey spoke fluent French and had served with the OSS in France and North Africa, but his knowledge of current conditions in Indochina was spotty. In a memorandum on French policy in the Far East, prepared for Detachment 404 in August 1945, Dewey made no mention of the nationalistic stirrings in Vietnam and Laos but devoted his attention exclusively to what the French might do. Like the French themselves, Dewey viewed the question of Indochina primarily as a problem for France, Britain, the United States, and China. Dewey pointed out that the French were worried about the possibility of a joint British-American-Chinese trusteeship for Indochina and were determined to place elements of their army in southern Vietnam as soon as possible.[73]

On 1 September the advance element of Embankment, a prisoner of war evacuation team under 1st Lt. Emile R. Connasse, was parachuted into Saigon. The men were greeted respectfully by the Japanese and allowed to proceed with their work.[74] Connasse dismissed the establishment by the Vietnamese of an independent government as "a drugstore revolution" but acknowledged that "for the present [its] control is complete."[75]

On the day after their arrival, the Americans witnessed a massive demonstration and parade by several hundred thousand men and women organized by the Provisional Executive Committee for the South. Intended by the Viet Minh as a demonstration of solidarity, the parade was soon manipulated by extremists into an attack on the French residents of the city. Dozens of French men and women were beaten up or arbitrarily thrown into jail, and many of their homes were looted.

This attack was the first serious breakdown of public order since the Committee for the South had taken control and would not be repeated until well after the arrival of the British and French.[76] Yet it gave the newly arrived Americans of the Embankment team a sense that the revolutionary government was naturally prone to violence and disorder. Many of its actions "appeared crazy or unexplainable."[77] The Americans commandeered the large Continental Palace Hotel as a refuge for French civilians, using the Japanese to guard it against attacks by the Vietnamese.[78]

Major Dewey arrived with the remainder of the Embankment team on 4 September and relieved Lieutenant Connasse, who returned to Ceylon. Dewey and his executive officer, Capt. Herbert J. Bluechel, continued to do their best to protect French civilians, but they also established close contact

---

[72]Ibid.

[73]Peter Dewey, Aug 45, French Policy in the Far East and Its Instrumentation, records of the OSS.

[74]Report of Embankment P.O.W. Evacuation Team, 8 Sep 45, records of the OSS.

[75]Ibid.

[76]Buttinger, *Vietnam: A Dragon Embattled*, 1:320 – 21; Hammer, *The Struggle for Indochina*, pp. 108 – 09.

[77]Interv, author with Frank White, 18 Feb 72, Historians files, CMH.

[78]Ibid.

with the leaders of the independence movement. After the arrival of the British and French, Dewey was under considerable pressure to break off those meetings with the Vietnamese.[79] General Gracey claimed that Dewey was going outside normal command channels and that his actions would be interpreted by the Vietnamese as evidence of official American support for the independence movement.[80] On 14 September Gracey formally ordered the Embankment team to cease all intelligence activities until its mission in Saigon was "clarified." Dewey complained bitterly about that directive to OSS headquarters and evidently continued his intelligence activities.

Although French and British relations with the Vietnamese were deteriorating, the Americans experienced little difficulty until 24 September, when Capt. Joseph Coolidge was ambushed along with a British officer on a trip to Dalat. Coolidge was seriously wounded and had to be evacuated to Ceylon. A more serious incident occurred on 26 September when Major Dewey and Captain Bluechel, while riding in a jeep, were fired upon without warning by a group of Vietnamese. Dewey was killed instantly, but Bluechel, who was slightly wounded, managed to fight his way back to a nearby villa where the OSS team had its headquarters. The Vietnamese then attacked the villa. Capt. Frank White and Sgt. George Wickes held them off until help arrived from a nearby British post.[81]

The motives of the Vietnamese who killed Major Dewey and attacked the villa were never determined. The ambushers could have been Viet Minh, members of the Binh Xuyen, or even hirelings of the French. Since General Gracey had forbidden the Americans to fly the American flag from their vehicle, Dewey might have been mistaken for a Frenchman. The major's body was never recovered. In 1981 a Vietnamese refugee in France told U.S. Defense Department officials that a band of Avant Garde Youth (a Viet Minh front movement) led by a man named Muoi Cuong had ambushed Dewey, burned his jeep, and dumped his body into a nearby well. Learning later that Dewey was in fact an American and fearing discovery, they removed the body from the well and disposed of it near the village of An Phu Dong. Both Muoi Cuong and his deputy Bay Tay, a renegade soldier of the French colonial troops who wore Dewey's Colt 12 pistol on his hip, were later killed fighting the French.[82]

Dewey was succeeded as commander of the Embankment team by Lt. James R. Withrow, Jr., U.S. Navy, a veteran of OSS operations in India. Withrow's mission was the same as Dewey's: to help repatriate Allied prisoners, hunt for war criminals, and report on the intentions and attitude of the

---

[79]Ibid.; Maj F. M. Small, Memorandum on Investigation of the Death of Major Peter Dewey, 25 Oct 45, and Msg, Dewey to HQ, 404, 14 Sep 45, both in records of the OSS.

[80]Interv, author with White, 26 Feb 72.

[81]Ibid.; Affidavits by Capt Herbert J. Bluechel and Sgt George Wickes, both in records of the OSS.

[82]Small, Memo on Investigation of the Death of Dewey, 25 Oct 45. Dewey was promoted posthumously to the rank of lieutenant colonel. Ltr to U.S. Embassy, Paris, 1981, copy in Historians files, CMH.

French.[83] Shortly after Withrow's arrival, the French forces in Saigon were reinforced by regular units under the command of General Jacques Leclerc. The French then began the reconquest of southern Vietnam in earnest. Withrow established contact with the local Viet Minh leaders but also maintained a close relationship with General Leclerc. In a private conversation with Withrow, Leclerc outlined his plans to regain control of Indochina and stated that he intended to ask the United States for arms and equipment to enable him to pacify the country.[84] When Withrow passed on that information to the State and War Departments, he was admonished not to interfere in French affairs.[85] The OSS role in southern Indochina had become one simply of observing the French conquest of Cochinchina and reporting the results to Washington.

Possible Trouble

In Hanoi, word of Major Dewey's death caused uneasiness among the Americans of General Gallagher's command. Prime Minister Ho Chi Minh hastened to the general's headquarters to express his regrets and assured the Americans that such an incident would occur in the north only "over my dead body."[86] The prime minister said he intended to write personally to the State Department to explain the incident.

At the same time, news of the turmoil in the south frightened and angered the Vietnamese population in Hanoi and led to beatings and even murders of members of the French community. At one point Major Sainteny, displaying a French flag on his car, was seized and imprisoned by a Vietnamese mob, but at American insistence he was soon released. Scattered rioting and unruly street demonstrations erupted, climaxing on 23 October when shots from a mob killed two French officers. The next day Vietnamese markets and stores declared a boycott on sales to the French. "The situation here," General Gallagher observed, "is pregnant with possible trouble." To General Lu Han he declared that "unless the Provisional government can demonstrate at once that it can control the population . . . you will be forced to assume direct control."[87] But Lu Han was no more anxious than before to assume responsibility for governing northern Vietnam. He was content to leave this thankless task to Ho Chi Minh.

Despite the tense atmosphere, General Gallagher and his staff proceeded with preparations to transport three of the Chinese armies to Formosa and Manchuria. When a naval task force arrived off the port of Haiphong in mid-October to load the Chinese, it was discovered that mines sown in the

[83]Interv, author with Withrow, 9 Mar 72.
[84]Ibid.
[85]Ibid.
[86]MFR, Ungern, 28 Sep 45, Gallagher Papers.
[87]MFR, 26 Oct 45, Gallagher Papers.

harbor by the U.S. Army Air Forces during World War II had never been cleared.[88] Since sweeping the mines would open the harbor to French troopships and thus possibly lead to war between the French and the Vietnamese, neither General Gallagher nor General Lu Han wanted the harbor cleared. The task force commander, Rear Adm. Elliott Buckmaster, suggested that only the outer approaches to the harbor be cleared and that the troops be put aboard from lighters.[89] Using commandeered Japanese minesweepers, Buckmaster completed the task by 22 October, and contingents of the 52d Army began to board seven Liberty ships. Through most of November, General Gallagher and his staff personally supervised the loading of the troops.

Returning to Hanoi on the 29th, Gallagher found a full-blown economic crisis in progress. This crisis was an outgrowth of Chinese occupation policy which, as practiced by General Lu Han, was essentially an opportunistic exploitation of the situation in Vietnam. One aspect of this policy was the deliberate manipulation of the Vietnamese currency system to enrich the Chinese. The exchange rate between the Chinese dollar and the Vietnamese piaster had been arbitrarily set at 1.5 piasters to 1 Chinese dollar, thus making the value of the Chinese dollar approximately three times greater in Hanoi than across the Chinese border in Kunming.[90]

The Chinese soon began to flood northern Vietnam with their currency. In one instance 60 million Chinese dollars were reported on a single flight from China. The Chinese bought hotels, shops, houses, and any other property that became available. At the same time, according to one estimate, they extracted some 400 million Bank of Indochina piasters.[91] This sum came from the poorer half of a country whose total gross national product in 1939 had been around $1.14 billion.

General Gallagher's civil affairs officer, Lt. Col. C. Radford Berry, early predicted that continued manipulation of the exchange rate, forced loans from the Bank of Indochina, and concurrent use of both Chinese and Vietnamese money as legal tender would result in the collapse of the currency of Indochina.[92] Attributing the Chinese practices to simple ignorance of the mechanics of finance, Berry suggested that General Gallagher dispatch a memo on the subject to Lu Han. Gallagher instead sent Lu Han a copy of Berry's memorandum. Berry observed that "it appears [my] memo has caused the Chinese to realize the gravity of the situation and provoked early action by them looking to a remedy."[93] Action proceeded—but not in the manner envisioned by Colonel Berry. The Chinese continued doing business as usual. At the end of October, General Gallagher felt compelled to warn Lu Han that "the situation with respect to currency . . . is growing steadily worse."[94]

[88]Ltr, Vice Adm Elliott Buckmaster to author, 6 Nov 71, Historians files, CMH.
[89]MFR's, 26 Oct and 29 Oct 45; Ltr, Gallagher to McClure, 26 Oct 45. All in Gallagher Papers.
[90]Chen, *Vietnam and China*, pp. 134–35.
[91]McAlister, *Vietnam: Origins of Revolution*, pp. 225–26.
[92]Ltr, C. Radford Berry to Gallagher, 18 Oct 45, FIC file, China Theater files.
[93]Ibid., 25 Oct 45, FIC file, China Theater files.
[94]Ltr, Gallagher to Lu Han, 31 Oct 45, Gallagher Papers.

Despite that warning, the Chinese on 14 November demanded that Major Sainteny arrange that the Bank of Indochina make available at least 600,000 piasters a day for exchange and grant an immediate loan of 40 million piasters to meet "urgent military needs."[95] Although protesting, Sainteny felt he had no choice but to accede to the Chinese demands.

The French authorities in Saigon, however, who were now professing authority over all of Vietnam, rejected any further Chinese levies. On 17 November the French high commissioner in Saigon issued a decree withdrawing all 500-piaster bank notes from circulation in Vietnam, devaluating them by 30 percent, and directing that they be deposited in the Bank of Indochina in special blocked accounts. He also declared all 500-piaster notes printed by the Japanese following their takeover in March to be of no value.[96] The 500-piaster note formed the backbone of Vietnamese currency, and many small tradesmen, merchants, and artisans had put their life savings into a few of them. The French decree thus caused consternation and panic among the people of Hanoi. There were demonstrations and riots, and large crowds besieged the Hanoi offices of the Bank of Indochina.[97]

Since the decree caught many Chinese officers and soldiers in possession of great numbers of 500-piaster notes and since the ethnic Chinese in Hanoi, a large portion of the city's tradesmen, were sharply affected, the Chinese command on 24 November not surprisingly notified Sainteny that the French high commissioner's decree was invalid north of the 16th Parallel. Two days later they told the manager of the Hanoi branch of the Bank of Indochina that unless the decree was rescinded immediately, they could no longer be responsible for the safety of the bank.[98]

The Viet Minh organized a mass demonstration outside the Bank of Indochina. When two Chinese guards were wounded, other guards opened fire on the crowd. After this fire apparently was returned, the Chinese responded by tossing hand grenades into the crowd. Six Vietnamese were killed. Blaming the French for the incident, the Viet Minh—with apparent encouragement by the Chinese command—organized another boycott; Vietnamese (and ethnic Chinese) merchants refused again to sell food or goods to members of the French community. Under pressure from the Americans, the Chinese continued to guard the bank, but when Sainteny, after conferring with French authorities, announced that "the invalidation of the 500 piaster note is a financial policy of the French government [and] no change will be made," the Chinese responded by taking the two officials of the bank into custody.[99]

Throughout the crisis, General Lu Han stayed away from the city, claiming ill-health. He failed to return even after General Gallagher sent him an urgent message from Haiphong saying his presence in the city was essen-

---

[95]Chen, *Vietnam and China*, p. 135.
[96]Decree of the High Commissioner of France for Indochina, Incl to Ltr, Sainteny to Gallagher, 21 Nov 45, Gallagher Papers.
[97]Reginald Ungern, History of the $500 [*sic*] Note Incident, Ms in Gallagher Papers.
[98]Chen, *Vietnam and China*, p. 136.
[99]Ibid., p. 137.

tial.[100] In his absence, his chief of staff, General Yin, was in charge. When General Gallagher returned to Hanoi, he met immediately with Yin. Pointing out that neither the officials of the bank nor any other local French official had authority to alter financial policies of the French government, Gallagher demanded immediate release of the two bankers, followed by a meeting between Chinese and French officials.[101] When the Chinese released the two the next afternoon, Major Sainteny agreed to meet with the Chinese on 1 December at General Gallagher's residence.

At the meeting, the Chinese generals reiterated that it would be very difficult to maintain local peace in view of the measures taken by the French.[102] Powerless to alter monetary policy directed by the French government, Sainteny had no choice but to stand firm. Seemingly unable to comprehend Sainteny's inability to act, the Chinese suggested that in exchange for French cooperation, they might be able to use their influence to end the Vietnamese boycott on selling to the French community. General Gallagher then interceded, arguing that the two sides "could not solve the banking problem by having women and children go hungry." Saying that he found it impossible to believe that the Chinese intended to do so, he asked approval of both sides for him to call personally on Ho Chi Minh to ask that the Vietnamese end the boycott.[103] Thus confronted, the Chinese agreed. Seeing that agreement as a concession by the Chinese, Gallagher told Sainteny that it left the French with a moral responsibility to try to solve the problem over withdrawal of the 500-piaster notes.

The meeting temporarily adjourned; Gallagher called on Ho Chi Minh, who agreed to try to stop the boycott but demanded that the French indemnify the families of the Vietnamese killed during the demonstration at the bank. When Gallagher next met with the French and Chinese, Sainteny announced that French financial experts with full authority to make an agreement would be sent from Saigon to confer with the Chinese.

After a few days of acrimonious discussion with these experts, the two sides finally agreed upon a joint proclamation declaring that the 500-piaster notes would continue in circulation north of the 16th Parallel. Persons possessing 500-piaster notes in amounts greater than 5,000 piasters were required to deposit them in special accounts in the Bank of Indochina but would be allowed a monthly withdrawal of up to 20 percent of their balance. As a part of a gradual effort to withdraw the notes printed by the Japanese, individuals possessing less than 5,000 piasters of those notes could exchange them at face value.[104] The immediate crisis was over, although Chinese exploitation of Vietnamese currency continued.

The 500-piaster crisis proved to be General Gallagher's last major prob-

[100]Ungern, History of $500 Note Incident, p. 3.
[101]MFR, 29 Nov 45, Gallagher Papers.
[102]Ibid., 2 Dec 45, Gallagher Papers.
[103]Ibid.
[104]Ltr, High Commissioner of France for Indochina to Gen Lu Han, 5 Oct 45, copy in Gallagher Papers.

lem in Vietnam. As early as 3 October 1945 the chief of the War Department's Operations Division, Lt. Gen. John E. Hull, had suggested to General Wedemeyer, in the wake of the Gallagher-Wang incident, that American advisers be withdrawn to "preclude further embarrassment and in consonance with U.S. policy that all matters pertaining to that area should be resolved between the Chinese and French governments."[105] Since early November the China theater itself had become increasingly anxious to withdraw its contingent from Vietnam in order to meet other personnel needs, while the State and the War Departments were becoming more concerned about persistent French complaints and accusations that American military men were interfering in Franco-Vietnamese and Franco-Chinese relations. Because General Gallagher believed that the presence of an American general officer in Hanoi was still advisable, he was permitted to remain in the capital with a steadily diminishing staff until 12 December 1945, when he was finally ordered to close out the American advisory mission.

General Gallagher's mission to Hanoi must certainly rank among the most difficult assignments of the immediate postwar period. Gallagher and his men viewed their role as a purely military one: to advise the Chinese Army. In Hanoi they found themselves caught up in a volatile political crisis which they only partially understood. They became the focus of extravagant hopes on the part of the French and the Vietnamese, and their every action was viewed as politically significant. In this situation they were inevitably doomed to disappoint both the French and the Vietnamese.

The Gallagher mission was the last and perhaps the most important of a series of American World War II military involvements with Indochina. During the period between 1943 and March 1945, American commanders felt compelled by their need for timely intelligence about Vietnam to cultivate the various political groups involved in the struggle for control of the country: the Free French, the Vichyites, the Nationalist Chinese, and the Viet Minh. The Japanese takeover in March 1945 destroyed many of the traditional American sources of intelligence and ultimately led to more direct and intensive U.S. involvement in Indochina. Finally the postwar Allied occupation of Vietnam led to American military participation as advisers in northern Vietnam.

That advisory role ended American involvement in Vietnam for a time, but a strong legacy of bitterness and mistrust toward the United States lingered among the French. The legend of so-called American double-dealing and collusion with the Viet Minh would later provide French officials, faced with American criticism of their policies and actions, with the convenient accusation that their postwar difficulties in Vietnam had stemmed from American obstruction of French efforts to regain Vietnam and alleged aid and encouragement to the Viet Minh. That Washington, more than three months before V–J Day, had virtually capitulated to French demands for the return of all of Indochina, that American material aid to the Viet Minh had been inconsequential, and that the very existence of the Viet Minh was largely a

[105]Ltr, Hull to CG, China Theater, 3 Oct 45, OPD 312.12, RG 165.

response to French exploitation and oppression were rarely acknowledged by the men who would lead France to Dien Bien Phu.

French Forces Move Against the Viet Minh

PART TWO
The Franco — Viet Minh War

5

"Heading Into a Very Bad Mess": Origins of Military Aid

When the last American officers and soldiers left northern Vietnam in December 1945, they did so with a feeling of relief. They had carried out their mission in the midst of revolution, famine, warlord feuds, and an incipient colonial confrontation and had helped to maintain a fragile peace. Less than five years later the U.S. Army would return to Southeast Asia during the Franco-Vietnamese conflict. In those five years the United States, impelled by the pressures and anxieties of the cold war, would move from concerned neutrality to active participation in the struggle for Vietnam.

A Reluctance to Intervene

As General Gallagher and his staff departed in December 1945, serious negotiations were already under way between the French and Chinese governments regarding the evacuation of Chinese troops from northern Indochina, a development which the Viet Minh watched warily. At the same time, meetings between the Viet Minh and the French, which General Gallagher and Major Patti had encouraged, became more frequent, although what the French had in mind for Vietnam was still unclear. In February 1946 Ambassador Jefferson Caffery advised the State Department from Paris that "all indications . . . point to the fact that the French Gov at this time favors . . . a moderate policy . . . [but] this does not mean . . . that they are thinking in terms of independence for Indo-China."[1]

Throughout this immediate postwar period the United States adhered to its hands-off policy. Although Ho Chi Minh appealed to Washington for support through letters to President Harry S. Truman and through conversations

[1]Telg, Ambassador in France (Caffery) to Secy of State, 6 Feb 46, Department of State, *Foreign Relations of the United States, 1946*, vol. 8, *The Far East* (Washington, 1971), p. 24.

Ho Arrives in France, 1946

with State Department officials in Hanoi, the American government made no reply, and in February 1946 the Department of State rejected a Chinese proposal for joint Chinese-American mediation of the Franco – Viet Minh dispute.[2] On the other hand, the United States was still unwilling to be involved in any way in a French reconquest of Vietnam. The government continued to prohibit American-flag vessels or aircraft from transporting troops, arms, and ammunition to or from French Indochina.

At the end of February 1946 the French and Chinese governments at last concluded a treaty providing for withdrawal of the Chinese occupation troops from northern Indochina. A few days later, on 6 March, Sainteny and Ho signed an agreement, subsequently accepted by the French government, which recognized the Viet Minh – controlled Democratic Republic of Vietnam as "a free state having its own government, its own parliament, its own army, and its own finances, forming a part of the Indo-China Federation and of the French Union." The question of the unification of the Democratic Republic of Vietnam with the other two regions of Vietnam—Annam and Cochinchina—was to be decided by plebiscite. The Vietnamese agreed to "welcome amicably"

---

[2]Telg, Counselor of Embassy in China (Smythe) to Secy of State, 28 Feb 46, Dept of State, *Foreign Relations, 1946: Far East*, 8:29 – 30.

the French Army back into Tonkin to "relieve" the Chinese. The number of French troops was fixed at 15,000, and they were to be gradually withdrawn over a five-year period.[3]

When Sainteny and Ho signed their agreement, British officials were negotiating with Indian and Burmese leaders on terms of independence for those former colonies, and the Dutch were beginning negotiations with the Republic of Indonesia, which, after many false starts and considerable bloodshed, would lead to an independent Indonesia in 1949.[4] Yet French Indochina did not follow the road of the other Asian colonies to early independence. Traditional colonial interest groups in France worked against a peaceful colonial settlement. They were reinforced by the desire of most Frenchmen "to bury the humiliating memory of 1940 by the establishment of a powerful closely-knit French Union" and the fear that independence for Indochina would lead to the unraveling of the entire French Empire.[5] The three national elections and two referendums which marked the birth of the Fourth French Republic in 1946 also left French leaders with neither the time nor the inclination to grapple with the problems of decolonization.

Almost at once there was trouble over the March agreements. The new French high commissioner for Indochina, Admiral Georges Thierry d'Argenlieu, insisted that the 6 March accords had no application to Cochinchina, which he claimed was a separate state within the Indochinese Federation, and on 1 June without consulting the government in Paris, he announced the formation of a provisional government for the Republic of Cochinchina. In August Ho and a Viet Minh delegation went to Paris for what were to be the definitive negotiations to settle the future relationship between Vietnam and France. D'Argenlieu, again without the approval of the French government, chose that time to convene a conference at Dalat on the future organization of the Indochinese Union, to which he invited representatives of the royal governments of Laos and Cambodia, of the Republic of Cochinchina, and of the ethnic minorities of the Central Highlands. This clear attempt to sabotage the Franco–Viet Minh negotiations in Paris led to heated protests by the Democratic Republic of Vietnam and a near rupture of the Paris conference.[6]

D'Argenlieu's action was a source of concern to American observers. The American vice-consul in Hanoi, James L. O'Sullivan, reported "an imminent danger of an open break between the French and Viet Nam," and predicted "that, although the French could quickly overrun the country, they could not—as they themselves admit—pacify it except through a long and bitter military operation."[7] The chief of the State Department's Division of Southeast Asian Affairs, Abbot Low Moffat, who had come to Vietnam in March to

---

[3]Hammer, *The Struggle for Indochina*, p. 153.
[4]Evelyn Colbert, *Southeast Asia in International Politics* (Ithaca: Cornell University Press, 1977), pp. 65–93, 105–07.
[5]Ronald E. Irving, *The First Indochina War: French and American Policy, 1945–1954* (London: Crown Helm, 1975), pp. 33–34.
[6]Ibid., pp. 23–28.
[7]Quoted in Memo, Chief, Southeast Asian Affairs (Moffat), to Director, Far Eastern Affairs, 9 Aug 46, Dept of State, *Foreign Relations, 1946: Far East*, 8:54.

Viet Minh Rally *in Hanoi, early 1946.*

observe the Franco-Vietnamese negotiations, warned that "the Annamese are faced with the choice of a costly submission to the French or of open resistance, and that the French may be preparing to resort to force."[8]

Although Ho signed a *modus vivendi* with the French on 14 September 1946 that temporarily averted a break, the agreement left most of the outstanding issues to be settled at a later conference, and when Ho returned to Vietnam in October he found both sides preparing for a showdown. During Ho's absence, Vo Nguyen Giap, the chairman of the Council of National Defense and minister of the interior, had swiftly neutralized the troops of the pro-Chinese political parties and had arrested or executed their leaders along with scores of other potential opponents of the Viet Minh regime.[9] By July he had scattered over 38,000 troops throughout northern Vietnam, generally in groups of 200 to 1,000. The largest concentrations were at Hanoi and Haiphong, with an estimated 4,500 and 3,000 troops, respectively.[10] Giap had little hope of

[8]Ibid.

[9]Hammer, *The Struggle for Indochina*, pp. 178−79; Irving, *The First Indochina War*, p. 29; Vo Nguyen Giap, *People's War, People's Army* (New York: Praeger, 1963), pp. xxiii−xxiv; Am Consul, Saigon, to Secy of State, No. 90, 19 Sep 46, 851G.00/9−1946, RG 59. The nominal Viet Minh head of government during this interlude was Huyn Thuc Khang.

[10]Am Consul, Saigon, to Secy of State, No. 90, 19 Sep 46.

Giap Addresses *a Viet Minh armed propaganda unit.*

achieving a peaceful settlement with France. Preparing for the worst, he reportedly had trained his forces using Chinese Communist advisers and had equipped them with arms smuggled by sea from Shanghai to Hong Kong and then to Haiphong.[11] By November the strength of the Viet Minh regular army was estimated at 60,000 men.[12]

On 8 November the Viet Minh—controlled National Assembly declared that northern, southern, and central Vietnam were "one and indivisible." On 20 November, after a minor incident involving the seizure of a Chinese junk by a French harbor patrol boat in the port of Haiphong, scattered fighting erupted between the French and Vietnamese in various parts of the city. A cease-fire was arranged by late the next day, but the French high commissioner in Saigon decided (with the approval of Paris) to use the incident as an excuse to seize control of the city. The French commander in Haiphong delivered an ultimatum to the local Viet Minh representatives demanding that all Vietnamese armed forces evacuate the city and that all the surrounding villages be disarmed. Without allowing the Vietnamese sufficient time to reply, the French opened a brutal bombardment of the city by naval guns,

[11]Am Consul, Hanoi, to Secy of State, No. 101, 1 Nov 46, 851G.00/11−146, RG 59.
[12]Buttinger, *Vietnam: A Dragon Embattled,* 1:421.

French Troops *search houses in Hanoi, January 1947.*

artillery, and fighter aircraft in which an estimated 6,000 Vietnamese civilians were killed.[13]

Not quite a month later, on 19 December, the Viet Minh launched an attack against the French in Hanoi. The attack began at 8:00 P.M. when Giap's troops attempted to isolate French forces in the Citadel by blocking off the only roads connecting the fortress with the main part of the city. The French, forewarned, managed to frustrate this attempt. Viet Minh militia put the electric power lines out of commission and attacked French posts and residential districts in the city, but these attacks were also contained. After 20 December fighting was concentrated in the Chinese and Vietnamese quarters of the city. Each building became a Viet Minh strongpoint. The battle was fought house by house, block by block, with the French employing point-blank artillery fire and occasional air attacks. Combat continued for almost

[13]Am Consul, Haiphong, to Secy of State, No. 9, 23 Nov 46, 851G.00/11–2346, No. 10, 24 Nov 46, 851G.00/11–2446, No. 12, 1 Dec 46, 851G.00/12–146; all in RG 59. The standard account of the Haiphong "incident" is Philippe Devillers, *Histoire du Viet Nam de 1940 a 1952* (Paris: Editions du Seuil, 1952), Chapter 19. The best English-language account is Joseph Buttinger, *Vietnam: A Dragon Embattled*, vol. 2, *Vietnam at War* (New York: Praeger, 1967), pages 424–30. These accounts are generally substantiated by the eyewitness reports of the American consul cited above.

sixty days, at the end of which over 2,000 Vietnamese soldiers managed to escape via an underground tunnel.[14]

Resistance was not confined to Hanoi. On the first day of the battle General Giap had issued orders to commanders of all units in the north, central, and southern portions of Vietnam to "Stand up in Unison/Dash into battle/Destroy the invaders and save the country."[15] Two days later, on 21 December, Ho Chi Minh broadcast an appeal for nationwide resistance in which he said that although the war would be a long and hard one, in the end "we are bound to win."[16]

The outbreak of general war was hardly a surprise to American officials, for Moffat and the American consuls had predicted for some time that a resort to force was likely. Writing in the first week of the conflict, John Carter Vincent, the director of the State Department's Office of Far Eastern Affairs, summarized the problems which were to bedevil the French for the next three years. They lacked the military strength to reconquer Vietnam, lacked strong public support for such a course, and were handicapped by a weak and divided government in Paris. Under these circumstances, Vincent concluded, guerrilla warfare could continue indefinitely.[17]

Washington nevertheless remained reluctant to intervene. The consensus was that attempting to pressure the French into making concessions to Vietnamese nationalism, which appeared the only way to end the fighting, might lead the French in turn to withdraw support for a Western European coalition aimed at containing the Soviet Union in Europe. As a State Department policy paper put it, "interest in maintaining in power a friendly French government to assist in the furtherance of our aims in Europe" took precedence over realizing American goals in Vietnam.[18]

Another reason for Washington's reluctance to pressure the French was that American misgivings about French policies in Southeast Asia were balanced by increasing American uneasiness about the apparent Communist nature of the Viet Minh. Throughout 1946 and early 1947 the question of Communist influence in Vietnam preoccupied American policymakers. The State Department's

[14]Am Consul, Hanoi, to Secy of State, No. 150, 24 Dec 46, 851G.00/12-2446, RG 59; Intel Rpt, Office of U.S. Military Attache, Bangkok, 5 Apr 47, R-72-47, G-2 ID file 860866 (this report is based on an account by United Press correspondent Emily Brown, who visited the sites of the fighting and interviewed eyewitnesses). See also Devillers, *Histoire du Viet Nam*, pp. 353-57, and Giap, *People's War, People's Army*, pp. 20-28.

[15]Order for Nationwide Resistance, in Gareth Porter, ed., *Vietnam: The Definitive Documentation of Human Decisions* (Stanfordville, N.Y.: Coleman Enterprises, 1979), pp. 133-34.

[16]Appeal by Ho Chi Minh for Nationwide Resistance, 21 Dec 46, in Porter, *Vietnam: Definitive Documentation of Human Decisions*, pp. 134-35.

[17]Memo, Director, Office of Far Eastern Affairs, for Under Secy of State (Acheson), 24 Dec 46, p. 76; Telg, Consul at Saigon (Reed) to Secy of State, 24 Dec 46, pp. 78-79; both in Dept of State, *Foreign Relations, 1946*, vol. 8, *Far East*. A poll (reported in Agences, France, Presse in February 1947) found only 37 percent of the Frenchmen felt that "force should be used to maintain order" in Indochina, while 22 percent favored "anything rather than war," and an additional 25 percent favored further negotiations. See Am Embassy, Paris, to Dept of State, No. 7836, 4 Mar 47, 851G.00/3-447, RG 59.

[18]Department of State Policy Statement on Indochina, 27 Sep 48, Department of State, *Foreign Relations of the United States, 1948*, vol. 6, *The Far East and Australasia* (Washington, 1974), p. 49.

concern extended even to questioning the Democratic Republic of Vietnam's adoption of a gold star on a field of red as the design for its national flag.[19] When Abbot Low Moffat prepared to meet with Ho in Hanoi in December 1946, Under Secretary of State Acheson cautioned him to "keep in mind Ho's clear record as [an] agent [of] international communism, absence [of] evidence [of] recantation [of his] Moscow affiliations. . . . Least desirable eventuality would be [the] establishment [of a] Communist-dominated, Moscow-oriented state [in] Indochina."[20]

Communist expansionism was being clearly demonstrated in various parts of the world. The tightening of Soviet control in Eastern Europe had produced a sharp increase in tension between the United States and the Soviet Union. In March 1946 the Americans and Russians had clashed bitterly over the continued presence of Russian troops in Iran, and a year later, on 12 March 1947, President Truman went before Congress to ask for military and economic aid to Greece and Turkey. Since "the people of a number of countries of the world have recently had totalitarian regimes forced upon them against their will," the president declared, "in the future . . . it must be the policy of the United States to support free peoples who are resisting attempted subjugation by armed minorities or by outside pressures."[21] A few weeks later State Department officials began work on a foreign aid program that would come to be known as the Marshall Plan. The Soviets responded in July 1947 by resurrecting the Communist International, the organization aimed at world revolution which they had ostensibly disbanded during World War II. That same month Ambassador Jefferson Caffery in Paris observed that "recent experiences have shown only too well how [a] relatively small, but well-trained and determined, minority can take over power in [an] area where democratic traditions are weak. Nor can remoteness of Moscow be regarded as [an] adequate safeguard."[22]

Given these developments, U.S. policy toward Indochina remained ambiguous and uncertain through 1947 and 1948. Secretary of State George C. Marshall candidly stated the predicament of American policymakers in May 1947. After criticizing France's "dangerously outmoded colonial outlook and method" and warning of Ho's "direct Communist connections," he concluded that "frankly we have no solution . . . to suggest."[23]

Meanwhile, the U.S. Army staff was developing its own position on the continuing unrest in Southeast Asia. On 3 July 1947, in a memorandum for the chief of staff, the director of the Intelligence Division, Lt. Gen. Stephen J. Chamberlin, observed that Southeast Asia was an important source of "strategic

[19]Airgram, Acting Secy of State to Consul at Saigon, 9 Oct 46, Dept of State, *Foreign Relations, 1946: Far East,* 8:61.

[20]Telg, Acting Secy of State to Consul at Saigon for Moffat, 5 Dec 46, Dept of State, *Foreign Relations, 1946: Far East,* 8:67.

[21]*Public Papers of the Presidents: Harry S. Truman, 1947* (Washington, 1963), pp. 178–79.

[22]Telg, Ambassador in France (Caffery) to Secy of State, 31 Jul 47, Department of State, *Foreign Relations of the United States, 1947,* vol. 6, *The Far East* (Washington, 1972), p. 128.

[23]Telg, Secy of State to Embassy in France, 3 Feb 47, Dept of State, *Foreign Relations, 1947: Far East,* 6:67–68.

resources" for the United States and that the fighting between the French and the Vietnamese nationalists in Indochina and between the Dutch and the Indonesian nationalists in the Netherlands East Indies threatened orderly economic development of those countries and the availability of their raw materials to the United States. Only the "mediation of a neutral power with sufficient authority and prestige to ensure honest implementation," General Chamberlin believed, could satisfactorily resolve the conflict in Vietnam. He suggested that the United States adopt a strong, positive approach to the problems of Southeast Asia and be prepared to undertake mediation if necessary.[24]

There was no direct response to that memorandum, but some weeks later, as Chinese Communist victories in Manchuria and North China appeared to presage the fall of the Nationalist regime of Chiang Kai-shek, the Army staff became concerned about the potential consequences of that fall for the countries bordering China. A study by the Plans and Operations Division in September on the "effect of a continually weakening China" on the situation in French Indochina predicted that a Communist victory in China would strengthen the Viet Minh and bring them more directly under the influence of international communism. Although the French could probably still hold Indochina, there would be little chance of ending the fighting in view of the French refusal to deal with the Viet Minh, the only nationalist group commanding broad allegiance from the people.[25]

The French Offensive of 1947

While Washington pondered, the fighting continued. In the northern part of Vietnam the Viet Minh, starting in December 1946, had at first laid siege to most of the principal towns, such as Hue, Vinh, Haiphong, and Nam Dinh, cutting off their communications. In the old imperial capital of Hue the Vietnamese had besieged a French battalion of 750 men for forty-seven days. As a relief column neared the city, the Viet Minh had systematically destroyed the entire French section, blown up bridges, mined the roads, and demolished most of the larger buildings before withdrawing.[26] Yet in the end, the poorly armed Viet Minh troops proved no match for superior French firepower. By March 1947 the French had reopened most of the main roads during daylight and had established control over Hanoi and the town of Son La in the north. At that time French forces in all of Vietnam totaled about 94,000 men, and 11,000 reinforcements were on the way from France.

Giap's regular forces in March totaled about 60,000 men, plus about

---

[24]Memo, Lt Gen S. J. Chamberlin for CofSA, 3 Jul 47, sub: Positive U.S. Action Required to Restore Normal Conditions in Southeast Asia, P&O 092 TS, RG 319.

[25]Current Situation in Indochina, 2 Sep 47, Intel Research Proj No. 3799, FIC, P&O 092 TS, RG 319.

[26]Intel Rpt, Office of U.S. Military Attache, Bangkok, 5 Apr 47.

100,000 militia and part-time guerrillas. The Viet Minh regulars were armed with a mixture of Chinese, Japanese, American, and French weapons. Crude but usable ammunition was produced in mobile workshops. A Red Cross representative who visited the Viet Minh positions around Hanoi in early 1947 found three concentric defensive lines. The first line of defense was manned by riflemen, the second by soldiers equipped with knives and spears, and the third by men armed with bows and arrows.[27]

In the spring of 1947 the Viet Minh turned to guerrilla warfare, which all along had been the pattern of fighting in the south. The regular units, organized into independent

Viet Minh Arms Factory

companies, were dispersed throughout northern Vietnam. A Viet Minh company had a strength of about 100 men plus the company commander, a political officer, and some communications personnel. It was organized into three combat sections, each consisting of three combat groups. The combat group included a leader with the rank of sergeant, an assistant group leader, a machine gunner and two assistants, three riflemen, and a grenadier. Aided by local militia forces, the independent companies—occasionally formed into battalions or regiments—conducted a campaign of hit-and-run attacks while gradually consolidating and extending their base areas.[28] "The soil of the fatherland was being freed inch by inch right in the enemy's rear lines," General Giap later wrote. "There was no clearly defined front in this war. It was there where the enemy was. The front was nowhere, it was everywhere."[29]

Vice-Consul O'Sullivan reported from Hanoi that the

destruction in Tonkin is literally appalling. Damage is due very largely to Vietnam Government policy of "scorched earth" although French bombing and shelling have contributed. Of small cities I have seen personally, Haiduong is about 60 to 70 percent destroyed, Hoabinh 100 percent razed, Hadong had perhaps a dozen buildings of several hundred standing. French aerial observers state that Tuyenquang and Thainguyen have been destroyed

[27]Dept of State, Circular Memo for Certain American Diplomatic and Consular Officers, 9 Jan 47, 851G.00/1—947, RG 59; Intel Rpt, Asst Mil Attache, Nanking, 24 Mar 47, R—186—47, G—2 ID file 357789.

[28]Intel Rpt, U.S. Naval Attache, Bangkok, 13 May 48, sub: FIC Vietnam Military Organization G—2 ID file 469139; Viet Minh Organizational System, Incl 1 to Am Consul, Hanoi, No. 122, 29 Jan 51, copy in G—2 ID file 763660. Edgar O'Ballance, *The Indo-China War, 1945—1954: A Study in Guerrilla Warfare* (London: Faber and Faber, 1964), pp. 77—84; McAlister, *Vietnam: Origins of Revolution*, pp. 313—15; Giap, *People's War, People's Army*, p. 23.

[29]Giap, *People's War, People's Army*, p. 23.

by [the] Vietnamese. . . . No estimate available of number of villages destroyed.[30]

The French were convinced that they had the situation in hand. In May 1947, French War Minister Paul Coste Floret observed "there is no military problem any longer in Indo-China . . . the success of French arms complete."[31] But if the French controlled most of the towns and cities, the Viet Minh controlled over half the countryside of Vietnam and were able to subject well over half the population to direct or indirect political control.

When the French government in March 1947 replaced d'Argenlieu as high commissioner with a civilian member of the French National Assembly, Emile Bollaert, American officials saw the change, with guarded optimism, as a signal that France had adopted a more flexible policy. Yet the stolid opposition of the French colonials in Vietnam, the French Army, and the political right in France had not weakened. Nor were Vietnamese nationalists of any political persuasion willing to accept the meager concessions proffered by Bollaert. Consul Reed in Saigon summed up the situation in a telegram of 23 May: "Bollaert trying [to] find satisfactory solution, but finding it all but impossible [to] treat with anyone except Ho; also finding it difficult [to] find formula [to] protect French interests, as [Bollaert] has no confidence in Ho or his group."[32]

By September 1947 it was clear to American observers in Indochina that, far from accepting compromise, the French were preparing a major military offensive designed to destroy the Viet Minh. Although the consuls in Hanoi and Saigon differed in their assessment of how successful a new military offensive might be, they agreed that an attempt to restore the prewar status quo by armed force would be "catastrophic to U.S. prestige in Asia."[33] Both called for active American intervention to prevent the French from taking that course.

Secretary of State Marshall directed Ambassador Caffery in France to make appropriate informal inquiries and to report promptly. Such an offensive, said Marshall, would have a serious negative effect on U.S. public opinion and on Congress, which would soon "be called upon to consider extensive financial aid for [the] western European nations, including France."[34] In response to Caffery's inquiries, the French Foreign Office on 27 October assured him that France was carrying out no major offensive but only "small scale raids" to seize Viet Minh broadcasting posts and arms caches and to seal off the Chinese frontier against arms smuggling. Total French losses, the Foreign Office added, had been less than fifty killed.[35]

[30]Telg, Vice-Consul at Hanoi (O'Sullivan) to Secy of State, 5 Jun 47, Dept of State, *Foreign Relations, 1947: Far East,* 6:101.
[31]Buttinger, *Vietnam: A Political History,* pp. 316–17.
[32]Telg, Consul at Saigon (Reed) to the Secy of State, 23 May 47, Dept of State, *Foreign Relations, 1947: Far East,* 6:100.
[33]Reed to State Dept, 9 Sep 47, 851G.01/9–947, and 26 Sep 47, 851G.01/9–2647; O'Sullivan to State Dept, 24 Sep 47, 851G.01/9–2447. All in records of Dept of State, RG 59.
[34]Telg, Secy of State to Embassy in France, 11 Sep 47, Dept of State, *Foreign Relations, 1947: Far East,* 6:136.
[35]Telg, Ambassador in France (Caffery) to Secy of State, 28 Oct 47, Dept of State, *Foreign Relations, 1947: Far East,* 6:145.

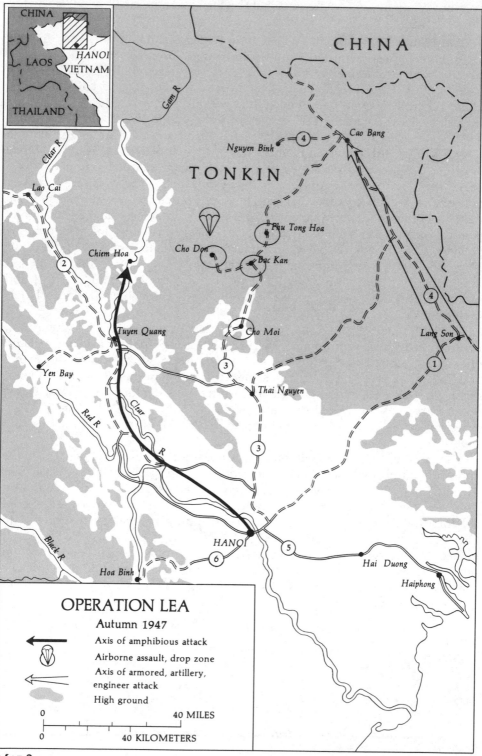

CHINA
LAOS
THAILAND
HANOI
VIETNAM

CHINA

TONKIN

Clear R.
Gam R.

Lao Cai

Nguyen Binh
Cao Bang

Chiem Hoa
Cho Don
Phu Tong Hoa
Bac Kan

Tuyen Quang
Cho Moi

Yen Bay
Red R.
Clear R.
Thai Nguyen

Lang Son

Hanoi
Hoa Binh
Black R.
Hai Duong
Haiphong

OPERATION LEA

Autumn 1947

Axis of amphibious attack
Airborne assault, drop zone
Axis of armored, artillery,
engineer attack
High ground

0   40 MILES
0   40 KILOMETERS

MAP 2

French officials were being less than candid, for the French offensive in Tonkin during late 1947 would involve close to 60,000 troops, which included three battalions of paratroopers, most of the French Air Force in the Far East, and small naval detachments. It was, noted a new American consul in Hanoi, Edwin C. Rendall, in January 1948, "a period of military activity far exceeding in scope and number of troops employed any previous French effort since [Francis] Garnier seized most of the Red River Delta with a few hundred men in 1874."[36] The French objectives, he reported, were to cut the flow of arms across the Chinese border, to kill or capture the principal Viet Minh leaders, and to destroy the Viet Minh army. The area of operations was due north and northwest of Hanoi near Thai Nguyen, Backan, Chiem Hoa, and Tuyen Quang.

In the first phase of the French offensive, Operation LEA, paratroopers descended on the Viet Minh headquarters area at Backan early in October. They captured large stores of food and ammunition as well as the Viet Minh broadcasting station, but all of the political and military leaders of the Viet Minh government escaped.[37] Meanwhile, a French armored column with artillery and engineer support pushed northward from the border fort of Lang Son along Route 4 toward the town of Cao Bang, and a river flotilla with two infantry battalions worked its way up the Red and Clear Rivers through Tuyen Quang and up the Gam River to Chiem Hoa. (*Map 2*) During the second stage of the campaign in late November and December, nine reinforced battalions from Hai Duong moved to clear the northern part of the Red River Delta east and northeast of Hanoi, while other formations operated in the region directly to the north of Hanoi.[38]

American officials were divided over the significance of the French effort. The Central Intelligence Agency interpreted the offensive as evidence that France had adopted a new policy of unrestrained military pressure in order to retain "undisputed control" of Vietnam. The American embassy in Paris suggested, instead, that the offensive should be viewed as an attempt at saving face, with the more limited aim of creating so much disorder and destruction in Viet Minh—held territory that the authority and prestige of the Ho Chi Minh government would be weakened, thus making possible an agreement with other nationalist groups.[39]

Whatever the French aim, the cost of these operations was high and the results were minimal. On 2 January 1948 Consul Rendall in Hanoi reported "no evidence that the 'hard core' of resistance on which the Viet Minh government relies has been broken. The fact that the Vietnamese may be dubious about the Viet Minh does not dispose him to seek salvation in the

[36]Ltr, Edwin C. Rendall to Secy of State, 24 Jan 48, sub: The French Autumn Military Campaign in Tonkin, 851G.01/1–2448, RG 59; State Department Division of Research on the Far East, Chronological History of Events in Indo-China Since 1948, 1 Apr 54, p. 47.

[37]Ltr, Rendall to Secy of State, 24 Jan 48, sub: French Autumn Military Campaign in Tonkin; Bernard B. Fall, *Street Without Joy*, 4th ed. (Harrisburg, Pa.: Stackpole Co., 1967), pp. 28–29. Fall erroneously reports that one of Ho's ministers was captured near Backan. This prisoner was, in fact, an aide to Finance Minister Le Van Hiem.

[38]Ltr, Rendall to Secy of State, 24 Jan 48, sub: French Autumn Military Campaign in Tonkin.

[39]Am Embassy, Paris, to State Dept, 2 Jan 48, 851G.01/1–248, RG 59.

French military—especially since the French frequently pursue their own scorched earth policy."[40] By the end of the offensive, over a thousand French troops had been killed and 3,000 wounded. An American military observer estimated, moreover, that the French would not be able to make another such large-scale military effort because their equipment was rapidly deteriorating. Morale also was admittedly low, and replacements for paratroopers, who had incurred especially heavy losses on the campaign, were, for the present, almost impossible to find.[41] The financial cost of the offensive was estimated to have been around $34 million a month.[42] By early 1948 military operations, except for patrol actions, were "at a standstill," and the Chinese border was "once more unguarded from Laokay to Caobang."[43] In April the American naval attache in Bangkok reported that the French military position in Indochina was steadily deteriorating.[44]

The French continued to hold some key towns and border posts in northern Vietnam, but their control of the countryside beyond these strongholds was tenuous. Beginning in 1948 the Viet Minh steadily increased the frequency and intensity of their attacks on French outposts and convoys. For a time during 1948 the French were obliged to dispense with the convoy system because of lack of manpower. Instead, they concentrated on patrolling a few key roads for limited periods of time to enable traffic to pass.[45]

The Bao Dai Experiment

Frustrated militarily, the French sought a political solution, one involving not the Viet Minh but the former emperor of Vietnam, Bao Dai, who had been living quietly in Hong Kong since March 1946 when he had had a falling out with the Viet Minh. Although he had a reputation of being something of a playboy and a *bon vivant*, he also was an intelligent and patriotic nationalist. Since early 1947 the French had been carrying on a diplomatic flirtation with Bao Dai in the hope of persuading him to collaborate with them against Ho, but he refused to enter into any serious negotiations unless he received firm assurances that the French would grant real independence to Vietnam. In the meantime, a few groups of non-Communist nationalists—veterans of the Dong Minh Hoi and VNQDD, leaders of the religious sects, and independents—formed a National Union and pledged support for Bao Dai. Although the National Union had no real base of support among the Vietnamese people, it did lend to Bao Dai the outward appearance of being the leader of a broad nationalist movement.

On 7 December 1947, in a meeting with French High Commissioner

[40]Ibid.
[41]U.S. Naval Attache (Lt William T. Hunter), Bangkok, to CNO, 27 Jan 48, records of Office of Naval Intelligence (ONI), RG 38.
[42]William C. Bullitt, "The Saddest War," *Life*, 29 December 1947, p. 64.
[43]Am Consul, Hanoi, to State Dept, 9 Feb 48, 851G.00/2–948, RG 59.
[44]Am Naval Attache, Bangkok, to CNO, 19 Apr 48, records of ONI, RG 38.
[45]Ibid., 10 Jun 48, records of ONI, RG 38; Maj Carmelo J. Bernardo, The Franco–Viet Minh War, 1946–54: Modern Arms and Revolutionary War, p. 8, Historical Manuscript file, CMH.

High Commissioner Bollaert and Emperor Bao Dai *sign the first Ha Long Bay Agreement, 1947.*

Bollaert aboard a warship in Ha Long Bay, Bao Dai concluded a protocol which became known as the Ha Long Bay Agreement. Although it contained a vague promise of Vietnamese "independence within [the] French Union," it left control of Vietnam's foreign relations and armed forces to France and said nothing about the separate colony of Cochinchina. Bao Dai was to return to Vietnam to form a new government for Tonkin and Annam that would exclude the Viet Minh.[46]

The French concessions at Ha Long Bay were so minimal that even Bao Dai's strongest supporters denounced the agreement. Unable to get further commitments from the French and disturbed by criticisms of his actions, he retired to Europe. On 5 June 1948, after pursuing the former emperor to many of the Continent's nightclubs and spas, the French prevailed upon him to return to Vietnam. In another meeting aboard ship in Ha Long Bay, Bao Dai signed a second agreement. France now declared its recognition of Vietnamese "independence," but it again failed to provide for unifying Vietnam, and France was still to retain control of foreign relations and armed forces. The agreement also left the transfer of governmental authority in other

[46]Telg, Ambassador in France (Caffery) to Secy of State, 16 Dec 47, Dept of State, *Foreign Relations, 1947: Far East*, 6:151.

areas to future negotiations.[47] After signing, Bao Dai almost immediately had misgivings and again exiled himself.

The American government at first viewed Bao Dai with little enthusiasm. In May 1947 Secretary of State Marshall told Ambassador Caffery that the State Department was "concerned lest French efforts [to] find 'true representatives [of] Vietnam' with whom [to] negotiate result " in the creation of a puppet government like that of Cochinchina. In addition the restoration of Bao Dai might be seen to imply that the democracies were reduced to resorting to "monarchy as a weapon against Communism."[48]

Yet the choices for the United States were becoming progressively narrower. By the beginning of 1948 the State Department had reached a consensus that the establishment of a Viet Minh–dominated state in Indochina would be contrary to American interests.[49] As one official declared, "it may not be certain . . . that Ho and Co will succeed in setting up a Communist State if they get rid of the French but let me suggest that from the standpoint of the security of the United States, it is one hell of a big chance to take."[50] Consul General Abbot in Saigon observed on 30 June that a French truce with Ho Chi Minh "would result in the non-communist elements [in Vietnam] being swallowed up on the Czech pattern."[51] Under Secretary of State Robert A. Lovett in turn wrote Abbot that a favorite strategy of the Communists in dependent areas was to pretend to champion the cause of local nationalists.[52]

The conviction that the Viet Minh were unacceptable ruled out any negotiated settlement on the model of Indonesia, where a U.N.-sponsored Good Offices Committee, strongly backed by the United States, was well on the way to achieving a final settlement of the Dutch-Indonesian conflict.[53]

These considerations, plus world events in 1948—the Berlin Blockade, the setbacks suffered by the Chinese Nationalist armies, and the Communist *coup d'etat* in Czechoslovakia—saw a shift in American policy toward what was becoming known as the Bao Dai experiment. Skepticism changed to qualified acceptance. Bao Dai, however, remained in Europe, adamantly refusing to return to Vietnam and take up the reins of government without some additional concrete concession from the French. In his absence the French installed a puppet government in Hanoi headed by the little-respected politician Nguyen Van Xuan.

The French blamed the Xuan government's lack of popular support on the refusal of Bao Dai to return to Vietnam, but the American consul in Hanoi believed the former emperor's return, if he could offer only vague hopes of future concessions, would have little effect on the local situation. What was

[47]Buttinger, *Vietnam: A Political History*, p. 305.

[48]Telg, Secy of State to Embassy in France, 13 May 47, Dept of State, *Foreign Relations, 1947: Far East*, 6:97.

[49]Gary R. Hess, "The First American Commitment in Indochina: The Acceptance of the 'Bao Dai Solution,' 1950," *Diplomatic History* 2 (Fall 1978):333–35.

[50]Marginal Comment, Woodruff Wallner to Memo, Director, Div of Philippine and Southeast Asian Affairs, for Office of Far Eastern Affairs, 18 Nov 47, 851G.00/11–1847, RG 59.

[51]Am Consul at Saigon to Secy of State, 30 Jun 48, 851G.00/6–3048, RG 59.

[52]Lovett to Am Consul, Saigon, 22 Sep 48, *U.S.-Vietnam Relations*, 8:141.

[53]Evelyn Colbert, "The Road Not Taken: Decolonization and Independence in Indonesia and Indochina," *Foreign Affairs* 51 (April 1973):608–28.

needed, Abbot suggested, was prompt and decisive action by the French to grant real independent powers to a Bao Dai government.[54] To the American embassy in Paris, Secretary of State Marshall noted that the department "believes nothing should be left undone which will strengthen truly national-ist groups [in] Indochina and induce [the] present supporters [of the] Viet Minh . . . to side [with] that group."[55] Yet for all the American urgings, the French neither liberalized their approach to Bao Dai nor succeeded in induc-ing him to return to Vietnam.

By early 1949 American policymakers were split into two groups—those who favored American support for Bao Dai as the only hope for non-Communist Vietnam, and those who were loath to hazard American money and prestige on what they were certain would be an unsuccessful experiment if the French refused to make far more substantial concessions. The differ-ences were evident in February 1949 when Secretary of State Acheson reiter-ated the belief of the State Department's Far Eastern experts that it would be unwise to give public support to any arrangement for Indochina "unless that arrangement also embodies means clearly sufficient for its success." He instructed the American embassy in Paris to explain to the French Foreign Office that the United States was unwilling to approve the Bao Dai solution in its current form.[56] There appeared to be little reason, as Under Secretary of State Lovett put it, to "irretrievably commit US to [the] support of [a] native gov which by failing [to] develop appeal among [the] Vietnamese might become virtually [a] puppet gov, separated from [the] people and existing only by [the] presence [of] French military forces."[57] Yet American diplomats in Paris saw the Bao Dai experiment as "the only non-communist solution in sight" and feared that the Acheson stance would only discourage the French from going further with the experiment.[58] From Saigon, Consul General Abbot pointed out that, while American prestige would suffer if Bao Dai were to fail after receiving American support, "the lack of our support would be a heavy handicap which might well eliminate any chance of success." The only alternative to a Bao Dai government, according to Abbot, would be a costly colonial war or a Communist-dominated government in a strategic area of Southeast Asia.[59]

By finally making a major concession, the French succeeded in winning Bao Dai's consent to a new accord, known as the Elysee Agreements, which consisted of an exchange of letters between Bao Dai and French President Vincent Auriol in March 1949. In the Elysee Agreements the French now sanctioned political unification of Vietnam, allowing Cochinchina to be united with Annam and Tonkin to form the State of Vietnam. Ending Cochinchina's status as a separate colony required an act of the French National Assembly,

[54]Telg, Consul General at Saigon (Abbot) to Secy of State, 28 Aug 48, Dept of State, *Foreign Relations, 1948: Far East and Australasia*, 6:39.
[55]Telg, Marshall to Am Embassy, Paris, 30 Aug 48, *U.S.-Vietnam Relations*, 8:140.
[56]Acheson to Am Embassy, Paris, 25 Feb 49, 851G.01/2−2549, RG 59.
[57]Telg, Lovett to Am Embassy, Paris, 17 Jan 49, *U.S.-Vietnam Relations*, 8:152.
[58]Ambassador in France (Caffery) to State Dept, 6 Mar 49, 851G.01/3−649, RG 59.
[59]Paper Prepared (31 Mar 49) for New Delhi Foreign Service Conference, George M. Abbot, 5 May 49, RG 59.

which was obtained after a hard struggle. Yet from the Vietnamese viewpoint, there were still deficiencies in the Elysee Agreements, for even though they provided for a Vietnamese police force and some Vietnamese military forces, they again stipulated that the French would retain control of Vietnam's military affairs and foreign relations. As before, the transfer of other governmental functions to the Vietnamese was left to later negotiations.

American officials were deeply divided over the significance of the Elysee Agreements. Although the embassy in Paris continued to insist that Bao Dai offered the only non-Communist solution for Indochina, the former vice-consul in Hanoi, O'Sullivan, doubted that the United States should commit itself completely to his cause.[60] The current chief of the State Department's Division of Southeast Asian Affairs, Charles E. Reed, similarly warned that Bao Dai might come to be seen merely as a puppet of the French; the United States, if publicly committed to him, would then be obliged "to follow blindly down a dead-end alley, expending our limited resources in money and most particularly in prestige in a fight which would be hopeless."[61] Adopting Reed's view for the moment, Secretary of State Acheson in May cautioned American diplomats in the Far East to "guard carefully against any action which might be seized upon as premature endorsement or de facto recognition by US of Bao Dai. . . . Dept desires [to] retain as much freedom of action . . . as possible without . . . giving the impression we oppose or wish to hinder ex-Emperor."[62]

When in June 1949 the French National Assembly ratified the Elysee Agreements, including the provision on Cochinchina, the State Department felt obliged to take some official notice of the agreements. In a note prepared by the Bureau of Far East Affairs, the department told the French government that the agreements provided insufficient incentive to win the support of most Vietnamese nationalists away from Ho's Democratic Republic of Vietnam.[63] Though couched in diplomatic language, this statement was the bluntest yet made by the United States government on the shortcomings of the Bao Dai experiment.

It was far too blunt for Ambassador Caffery's successor, David K. E. Bruce, who successfully advised against delivering the note in its existing form. Bruce's staff believed the department's note unfairly prejudged the outcome of the experiment before it had even begun, and was unrealistic in its expectation of further concessions by France. They feared that the note's effect on French officials who were "battered and bruised by the long struggle to get passage of the Cochinchina bill" would be "the opposite of constructive."[64] The counselor of the State Department, Charles E. Bohlen, who was

---

[60]Memo, Chief, Southeast Asian Affairs Div (Charles E. Reed), for Chief, Office of Far Eastern Affairs, 14 Apr 49, RG 59.

[61]Ibid.

[62]Telg, Acheson to Am Consul, Saigon, 2 May 49, *U.S.-Vietnam Relations*, 8:153.

[63]W. Walton Butterworth to David K. E. Bruce, Am Ambassador, Paris, 6 Jun 49, *U.S.-Vietnam Relations*, 8:200–16.

[64]Bruce to State Dept, 13 Jun 49, 851G.01/6–1349; Ltr, Douglas MacArthur II to Chief, Bureau of Western European Affairs, 19 Jun 49; both in RG 59.

in Paris for talks with the French government, characterized the department's note as "a combination of 'holier than thou' lecture plus suggestions which, in view of the March 8 [Elysee] agreements, are completely hopeless of French acceptance."[65]

The controversy over the Elysee accord was another manifestation of the continuing differences between the Bureau of Far East Affairs and most of the rest of the foreign policy establishment, whose orientation was toward Europe. One State Department Far East expert, Charlton Ogburn, complained bitterly that the United States had been needlessly "gagged" and "hogtied" by its anxiety to avoid placing undue pressure on the French government. He warned that "we are heading into a very bad mess in the policy we are now following toward Indochina."[66] Yet by mid-1949 most policymakers felt that the options open to the United States in regard to Vietnam had been reduced to two: to remain neutral, or to recognize Bao Dai. A third choice, to press for an accommodation with Ho, had already been ruled out in 1948, and the fall of China and Communist activities in other parts of the world had only further steeled the American public against any reversal of that decision. As Dean Acheson bluntly asserted in May, "all Stalinists in colonial areas are nationalist," but "with the achievement of national aims (i.e., independence) their objective necessarily becomes subordination [of the] state to Commie purposes. . . . On the basis [of the] examples [in] Eastern Europe it must be assumed such would be [the] goal [of] Ho and [his] men."[67]

As for a neutral, wait-and-see stance, pressures also were mounting against that alternative. The apparent menace of Communist China, whose troops were approaching the borders of Tonkin, weighed heavily on American minds. In April 1949 the American consul in Hanoi had reported that the Viet Minh were cooperating militarily with the Chinese People's Liberation Army.[68] That same month there was a flurry of anxiety in Washington about the apparent attempt by French officials in Indochina, Thailand, and Washington to query American diplomats about the likely U.S. attitude in the event the French reopened negotiations with Ho Chi Minh.[69] Indeed, French officials repeatedly played on American fears regarding the spread of communism. In June a French cabinet minister told the American military attache in Paris that "the U.S. does not seem to appreciate that France's fight in Indo-China is not a question of combatting nationalism but concerns a fight against international communism. The U.S. must decide where the southward drive of communism is to stop. She must assist the French in 'drawing a line somewhere' and it is hoped that the line will be at least north of the Sino – Indo-Chinese border."[70]

[65]Bohlen to State Dept, 13 Jun 49, 851G.01/6–1349, RG 59.
[66]Memo, Charlton Ogburn for Reed and O'Sullivan, 28 Jun 49, files of Office of Philippine and Southeast Asian Affairs, Lot 54D190, RG 59.
[67]Acheson to Am Consul, Hanoi, 20 May 49, *U.S.-Vietnam Relations*, 8:196–97.
[68]Am Consul, Hanoi (Gibson), to State Dept, 2 Apr 49, 851G.01/4–249, RG 59.
[69]Memo, Charles E. Reed for W. Walton Butterworth, 27 Apr 49, sub: Paul Mus, files of Office of Philippine and Southeast Asian Affairs, RG 59.
[70]Msg, USARMA (U.S. Army Attache), Paris, to ACofS G–2, 10 Jun 49, records of ACSI.

In April 1949 twelve European nations had signed the North Atlantic Treaty. Aware of American hopes for the North Atlantic Treaty Organization (NATO), in which French forces were to play a vital role, French leaders repeatedly emphasized the drain which the Indochina fighting imposed on their military resources. Over 150,000 ground troops and sizable air elements were in the Far East by 1949, including most of the experienced officers and noncommissioned officers. Since no conscripts could be sent to Indochina under French law, training programs and general military efficiency had been adversely affected.[71]

During 1948 the French had suffered over 8,000 casualties in Vietnam, and by 1949 they had incurred a total of more than 30,000 casualties since the fighting had begun. French authorities frequently asserted that the annual casualty rate among officers in Vietnam was equal to the total number graduated from the French military academy each year. The situation in regard to experienced noncommissioned officers was even more serious. These career soldiers had suffered particularly heavy losses, and many chose to resign rather than return to the Far East for a second tour. The shortage of noncommissioned officers was aggravated by the necessity to transfer many of them to the separate army which the French were attempting to form for the State of Vietnam. Meanwhile, French forces in Europe had to rely mainly on recently conscripted noncommissioned officers.[72]

In the fall of 1949, after the final Communist triumph in China, Ho exchanged cordial messages with Mao Tse-tung, and in late January 1950 both the People's Republic of China and the Soviet Union recognized the Democratic Republic of Vietnam. For American policymakers these events were final proof of the Communist nature of Ho's government. As Secretary Acheson put it, the recognition removed any illusions as to the nationalist nature of Ho Chi Minh's aims and revealed Ho "in his true colors as the mortal enemy of native independence in Indo-China."[73]

Having decided that the Bao Dai experiment was the only alternative left to the United States, the State Department tried to persuade Asian states such as India to take the lead in recognizing a Bao Dai regime; but by early 1950 the need to act became paramount. On 2 February 1950 Acheson recommended to President Truman that the United States recognize the legally constituted non-Communist governments of Vietnam, Laos, and Cambodia.[74] Two days later the United States officially recognized the Bao Dai regime.

On 17 February U.S. Ambassador Loy W. Henderson declared to the Indian Council of World Affairs that "the United States is convinced that the

[71]USARMA, Paris, to Director of Intelligence, R–1039–49, 10 Nov 49, G–2 ID file 10669649; USARMA, Saigon, to DEPTAR (Department of Army), R–716, 28 Jul 52, sub: Casualty Tabulation, 1945–46, 1947, 1948, 1949, 1950, 1951, 1952, records of ACSI.

[72]Memo, Col Harris [1949]; Memo, SY for Mr. Band, 18 May 50; both in files of Office of Philippine and Southeast Asian Affairs. The beginnings of the Vietnamese National Army are discussed in Chapter 7.

[73]Department of State *Bulletin*, 13 February 1950, p. 244.

[74]Memo, Acheson for President, 2 Feb 50, sub: U.S. Recognition of Vietnam, Laos, and Cambodia, *U.S.-Vietnam Relations*, 8:276–77.

Bao Dai government . . . reflects more accurately than rival claimants the nationalist aspirations of the people of that country. . . . My government felt therefore that Bao Dai offered more opportunity to the Vietnamese people than a leader, who, in accordance with his political creed, must obey the orders of international communism."[75] Less than three years earlier Secretary of State Marshall had warned of the dangers in accepting a Bao Dai government, but now the United States, spurred on by its fears and misconceptions, had embarked on that very course.

American Aid

During the long debate over recognizing a Bao Dai government, both the Americans and the French seemed to assume that American aid of some type would naturally follow recognition. As early as September 1948, French Minister of National Defense Paul Ramadier told Ambassador Caffery in Paris that the operations in Vietnam were "costing much more money than the government could afford," a statement which Caffery interpreted as an "appeal to us for assistance."[76] In January 1949 the director of the Division of Political Affairs of the Ministry of Overseas France told Caffery informally that the rapid economic rehabilitation of Vietnam could be the key to Bao Dai's success and that the French hoped the United States would consider extending Marshall Plan aid directly to Vietnam and the rest of Indochina. Not quite two months later one of Bao Dai's close advisers, Tran Van Huu, asked the United States to give serious consideration to directly supplying arms for a new Vietnamese army. To all the requests Caffery replied noncommittally that the United States had the question under study.[77]

The collapse of Nationalist China had influenced official American thinking not only on recognition but also on aid. In late 1949 congressional lawmakers were attempting to sort through the wreckage of U.S. Far Eastern policy to find what, if any, pieces might be salvaged. A group of diehard supporters of the Chinese Nationalist regime, led by Senator William Knowland, proposed an amendment to the Mutual Defense Assistance Act which would have provided funds for assistance to "the non-communist areas of China." At this time the only remaining "non-communist areas of China" were the island of Hainan, soon to fall, and the Nationalist stronghold of Taiwan which also appeared likely to fall.[78] Since the State Department had little enthusiasm for additional aid to Chiang Kai-shek's defeated regime, and since there appeared to be no way to derail Knowland's proposal, it was astutely shunted onto a different track by Secretary of State

---

[75]State Dept Press Release, 17 Feb 50, RG 59.
[76]Caffery to State Dept, 26 Sep 48, 851G.01/9–2648, RG 59.
[77]Ibid., 11 Jan 49, 851G.00/1–1149, and 19 Mar 49, 851G.01/3–1949; both in RG 59.
[78]U.S. Congress, Senate, *Hearings Held in Executive Session Before the [Senate] Committee on Foreign Relations on Economic Assistance to China and Korea: 1949–50, Historical Series* (Washington, 1974), pp. 56–61, 193–99, passim.

Acheson and the chairman of the Senate Foreign Relations Committee, Senator Tom Connally. What emerged from the Senate's deliberations was Section 303 of the Mutual Defense Assistance Act, authorizing a sum of $75 million to be used in "the general area of China."

This broad geographical reference obviously could be interpreted to include French Indochina, where, Acheson explained to Senator Claude Pepper of Florida,

the situation has improved a great deal . . . in the last year. . . . The French Army has been reorganized and moved up to the border, where the morale is high, its equipment is good and it is a pretty efficient outfit. . . . conditions in the area are very much improved. The whole delta region is . . . pacified and is now under cultivation again, which is a great improvement, and the Vietnam system of blockhouses has kept the raiders pretty successfully in the hills. So it looks better—much better.[79]

· Acheson's view of conditions in Indochina was far more optimistic than that of American observers on the scene. As early as February 1949 the U.S. naval attache in Hanoi, Lt. William H. Hunter, had predicted that the French would probably abandon all but the coastal areas of Tonkin.[80] In late March the American consul in Hanoi, William H. Gibson, reported that the French military position in the border areas of northern Vietnam was serious and deteriorating, and that the current French losses of about five hundred killed and wounded per month could not be sustained without reinforcements. Gibson described Hanoi as "subject to increasingly daring terroristic attacks . . . which the present Hanoi garrison is apparently unable to restrict," and in July the consul expressed the fear that Bao Dai's prestige in Hanoi was rapidly declining.[81]

Yet in the wake of the China debacle legislators in Washington were apparently inclined to grasp any possible reason for optimism about the Far East. In January 1950 the House and Senate readily voted the $75 million with the hope that things were indeed looking "much better."

Well before Section 303 became law, Secretary of Defense Louis A. Johnson, anticipating the Senate's action and concerned about the situation in Asia, had requested the Joint Chiefs of Staff to study the problems involved in military assistance to countries "in the general area of China."[82] On 17 December 1949 the Joint Staff had submitted to the Joint Chiefs a draft report on American assistance to Southeast Asia. East Asia, especially Southeast Asia, had for long ranked low on the Joint Chiefs' list of probable areas of conflict. Military planners since 1946 had been preoccupied with planning for a global conflict with the Soviet Union as the hypothetical enemy. In such a war, the United States would endeavor to hold Japan, the Ryukyus, and Formosa; from these island bastions it would deliver air and sea attacks

[79]Ibid., p. 216.
[80]Am Consul, Hanoi (William H. Gibson), to Charles E. Reed, 9 Feb 49, 851G.01/2–949, RG 59.
[81]Gibson to State Dept, 27 Mar 49, 851G.00/3–2749, 30 Mar 49, 851G.00/3–3049, and 8 Jul 49, 851G.00/7–849; all in RG 59.
[82]Memo, Johnson for Joint Chiefs of Staff, 13 Sep 49, cited in Incl to JCS 1721/42, 17 Dec 49, CCS 452 China (4–3–45), JCS records.

against the Soviet Union. Later, in 1948, the Philippines were added to the list of island bases to be held.[83]

The Joint Staff planners undoubtedly had reference to these earlier studies in preparing their 1949 report. In it they expressed the view that the Communist success in China constituted a grievous defeat for the United States and warned that "if Southeast Asia is also swept by Communism, we shall have suffered a rout the repercussions of which will be felt throughout the rest of the world." The Joint Staff observed that "in the last analysis the United States is the only nation which can offer a major check to the influence of the USSR in Asia," and that it was necessary for the United States to "maintain at least a minimum position in Asia if a successful defense is to be achieved against Soviet aggression, either directly, or in the guise of international communism." The minimum position in Asia involved the offshore island chain stretching from Japan south to Okinawa, Taiwan, and the Philippines.[84] The planners recommended formulating as early as possible a program to utilize the $75 million that likely would be authorized in Section 303. The object of the program would be to "slow the communist advance with a view to eventually stopping it and causing it to retreat" and to minimize its penetration of Southeast Asia.[85]

In reviewing the Joint Staff's report, U.S. Army Chief of Staff J. Lawton Collins took a different view of the problem. While recognizing that there were "strong implications in the events now taking place throughout the Far East," Collins cautioned that "the prospect of military disadvantage to the U.S. . . . does not alone justify the seeking of a solution through a primarily military effort." General Collins believed that an integrated package of "political, economic, and psychological programs" would be more appropriate for Southeast Asia than "a program in which the primary effort would be restricted to military assistance."[86]

Whether the struggle was to be political and psychological or military, the American view of events in Southeast Asia had undergone marked change. Until the fall of China, American interest had been primarily in maintaining the goodwill of the peoples of the area and in ensuring continued American access to the raw materials of the region. Although the State Department had also been concerned about the growing threat of Communist subversion and penetration in the area, its prescription for meeting this danger had been modest. As late as mid-1948 its position was that the United States should step up its information and educational exchange programs to counter Soviet propaganda and encourage settlement of outstanding colonial-nationalistic disputes.[87]

The change that developments in China caused was illustrated by a draft

[83]Roger Dingman, "Strategic Planning and the Policy Process: American Plans for War in East Asia, 1945–50," *Naval War College Review*, November-December 1979, pp. 5–19.
[84]JCS 1721/42, 17 Dec 49, CCS 452 China (4–3–45), JCS records.
[85]Ibid.
[86]Memo, Chief of Staff, Army, Dec 49, in JCS 1721/42, 17 Dec 49.
[87]Memo, K. P. Landon, 29 Jun 48, sub: Southeast Asia: Communist Penetration, and Memo, W. S. B. Lacy for Charles Reed, 4 Aug 48, sub: Long Range Policy With Respect to Emergent Nations; both in files of Office of Philippine and Southeast Asian Affairs, RG 59.

policy paper prepared for the National Security Council (NSC) during late 1949, The Position of the United States With Respect to Asia (NSC 48/1). The Soviet Union in Europe was "now and in the foreseeable future" the greatest menace to freedom, but the Communist victory in China threatened Southeast Asia. China, with its support from Russia, thus constituted a more immediate danger. Viewed in this light, the French struggle in Indochina was no longer an old-fashioned war between a colonial power and a subject people, no longer a mere embarrassment to American interests in Asia, but a contest between an American ally and a Communist-controlled insurrection supported by China.[88]

This change of emphasis could be observed also in the reaction by the Joint Chiefs of Staff to NSC 48/1. The draft made little specific mention of Vietnam and addressed only in general terms a need to resolve the colonialist-nationalist conflict in such a manner as to satisfy nationalist demands with minimum strain on the colonial powers.[89] Such generalities held no satisfaction for the Joint Chiefs of Staff, who called for the "determination, development, and implementation of definite United States steps in Asia." The first of those steps would be the implementation of the Joint Staff's recommendation—the programming and spending of the Section 303 funds.[90] Adopting the Joint Chiefs' view, the National Security Council revised NSC 48/1, calling on the United States to "support non-communist forces in taking the initiative in Asia" and to pay particular attention "to the problem of French Indo-China."[91] The Joint Chiefs also received approval for programming the Section 303 funds.

On 5 January 1950, the director of the Office of Military Assistance, Maj. Gen. Lyman L. Lemnitzer; the foreign affairs adviser to the Secretary of Defense, Najeeb Halaby; and Under Secretary of State Dean Rusk formulated a number of questions concerning the limitations on and the uses of the funds. The Joint Chiefs assigned the task of answering the questions and formulating a specific aid program for Asia to an ad hoc committee headed by Maj. Gen. Robinson E. Duff.[92] General Duff's committee accepted the earlier position of the Joint Staff that the United States had to retain control of the offshore island chain as a minimum defensive position, but it concluded that the chain would be unable to stand alone against an integrated, Soviet-controlled Asia. Japan and the other island nations required a stable, non-Communist Southeast Asia from which to obtain food and raw materials. The minimum position was thus too minimal; a non-Communist Southeast Asia was required to maintain the stability of the island chain.

Mainland Southeast Asia was particularly "vulnerable to military attacks despite important terrain barriers," the committee added, and was politically and psychologically susceptible to Communist subversion. Unless outside

[88]*U.S.-Vietnam Relations*, 8:227.
[89]NSC 48/1, *U.S.-Vietnam Relations*, 8:271.
[90]JCS 1992/7, 29 Dec 49, CCS 092 Asia (6–25–48).
[91]*U.S.-Vietnam Relations*, 8:266, 271.
[92]Memo, K. T. Young for Rear Adm A. C. Davis, 6 Jan 50, CCS 452 China (4–3–45), sec. 7, pt. 7, JCS records.

influence was applied, the local Communists would likely succeed. To reverse this trend, the Duff committee recommended a program of overt assistance and covert operations in the general area of China to be initiated as early as possible. Indochina, where the need was seen to be most critical, should receive first priority and $15 million of Section 303 aid, an amount second only to that allotted for Taiwan. The committee recognized hatred of colonialism, rather than fear of communism, as the dominant political concern of most of the peoples of Southeast Asia, and was aware that by aiding French Indochina "the United States might come to be identified with the colonial countries of Europe," but the members believed "careful maneuvering and determined handling of the psychological factors in the individual countries" could overcome this obstacle.[93]

Secretary of State Acheson had now come to much the same view. On 23 January he told the National Press Club that American military assistance to Southeast Asia might well provide "the missing component in a problem which might otherwise be unsolved."[94] An important consideration for Acheson was the serious effect continued involvement in Vietnam was having on France's ability to contribute to the defense of Western Europe. Every franc spent in Vietnam was one franc less for French forces in the North Atlantic Treaty Organization.[95] He thus acknowledged the French position; the current French commander in Vietnam, General Marcel Carpentier, for example, complained to an American visitor, "the flower of the French Army was in Indo-China instead of on the Rhine."[96] The respected foreign affairs analyst C. L. Sulzberger echoed Acheson's concern in the *New York Times* on 23 January when he wrote that "the disciplined machinery of international communism, directed by Moscow, is carrying out perhaps the most brilliant example of global political warfare so far known by draining the potential strength of France in the Indo-China civil war and thus . . . simultaneously weakening the Western Powers' position in Europe and Asia."[97] That same day the *Times* reported that "highly competent military authorities in Tokyo" believed "the French might be able to hold off a concerted communist thrust [in Indochina] if properly equipped."[98]

Yet official American thinking about Indochina was less than unanimous. From Bangkok, the new head of the State Department Far East Division, W. Walton Butterworth, sent a blunt warning that economic and military aid did not constitute the "missing components" in solving the problems posed by Asia. The impression held by some Americans that aid to Indochina would be as effective and successful as had been American aid to Greece was, said Butterworth, a dangerous delusion.[99]

[93]Report of Ad Hoc Committee, Duff to Secy, JCS, 14 Jan 50, CCS 452 China (4−3−45), sec. 7, pt. 7, JCS records.
[94]Department of State *Bulletin*, 23 January 1950, p. 114.
[95]Gaddis Smith, *Dean Acheson* (New York: Cooper Square, 1972), pp. 313−14.
[96]Am Consulate, Saigon, to State Dept, 31 Jan 50, 751G.02/1−3150, RG 59.
[97]C. L. Sulzberger, "Red Blow to West in Indochina Seen," *New York Times*, 23 Jan 50.
[98]"Indo-China Viewed as Key Asia Point," *New York Times*, 23 Jan 50.
[99]Telg, Butterworth to Secy of State, 17 Feb 50, *U.S.-Vietnam Relations*, 8:280.

101

Second thoughts about committing American military resources to Southeast Asia also arose within the Plans and Operations Division of the Army staff. In February 1950 the planners took issue with the conclusions of a draft prepared by the staff of the National Security Council. Entitled "The Position of the United States With Respect to Indochina," the paper declared that Indochina was important to U.S. security interests and that all practical measures should be taken to protect it. The Army planners countered that "to condition a course of action on the security interest of this place is false and narrow" because it was not clear "that the U.S. has a vital security interest in this immediate area." The Plans and Operations Division contended that while the United States had a strategic interest in Southeast Asia as a whole, this interest was basically limited, in terms of required action, to guaranteeing Japan's access to the food supplies of the area. The paper noted the importance of denying resources to Communist China, but it argued that doing so was important not because of the need to defend against Communist aggression but because "China's failure to control this area may increase her dependence on the Western bloc [for food and raw materials] and serve as a stimulus for a durable long-term Western orientation."[100]

As for Indochina (and Vietnam, specifically), the Plans and Operations Division recommended support "on a limited basis provided that France agrees to a more complete transfer of sovereignty to Bao Dai, a relinquishment of its colonial tenets and an acknowledgment that the Military pacification of Indo-China is not possible." Although the Army planners recognized that Bao Dai had the support of no more than a small proportion of the population, they believed the United States had no choice but to back him. "The time has passed when the United States could pursue an attitude of complete neutrality. Our recognition of Bao Dai cast the die. French prestige is at stake and requests from them for . . . assistance will probably be forthcoming shortly."[101]

The old argument about support for Bao Dai had thus taken a new turn. For two years advocates of the Bao Dai experiment had argued that the United States had to recognize Bao Dai or his regime would fail. With recognition a fact, the Army planners now reasoned that keeping Bao Dai from failure was necessary because the United States had recognized him.

As discussions of military aid continued in the Pentagon, a State Department working group was attempting to put forward some broad guidelines for American assistance, both military and economic. The working group members cautioned against a program so large that it would shift the burden of supply for the Indochina conflict from France to the United States. They believed that the United States should be willing to consider requests from the French only for "unique items of military equipment," that is, items not available from Europe. These supplies could be financed by the 303 funds, although the United States should do nothing to invite France to apply for

---

[100]Memo for Gen Schuyler, 24 Feb 50, sub: Position of the United States With Respect to Indochina, OPS 337, RG 319.
[101]Ibid.

military or economic aid under Section 303. Within a few months all these criteria had gone by the board.[102]

While the form of American aid for Indochina was still being discussed, the long-anticipated formal request for aid arrived from the French. On 16 February Ambassador Henri Bonnet met with the secretary of state to present an aide-memoire urging the American government to affirm publicly its solidarity with France in the face of the Communist menace in the Far East and to begin an immediate program of military and economic aid to France and the Associated States of Indochina.[103] Six days later the French told American officials in Paris that without a long-term program of American military assistance, they might find it necessary to cut their losses and withdraw from Indochina.[104]

Although the United States was already moving toward aid for Indochina, American officials were anxious to exploit fully the bargaining leverage presented by the French requests for help. They hoped specifically to compel the French to grant real power and independence to Bao Dai's regime in Vietnam. To Ambassador Bonnet, Secretary of State Acheson suggested that an American statement of solidarity with France in Asia would be more effective if coupled with a public French statement that the Elysee Agreements of 8 March 1949 "represented only a step in an evolving process" of gradual independence for Vietnam.[105] Acheson privately expressed to his staff a concern that "our bargaining power with the French disappears the moment we agree to give them aid for Indo-China."[106]

The French responded to the American pressure for further concessions with a warning: unless American support was forthcoming, they would have to abandon Vietnam and the rest of Indochina to communism. French Foreign Minister Robert Schuman told reporters he was "amazed that the United States insisted upon discussing future Vietnamese independence from France when Vietnamese independence from communism was at stake."[107]

Despite this French refusal to make changes in their Vietnam policy, the pressure in America for aid continued. Since Section 303 funds were now available, the service secretaries on 1 March urged approval of the $15 million allocation to Indochina recommended by the Joint Chiefs of Staff, and on the same day the National Security Council recommended an immediate military aid program to Indochina and Thailand.[108] President Truman approved the $15 million military aid recommendation on 10 March 1950. Thus, despite General Collins' earlier warning against trying to solve the problem of Indo-

[102]Min, PSA-WE Working Groups, 17 Jan 50, files of Office of Philippine and Southeast Asian Affairs, RG 59.

[103]Memo of Conversation, Secy of State, 16 Feb 50, Incl to JCS 1992/10, CCS 092, Asia, sec. 3, JCS records.

[104]Telg, Ambassador in France (Bruce) to Secy of State, 22 Feb 50, Department of State, *Foreign Relations of the United States, 1950*, vol. 6, *East Asia and the Pacific* (Washington, 1976), p. 740.

[105]Memo of Conversation, Secy of State, 16 Feb 50.

[106]Smith, *Acheson*, p. 310.

[107]*New York Times*, 4 May 50.

[108]Memo, Adm A. C. Davis for Col Shell, 1 Mar 50, CCS 092 Asia, sec. 3, JCS records.

china primarily through military assistance, the first American response to the problem was essentially military in nature.

The transition from recognition of Bao Dai to supplying military aid to his government and its French patron seemed a logical, easy, and natural one. From early 1948, when Washington reached the conclusion that a Viet Minh – dominated, and therefore Communist, Vietnam was unacceptable, to early 1950, when military aid was extended, the cost of avoiding the unacceptable was never calculated. Yet the cost was already beginning to rise: from diplomatic support for Bao Dai, to formal recognition, to $15 million of military aid. The cost was, in fact, open-ended, for if a Viet Minh victory was unacceptable, then a French defeat had to be forestalled no matter what the price. Any hint from Paris that the French were faltering in their will to stay in Vietnam and keep fighting usually produced in America political concession or additional aid or both. In time, avoiding French defeat would become more important to the United States than to France. It was, as Charlton Ogburn had foreseen, the beginning of "a very bad mess."

6

Establishing a Military Assistance Program

On 16 March 1950 the French government delivered to the U.S. embassy in Paris a list of urgently needed supplies and equipment for Indochina. Heading the list were radios and radio equipment. Radio was the primary means of communication in Indochina and the only link between widely separated cities such as Hue and Saigon, which had no telephone connections. Also critically needed were bulldozers and other types of construction equipment to improve and expand the primitive road network, light planes or helicopters for medical evacuation, and spare parts for aircraft. The cost of these arms and equipment totaled about $94 million. Included were $11 million for ammunition, $32 million for automotive equipment, $2 million for medical supplies, $8 million for engineering equipment, and $8 million for signal equipment.

General Duff of the Joint Chiefs' ad hoc committee on aid for Southeast Asia characterized the French request as modest and appropriate in view of the military situation in Vietnam.[1] Aid to Indochina on such a scale, however, called for a more substantial and lasting commitment to the area than what was contemplated in Section 303. That a fuller commitment might be forthcoming could be inferred from the fact that in late February 1950 the State Department had announced plans for an economic survey mission to Southeast Asia. Headed by Robert A. Griffin, an official of the Economic Cooperation Administration and a veteran of aid programs in China, the mission was to determine the nature, scope, and appropriateness of American economic and technical assistance to Southeast Asia.[2]

The Griffin Mission

The Griffin mission arrived in Saigon around the same time that units of the U.S. Seventh Fleet, at State Department behest, were paying a cour-

---

[1]Consul General, Saigon, to State Dept, 18 Mar 50, 751G.5MAP/3–1850; Charge d'Affaires, London, to State Dept, 22 Mar 50, 751G.01/3–2250; State Dept to Am Legation, Saigon, 31 Mar 50, 751G.5MAP/3–3150. A11 in records of Dept of State.
[2]Ltr, Under Secy of State to Griffin, 1 Mar 50, U.S.-Vietnam Relations, 8:286–87.

tesy visit to Vietnam.[3] It included two military officers, Army Col. E. A. Duff and Navy Capt. W. Warder, who spent much of their time conferring with French military authorities.[4] French High Commissioner Leon Pignon told the mission that French problems in Vietnam were primarily military. Only the rapid improvement of the weapons and equipment of the French forces, he argued, would permit a return of military confidence, and only the prospect of ultimate military success would make further political and economic progress possible.[5]

French forces in Indochina were armed with a mixture of World War II British, American, French, and German weapons and equipment. Most of the British and American small arms, which constituted about 40 percent of those possessed by the French Army and auxiliary forces in Indochina, were worn-out or unserviceable due to a shortage of spare parts. A lack of suitable ammunition also limited the number of machine guns that could be kept in service. The French field artillery units possessed about 400 fieldpieces, ranging in size from French 75-mm. types to a handful of American World War II 155-mm. howitzers, but about 22 percent of all the artillery was worn-out or unserviceable.[6] The situation in regard to aircraft was no better. An American general who was invited to observe a French bombing mission rode in an antique German aircraft which "actually had telephone wire tying things up." There were no bomb racks; the 100-pound bombs were tied down with wire until needed, then pitched out the door.[7] When Captain Warder accompanied French forces on an amphibious assault against the Viet Minh, he was impressed with the high morale of the troops, but he noted a lack of sufficient air cover and a shortage of officers.[8] The members of the survey mission quickly concluded that the aid requirements for French Indochina would far exceed the money available from Section 303 funds.[9]

A Growing Commitment

While the Griffin economic survey mission was in Asia, the State and Defense Departments began to formulate long-range assessments of the status of Indochina and of its importance to the United States. On 10 April 1950 the Joint Chiefs of Staff submitted a memorandum to Secretary of Defense Johnson on the strategic importance of Southeast Asia. In contrast to the rather cautious approach of General Duff's ad hoc committee and the

[3]Edwin Bickford Hooper, Dean C. Allard, and Oscar P. Fitzgerald, *The United States Navy and the Vietnam Conflict*, vol. 1, *The Setting of the Stage to 1959* (Washington, 1976), p. 173.
[4]Colonel Duff had served on the JCS ad hoc committee headed by Maj. Gen. Robinson Duff.
[5]Statement, M. Leon Pignon, French High Commissioner Indochina, Incl 4 to U.S. Army Attache, Saigon, to ACofS G – 2, 2 Aug 50, records of ACSI.
[6]U.S. Army Attache, Saigon, to ACofS G – 2, 12 Jul 50, sub: Arms and Armament of the French Army in Indochina, R – 13 – 50, OARMA 056, records of ACSI.
[7]Oral Hist Interv with General Graves B. Erskine, 1969 – 70, U.S. Marine Corps Historical Center.
[8]Min, Foreign Military Assistance Coordinating Committee Meeting, 6 May 50, M – 17, Lot 54D5, records of Dept of State.
[9]Ibid.

even more circumspect approach of the Army staff, the Joint Chiefs firmly declared that mainland Southeast Asia was of critical strategic importance to the United States.

Although military leaders earlier had viewed Southeast Asia as important chiefly because of its relationship to the island chain of Japan, Okinawa, Taiwan, and the Philippines, the Joint Chiefs now saw Southeast Asia as strategically important in its own right. The area was a major source of certain "strategic materials" required by the United States and was a "cross-road of communications" and a "vital segment in the line of containment of communism stretching from Japan southward and around to the Indian Peninsula." Should Southeast Asia fall to communism, the Joint Chiefs noted, the security of Japan, India, and Australia would be threatened. Indochina was the key because its fall would undoubtedly bring about the fall of Burma and Thailand, and probably of the Philippines, Malaya, and Indonesia. The Joint Chiefs of Staff urged that funds allocated for aid to Indochina be programmed as soon as possible and that an additional appropriation of at least $10 million be sought for fiscal year 1951.[10]

The State Department was thinking along similar lines. "The Department's policy with respect to Southeast Asia," declared Deputy Assistant Secretary of State Livingston T. Merchant, "is to stop Communism at the southern border of China." The fate of French Indochina was crucial. Should it come under Communist control, Burma would be outflanked, Thailand would change sides, and Malaya would be gravely threatened. The psychological effects would be felt even beyond Southeast Asia.[11]

Such views found expression also in a new National Security Council memorandum, the first to deal exclusively with the question of Indochina. That memorandum, NSC–64, approved by the president in March 1950, defined Indochina as a key area of Southeast Asia and predicted, much as the Joint Chiefs would do, that if Indochina succumbed to Communist domination, Thailand and Burma could also be expected to fall. The rest of "Southeast Asia would then be in grave hazard."[12]

The concepts embodied in the April memorandum from the Joint Chiefs and in NSC–64 would form the basis of American policy in Southeast Asia for at least the ensuing decade. The goal of containing communism in China and the related idea that the loss of one country in Southeast Asia would inevitably lead to the loss of others—eventually known as the domino theory—gradually took on the aura of a kind of dogma. Yet the writers of these two pivotal documents probably intended them more as arguments for immediate American aid to Indochina than as long-range geopolitical analyses.

[10]Memo for Secy of Defense, 10 Apr 50, sub: Strategic Assessment of Southeast Asia, *U.S.-Vietnam Relations*, 8:308–13.
[11]Memo, Merchant for W. Walton Butterworth, 7 Mar 50, sub: French Indochina, files of Office of Philippine and Southeast Asian Affairs, Lot 54D190, records of Dept of State.
[12]Draft report by the National Security Council on the Position of the United States With Respect to Indochina, NSC–64, *U.S.-Vietnam Relations*, 8:285.

Although agreement was fairly general that American military aid was needed in Indochina, the question remained: Aid to whom? One obvious way of increasing American influence in Indochina while avoiding the stigma of supporting French colonialists was to give the aid directly to Bao Dai. Robert Griffin in March advised the State Department that such a course would greatly bolster the Bao Dai government by "increasing its appearance of independence [and] its local and international prestige."[13]

To Bao Dai's government, the advantages were just as obvious. Consul General Edmund Gullion in Saigon reported on 18 March, for example, that responsible Vietnamese officials believed direct access to American military aid would give them a "whip hand with the French."[14] To the commander of the U.S. Seventh Fleet, Vice Adm. Russell S. Berkey, Bao Dai explained that direct American aid would be useful in obtaining greater military independence from the French, and that greater independence was "the key to the situation."[15] His defense minister, Phan Huy Quat, proposed to Gullion on 25 March that the United States assume direct responsibility for training and equipping a Vietnamese army.[16]

Both Gullion and Admiral Berkey, however, were skeptical about direct military aid to Bao Dai. Berkey noted that while the French had submitted a detailed and specific list of their needs, the Vietnamese had been unable to furnish more than hazy ideas about their military requirements. Gullion dismissed Phan Huy Quat's proposal as "fantastic" and suggested that the early arrival of U.S. aid in Indochina was more important than "some evolutionary or renunciatory declaration to be wrung from the French."[17]

Predictably, the French made clear that they would reject any plan to provide direct military aid to the Vietnamese. General Carpentier, for example, told the *New York Times* that he would never agree to military equipment going directly to Bao Dai and declared that if it did he "would resign within twenty-four hours." "The Vietnamese," said Carpentier, "have . . . no military organization which could effectively utilize the equipment. It would be wasted, and in China, the United States has had enough of that." French High Commissioner Leon Pignon explained that only the French military could handle the complex technical problems involved in the reception and distribution of arms and equipment.[18]

Always present in the background was the implied, and sometimes explicit, threat that France might, as French Foreign Office Secretary Alexandre Parodi told the U.S. ambassador in February, "cut her losses" and quit Indochina if the United States failed to provide aid or if France was pressured to make too many concessions to Bao Dai. Although there was doubtless an element of bluff in the French threats, they seldom failed to elicit vigorous hand-wringing from American officials. Parodi's statement itself evoked an immedi-

[13]Griffin to Secy of State, 16 Mar 50, *U.S.-Vietnam Relations,* 8:292.
[14]Gullion to State Dept, 18 Mar 50, 751G.00/3–1850, records of Dept of State.
[15]Cmdr, Seventh Fleet, to CNO, 25 Mar 50, CCS 452 China, sec. 7, pt. 8, JCS records.
[16]Gullion to State Dept, 25 Mar 50, 751G.00/3–2550, records of Dept of State.
[17]Ibid., 18 Mar 50, and 25 Mar 50.
[18]*New York Times,* 9 Mar 50.

ate demand from Washington that France vow not to give up the war.[19] But in May Robert Griffin warned that the French might still withdraw entirely "if [the] pressure . . . for 'evolutionary' treatment . . . became too severe."[20]

Given this wariness about French reactions, the idea of using aid to the Vietnamese as a lever to pry further concessions of local autonomy was quietly abandoned. The State Department continued to hope that France would make a public declaration at least of its intent in time to grant greater authority to the Bao Dai regime, but the French government refused even this minimal concession under the pretext such a statement would cast doubt on the validity of the Elysee Agreements.[21]

Even though the question of who should receive aid remained, the movement for a large-scale American commitment to Indochina had acquired a momentum of its own. The Joint Chiefs of Staff in April and May advised that although the establishment of political and economic stability would be the most important factor in the long-run struggle for Southeast Asia, the military situation there was of "pressing urgency." They recommended "immediate and positive steps to achieve the initiative in the present conflict."[22] From Saigon, Consul General Gullion added the warning "that most of the colored races of the world will, in time, fall to the communist sickle if Indochina is taken over."[23] On his return from Indochina, Robert Griffin reiterated his view that American aid to Bao Dai would help him win over the non-Communist elements of the Viet Minh and the "numerous fence sitters." Ambassador-at-Large Philip C. Jessup, meanwhile, told a closed session of the Senate Foreign Relations Committee that the French would have a chance of gradually defeating the Communist forces if supplied with sufficient American economic and military aid.[24]

There were a few notes of caution. The chief of the State Department's Southeast Asia Branch, Charlton Ogburn, pointed out that Griffin, Jessup, and some of the other supporters of large-scale aid had only a brief and superficial familiarity with Southeast Asia and that even Consul General Gullion had been at his post less than two months. "The trouble is that none of us knows enough about Indochina," Ogburn explained. "We have had no real political reporting from there since [Charles E.] Reed and [James L.] O'Sullivan left two years ago." Ogburn doubted that the introduction of American military aid would make any decisive difference in the Franco-Vietnamese conflict. Ho's forces had fought the 150,000-man French Army in Vietnam to a draw after four bitter years and were unlikely "to wilt under the psychological

[19]Ambassador in France to State Dept, 22 Feb 50, 751G.00/2-2250, records of Dept of State.

[20]Memo, Griffin for Secy of State, 4 May 52, sub: Conference on Indo-China—May 2, 1950, Department of State, *Foreign Relations of the United States, 1950*, vol. 6, *East Asia and the Pacific* (Washington, 1976), p. 797.

[21]Telg, Acheson to Am Embassy, Paris, 29 Mar 50, *U.S.-Vietnam Relations*, 8:301-03.

[22]Memo for Secy of Defense, 10 Apr 50, sub: Strategic Assessment of Southeast Asia, *U.S.-Vietnam Relations*, 8:310; ibid., JCS for Secy of Defense, 2 May 50, sub: Southeast Asia, same volume, 8:318.

[23]Gullion to State Dept, 6 May 50, 751G.00/5-650, records of Dept of State.

[24]Smith, *Acheson*, p. 313.

impact of American military assistance." Even if American military aid on a large scale could turn the tide, the Viet Minh, Ogburn surmised, would merely return to scattered guerrilla resistance and bide their time.[25]

Although Ogburn's skepticism was to prove well founded, there was little inclination in Washington to undertake the careful reexamination of American policy that Ogburn was suggesting. By May 1950, when Secretary of State Acheson flew to London for meetings with NATO foreign ministers, it was apparent that an open-ended American commitment to Indochina much greater than that provided for by the Section 303 funds was in the offing. Policymakers were now convinced that large-scale military aid was essential and inevitable. Secretary Acheson was worried about France's continued participation in the North Atlantic alliance, the Army was disturbed by the drain on France's NATO forces, and the Joint Chiefs wished to "achieve the initiative" in the battle for Southeast Asia.

In London, French Foreign Minister Robert Schuman flatly told Acheson that France would be unable to meet its NATO military commitments in Western Europe so long as the Indochina conflict continued to drain French resources. When Acheson again raised the question of more autonomy for the Bao Dai regime, Schuman replied blandly that "if the United States gives France its support in the military field and trusts it for the internal development of its policy, a happy ending will be achieved."[26] Acheson and Schuman finally agreed that $20 to $30 million in American aid would be furnished forthwith and an indeterminate amount during the next fiscal year. "The United States Government," Acheson told the press on 8 May, "convinced that neither national independence nor democratic evolution exists in any area dominated by Soviet imperialism, considers the situation such as to warrant its according economic aid and military equipment to the Associated States and France."[27]

The French had won the first round of bargaining over aid, as they would continue to do in all subsequent rounds until their final defeat in Vietnam, for the American negotiating position was fundamentally untenable. Although American officials agreed that the war could be won only if Bao Dai had sufficient authority and independence to attract substantial portions of Ho's adherents and to subdue the others militarily, they were also convinced that real independence for Vietnam would mean a loss of all French incentive to continue the war.

Ambassador David Bruce recognized the problem when he pointed out that the success of American policy depended upon both a continued French effort in Indochina and a steady growth in the authority and prestige of non-Communist Vietnamese nationalists. "Yet," he added, "these two forces . . . are inherently antagonistic and the gains of one will be at the

---

[25]Ltr, Ogburn to W. Walton Butterworth, 21 Mar 50, 751G.00/3 – 2150, records of Dept of State.
[26]Documentary History of U.S. Policy Toward Indochina (compilation by the State Dept Historical Div), doc. B – 47, Acheson-Schuman Conversations, 8 May 50.
[27]Smith, *Acheson*, p. 314.

expense of the other."[28] Instead of drawing the conclusion that the task was impossible, Bruce merely spoke of the need for officers of exceptional tact and judgment to be assigned to Indochina.

The Melby-Erskine Mission

While policymakers in Washington pondered the problems of Indochina, the machinery of the American military aid program was gradually being assembled in Saigon. Saigon was chosen instead of Hanoi because of the location there of the French military headquarters and the seat of the Bao Dai government. Although American military representatives would play a major role in ensuring the efficient and timely delivery of aid to the French, they would not be able to exercise much influence upon the conduct of the war or even upon French use of the American material. During the first two years of the aid program, Americans in Saigon would prove no more able than Americans in Washington or Paris to use military aid to exercise leverage on the French.

The counselor and second secretary of the American legation in Saigon spent the weeks immediately after the decision to supply military aid to the French negotiating military aid requests. That work was already well along when another survey mission arrived in Saigon on 15 July. This joint survey team, composed of representatives of the Defense and State Departments, was charged with determining the long-range nature and objectives of the aid program and the best organization for carrying it out. John F. Melby of the State Department headed the team. Maj. Gen. Graves B. Erskine, U.S. Marine Corps, was in charge of its military component.[29] Shortly after the Americans' arrival three terrorist bombs wrecked the lobby of their hotel. Fortunately, the members of the team were absent at the time, but General Erskine suspected that the incident had been arranged by the French to persuade the team not to spend too much time looking into affairs in Indochina.[30]

The members of the team received over 5,000 pages in reports from the French for study, but the U.S. legation's overworked staff of three translators took so long to provide translations that the reports proved of little practical use. At the same time, General Erskine, a crusty veteran of the Pacific campaigns of World War II with no knowledge of French, was outspokenly annoyed at the amount of time that the French wished him to spend at formal briefings, military reviews, and social occasions. Both Erskine and Melby were also worried by the apparent lack of hard intelligence on the enemy. The French military dispositions were not the problem, Melby recalled, for "we were free to look at them any place we chose and did so." The problem "was the strength and disposition of the Communist-led

[28]Bruce to Secy of State, 31 May 50, 751G.00/5–3150, records of Dept of State.
[29]Am Minister, Saigon (Donald Heath), to State Dept, 5 Jan 51, 751G.5MAP/1–551, records of Dept of State.
[30]Erskine Interv, pp. 471–72.

Vietminh forces. It became increasingly clear that the French did not know this and that what they thought they knew just as likely as not was wrong."[31]

Erskine was determined to see and judge for himself the state of the French military effort and "to find out just what the hell their ability was to use the equipment." The French, he told U.S. Minister Donald R. Heath, "haven't won a war since Napoleon so why listen to a bunch of second raters when they are losing this war. They are going to show down [*sic*] with me or I'll recommend they don't get a damn penny."[32] Such talk appalled the minister and his staff, but in the end the general and his aides did manage to see a

General Erskine

good bit of the war. The joint survey team remained in Indochina for three weeks, visiting military installations in the Saigon area, participating as observers in a number of French military operations, touring the Red River Delta and the Chinese border in Tonkin, and making brief visits to Laos and Cambodia. When one of Erskine's aides, Capt. Nick Thorne, U.S. Marine Corps, secured permission, with considerable difficulty, to accompany a Vietnamese unit of the French Expeditionary Corps on a night ambush to capture prisoners for interrogation, he was impressed by the combat performance of the Vietnamese troops. The mission, however, was a failure because the Vietnamese "refused to bring back heads with bodies still attached to them."[33]

At the time of the team's visit, French forces were engaged in three types of military operations. The first, pacification operations, consisted of cordoning off a region and securing the main lines of communication within the area. French and Vietnamese authorities then attempted to establish a working civil government and police force. This slow process absorbed many troops. A second type of operation involved offensive probes against the Viet Minh. The French admitted that enemy regular forces were hard to find. These large-scale attacks seldom resulted in heavy fighting against organized units, although small-scale, vicious, hand-to-hand encounters were common. The majority of French casualties on these offensive probes were caused by skillfully planted mines and night sniper fire.

Protection of convoys, which were vulnerable to mines and to ambushes,

[31]John F. Melby, "Vietnam—1950," *Diplomatic History* 6 (Winter 1982):99.
[32]Erskine Interv, p. 473; Ltrs, Heath to W. S. B. Lacy, 2 Aug 50, and 16 Jan 51, both in Lot 58D207, records of Dept of State.
[33]Melby, "Vietnam—1950," p. 101; Erskine Interv, p. 477.

French Convoy *near Ninh Hoa.*

constituted a third type of operation. Since Viet Minh ambushes often employed up to 6,000 men along a 3- to 5-kilometer section of a convoy route, convoys had to be heavily escorted by strong infantry forces and armored cars. To escort a convoy of 200 vehicles required up to 5 infantry battalions, 2 artillery groups, and 2 squadrons of armored cars. Even smaller convoys required a minimum of 2 infantry battalions. Supply convoys on the 200-kilometer stretch of road between Cao Bang and Lang Son near the Chinese border took an average of fourteen days to reach their destination.[34]

The Viet Minh were now employing up to six or seven battalions in their major offensives and were able to sustain their attacks for almost a week. Improved Viet Minh capabilities obliged the French to alter their method of fortifying posts. Simple barbed wire or bamboo fences were no longer sufficient; concrete pillboxes were now necessary to deal with the increasing enemy numbers and firepower.[35]

The military members of the Melby-Erskine team quickly concluded that the Viet Minh, not the French, controlled the major portion of Indochina and

[34]Staff Discussions Between the Birtish Service Authorities in Singapore and the French Service Authorities in Indo-China, Incl 1 to Army Attache, Singapore, to ACofS G – 2, 11 Sep 50, records of ACSI.
[35]Viet Minh Document on Military Tactics, 9 Apr 54, Incl 29 to U.S. Army Attache to ACSI, 8 Jun 54, records of ACSI.

"for all practical purposes have the French forces pinned to their occupied areas." The French appeared to have "lost most of their offensive spirit." Their efforts were stalemated and their casualties were very high.[36] While inspecting the French border fortress at Dong Dang, General Erskine discovered that the French had only about five units of fire for their machine guns and that the fort's water storage area was empty. No terrain obstacles or traps had been erected to bar likely avenues of attack even though bamboo and other types of wood were plentiful. "They had a brigadier in command of the area," Erskine recalled, "who gave me the impression he couldn't make a decent corporal."[37]

The joint survey team concluded that "military action alone cannot solve the internal security problems" in Vietnam, which they attributed less to technical military errors on the part of the French than to "the deep-seated hatred and suspicion" with which the Vietnamese people regarded their former colonial rulers. The French could overcome that hostility only by persuading the Vietnamese that cooperation with France was a more certain road to independence than support of the Viet Minh. That, in turn, could only be accomplished by further French concessions and reforms and early implementation of the provisions of the Elysee Agreements.

Once again the old paradox emerged: if the French were to do all those things, they would have little incentive to continue the war; yet if they failed to do them, the Vietnamese would have little reason to oppose the Viet Minh. After private conversations with General Carpentier and other French and Vietnamese officials, Melby concluded that "the political interests of France and the Associated States are not only different, they are mutually exclusive." Despite that recognition, the team failed to conclude that the inherent contradictions made the war fundamentally unwinnable; Melby and Erskine declared, instead, that "the Vietnamese and the French must be persuaded to rise above their parochial political interests."[38] Since those "parochial political interests" were the principal reasons for the war, the American job of persuasion would be difficult indeed.

In terms of the immediate military situation, the Melby-Erskine mission concluded that, with the troops and equipment then available, the French might be able to hold their own in the face of a large-scale Viet Minh offensive but not against an attack in force by the Chinese Communists. The military aid received from the United States to that point was inadequate to meet the needs of the situation. More equipment and supplies were urgently needed.[39]

With their recommendations for aid, General Erskine and his staff included

[36]Rpt of Joint MDAP Survey Mission, 24 Aug 50, CCS 092 Asia, BP (Bulky Package) 1, JCS records.
[37]Erskine Interv, pp. 478 – 79.
[38]Rpt of Joint MDAP Survey Mission, 24 Aug 50.
[39]The seriousness of the French supply problem was pointed up a few weeks later, when an American officer discovered that the poor marksmanship of many Vietnamese and Laotian soldiers in the French forces was attributable to the lack of ammunition for target practice. See Ltr, Gillespie to Secy of Defense, 4 Sep 50, G – 3 091 Indochina, RG 319.

a proposal that an American military assistance advisory group for Indochina be established as soon as possible. French leaders in Vietnam had repeatedly indicated their strong opposition to such a group. They argued that French soldiers were already familiar with U.S. World War II equipment, and they added that the presence of an advisory group would allow disruptive native politicians to play off the United States against the French and might suggest to some people that America was simply taking over in Vietnam.

U.S. representatives in Saigon, firmly backed by the director of the Defense Department Office of Military Assistance, General Lemnitzer, nevertheless insisted that a military advisory group was necessary to assure proper requisitioning, procurement, and receipt of supplies. The advisory group could also serve as a point of contact for U.S. and French military leaders and might prove of great practical value to the latter if the United States, as most people anticipated, decided to furnish the French with new, post—World War II types of equipment and weapons.[40]

General Erskine and his staff recommended that the military assistance advisory group be fairly small since it would have few training responsibilities and would be concerned mainly with processing requests for aid and occasionally inspecting military installations to observe end-use, pilferage, and loss of equipment through combat. The advisory group also was to "evaluate French tactical efficiency in the use of U.S. equipment." Given those limited duties, General Erskine personally believed the group would require no more than 30 members, but the Erskine-Melby report of 24 August recommended a joint service advisory group of 38 officers and enlisted men, headed by a general officer; the Army contingent was to consist of a colonel and 3 other officers, along with 6 enlisted men and 4 civilian clerks.[41]

Another of General Erskine's recommendations—that a regional military assistance advisory group headed by a two- or three-star American general be established for the entire Southeast Asia area—was opposed by the State Department. The latter believed that such a group might impinge on the prerogatives of ambassadors as heads of their respective missions, and it was successful in blocking the measure.[42]

The Military Assistance Advisory Group

When the Military Assistance Advisory Group (MAAG), Indochina, was approved, General Erskine appointed the U.S. military attache, Col. Lee V. Harris, as acting chief. In September 1950 the first contingent of

---

[40]Min, Foreign Military Assistance Coordinating Committee Meeting, 6 May 50; Memo, U.S. Army Attache, Saigon, for Chief, U.S. Mission, 28 Jul 50, sub: Conference With General Carpentier, Incl to U.S. Army Attache, Saigon, to ACofS G–2, 1 Aug 50, 281750Z, records of ACSI.

[41]Memo, J. T. Forbes for Head, U.S. Survey Mission to SE Asia, 2 Aug 51, G–3 091 Indochina, RG 319.

[42]Marginal Note on Ltr, Heath to W. S. B. Lacy, 3 Jan 51, Lot 58D207, records of Dept of State.

officers and enlisted men arrived in Saigon and took up temporary quarters at the Base Militaire. Col. P. J. Gillespie, who was senior to Colonel Harris, assumed temporary command, and at the end of the month the Department of Defense selected Brig. Gen. Francis G. Brink as the commander.[43]

Few American officers had gained more experience in Asia than General Brink. Fifty-seven years old at the time of his appointment, he had served three years in the Philippines before World War II, and during the war he had been a military observer in Singapore, the Dutch East Indies, and Burma and then chief of the Operations Division of the Southeast Asia Command. As chief of the Army Advisory Staff in China in 1948 and 1949, he had witnessed the defeat of Chiang Kai-shek's forces. Given that background, General Brink, as he stepped from a plane at Tan Son Nhut Airport on the outskirts of Saigon on 9 October 1950, likely had few illusions about the difficulty of his assignment.

By that time the Military Assistance Advisory Group had grown to about 65 officers and enlisted men and a civilian clerk. The Army section, headed by a colonel, was divided into five branches: Aid Supply, Transport, Technical Services, Logistics, and Operations. Each branch was small, about 6 officers and enlisted men. The single civilian, a clerk-stenographer borrowed from the American legation, was unequal to the large load of administrative paperwork generated by the group, and even after 6 more clerks were added in February 1951 the clerical and administrative staff remained too small.[44]

A serious consequence of the small staff was that the Military Assistance Advisory Group could not monitor adequately the distribution of military equipment. With no one assigned to that job, American officials had to rely on receipts furnished by the French. The advisory group's observation and supervision activities usually amounted to little more than obtaining a French signature for equipment and hoping that the equipment would be distributed as agreed.[45]

The few men of the MAAG Army section worked as inspection teams to observe the use of American equipment by French and Vietnamese military units. According to the terms of the Pentalateral Mutual Defense Assistance Pact—signed by France, the United States, and the Associated States of Indochina on 23 December 1950—which set the ground rules for military assistance, the French were to extend facilities to the advisory group "freely and fully to carry out their assigned responsibilities [for] observation of the progress and the technical use made of the assistance granted."[46] But French officials gave that provision a peculiar interpretation that made the Army inspections far from successful. They allowed no observation of units in

[43]WAR 92946, 28 Sep 50, records of MAAG Indochina, RG 218.

[44]Country Statement for 1951, USMAAG, Indochina, 12 Oct 51, records of MAAG Indochina, RG 218; Heath to Secy of State, 18 Jan 51, 751G.5MAP/1 – 1851, and State Dept to Heath, 2 Feb 51, 751G.5MAP/2 – 251, both in records of Dept of State.

[45]Synopsis of Interv with Lt Col S. Fred Cummings, Logistics Officer, MAAG Army Section, 1 Nov 54, JCS Historical Div files.

[46]Mutual Defense Assistance in Indochina, *Treaties and Other International Acts to Which the United States Is a Party*, Series 2447 (Washington, 1953), p. 4.

combat operations, and inspections in the rear areas had to be arranged two months in advance. If the request was approved, the American inspection team, usually an officer and an enlisted man, had to make a formal, almost ceremonial inspection, with the entire unit turned out in formation.[47] A further complication was that few of the inspecting officers and noncommissioned officers spoke French, and none spoke Vietnamese, so most questions and remarks had to be filtered through an interpreter. Under these circumstances, almost all units received ratings of "very good" or "excellent."

General Brink

In contrast, the MAAG Air Force and Navy teams were far more critical of French methods of utilizing aid equipment. French air and naval bases were located in secure areas, and their air and naval craft normally operated from the same bases for weeks or months at a time. The use and maintenance of their equipment thus could be checked more adequately and more frequently.

In mid-1951 the Air Force section was reporting the "bad operational habits" of French mechanics, citing in particular "the lack of appreciation of safety precautions, lack of respect for preventive maintenance," and the "standard French procedure of drinking while working."[48] Later in the year Air Force observers reported that French aircraft were so dirty that checking them thoroughly before and after flights was impossible. Another report noted that insufficient maintenance was draining spare parts: "Under these conditions," the observers concluded, "no amount of logistical support supplied [to the French] . . . will greatly reduce the difficulties now being experienced by the French Air Force in maintaining sufficient aircraft at operational level."[49] Similarly, MAAG Navy inspectors reported in May 1952 that American vessels which had been turned over to the French in excellent condition were now rusty and dirty. The French sailors were also "sloppy and unkempt."[50]

The problem of misuse of equipment was compounded by a tenuous supply line that stretched halfway around the world. The advisory group often had to cope with unexpected shortages or delays. During heavy fighting

[47]Country Statement for Presentation of 1954 MDA (Mutual Defense Assistance) Program, 17 Feb 53, records of MAAG Indochina, RG 218.
[48]MDAP Monthly Rpt, Jun 51, Air Force Sec, records of MAAG Indochina, RG 218.
[49]Ibid., Nov and Dec 51, records of Dept of State.
[50]Ibid., May 52, records of Dept of State.

in 1951 around the town of Vinh Yen, for example, General Brink had to fly to Far East Command headquarters in Tokyo to obtain critical supplies for the French. In June of that year, during fighting in the town of Phat Diem, the French suddenly ran dangerously short of 105-mm. howitzer ammunition. Again General Brink flew to Tokyo to work out an emergency arrangement whereby the French would get ammunition directly from the stockpiles of the Far East Command.[51]

Keeping track of the large amount of equipment continually arriving in Vietnam was even more difficult than coping with shortages. The equipment was shipped directly from the United States, from Japan, from the Joint U.S. Military Assistance Advisory Group in France, and from other parts of Europe. Many shipments, especially those from outside the United States, were so inadequately documented that the MAAG personnel could not identify exactly where they came from.[52]

Moreover, despite repeated requests, the French refused to produce any detailed accounting of the American equipment they had received from sources other than the continental United States.[53] Because of an archaic record-keeping system, they were perhaps simply unable to provide the detailed information needed. The first MAAG logistics officer, Lt. Col. S. Fred Cummings, Jr., for example, discovered to his surprise that the French had no stock-control system. "Requisitions were filled," he noted, "without giving recognition to previous unfilled requests." By parceling out his six enlisted men to the principal French supply depots, Cummings succeeded in a few months in establishing at least a makeshift stock-control system.[54]

Another principal MAAG function was to screen aid requests from the French in the light of criteria established by the Joint Chiefs of Staff, by budget ceilings, and by authorized force levels. Yet the group had little information to use in evaluating French requests, since the French from 1951 through 1953 never discussed their strategic plans with the Americans. "We were not too certain just what program the French and Associated States had for Indochina," recalled Colonel Cummings. "They never even provided us with an order of battle."[55]

When they received a draft program or request from the French, American officers would carefully review it, blue-pencil questionable items, and then ask the French to provide more information on those items.[56] Yet even when the information did not come, American examiners seldom went so far as to delete an item. "When there was doubt," one officer recalled, "material was left in the program."[57]

[51]Ibid., Jun 51, G – 3 091 Indochina, RG 319.
[52]Inspector General's Rpt, Apr 51, MAAG Indochina, 54, Tab F, RG 218.
[53]Ibid.
[54]Interv with Cummings, 1 Nov 54.
[55]Ibid.
[56]William J. Donovan, Report on Indochina, 1952, in Donovan Papers, RG 84, Box 5, records of Dept of State; see also Interv with Cummings, 1 Nov 54.
[57]Synopsis of Interv with Maj H. L. St. Onge, Adjutant to Gen Brink, 24 Oct 54, JCS Historical Div files.

Even that light-handed policy failed to satisfy the French. In January 1951, General Jean de Lattre de Tassigny, then commander in chief in Indochina, heatedly complained to Minister Heath that subordinate MAAG officers were requiring "excessive justification" for French aid requests. Many of the French requests had been turned down, he said, and the Americans "appeared to have lost interest in Indochina." They now seemed to be "more interested in arming Europe." After a thorough investigation, General Brink could find no evidence to substantiate de Lattre's charges. As far as he could determine, no member of the advisory group had ever refused to consider French requests for military equipment.[58]

General de Lattre's accusation was but a symptom of French suspicion and resentment. The Military Assistance Advisory Group was a continuing reminder that the French could no longer go it alone in Southeast Asia. It was also tangible evidence to the Vietnamese, Cambodians, and Laotians that their French patrons were themselves dependent upon a far more powerful patron, one that might someday replace the French as protectors of Indochina. Even before the last contingents of the advisory group had arrived, the French commander in chief at the time, General Carpentier, had already complained that the group was too large. He was, Consul Gullion noted, at best lukewarm over the prospect of American aid.[59]

The refusal of the French to recognize the importance, or even the necessity, of an adivsory group hindered all aspects of the group's operations. The American headquarters building, for example, at 284 Rue Cai May in the Cholon section of Saigon, was old and inadequate. The rickety five-story structure was located next door to a brothel much favored by troops of the French foreign legion. Around five o'clock each afternoon the noise in the crowded Rue Cai May would rise to a crescendo as trucks and busloads of legionnaires trooped into the house.[60]

No billets were provided for officers, enlisted men, or dependents. Members of the advisory group lived in old hotels described by the embassy as unfit to live in and bad for the morale, efficiency, and health of the personnel billeted in them.[61] The Army inspector general noted that billeting facilities in Vietnam for enlisted men without dependents were especially poor and that medical support for dependents was almost nonexistent except for that provided by local civilian doctors.[62] When Minister Heath raised the question of more adequate housing with the French high commissioner, he was gruffly asked, "Yours is a rich country, why don't you build houses?"[63]

In a host of minor ways the French made life difficult for the advisory group. The entire cost of renovating and remodeling the headquarters, for

---

[58]Heath to State Dept, 9 Jan 51, 751G.5MAP/1–951, records of Dept of State.

[59]MDAP Monthly Rpt, Oct 50, G–3 091 Indochina, RG 319.

[60]Interv, author with Col Donald W. Dunn, U.S. Army Reserve (Retired), Aide to Gen Brink, Bethesda, Md., 27 May 80, Historians files, CMH.

[61]Gullion to State Dept, 7 Sep 51, 751GMAP/9–751, records of Dept of State.

[62]Inspector General's Rpt, FY 53, 12 May 53, RG 218.

[63]Telg, Heath to Secy of State, 15 May 51, Department of State, *Foreign Relations of the United States, 1951*, vol. 6, *Asia and the Pacific, Part I* (Washington, 1977), p. 419.

example, was charged to the Americans even though the French retained title to the property. The French also billed the United States for such items as telephones, other utilities, and janitorial services, despite Minister Heath's protest that these items were normally charged against the governments of countries receiving American aid.[64] The French also imposed a stiff luxury tax and an import duty on such equipment as fans, washing machines, and refrigerators, even though the items were the property of the advisory group rather than of individuals.

After General de Lattre arrived and the Communists opened large-scale offensives in the fall and winter of 1950, the French attitude underwent some change. Consul Gullion attributed the change to "recognition that the recent Viet Minh assaults were repulsed only with [the help of] American weapons." In public statements, General de Lattre duly credited the part played by American military equipment in the victories at Vinh Yen and Mao Khe. After a time de Lattre even conceded to the Americans the right to know some details of his tactical plans, a concession never made by his predecessors. Yet once the first flush of those victories passed, General de Lattre and his staff came to adopt a "somewhat more grudging attitude toward U.S. aid."[65] De Lattre was heard to remark that Minister Heath "was a dupe, presenting an honest face while all sorts of American machinations were transpiring behind our backs." The American legation observed that "we are confronted with a sudden access of suspicion and objection to American operations and policy in Vietnam."[66] In April 1951 de Lattre told Heath that there were "entirely too many Americans in Indochina." He placed the figure at around 700, more than three times the actual number.[67]

De Lattre directed much of his hostility and suspicion at an American group known as the Special Technical and Economic Mission (STEM). The purpose of this mission was to "provide direct support to the Franco-Vietnamese forces" through a variety of social, medical, technical, and civil works programs. Its varied projects included road repair, bridge construction, public health, agricultural assistance, land reclamation, and technical training. Unlike military aid projects, STEM projects were negotiated directly with the governments of the Associated States, and they were administered jointly by the Americans and those governments.

That direct contact between American and Vietnamese officials worried French authorities. Some members of the special mission, they asserted, "may have been taken in by the more extreme nationalists."[68] STEM technicians and administrators did tend to be considerably less sympathetic to the problems of the French, and more concerned with promoting the self-reliance of the Bao Dai government than were members of the advisory group.[69] The

---

[64]Heath to State Dept, 11 May 51, 751GMAP/5 – 1151, records of Dept of State.
[65]MDAP Monthly Rpt, Mar 51, records of Dept of State.
[66]Heath to State Dept, 8 Mar 51, 851G.00/3 – 851, records of Dept of State.
[67]MDAP Monthly Rpt, Apr 51, records of Dept of State.
[68]Ibid., May 51, records of Dept of State.
[69]Interv, author with Austin Ivory, International Division, Office of Management and Budget, 8

sheer size and expense of many STEM projects also were disconcerting to the French. In the Cholon area of Saigon, for example, the mission built a demonstration low-cost housing project, the Cite Nguyen Tri Phuong, with over a thousand housing units, forty-four commerical buildings, a school, a dispensary, and a police station. That kind of project, the French complained, "belittled them in the eyes of the Vietnamese."[70] When the French tried to counter STEM influence with whispering campaigns and with planted anti-American articles in the controlled local press, the resulting general atmosphere of jealousy and suspicion only complicated the task of the Military Assistance Advisory Group to establish effective Franco-American cooperation.

In Washington, meanwhile, the National Security Council had established an interdepartmental Southeast Asia Aid Policy Committee in 1950 to develop basic policy guidelines for all American assistance to Southeast Asia. The committee was primarily a consultative group. It monitored the workings of the Mutual Defense Assistance Program and the Economic Aid and the Technical Assistance ("Point 4") Programs administered by the Economic Cooperation Administration. The Aid Policy Committee had no direct operational responsibility for any of those programs, but it was responsible for ensuring that major policy directives in regard to Southeast Asia aid programs were carried out.[71]

Military assistance for Southeast Asia was also subject to the supervision of the interagency Foreign Military Assistance Coordinating Committee, which directed all American military assistance abroad. The relationship between this committee and the Southeast Asia Aid Policy Committee was never clearly spelled out, but the latter exercised a vague mandate to ensure that the military assistance programs implemented by the Foreign Military Assistance Coordinating Committee produced no unfavorable political repercussions.[72] Within the Department of Defense the military assistance program was administered by the Office of Military Assistance under the direction of the Office of the Secretary of Defense. With the completion of these arrangements in Washington, the mechanics of American aid were settled, yet many observers wondered whether French forces in Indochina, with Chinese Communist troops just to the north, would survive long enough to benefit from that aid.

Mar 74, Historians files, CMH; see also Memo, Deputy Asst Secy of State, Far Eastern Affairs, for Asst Secy, 27 Jul 51, Dept of State, *Foreign Relations, 1951; Asia and the Pacific, Part I,* 6:463.
  [70]MDAP Monthly Rpt, Mar 51; Rpt of Mutual Security Evaluation Team, Jun 54, records of Bureau of the Budget.
  [71]Southeast Asia Aid Policy Committee, Meeting of 13 Jul 50, files of Office of Philippine and Southeast Asian Affairs, RG 59.
  [72]Ibid.

7

Defeats in Tonkin, Deliberations in Washington

The period from October 1950 to February 1951 was a time of shock and anxious deliberation for American leaders. A series of powerful Viet Minh attacks in Vietnam brought the French to the verge of defeat at the very time that American forces in Korea were fighting desperately to halt the advance of massed Chinese armies. These crises not only increased American concern for the security of Vietnam but also led a few leaders to question the very logic and feasibility of the U.S. commitment there.

The Korean War broke out on 27 June 1950, three weeks after the United States announced its aid program for Indochina. Some observers have seen that war as an important factor in the shaping of American policy toward Vietnam, but the basic decisions related to that policy had already been made. The Korean War thus led to a change in degree rather than kind in the American commitment to Southeast Asia.[1] Although the basic assumptions behind American aid to the French remained unchanged, the aid itself increased dramatically. On the first day of the North Korean attack, President Truman ordered an acceleration and increase in aid to Indochina, and on 30 June, the day that U.S. ground troops were committed to combat in Korea, eight C–47 transports arrived in Saigon with the first shipments of American materiel for the French. By 31 July military supplies sufficient to equip twelve infantry battalions were en route by ship to Vietnam.[2]

Yet time was running out. The Viet Minh were being heavily aided and supported by the Chinese People's Liberation Army. By the summer of 1950 "substantial and increasing quantities of small arms" and "large consign-

---

[1]Indeed, it might be argued that American apprehensions about Vietnam in the months preceding the North Korean invasion had tended to cause American officials to underrate the danger to South Korea. In March 1950, for example, the Army G–2, Maj. Gen. Alexander R. Bolling, had predicted that Communist military moves in Korea "will be held in abeyance pending the outcome of their program in other areas, particularly Southeast Asia." See James F. Schnabel, *Policy and Direction: The First Year*, United States Army in the Korean War (Washington, 1972), p. 63.

[2]MDAP Status Rpt, Jul 50, G–3 091 Indochina, RG 319.

ments of artillery pieces, 'bazookas,' and anti-aircraft guns" were reaching the Viet Minh forces by land from Kwangsi Province and by sea from Chinese-controlled Hainan Island in the Gulf of Tonkin. The Chinese were active also in the repair and construction of land communications leading into Vietnam.[3] In late March 1950 the French had reported that all major roads leading from China to Tonkin had been repaired, and that one had been banked for high-speed traffic.[4]

By mid-1950 the Viet Minh army had grown to a force of some 250,000 men organized in three components: regular forces, regional units, and popular, or irregular, forces. The regular forces, with an estimated strength of 120,000, were organized into divisions, each consisting of three infantry regiments, an artillery battalion, an antiaircraft battalion, and staff and support elements. The regular army's mission was exclusively offensive. All defensive and security tasks were assigned to the regional and popular troops.

Vo Nguyen Giap, who now bore the formal titles of General of the Army, Commander in Chief of the Armed Forces, and Minister of Defense, was assisted by Chief of Staff Maj. Gen. Hoang Van Thai and a general staff that included Maj. Gen. Van Tien Dung as political commissar. The entire country was split into three main divisions: Tonkin on the north, Annam in central Vietnam, and Cochinchina in the south. These were subdivided into regions or sectors, and still smaller "fronts." Each front commander exercised direct operational control over units in his area.[5]

Each province and district was responsible for raising and equipping its own units of regional troops, who served as a cadre and sometimes as a general reserve for the regular army. These regional troops also served as a link between the popular forces and the regular troops and were responsible for the military training of the popular forces. The latter constituted a kind of village militia. Unarmed or lightly armed, they were mainly assigned to such duties as intelligence, transport, and sabotage. A better armed element of the popular forces, the *Dan Quan du Kich*, or "elite irregulars," was equipped with rifles, grenades, mines, and a few automatic weapons. It took part with the regional forces in local operations. The French estimated that the regional forces had a strength of about 40,000 and the armed local forces about 85,000, but those estimates were almost certainly low.[6]

Although the Chinese refrained from sending major units to Vietnam and failed to provide the Viet Minh with appreciable numbers of the more sophisticated weapons in their arsenal, their assistance was of great value to Ho Chi Minh's forces. An estimated 15,000 Chinese advisers and technicians helped to train and organize the Viet Minh regulars, and Vietnamese troops used training installations and artillery ranges at Chinghsi and Paise in Kwangsi

[3]Arms Supply to Viet Minh Forces, 8 Aug 50, G – 3 091 Indochina, RG 319.
[4]Ltr, U.S. Army Attache, Paris, to ACofS G – 2, 5 Apr 50, sub: Situation in Indochina, G – 2 ID file 653146.
[5]Viet Minh Military Forces, 15 Jan 51, G – 2 ID file 761741; Viet Minh Armed Forces Order of Battle and High Command, 6 Feb 51, G – 2 ID file 643165.
[6]The Viet Minh Army, FEC (Far East Command) Intelligence Digest, 16 – 30 Nov 50, FEC records; Appendix to National Intelligence Estimate, NIE – 35, 7 Aug 51, VI:476.

124

Province inside China.[7] Equally helpful were the large quantities of military equipment that the Chinese did make available. The French estimated that in one month the Viet Minh had received 50,000 rifles, 150 automatic rifles, 95 machine guns, 30 mortars, 32 75-mm. field guns, 8 37-mm. guns, and 4 130-mm. field guns.[8]

There was a sense of growing danger in both America and France. In March the French Chiefs of Staff Committee had recommended a regrouping of French forces "for the purpose of avoiding the present risk of a military catastrophe in case of intensified external aggression."[9] The isolated and exposed French posts along the Chinese border, however, had not been evacuated, allegedly because High Commissioner Pignon and General Alessandri feared a "loss of face."[10] By June 1950 U.S. Army intelligence warned that "in a year's time it is quite possible that Viet Minh capabilities will be sufficiently enhanced through receipt of Chinese communist aid that the French may be forced out of northern Indochina."[11] At the end of August the Joint Intelligence Committee generally endorsed the Melby-Erskine survey team's warning about the military situation in Vietnam and predicted a large-scale Viet Minh attack sometime after the first of September.[12]

The catastrophe feared by the French Chiefs of Staff Committee came in the autumn of 1950. On 18 September Viet Minh forces, supported by newly acquired artillery and mortars, overran a French fortress at Dong Khe on the Chinese frontier. A few days later a French force of almost 4,000 men was completely destroyed in a series of Viet Minh ambushes along the frontier near the town of Cao Bang. One by one, the other isolated French posts along the border were captured by the Viet Minh or were abandoned in panic by their garrisons. The French lost as many as 6,000 men killed or captured and over 10,000 rifles, mortars, and machine guns.[13]

The frontier between China and Vietnam, U.S. Minister Heath observed, "has ceased to exist." He predicted that the Viet Minh would soon "be able to hurl tank-led plane-covered assault[s] against" the populous areas of northern Vietnam.[14] The American consul in Hanoi warned that "unless reinforcements in the form of mobile battalions are provided, there is danger American

[7]Am Consul, Hanoi, to Dept of State, 10 Oct 50, G–2 ID file 728120; CIA Information Rpt, sub: Sino–Viet Minh Military Activities, 22 Nov 50, G–2 ID file 652176; Ltr, Col Hamilton H. Howze to Maj Gen A. C. Short, 20 Dec 51, G–2 350.05 Indochina, records of ACSI; O'Ballance, *The Indo-China War, 1945–1954*, p. 116.
[8]Arms Supply to Viet Minh, Incl to JCS 1992/22, 11 Sep 50, G–3 091 Indochina, RG 319.
[9]Dossier O, Notes de C. Cheysson, A: Jugements sur la situation politique et militaire en Indochine au debut de 1954. [French documents collected by Dr. Trumbull Higgins during his research in France and presented to the Center of Military History in 1975. Hereafter cited as French Documents Collection.]
[10]Ltr, U.S. Army Attache, Paris, to ACofS G–2, 8 Nov 50, sub: Indochina, S–83–50, records of ACSI.
[11]Probable Developments in the Far East in 1950, 6 Jun 50, G–2, GSUSA, OPS 092 Asia, 10 Apr 50, RG 319.
[12]History of Indochina Incident, 1940–1954, p. 175, manuscript in JCS Historical Div files.
[13]O'Ballance, *The Indo-China War, 1945–1954*, p. 118.
[14]Telg, Minister at Saigon to Secy of State, 17 Oct 50, records of Dept of State; ibid., 15 Oct 50, Dept of State, *Foreign Relations, 1950: East Asia and the Pacific*, 6:894.

arms may fall into the hands of the Vietminh."[15] A young French Army officer described the civilian population in Hanoi and Haiphong as being "in a psychosis of fear."[16] In the absence of any official government information on the military situation, rumors multiplied and most people had only the Viet Minh radio as their source of news.[17]

Yet the French, whether they knew it or not, were being afforded a breathing spell. The Viet Minh high command was unable to take full advantage of its successes at this time because of shortages of supplies and the need to train more troops. The next big offensive would have to await the correction of these deficiencies.[18]

The French defeats puzzled some American leaders. Meeting with President Truman at Wake Island, the head of the Far East Command, General of the Army Douglas MacArthur, observed, "the French have 150,000 of their best troops there with an officer of the highest reputation in command. . . . I cannot understand why they do not clean it up. They should be able to do so in four months yet we have recently seen a debacle. . . . They have the flower of the French Army in Indochina and they are not fighting." The president replied, "I cannot understand it either."[19] The U.S. Army's chief of staff, General J. Lawton Collins, went further, saying that it appeared that "France will be driven out of Indochina, at the very least out of Tonkin and they are wasting men and equipment trying to remain there."[20]

American military observers closer to the scene took a less pessimistic view. The newly appointed chief of the U.S. Military Assistance Advisory Group, General Brink, for example, attributed the French reverses to poor intelligence, improvement of the Viet Minh forces, static French defensive dispositions, a lack of coordination between air and ground forces, and failure to organize forces larger than battalions. These factors, however, were not insurmountable. He still expected the French to be able to hold the Hanoi-Haiphong delta area "if adequate military aid arrives within [the] next two months and French forces in Tonkin receive an additional 9 battalions and are reorganized and properly trained as the French plan."[21]

Increasing Aid and Continuing Debate

The shattering defeats in Tonkin produced calls for additional American military aid. On 12 October French Defense Minister Jules Moch told

[15]Am Consul, Hanoi, to State Dept, 27 Oct 50, 751G.00/10–2750, records of Dept of State.

[16]Ltr, Bernard de Lattre to Gen Jean de Lattre, 6 Nov 50, de Lattre Papers (in the possession of Madame la Marechale de Lattre de Tassigny, Paris).

[17]CIA Information Rpt 54624, 16 Nov 50, sub: Political and Military Situation in Tonkin, G–2 ID file 750342.

[18]Ibid.

[19]Substance of Statements Made at Wake Island Conference, 15 Oct 50, Department of State, *Foreign Relations of the United States, 1950*, vol. 7, *Korea* (Washington, 1976), p. 957.

[20]U.S. Min of U.S.-U.K. Political-Military Conversations, 26 Oct 50, Department of State, *Foreign Relations of the United States, 1950*, vol. 3, *Western Europe* (Washington, 1977), p. 1696n.

[21]Msg, Chief, MAAG, to CofSA, Saigon 763, 4 Nov 50, *U.S.-Vietnam Relations*, 8:408; MDAP Monthly Rpt, Oct 50, G–3 091 Indochina, RG 319.

officials of the Defense Department that the current level of American aid was inadequate to meet the increased threat in Vietnam. Moch pressed for faster delivery of American equipment already programmed and for immediate transfer of two squadrons of B–26 light bombers. He also stressed the French need to know as soon as possible the exact size and nature of the military aid program planned by the United States. On 23 October President Truman and Budget Director Frederick J. Lawton agreed to a military aid program of $33 million. Although the Joint Chiefs of Staff had advised that B–26 bombers could not materially affect the situation in Vietnam, the program included, at the instigation of the secretaries of state and defense, who were anxious to bolster French morale, twenty-one B–26 aircraft already en route to the Far East Air Forces.[22] These commitments made the size of the military aid program for Indochina second only to the support for American combat forces in Korea.

To Minister Heath and other Americans in Vietnam, the decision on future aid called for a greater American voice in French political and military policy toward Vietnam. As Heath noted, information supplied by the French to the legation during the course of the military reverses had been fragmentary, tardy, and misleading. The French command, for example, had continued to deny that Cao Bang had been abandoned long after it had fallen.[23] "Nowhere else in the world," Heath remarked in November, "have we been willing to spend the sums and make the effort now required [in Vietnam] without substantial and continuing opportunities to influence [the] directions and course of national enterprises we are supplementing."[24]

Although Heath had no desire for Americans to assume management of the war, he did believe that an advisory and consultative role was a necessity. He wanted General Brink, as chief of the new Military Assistance Advisory Group, Indochina, to act as an unofficial and unadvertised adviser to the French high command, while the American legation similarly advised the French high commissioner and the Bao Dai government. Yet such a relationship with the United States was precisely what the French were determined to avoid. It would be years before any French government would be willing to consider the type of relationship in Vietnam proposed by Heath.[25]

In the meantime, officials in Washington were becoming increasingly concerned about the slow pace of progress toward self-government for the Associated States of Indochina. A conference between France and the Associated States had been in session at Pau, France, since June. Under the provisions of the Elysee Agreements, it was to determine the scope and nature of authority to be exercised by France and the Associated States in such areas as communica-

[22]Acheson to Frederick Lawton, 20 Oct 50, records of Dept of State; Memo, JCS for Secy of Defense, 13 Oct 50, G–3 091 Indochina, RG 319; Memo, Gen Lyman Lemnitzer for Dir, MDA, State Dept, 16 Oct 50, JCS 1992/32, 16 Oct 50, CCS 092 Asia (6–25–48), sec. 6.

[23]MDAP Monthly Rpt, Oct 50; Heath to Secy of State, 13 Oct 50, Dept of State, *Foreign Relations, 1950: East Asia and the Pacific*, 6:890–93.

[24]Telg, Minister at Saigon (Heath) to Secy of State, 15 Nov 50, Dept of State, *Foreign Relations, 1950: East Asia and the Pacific*, 6:922.

[25]Irving, *The First Indochina War*, pp. 102–06, passim.

tions, foreign trade, and customs, but the meeting had dragged on with increasing acrimony and with little apparent progress. In September the American legation in Saigon had reported that the "net effect" of the conference thus far had been "a serious erosion of public confidence in the 'Bao Dai formula' among the Vietnamese."[26]

Bao Dai himself was again in Europe, ostensibly to guide the conduct of his ministers at the Pau negotiations, but on the eve of his departure for Pau, the emperor had been extremely pessimistic in a meeting with Consul General Gullion and the head of the U.S. Economic Aid Mission to Indochina, Robert Blum. He had received his two visitors dressed in Vietnamese clothes instead of his usual European business suit, a sure sign, according to Gullion, that he was severely depressed. The emperor said that he no longer believed that the French had any intention of ever relinquishing their hold on Vietnam and that the measures they had taken thus far had been a sham. " 'This independence, what is it? Where is it? Do you see it? Is a government independent without a budget?' "[27]

Most American officials continued to see the solution in Vietnam as political.[28] After conducting a detailed study for the Joint Chiefs of Staff, the Joint Strategic Survey Committee concluded that "in view of the unrest in Indochina, any military victory over the Communists would be temporary in nature. The long-term solution to the unrest in Indochina lies in sweeping political and economic concessions by France." Urging that the United States employ every possible pressure to convince the French to make concessions, the committee noted that "the more aid and assistance furnished to France before reforms are undertaken, the less the probability that France of its own accord will take the necessary action."[29]

The committee warned against even a minor commitment of American military forces in Vietnam lest pressures build up for additional commitments. Although Indochina was "of some strategic importance to the United States," the committee noted, it was not important enough, in view of the current Soviet threat, to warrant the United States' intervening and "dissipating its forces." Should Communist China intervene, said the committee, the French should bring the matter before the United Nations.[30]

The view of the Joint Strategic Survey Committee reflected a common concern among American policymakers during the early months of the Korean War: that the Communist attack in Korea might be but the prelude to a series of worldwide military moves engineered or conducted by the Soviet Union.[31]

[26]MDAP Monthly Rpt No. 2 for Sep 50, 6 Nov 50, G–3 091 Indochina, RG 319.

[27]Telg, Charge at Saigon to Secy of State, 18 Jun 50, Dept of State, *Foreign Relations, 1950: East Asia and the Pacific*, 6:824.

[28]See, for example, Secy of State (Acheson) to Am Legation, Saigon, 1 Sep 50, records of Dept of State, and Memo, Gen Omar Bradley for Secy of Defense, 7 Sep 50, sub: Indochina, CCS 092 Asia (6–25–48), sec. 6, JCS records.

[29]Rpt, JSSC to JCS, 7 Oct 50, sub: Possible Future Action in Indochina, G–3 091 Indochina, RG 319.

[30]Ibid.

[31]Smith, *Acheson*, p. 184; Malcolm W. Cagle and Frank A. Manson, *The Sea War in Korea* (Annapolis: U.S. Naval Institute, 1957), p. 34; Schnabel, *Policy and Direction*, p. 67.

Many experts therefore believed that the obvious course for the United States would be to husband its military resources for the eventual showdown with Russia, not to expend its resources in other peripheral involvements. The acting director of the State Department's Office of International Security Affairs, John H. Ohly, for example, called for a "reappraisal of U.S. policy with respect to Indochina." Continuing the current policy toward Indochina, said Ohly in November, would probably require some $500 million in military equipment in the immediate future and more later. Providing that level of aid would have a substantial impact on U.S. military assistance to Western Europe, Greece, Turkey, and Iran and could well make it impossible to fulfill some mutual defense goals in these areas.[32] Accordingly, Ohly maintained that the United States had to decide its long-term objective for Indochina. "Was it long-run, non-communist control of the area, temporary non-communist control, or simply a continuance of the present situation?" Once that goal was defined, planners would have to answer other questions. Were enough manpower and equipment available to attain U.S. objectives? Did the French and Vietnamese have the necessary will, morale, and leadership to continue the fight, and, most important, would it be possible to "prevent a political deterioration which will nullify any accomplishments in the military field?"[33] Ohly subsequently called for a task force of the National Security Council to study the subject.[34]

Yet other analysts emphasized the possible consequences of a French defeat. While noting that Indochina would be of little importance in a global conflict, U.S. Army planners in October 1950 maintained that it was "of critical, if not vital, strategic importance to the United States in the Cold War." They reiterated the oft-expressed belief that "the loss of Indochina to the Communists could initiate a train of events that could deal a staggering blow to our position in the whole of Asia," leading to the fall of Burma and probably Thailand. Their fall in turn would place Indonesia and the Philippines in an extremely tenuous position and directly threaten India and Pakistan.[35] So important did Army Chief of Staff J. Lawton Collins consider Indochina that he recommended to the Joint Chiefs of Staff that "if all fails the United States [should] be prepared to commit its own armed forces to the defense of Indo-China provided this could be done in concert with other United Nations members and without endangering the U.S. capability to conduct a general war."[36]

Further pointing up the contradictions in the view of American policymakers, the Joint Chiefs of Staff, in a memorandum prepared as a suggested statement of U.S. policy, emphasized the strategic importance of Indochina to the United States in the cold war but warned that the United States should

[32]Memo, Ohly for Secy of State, 20 Nov 50, sub: Reappraisal of U.S. Policy With Respect to Indochina, records of Dept of State.
[33]Ibid.
[34]Ltr, Ohly to Secy of State, 16 Jan 51, records of Dept of State.
[35]Draft Study, G–3 Plans Div, 17 Oct 50, sub: Indochina, G–3 091 Indochina, RG 319.
[36]Memo, CofSA, 18 Oct 50, sub: Possible Future Action in Indochina, JCS 1992/29, 7 Oct 50, CCS 092 Asia (6–25–48), sec. F, JCS records.

French Officer *trains Vietnamese Army troops to use 57-mm. recoilless rifle.*

not permit itself to become engaged in a general war with Communist China. The Joint Chiefs repeated earlier calls for pressure on France to eliminate its policy of colonialism and for an accelerated program of self-government, but at the same time they worried that France might abandon its military position in Indochina.[37]

In commenting on the memorandum, the State Department's Office of Philippine and Southeast Asian Affairs suggested that the recent French reverses in Vietnam were due mainly to the extensive military assistance which the Viet Minh had received from China and minimized the importance of popular support of the government by the Indochinese people. "The history of [Communist] satellites has proven," that office noted, "that they were established without 'popular support.' To therefore state categorically that popular support of an anti-Communist government is essential may not be entirely correct."[38]

The position of the two sides was thus paradoxical, with the political agency stressing the importance of military actions and the military agency—

[37]Memo, JCS for Secy of Defense (Marshall), 28 Nov 50, sub: Possible Future Action in Indochina, Dept of State, *Foreign Relations, 1950: East Asia and the Pacific,* 6:945–48.
[38]Memo, Robert E. Hoey for Ambassador-at-Large (Jessup), 27 Dec 50, sub: Our Comments on NSC 64/1, Dept of State, *Foreign Relations, 1950: East Asia and the Pacific,* 6:956–58.

the Joint Chiefs—stressing the political. Another illustration of that paradox occurred in January, when Deputy Assistant Secretary of State Livingston T. Merchant observed, after noting Ohly's call for a policy reassessment, that "the Joint Chiefs of Staff are the proper arbiters of the military aspects of the problem and [they] have in fact resolved it by approving an expanded aid program for Indochina. . . . I see no point in reopening the debate or even in troubling the Secretary [of state] about it."[39] Merchant's note, in effect, left to the military the essentially political question of whether there should be aid for Indochina and how much it should be.

Toward a Vietnamese Army

The one point on which all American leaders could agree was a need to form indigenous national armies in the Associated States of Indochina, particularly in Vietnam. Since the disasters at Cao Bang and elsewhere had pointed up the limits of France's military resources, Minister Heath and the State Department argued, a strong Vietnamese army was the only alternative to either a French defeat or the commitment of American troops.[40] The Erskine-Melby mission had already made weapons and equipment for a Vietnamese army a high priority, second only to filling shortages in the French Expeditionary Corps.[41]

Although the French in 1948 and 1949 had taken a few faltering steps in the direction of a Vietnamese army, and sometimes referred to "the armed forces of the Associated States," the French high command retained sole responsibility for the conduct of operations and for internal security in Vietnam.[42] In May 1950 the existing Vietnamese forces numbered only about 16,000 regulars. There were no higher headquarters or staffs, and only about three battalions were officered exclusively by Vietnamese. The French program called for twelve battalions to be activated by the end of 1950.[43] French attitudes toward the project were well illustrated by General Carpentier's reaction to a suggestion by General Erskine that the former increase the number of Vietnamese under arms. According to Erskine, Carpentier "threw up his hands and said 'they are absolutely unreliable; you can't trust them, they'd never make good soldiers.' I said, 'General Carpentier, who in hell are you fighting but Vietnamese!' "[44]

---

[39]Memo, Merchant for Rusk, 17 Jan 51, records of Dept of State.
[40]Heath to State Dept, 5 Sep 50, 751G.00/9 – 550, records of Dept of State.
[41]Memo, Col F. J. Gillespie, Chief, Army Section, MAAG, Indochina, for Lt Col Stern, 20 Mar 51, records of MAAG Indochina.
[42]Irving, *The First Indochina War*, pp. 92 – 93; Memorandum on the Relations Between the French Command and the Armed Forces of the Associated States, Incl 1 to Army Attache, Saigon, to ACofS G – 2, 21 Jul 50, OARMA 052, records of ACSI.
[43]Acting Army Attache, Saigon, to ACofS G – 2, 5 Jul 50, sub: Armies of the Associated States, 50816930, G – 2 ID files.
[44]Erskine Interv, p. 174.

Prime Minister Huu With Emperor Bao Dai

The Foreign Military Assistance Coordinating Committee complained that the French had not brought the training and combat efficiency of the Vietnamese up to the level necessary for the latter to utilize the American military equipment being supplied to Vietnam. The committee recommended that the Military Assistance Advisory Group in Saigon be instructed to inform Bao Dai that a favorable reception would be accorded to requests for United States training of Vietnamese forces.[45] Estimates by the Central Intelligence Agency (CIA) supported the committee's view. In a briefing for Secretary of Defense Marshall, the agency reported that although there were considerable risks in entrusting the inexperienced Vietnamese with full responsibility for their own affairs, they had nevertheless already demonstrated considerable "resourcefulness, fighting capability and capability for organization under Ho Chi Minh and ought to be able to do the same fighting against him."[46] The CIA suggested that French participation in the development of an indigenous Vietnamese fighting force be limited to paid advisers and technicians operating within the framework of the Bao Dai government.[47] That type of arrange-

[45]Memo, Maj Gen S. L. Scott for Gen Duff, Dep Asst G–3, 17 Nov 50, G–3 file 350–2, RG 319.
[46]Recent Developments in Asia, 12 Oct 50, G–3 092 Pacific, RG 319.
[47]JCS 1992/32, 18 Oct 50, CCS 092 Asia, sec. 6, JCS records.

ment was precisely what Bao Dai had sought since the previous March. Yet many Americans suspected—with good reason—that the French would never consent to such an arrangement or that, if they did, they would have that much less incentive to continue the war. Moreover, U.S. Army officials doubted whether the Vietnamese had the logistical and technical capability to handle the variety of weapons and equipment needed for their army.

Faced with these conflicting considerations, the Joint Chiefs of Staff suggested a compromise: that American aid should continue to be delivered to the French "with such participation by the governments of Vietnam, Laos and Cambodia as the Secretary of State may deem wise."[48] This compromise in reality left effective control in the hands of the French with some nominal Vietnamese participation as window dressing. In practice, all equipment for the Vietnamese was turned over to the French, and the French commander in chief retained the right under the Pentalateral Agreement to divert that equipment to other uses if he found it necessary for mutual defense. Representatives of the Bao Dai government were seldom even present when the equipment for their forces was received at Saigon or Haiphong.[49]

Adoption of the compromise demonstrated that, even in the face of French defeats, American military leaders were unwilling to risk a French pullout by openly backing an indigenous Vietnamese army. Minister Heath angrily observed that, if Indochina was really vital to the defense of the West, the United States had only three options: to rely on the French to achieve a military victory (a dubious possibility by late 1950), to help non-Communist Vietnamese form major military forces of their own, or to commit American troops as in Korea.[50] Yet in 1950 few Americans were willing to accept such stark choices; instead, most continued to hope somehow to obtain the best of both worlds: a continued French military presence along with political and military independence for Bao Dai.

It did seem for a time that the French, shaken by the autumn setbacks, were prepared to be more flexible. The Pau Conference concluded in November with apparent significant concessions to the Vietnamese. Control of finances, communications, immigration, foreign trade, and customs, all of which previously had been administered directly by the French high commissioner for Indochina, was to be vested in a group of joint agencies composed of representatives of Vietnam, Laos, Cambodia, and France.

Although a step forward from the old colonial system, these concessions were in no sense a complete transfer of sovereignty to the Associated States. In a long report entitled Vietnam Is Not Actually Independent, Edmund Gullion, then the counselor of the American embassy in Saigon, noted various factors which still circumscribed Vietnamese sovereignty, including compulsory membership in the French Union, French control of military equipment, guarantees of French private property, and compulsory monetary union

---

[48]Ibid.
[49]Memo, Gillespie for Stern, 20 Mar 51.
[50]Heath to State Dept, 5 Sep 50.

with France.[51] The French had representatives on all the joint agencies of the Associated States, and since most decisions of these agencies required a unanimous vote, the French could veto any proposal they disliked. Prime Minister Tran Van Huu had complained to American Minister Heath that "the mechanism of the commissions including French membership was illogical, unworkable, and . . . would put more checks on Vietnamese freedom than had existed before."[52]

Nevertheless, many Americans still saw the Pau agreements as a sign of a new and more liberal French attitude toward Indochina. In addition, the U.S. Army and the Joint Chiefs of Staff were pleased by a French decision to take further steps toward the creation of an independent Vietnamese army. At Dalat on 8 December 1950 the French concluded a military convention with the Bao Dai government. Most of the officers and noncommissioned officers of the new Vietnamese National Army would be French, but they would wear Vietnamese uniforms and be subject to the order of the emperor, who would serve as supreme commander of the army. The great majority of Vietnamese officers and enlisted men then serving in the French Army were transferred to the Vietnamese Army during the following month.

Like the Pau agreements, the Dalat military arrangements represented a step forward but not nearly as big a step as the United States wanted. Significantly, even though the success of the Vietnamese Army would depend on substantial quantities of U.S. military aid, the United States had not been invited to participate in the Dalat discussions. That exclusion said much about the French view of the proper sphere of American activity in Indochina.

[51]Gullion to State Dept, 29 Jan 51, 751G.00/1–2951, records of Dept of State.
[52]Am Legation, Saigon, to State Dept, 27 Jan 51, 751G.00/1–2751, records of Dept of State.

8

The de Lattre Interlude, 1950—1951

Questions of political and military policy seemed less urgent in late 1950 than the problem of stemming the tide of French defeat in Tonkin. By November the chief of the Military Assistance Advisory Group, Indochina, Brig. Gen. Francis G. Brink, was reporting that the French would need nine additional battalions merely to hold their own in the Red River Delta and that a counteroffensive was "out of the question for the predictable future."[1] Paris acted quickly to shore up its faltering army in Vietnam. During November and December reinforcements—including an armored regiment, an antiaircraft artillery regiment, a parachute battalion, two artillery battalions, and five battalions of colonial infantry from North Africa and Senegal—sailed for the Far East.[2]

Yet the most important French "reinforcement" proved to be a new commander in chief, General Jean de Lattre de Tassigny. Unlike General Carpentier, de Lattre also held the position of high commissioner and thus had both civil and military authority. A popular and romantic figure (he had taken part in one of the last cavalry charges in history), de Lattre had been the youngest general in the French Army at the beginning of World War II. After escaping from Vichy France in 1943 to join General de Gaulle, he had led the First French Army in its drive to the Rhine and the Danube.[3] An American officer who knew the general well described de Lattre in 1950 as

probably the chief military personality in France today. . . . Based on grade he ranks second of the five star generals. The fact that he commanded the First French Army has not been forgotten by the French people, nor have they been permitted to forget it. He has kept up his asssociation with veterans organizations of the "Rhine Danube" Army on an extensive scale. By virtue of his post as commander Ground Forces, Western Europe he has kept

---

[1]Brink to CofS, Army, 4 Nov 50, 751G.00/11−450, records of Dept of State.
[2]Ltr, Ch, MAAG, France, to ACofS G−3, 4 Dec 50, sub: French Reinforcements Scheduled for Indochina, MAAG 00618, copy in files of Office of Philippine and Southeast Asian Affairs, RG 59.
[3]Pierre Darcourt, *de Lattre au Viet Nam: Une Annee de Victoires* (Paris: La Table Ronde, 1964), p. 38.

on the move visiting various commanders, capitals and installations of Western European countries. . . . The majority of military men in high position are his people. . . . His appeal for the average French soldier or civilian is comparable to the appeal which Eisenhower and Patton have for the average American.[4]

De Lattre assiduously cultivated newsmen and often held off-the-record briefings and conversations with them. As a consequence, the American press usually treated him more favorably than other French officials in Indochina.[5]

De Lattre knew that his first task was to restore the morale and the shattered confidence of the French forces in northern Vietnam. Disembarking from his plane at Hanoi in full-dress uniform, he dramatically announced to reporters, "I am proud to again find myself at the head of a French army in battle."[6] He promptly canceled a planned evacuation of French civilians from Hanoi, installed his wife in the governor-general's palace, and left on a whirlwind tour of the battlefront. Everywhere de Lattre galvanized the disorganized and disoriented French into action, ruthlessly weeding out incompetents and inspiring others with his confidence and enthusiasm.[7] "His military tactics of blunt and occasionally brutal criticism of subordinates' actions," reported Minister Heath, "frequently resulted not in resentment but in the admiration and loyalty of the latter, who appreciated [his] courage, unremitting energy, ability and honesty. He is an effective orator and continually refers to the theme that Vietnam is at last free and that it is his task to protect this freedom."[8] In addition to restoring the morale of the Expeditionary Corps, de Lattre intended to reorganize French forces into more effective units, create an able Vietnamese National Army, use American aid efficiently, defend Tonkin, and recapture the initiative from the Viet Minh.[9]

Viet Minh Offensives in Tonkin

De Lattre had barely begun that ambitious program when the Viet Minh launched a major new offensive near the town of Vinh Yen north of the Red River and northwest of Hanoi. If Vinh Yen fell, the road to Hanoi would be open. On 13 January 1951, two Viet Minh divisions attacked French strongpoints in and around the town, which were manned by about 6,000 French troops. General de Lattre deployed all available reserves to reinforce Vinh Yen and employed almost all the French Air Force planes in the country. Against Viet Minh troops attacking in human-wave assaults, the French for the first time used American-made napalm bombs. For four days fierce fighting raged around the town. Viet Minh strength rose to twenty-one battalions as Giap fed in reinforcements, but the French superiority in avia-

[4]Ltr, Brig Gen J. J. O'Hare to ACofS G – 2, 20 Nov 50, sub: General de Lattre de Tassigny's Aspirations in NATO, S – 93 – 50, G – 2 ID file 735636.
[5]Cf. Tilman Durdin, "Fighter on a Mission," *New York Times Magazine*, 18 February 1954, pp. 19 – 21.
[6]Ltr, O'Hare to ACofS G – 2, 20 Nov 50, sub: General de Lattre Tassigny's Aspirations in NATO.
[7]Durdin, "Fighter on a Mission," pp. 19 – 21.
[8]Heath to State Dept, 14 Jan 51, 751G.00/1 – 1451, records of Dept of State.
[9]De Lattre to Comite de Defense Nationale, 17 Mar 51, de Lattre Papers.

tion and artillery proved decisive. When the Viet Minh withdrew on 17 January, they left behind about 500 prisoners and some 1,500 dead on the battlefield. Yet French casualties were so heavy that de Lattre's forces were in no condition to follow up their success. One "mobile group" of three battalions, totaling about 2,000 men, had suffered 540 losses.[10]

The narrow French victory at Vinh Yen would have been impossible without the timely arrival of American weapons and equipment, particularly napalm bombs and 105-mm. howitzers.[11] In a single week during January 1951 the French received from the United States 20 M24 tanks, 40 105-mm. howitzers, and 250 conventional bombs, as well as napalm bombs, 105-mm. ammunition, automatic weapons, and small arms.[12] At the height of the Vinh Yen battle, General Brink flew to Japan to arrange for direct shipment of war materials from the Far East Command to Vietnam.[13]

Two months after the attack at Vinh Yen, the Viet Minh moved against French garrisons around the coastal village of Mao Khe, some thirty kilometers northeast of Haiphong. Although outnumbered almost three to one, the French again repulsed the attack. Losses on both sides were high. Three French battalions sustained casualties of over 25 percent; the French took 483 prisoners, and the Viet Minh left more than 1,500 bodies on the battlefield. As at Vinh Yen, it was French superiority in aviation and artillery that enabled half a dozen French battalions to blunt an attack by twenty-one Viet Minh battalions.[14]

In June 1951 the Viet Minh attempted to overrun Catholic-dominated districts in the southwest corner of the Red River Delta around the towns of Ninh Binh and Phat Diem. The Viet Minh divisions, fighting in the open delta plain for the first time, lost heavily to French artillery and air power, while French control of the strategic Day River successfully choked off Viet Minh supply lines. By 10 June the Viet Minh forces had begun to withdraw across the Day River, leaving the French in possession of the southwest delta.

General de Lattre reported that "these three violent battles seriously eroded enemy strength," and Frenchmen tended to look upon their successes at Vinh Yen, Mao Khe, and Phat Diem as glorious victories.[15] American observers were more cautious. Edmund Gullion warned that "it would be wrong to view the victories . . . as turning points in the Indochina struggle, or to overlook the special and non-duplicative factors which made them possible." At Vinh Yen the Viet Minh had faced modern American military equipment for the first time, and their daytime attack had enabled the French to employ the new weapons to maximum effect. Lacking air, armor, or heavy artillery support, the Viet Minh had nevertheless inflicted heavy losses on the French and had gained experience in delta fighting; as Gullion stressed, they

---

[10]Am Consul, Saigon, to Dept of State, 21 Jan 51, 751G.00/1–2151, records of Dept of State.
[11]MDAP Monthly Rpt for Jan 51, 23 May 51, G–3 091 Indochina, RG 319.
[12]Consul, Hanoi, to State Dept, 4 Jan 51, 751G.00/1–451, records of Dept of State.
[13]MDAP Monthly Rpt for Jan 51, 23 May 51.
[14]Am Consul, Saigon, to Dept of State, 21 Jan 51.
[15]Expose du General de Lattre, Comite de Defense Nationale, 15 Oct 51, de Lattre Papers.

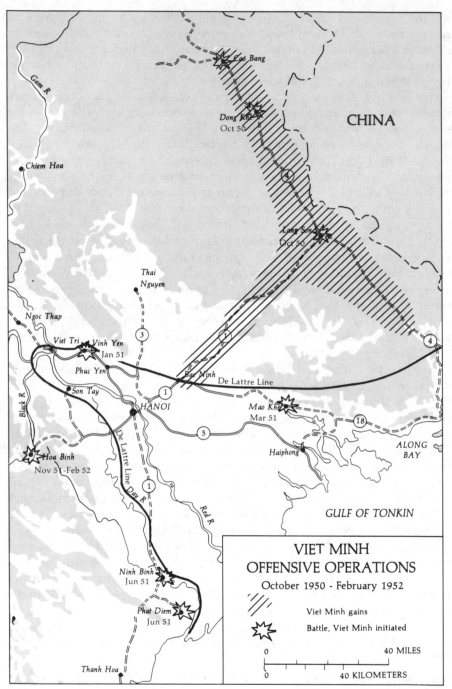

**VIET MINH
OFFENSIVE OPERATIONS**

October 1950 - February 1952

///// Viet Minh gains

✦ Battle, Viet Minh initiated

0   40 MILES

0   40 KILOMETERS

MAP 3

also still held the initiative.[16] *(Map 3)* The Joint Intelligence Committee agreed that the Viet Minh had not been decisively defeated and warned that the delivery of American military assistance to the French would probably be counterbalanced by increased aid to the Viet Minh from China.[17]

These powerful Viet Minh attacks in Tonkin followed closely the massive intervention of the Chinese People's Liberation Army in Korea. By early December 1950, United Nations forces in Korea had appeared to be facing a disastrous defeat, perhaps even annihilation. Policymakers in the State and Defense Departments consequently began to consider pulling American forces in Korea back into narrow defensive beachheads, evacuating them to Japan, or making important political concessions to the Communists in return for a cease-fire.[18] The reverses in Korea, particularly when combined with the Communist display of strength and resourcefulness in Vietnam, reinforced the fears of many American political and military leaders that the Soviet Union was now moving "to conquer the world."[19] Public opinion polls revealed that more than 50 percent of the American people believed that World War III was imminent.[20]

A particular concern by the end of 1950 was that China might intervene directly in Indochina. Columnist Joseph Alsop declared that "the Kremlin [has] speeded up its timetable in a way the worst pessimists never anticipated." He reported that a Chinese army of "200,000 seasoned troops" supported by Russian military advisers stood poised at Nanking to attack Indochina, and "every element of the pattern of preparation for the onslaught in Korea is now visible again in this even more important region to the southward."[21] Shortly thereafter, the State Department reported that its intelligence from Taipei, Hong Kong, Bangkok, and Hanoi predicted an invasion of Indochina by Chinese "volunteers" about the end of May 1951.[22] The Central Intelligence Agency and U.S. Army intelligence, however, were more sanguine; neither believed a Chinese invasion likely. The Army G−2, Maj. Gen. Alexander R. Bolling, commented in December that since the Viet Minh seemed to be doing very well on their own, massive Chinese intervention on the pattern of Korea was both unnecessary and improbable.[23]

As American policymakers debated, the worst of the immediate crisis

[16]Gullion to State Dept, 9 Feb 51, 751G.00/2−951, records of Dept of State.

[17]Estimate of the Indochina Situation, 20 Jul 51, Incl to Memo, Col C. E. Booth for Cabot, 21 Jul 51, G−3 091 Indochina, RG 319.

[18]Schnabel, *Policy and Direction,* pp. 290−91; Smith, *Acheson,* pp. 225−26; Dean Acheson, *Present at the Creation: My Years in the State Department* (New York: W. W. Norton, 1969), pp. 472−75.

[19]Schnabel, *Policy and Direction,* p. 298.

[20]David Rees, *Korea: The Limited War* (New York: St. Martin's, 1964), p. 172.

[21]Joseph Alsop, "In the Dark Shadow," *Washington Post,* 11 Dec 50.

[22]Memo, FE Div for Secy of State, 19 Dec 50, records of Dept of State.

[23]Bolling to CofS, 11 Dec 50, CCS 091 Indochina, RG 319. The more general mood of pessimism was indicated by Rear Adm. Arthur C. Davis, who suggested that the Joint Chiefs begin planning to aid in a possible French evacuation from Tonkin. He warned that since the French lacked the strong sea and air support available to U.S. forces in Korea, the French army might conceivably "be driven into the sea and destroyed." Davis to Joint Staff Planners, 2 Jan 51, JCS 1992/45, CCS 092 Asia, BP 9, JCS records.

passed. In Korea, United Nations forces halted the enemy advance, inflicted heavy losses on the Chinese, recaptured the capital of Seoul, and established a strong defensive line north of the 38th Parallel. The much-feared Chinese attack on French forces in Vietnam had failed to materialize. By the late spring of 1951 General de Lattre had constructed a strong chain of defensive positions stretching from Along Bay to Vinh Yen in the west and to Phat Diem and the sea in the south. That so-called de Lattre Line was designed to protect the Red River Delta and the cities of Hanoi and Haiphong from "the initial shocks of a Chinese invasion" and to serve as "mooring points for offensive operations."[24]

De Lattre formed all French forces not engaged in defense of the de Lattre Line into "mobile groups," combined arms units roughly equivalent to the American regimental combat team. Like many of de Lattre's other military innovations, the mobile groups would have been impossible without American aid. American tanks and half-tracks formed the backbone of their striking power.[25] Yet the groups were mobile only in the sense that they were motorized or mechanized, for their tanks, trucks, half-tracks, and armored cars were of little use in the mountainous jungles that covered much of northern Vietnam. The mobile groups were intended as both a quick-reaction defensive and an offensive force, but through the summer of 1951 the French conducted relatively few offensive operations. The main underpinning of de Lattre's long-range military strategy was the rapid mobilization and training of a Vietnamese National Army, but although the general talked enthusiastically of the excellent combat potential of the Vietnamese and outlined ambitious plans for an army of 60,000 troops by 1952, little apparent progress had been made toward that end.[26]

In his political role as high commissioner, de Lattre had fared even less well, despite a ringing declaration to the Vietnamese people in a speech at Vinh Yen: "I have come to accomplish your independence, not to limit it." De Lattre genuinely believed that his mission was to eliminate old-style colonialism. "The basis of all my work," he told the NATO commander, General of the Army Dwight D. Eisenhower, "ought to be the ruin of the arguments which yet permit of the claim that we are conducting a colonial war in Indochina."[27] But his concept of "independence" was limited. As he explained to a surprised Minister Heath, "[the] Associated States could not enjoy the same status as former British colonies within the commonwealth since France had spent too much wealth and blood in protecting them."[28]

Impatient with the leisurely pace of Vietnamese politics and adminstra-

---

[24]Expose du General de Lattre, Comite de Defense Nationale, 15 Oct 51.

[25]Interv, author with Dunn, 27 May 80.

[26]De Lattre, Secret Note on the Mobilization Proclamation of 25 July 1951, 24 Jul 51, No. 4601/564, de Lattre Papers; Telg, Heath to Secy of State, 23 May 51, and Minutes of Second Meeting With General de Lattre de Tassigny, 17 Sep 51, both in Dept of State, *Foreign Relations, 1951: Asia and the Pacific, Part I*, 6:421 and 6:512, respectively.

[27]Notes sur les Entretiens avec le General Eisenhower le 4 Septembre 1951, de Lattre Papers.

[28]Telg, Heath to Secy of State, 8 Mar 51, Dept of State, *Foreign Relations, 1951: Asia and the Pacific, Part I*, 6:390.

tion, de Lattre could not resist the temptation to intervene, sometimes rather heavy-handedly, in Vietnamese governmental affairs to the annoyance and embarrassment of Bao Dai and Prime Minister Huu. In June 1951 de Lattre refused at the last moment to permit the Vietnamese government to sign an economic agreement with the United States. Since that agreement was the first separate treaty negotiated and signed by the "independent" Bao Dai government, de Lattre's refusal was particularly disturbing.[29]

The de Lattre Visit

In September 1951 General de Lattre visited the United States for talks with American political and military leaders. Prior to his arrival, official assessments of de Lattre were mixed. Some leaders, impressed by his military achievements and apparent progress in creating an autonomous Vietnamese state and National Army, argued that the United States ought to try, as far as possible, to mollify his outspoken complaints about U.S. policies in Vietnam. Minister Heath, who during the military crisis in the fall of 1950 had called for a greater U.S. voice in French policy, now believed that de Lattre's military successes and French political concessions had changed the military situation, "almost overnight, for the better." Indochina was no longer easy prey for Communists. American policy should henceforth be to "supplement but not to supplant" French efforts in Indochina. To assuage de Lattre's suspicion of American actions in Vietnam Heath suggested discussing Special Technical and Economic Mission projects in advance with French officials, assuring them that the CIA would conduct no clandestine operations in Indochina without French consent, and instructing the staff of the U.S. mission in Vietnam not to "listen to, or give encouragement to, improper criticism of French sacrifices and intentions."[30] U.S. Ambassador to France David Bruce endorsed Heath's ideas, pointing out that it "is only French arms and resources which can . . . hold this area and serve as check to Commie advance." The United States should therefore "exert every care to avoid any actions which would tend to mar that common effort."[31]

Other Americans were troubled by Heath's proposals, which they saw as giving a blank check to the French and placing the United States "in the position of the 'Hear No Evil' monkey." The State Department Office of International Security Affairs wondered how, under Minister Heath's plan, the United States could persuade or pressure the French to move faster in strengthening the independence of the Associated States. STEM director Robert Blum pointed out that while the United States ought to do everything it could to avoid undermining the French position, "this undermining is the

[29]Ibid., 30 Jun 51, Dept of State, *Foreign Relations, 1951: Asia and the Pacific, Part I*, 6:439–40.
[30]Ibid., 29 Jun 51, Dept of State, *Foreign Relations, 1951: Asia and the Pacific, Part I*, 6:433, 437.
[31]Telg, Ambassador in France (Bruce) to Secy of State, 5 Jul 51, Dept of State, *Foreign Relations, 1951: Asia and the Pacific, Part I*, 6:443–44.

work of the Viet themselves, brought on in part by French mistakes, and has been going on for many years."[32]

Reviewing the divergent arguments, Deputy Assistant Secretary of State Livingston Merchant observed that much would depend on the "nature and sincerity of French intentions" and of General de Lattre. Merchant suggested postponing decisions until de Lattre's visit, since it "should enable us collectively to assess de Lattre and his intentions."[33]

To the Joint Chiefs of Staff the most worrisome aspect of de Lattre's impending visit was not his insistence on equal priority for aid to Indochina but the possibility that he would try to induce the United States to agree to a combined British-French-American command arrangement for the defense of all Southeast Asia. Their unhappy experience with the Southeast Asia Command in World War II and their desire to preserve their freedom of action in any future large-scale conflict were probably responsible for the chiefs' lack of enthusiasm for any such formal tripartite defense arrangements for Asia. At State Department urging the chiefs had reluctantly agreed to allow the Commander in Chief, Pacific, to attend military consultations at Singapore in May 1951 with British and French Far East commanders. Although little of importance was decided, the conference served to reinforce the Joint Chiefs' determination to keep allied military collaboration to a minimum.[34] There is little evidence that de Lattre was much concerned with this subject, but the Joint Chiefs strongly suspected that he was.[35]

De Lattre planned his visit to the United States with care and foresight. From the beginning of his mission in Indochina he had understood the importance of the "development in the United States of certain general attitudes, whose acceptance by the leaders and the public would condition the granting of supplementary aid."[36] His objective was to convince American leaders that the Indochina War and the Korean conflict were "one war" and that they deserved equal priority. In the process he contended that the American stake in the Indochina War was as great as the stake in Korea.

De Lattre arrived in New York aboard the *Ile de France* in September 1951, posed for pictures with Humphrey Bogart and Lauren Bacall in front of the Statue of Liberty, and immediately began his successful courtship of the press. "The war in Indochina is not a colonial war," he told reporters in New York. "It is a war against Red colonialism. As in Korea . . . we are fighting on a Red battlefield for liberty and peace." In a cover story on de Lattre *Time* observed, "In Indochina the battlelines of Asia and Europe merge. This is the

---

[32]Memo, Asst Dir for Non-European Affairs, Office of International Security Affairs (Bingham), for Asst Secy of State for Far Eastern Affairs (Rusk), 12 Jul 51; Telg, Chief, STEM, to ECA Administrator, 12 Jul 51. Both in Dept of State, *Foreign Relations, 1951: Asia and the Pacific, Part I,* 6:447–52.

[33]Memo, Deputy Asst Secy of State for Far Eastern Affairs (Merchant) for Asst Secy (Rusk), 27 Jul 51, Dept of State, *Foreign Relations, 1951: Asia and the Pacific, Part I,* 6:462–64.

[34]History of the Indochina Incident, pp. 211–14.

[35]Ibid.

[36]Note sur la Mission du General de Lattre aux Etats-Unis, de Lattre Papers.

Seated, President Truman and General de Lattre. *Standing, Ambassadors Bonnet and Heath. De Lattre wears black arm band in mourning for his son killed in Vietnam.*

crucial point which Douglas MacArthur fought to prove; that communism cannot go unchecked in Asia and still be defeated in Europe."[37]

In Washington the general called on President Truman and held lengthy discussions with State and Defense Department officials. To the president, de Lattre "emphasized the oneness of [the] anti-commie struggle [in] Korea, Europe and [Indochina]." President Truman, according to the State Department summary, "expressed warm interest in [the] General's exegesis."[38] At the Pentagon the French commander was even more graphic in his warnings. " 'If you lose Korea, Asia is not lost; but if I lose Indochina, Asia is lost.' Tonkin is the key to Southeast Asia, if Southeast Asia is lost, India will 'burn like a match' and there will be no barrier to the advance of communism before Suez and Africa. If the Moslem world were thus engulfed, the Moslems in North Africa would soon fall in line and Europe itself would be outflanked."[39]

[37]*Time*, 25 September 1951.
[38]Telg, Acting Secy of State to Am Legation, Saigon, 18 Sep 51, Dept of State, *Foreign Relations, 1951: Asia and the Pacific, Part I*, 6:515–16.
[39]Record of a Meeting at the Pentagon Building, Washington, September 20, 1951, Dept of State, *Foreign Relations, 1951: Asia and the Pacific, Part I*, 6:517.

After completing talks in Washington, de Lattre embarked on a tour of American military installations. In one week he visited the naval and military academies, the Army Infantry School at Fort Benning, and Langley Air Force Base, and he laid a wreath at the tomb of the Unknown Soldier. Everywhere his message was the same: Indochina and Korea were two fronts in one war against communism, a war which France could win in Indochina with American help.[40] "I am absolutely sure," he told reporters on "Meet the Press" (viewed by an audience estimated at ten to twelve million) "that it is a question of months, perhaps one or two years, but we shall dominate the problem surely."[41]

De Lattre's campaign came at a time when the American public and its leaders were unsettled and frustrated over recent events in Korea and indeed over the whole course of American foreign policy.[42] In April 1951 General MacArthur had been recalled from Korea, and during the summer the Senate Foreign Relations and Armed Services Committees opened joint hearings on the military situation in the Far East. Many Americans were inclined to agree with MacArthur and his Republican supporters that Asia rather than Western Europe was the decisive area of conflict with world communism.

Yet though American leaders were willing to accept de Lattre's concept of one war, they were unenthusiastic about taking any practical steps toward establishing a unified Franco-American war effort in the Far East. Whatever the logical appeal of de Lattre's geopolitical analysis and the level of official acceptance of his theories, the fact remained that the American public did not view the colonial conflict in Vietnam in the same light as the Korean War. Moreover, the British government, highly nervous about the Korean commitment, would be adamantly opposed to any combined military ventures in Indochina.[43] As the Joint Chiefs of Staff observed, although the struggles in Korea and Indochina were "but two manifestations of the same ideological conflict between the USSR and the Western World . . . it would be wholly unacceptable under existing circumstances to integrate the forces of the Western World engaged in the two wars."[44]

Solving the Supply Problem

De Lattre was more successful in accomplishing a second objective: to increase the amount and speed of delivery of U.S. military supplies. In meetings with American officials he vividly described his supply difficulties. In the battles of May and June there were at times less than 6,000 artillery

---

[40]Jean de Lattre de Tassigny, "Indochina 1951: Ma Mission aux Etats-Unis," *La Revue Deux Mondes*, December 1951, pp. 387 – 89.

[41]"Meet the Press," NBC-TV, 16 Sep 51; Telg, Acting Secy of State to Legaton at Saigon, 18 Sep 57, Dept of State, *Foreign Relations, 1951: Asia and the Pacific, Part I*, 6:516.

[42]Rees, *Korea*, pp. 196 – 229.

[43]Smith, *Acheson*, p. 323.

[44]Memo, JCS for Secy of Defense, 19 Nov 51, sub: Combat Opns in Indochina, CCS 092 Asia (6 – 25 – 48), sec. 19, JCS records.

shells in all of Indochina. During one eight-day period it had been impossible to counterattack because of lack of reserve ammunition. French paratroop operations were limited by lack of airlift, and French Hellcat fighter-bombers were "finished" and needed to be replaced by F−86 jets to impress the Vietnamese and deter Chinese aggression.[45]

De Lattre's complaints were in part justified, for during the summer of 1951 deliveries to Vietnam had in many cases lagged. That problem was especially acute for military vehicles. Only 444 of a scheduled 968 jeeps and 393 of 906 programmed 6 x 6 trucks had been delivered during fiscal year 1951.[46] Secretary of Defense Robert Lovett attributed the slow pace to a dearth of production capacity and skilled workers in certain areas, strikes in defense industries, shortages of machine tools and critical materials, and lack of experience in producing new types of equipment. Uncertainty within the Defense Department about the precise extent and nature of the Indochina aid program and the availability of funds to support it also had delayed deliveries.[47] Part of the problem, however, was attributable to the French themselves, particularly their inadequate maintenance practices. If de Lattre's planes were indeed "finished," a lack of preventive maintenance was probably as much a cause as the wear and tear of combat. Also, as General Brink reported from Saigon, the French were far behind in distributing material already delivered.[48] Because supplies could be moved within Vietnam only by armed convoys, whether by water or road, delivery of equipment to units in the field was inherently slow, a fact that made it essential to maintain stocks in forward areas at higher than normal levels.[49]

Army Chief of Staff J. Lawton Collins assured de Lattre that everything possible would be done to speed deliveries. Collins promised specifically that the Army staff would arrange for 4,500 general-purpose vehicles to be delivered in January rather than in March so they would be available before the start of the rainy season. He also promised to expedite delivery of combat vehicles and Thompson submachine guns and noted that the Army staff would carefully review reserve levels in Korea to determine if materiel stored there might be made available.[50]

General de Lattre left New York for France in early October well satisfied with the results of his trip. Although he had failed to persuade the American government to adopt a one-war strategy, his visit nevertheless represented a public relations success. If he had not "radically changed" American thinking about Indochina, as he later claimed in a letter to Bao Dai, he had left behind a greater awareness of, and respect and sympathy for, the French

[45]Memo, Maj Mitchell, 20 Sep 51, sub: Memorandum of Convs With de Lattre, G−3 091 Indochina, RG 319.

[46]Memo, Livingston Merchant for Robert A. Lovett, 20 Sep 51, 751G.5−MAP/9−2051, records of Dept of State.

[47]Memo, Lovett, 30 Oct 51, in JCS 2099/138, CCS 092 (8−22−46), sec. 61, JCS records.

[48]Air Force Section, MDAP Monthly Rpt, Aug 52, G−3 091 Indochina, RG 319; Ltr, Brink to DA, 4 Jan 52, 751GMSP/1−452, records of Dept of State.

[49]MDAP Monthly Rpt, Jun 52, G−3 091 Indochina, RG 319.

[50]Memo, Maj Mitchell, 20 Sep 51, sub: Memorandum of Conv With de Lattre; Memo, Merchant for Secy of State, 4 Jan 52, 751G.5-MAP/1−452, records of Dept of State.

Chief of Staff Collins *reviews French Expeditionary Corps tankers, left, and Vietnamese National Army troops, background, in Hanoi, 1951. Tanks still bear U.S. markings.*

effort there.[51] The most dramatic effect of the general's visit was a marked increase in the size and speed of American aid deliveries to Saigon. Between de Lattre's visit and February 1952, the French received over 130,000 tons of equipment, including 53 million rounds of ammunition, 8,000 general-purpose vehicles, 650 combat vehicles, 200 aircraft, 3,500 radio sets, and 14,000 automatic weapons.[52]

To cut down on the amount of supplies that had to be shipped thousands of miles across the Pacific, the Military Assistance Advisory Group and the American legation in September 1951 suggested the possibility of manufacturing certain simple items of military equipment in Vietnam. They pointed out that manpower, coal, and wood were in ample supply in Vietnam and that the Cao Dai religious sect was already producing its own small arms, mines, mortars, and hand grenades.[53] The advisory group believed that with relatively simple, even obsolete, U.S. machine tools, the Vietnamese might pro-

---

[51]MDAP Monthly Rpt, Oct 51, G–3 091 Indochina, sec. 1, RG 319.
[52]Am Legation, Saigon, to Embassy in Paris, 28 May 52, 751G.00/5–2852, records of Dept of State.
[53]Ibid. to State Dept, 23 Sep 51, 751G.00/9–2351, records of Dept of State.

duce such items as cartridge clips, canned rations, and small arms ammunition, probably at lower cost due to comparatively low wage levels in Saigon.[54] Local military production might also be of long-range benefit to the Associated States since it would constitute a step toward industrialization and lessen their dependence upon the French.

American officers offered to open discussions on the subject with the French, although recognizing that the latter were hardly likely to be enthusiastic about a plan that might weaken their control over the distribution of military equipment. To counter French misgivings, the advisory group planned to limit the proposal to items for use by French forces only. On 10 October the State Department asked the American legation to prepare a report on "facilities for production of military and paramilitary items in Indochina."[55] Although Minister Heath wrote to General de Lattre requesting information on the amount and types of equipment then being procured locally by the French and on the state of existing production facilities, General de Lattre never replied to the letter and failed even to show it to his staff.[56]

Despite that evidence of French apathy to local procurement, Minister Heath in January 1952 reported that the legation and the advisory group were impressed with the possibilities for light industry in Indochina and believed that the Associated States would be in a strong competitive position *vis-a-vis* France in the manufacture of certain products.[57] A month later, after making a joint study with the advisory group and the Special Technical and Economic Mission, the legation reported it was practical to establish manufacturing facilities in Indochina for small arms and small arms ammunition, tires and tubes, tarpaulins and webbing, camouflage nets, dock fenders, and canned rations. The cost of establishing the appropriate production facilities was estimated at $5.1 million.[58]

Yet by that time it was apparent that the French had no interest in or enthusiasm for local procurement. The French high commissariat had frequently "volunteered numerous reasons why the whole idea of such a program should be considered impracticable. Nor have the Associated States shown any great alacrity in seizing this opportunity." The real question, observed Heath, was whether the program was important enough to warrant a major American effort to obtain French concurrence or at least acquiescence.[59]

The answer, as the next six months were to demonstrate, was no. As had other schemes to improve the military aid program, the local production project foundered on the rocks of French indifference. Although discussions of local production between the advisory group and the French continued intermittently, with the French often promising to study the matter further, few concrete results were achieved. The continued military dependence of the

[54]Ibid. to State Dept, 21 Sep 51, 751G.9MAP/9–2151, records of Dept of State.
[55]Secy of State to Am Legation, Saigon, 10 Oct 51, 751G.00/10–1051, records of Dept of State.
[56]MDAP Monthly Rpt, Nov 51, G–3 091 Indochina, RG 319.
[57]Ibid., Jan 52, G–3 091 Indochina, RG 319.
[58]Memo, Heath, 8 Feb 52, sub: Capabilities for Production of Military Items, records of Dept of State.
[59]Ibid.

Associated States upon France was far more important to the high commissariat than any savings to the United States or any gains to the Vietnamese economy that might result from Vietnamese military industries.

From the short-range military viewpoint, the impact of American aid in Indochina was enormous. Contemporary observers were undoubtedly correct in attributing the narrow French victories in the winter and spring of 1950 – 51 to the timely arrival of American weapons and equipment. The responsiveness and efficiency of the military aid program were in turn the result of the extraordinary efforts of the Military Assistance Advisory Group. Yet it could do little more than deliver the goods. The advisory group's position with the French was little changed from the early months of 1950. Among themselves advisory group officers might fume at French waste or sloppiness or express impatience with "outmoded strategy and tactics," but they could exert little influence on the conduct of the war.[60] They could only ensure that the French would be able to conduct it their way a little longer.

[60]Interv, author with Dunn, 27 May 80.

9

Looking for a Way Out, January 1952 — February 1953

During 1952 and early 1953 it became apparent to nearly all American leaders that the conflict in Vietnam was a stalemate. Although the massive infusion of American aid and de Lattre's military successes had prevented a decisive Viet Minh victory in 1951, the French had failed to devise any political or military programs to defeat the Communists, and the prospect of important new French initiatives was bleak. From early 1952 to the end of the Truman administration in January 1953, American officials sought some means to break the deadlock in Indochina and to end the increasingly severe drain on American money and arms. In their search they set in motion a number of expedients and policies that would come to fruition under the Eisenhower administration and would mark the climactic phase of the Franco-American collaboration in Vietnam.

In January 1952 General de Lattre died of cancer in Paris. His death produced a feeling of pessimism and despair among the French. "Many had come to believe that he was the last chance for a solution in Indochina," the American embassy reported. "They now fear that the gains he has achieved might fall away."[1] General Brink tried to be more optimistic. "Although in places the [Vietnamese] government appears to be coming apart at the seams," he noted, "perhaps it would be better to say that not all seams are sewn together yet."[2]

Almost as disheartening as de Lattre's death was a development at the town of Hoa Binh on the Black River, west of Hanoi. De Lattre had occupied Hoa Binh in force in November 1951, ostensibly to cut Communist supply lines running southeast to a Viet Minh stronghold near Thang Hoa and to maintain the loyalty of the Muong tribesmen, whose principal town was Hoa Binh. As the American legation in Saigon observed, the offensive was as much political as military, for de Lattre hoped to impress the French government, preparing to debate the Indochina budget, with his vigor and enter-

---

[1] MDAP Monthly Rpt, Jan 52.
[2] Ibid.; Ltr, Brink to Maj Gen George H. Olmstead, OMA, 29 Mar 52, OMA 091.3 Indochina,

prise and to show the Americans that their military equipment was being put to good use. Some American observers, however, thought the move to Hoa Binh put French forces in a dangerously extended position and predicted a swift, vigorous Communist reaction.

The seizure of Hoa Binh probably caused the Viet Minh high command to cancel plans for its own offensive elsewhere in the north and to concentrate on dislodging the French. To divert French forces from the Hoa Binh sector the Viet Minh infiltrated some 25,000 regulars into the Red River Delta region. These forces in turn recruited and trained new members of the regional and popular forces. In the meantime General Giap assumed personal command of three divisions and supporting artillery that he had concentrated in the Hoa Binh area and between December 1951 and early February launched a series of heavy attacks against the French strongpoints around Hoa Binh. Although unsuccessful in taking the strongpoints, the Viet Minh were able to cut first the water and then the land routes into Hoa Binh. Attempts to reopen communications cost the French heavy losses in men and equipment. By this time the security situation in the delta had so deteriorated that on 24 February 1952, after having lost almost as many troops as in the border battles of 1950, the French abandoned Hoa Binh to concentrate on the delta. The French completed the evacuation with relatively light casualties, but had to blow up over 150 tons of supplies and ammunition at Hoa Binh because they lacked the means to transport them back to the delta.[3]

In the Hoa Binh battles the Viet Minh demonstrated a new degree of military sophistication. Their logistical support was much improved, enabling them to continue fighting at Hoa Binh for weeks at a time. They possessed a sophisticated intelligence apparatus including a radio intercept unit to supply Giap and his staff with timely information. Finally, they made effective use of field and antiaircraft artillery with the aid of Chinese advisers and technicians.[4]

The retreat from Hoa Binh led to speculation that the French might lack the resolve to continue the struggle in Vietnam. State Department officials observed that "it is now clear that the prospect of any offensive to clear out the Viet Minh in Tonkin, as promised by de Lattre, does not exist," and the CIA reported that "over the long term the combat effectiveness of the Viet Minh [will] probably continue to improve." The agency believed that growing domestic pressures and the difficulty of supporting a military effort in the Far East while fulfilling NATO commitments would eventually lead France to withdraw from Vietnam.[5] There were rumors of an impending French deal

RG 330, Secy of Defense records.

[3]This account of the Hoa Binh operation is based on the following sources: Rapport du general de Corps d'Armee Salan sur les operations menees sur la Riviere Noire a Hoa Binh et sur la R.C. 6 . . ., Incl 3 to USARMA, Saigon, to ACofS G – 2, R – 111 – 52, 29 May 52, G – 2 ID file 1054654, pt. II; Ltr, USARMA to ACofS G – 2, 27 Feb 52, records of ACSI; MDAP Monthly Rpt, Dec 52, G – 3 091 Indochina, RG 319; Fall, *Street Without Joy,* pp. 47 – 60.

[4]Rapport du General Salan.

[5]Memo, Far East Div for Western European Div, 28 Feb 52, records of Dept of State; National Intelligence Estimate 35/1, 28 Feb 52, G – 3 091 Indochina, RG 319.

French Forces Near Hoa Binh

with Ho Chi Minh and much talk of French loss of nerve. In February the Paris newspapers carried an interview with the minister for Relations with the Associated States, Jean Letourneau, in which he admitted that France had no hope of winning in Indochina.[6] At the end of March Secretary of State Dean Acheson found it necessary to assure British Ambassador Sir Oliver Franks that the United States had no evidence or reason to believe that the French were negotiating with the Viet Minh.[7]

U.S. Army officials were less pessimistic. General Brink reported that although the French had not dealt adequately with the grave political and economic problems confronting them, there was no sign of a French slackening.[8] The Army's acting chief of intelligence, Brig. Gen. John Weckerling, also believed a French withdrawal unlikely. Although the struggle severely strained French resources and the French budget, he noted, "any government that pulled out [of Vietnam] would fall" and France would "lose prestige throughout her Empire."[9]

[6]Army Attache, Paris, to ACofS G−2, 27 Feb 52, sub: Press Interview of M. Letourneau, 52, records of ACSI.
[7]Memo of Conversation, Acheson with Sir Oliver Franks, 28 Mar 52, in Historical Division, State Department, Documentary History of U.S. Policy Toward Indochina, 1940−1953, doc. C−46.
[8]Ltr, Brink to Maj Gen Reuben E. Jenkins, 1 Apr 52, Incl to Jenkins to CofSA, 12 May 51, G−3 091 Indochina, RG 319.
[9]Memo, Weckerling for CofSA, 2 Jan 52, sub: Current French Position in Indochina, G−3 091

American policymakers during the early months of 1952 also continued to worry that the Chinese would invade Vietnam. That fear persisted although both the CIA and the Joint Intelligence Committee of the Joint Chiefs of Staff had concluded in early 1952 that despite improved Chinese military capabilities along the Vietnamese border, an invasion was unlikely.[10] The Joint Chiefs of Staff and the National Security Council believed that in any event it was important to agree upon a course of action should the Chinese move. At a meeting of the American, British, and French Chiefs of Staff in Washington in January 1952, the American chiefs suggested that the three powers agree on such a course.[11] The conferees appointed an ad hoc committee composed of the military representatives of the three powers plus Australia and New Zealand to discuss what collective military measures might be taken.[12]

A meeting of the committee a few weeks later revealed that the allies could reach no real agreement about the best response to a Chinese attack. The Americans favored air attacks and a blockade of the Chinese coast, measures opposed by the French because they disapproved any diversion of resources from Vietnam and by the British because they wanted to avoid provoking the Chinese into moving against their colony at Hong Kong. The British and French desired a combined command for Southeast Asia, but the Americans did not want U.S. forces under British or French command. As the Joint Chiefs' representative, Vice Adm. Arthur C. Davis, complained, "They would like not only to determine what we shall do with our own forces in the event of our taking military action with respect to the Southeast Asia situation, but also to command our forces while these limited actions are being taken."[13]

Despite the disagreement, President Truman and the National Security Council decided in June 1952 to continue planning for air and naval action against China. NSC 124/2, United States Objectives and Courses of Action with Respect to Southeast Asia, adopted on 25 June 1952, called for the United States to contribute air and naval support for the defense of Indochina, to interdict Chinese Communist lines of communications, including those in China, and to blockade the Chinese coast. If those "minimum" measures proved to be insufficient, the United States would "take air and naval action in conjunction with at least France and the U.K. against all suitable military targets in China." If Britain and France refused to participate, the United States "should consider taking unilateral action."[14] Still, the chairman of the Joint Chiefs of Staff, General of the Army Omar N. Bradley, explained to the State Department that the service chiefs did not really expect

Indochina, RG 319.

[10]National Intelligence Estimate 35/1, 28 Feb 52; JIC 529/10, 9 Jan 52, CCS 092 Asia (6–25–48), BP pt. 3, JCS records.

[11]Notes Recorded by Secy and Dep Secy, JCS, at the U.S.-U.K.-French Chief of Staff Talks on Southeast Asia, 11 Jan 52, CCS 092 Asia (6–25–48), sec. 22.

[12]History of Indochina Incident, pp. 241–42.

[13]Memo, Adm Davis, 5 Feb 52, sub: Report of the Five Power Ad Hoc Committee on Southeast Asia, CCS 092 Asia (6–25–48), sec. 24, JCS records.

[14]NSC 124/2, *U.S.-Vietnam Relations*, 8:531–34.

air and naval attacks alone to be decisive. The point in limiting reaction to a blockade and aerial bombardment campaign was to avoid getting too deeply involved in another Asian ground war.[15]

Problems of a Vietnamese Army

Despite the attention paid to China, the primary threat to Vietnam remained France's inability to cope with the Viet Minh revolution.[16] The long weeks of discussion and debate which accompanied the drafting of NSC 124 had revealed the dissatisfaction of many American officials with the course of events in Vietnam and their desire to reverse the pattern of drift and stalemate. Yet the only new development of any promise was the formation of an indigenous Vietnamese army, under the control of the State of Vietnam. Such an army, if it were able to play at least a secondary role in combating the armed forces of the Viet Minh, would greatly increase the prestige and power of the Bao Dai government, demonstrating to the Vietnamese people and to the world that Vietnam was truly independent and able to defend itself against insurrection and subversion.

However promising the idea, realizing it proved to be difficult. Even though France expected the United States to provide much of the money and equipment for the undertaking, the French insisted that creating a Vietnamese army was a matter wholly between them and the Bao Dai government. Recurrent cabinet crises in Paris and Saigon and squabbling between the Vietnamese and the French over the amount of money each should contribute also delayed the project. Prime Minister Huu had complained to Consul General Gullion in January 1951 that the Vietnamese government could not possibly meet its assigned share of the financial burden until it assumed control of customs services as provided for in the Elysee Agreements.[17] The French also persisted in recruiting Vietnamese for their own forces in Vietnam, a practice which angered the Bao Dai government and made recruiting for a Vietnamese army more difficult.

By May 1951 the Vietnamese National Army had less than 40,000 men. Only 24 of a projected 34 battalions existed, even on paper, and only 7 of those had Vietnamese officers.[18] Yet small as it was, the Vietnamese Army was already beyond the means of the French and Vietnamese to support. By June 1951 the Vietnamese were talking of slowing the activation of the army to cope with soaring costs.[19]

In July the Huu government tried a new strategy by decreeing a "general

---

[15]Memorandum of Conversation Between General Bradley and Under Secretary of State, 12 May 52, records of Dept of State.

[16]NSC 124/2, *U.S.-Vietnam Relations,* 8:524.

[17]Gullion to State Dept, 27 Jan 51, 751G.00/1−2751, records of Dept of State.

[18]Brig Gen Francis Brink, A Study of the Vietnamese Army, 21 Mar 51, updated 7 May 51, records of Dept of State.

[19]MDAP Monthly Rpt, Jun 51.

mobilization" to conscript 60,000 men in four increments for two months of training. Although de Lattre saw the decree as a major step forward "which cannot fail to produce a very strong impression on the majority of Vietnamese fence-sitters," American observers dismissed it as "an expensive gesture" and pointed out that two months were far too short to prepare an adequately trained reserve.[20] The small number of officer candidates (1,000) and specialists (600) who were to be drafted under the plan constituted less than one-fourth the number needed. American officials believed that the Vietnamese government was proceeding so conservatively because it doubted whether it could compel any large proportion of the population to answer the call to the colors.[21]

Modest and inadequate as was the planned mobilization, it soon ran into difficulties. The first increment of 6,000 men was released after only about six and a half weeks of service instead of the planned two months. Only half of the 500 student reserve officer candidates handpicked by the Ministry of Defense ever reported for duty at the officer training schools in Thu Duc and Nam Dinh. The second increment of draftees was released after only five weeks of training, and the third increment was never called at all. Less than 10 percent of the Vietnamese who underwent training could be induced to enlist in the regular long-service Vietnamese Army.[22]

To stimulate recruiting, the Military Assistance Advisory Group and the United States Information Executive (a predecessor of the U.S. Information Agency) produced a booklet, *Phu Joins the Army*, and through Vietnamese government information services distributed 200,000 copies to potential recruits. The U.S. Information Executive optimistically predicted that "this type of propaganda . . . would carry a great impact," but *Phu Joins the Army* was more a reflection of American hopes for the Vietnamese Army than a successful stimulant to recruiting. The booklet's hero, Anh Phu Tung Quan, becomes acquainted with the National Army when its soldiers liberate his village from the Viet Minh. The villagers note that the soldiers are "correctly dressed, well disciplined, helpful and considerate to the people." They aid the people in rebuilding their homes and roads. When an officer informs the villagers of the establishment of the State of Vietnam under the leadership of Bao Dai, "the crowd, very happy to learn this, unanimously swears total support to Bao Dai and to the Army." After enlisting in the army, Anh Phu is heroically wounded in battle and awakens in a hospital bed where, "looking over at the wall he saw a picture of His Majesty, Bao Dai, and deeply moved, he prayed for His Majesty's health."[23]

As recruiting continued to lag, in January 1952 the Vietnamese reduced the quota for enlisted specialists from 800 to 500 and cut the training period for officer candidates from twelve to eight months. Of 1,000 officer candidates

---

[20]De Lattre Note, 24 Jul 51, No. 4601/SG4, de Lattre Papers.
[21]MDAP Monthly Rpt, Aug 51, G – 3 091 Indochina, RG 319.
[22]Ibid., Oct, Nov, Dec 51, G – 3 091 Indochina, RG 319.
[23]USIE (U.S. Information Executive) Translation, Nov 51, records of Dept of State.

projected in the mobilization plan only 690 were actually enrolled.[24] The little army's credibility as a viable military force suffered also from the lack of a general staff, a chief of staff, or even a full-time minister of defense. Few senior officers were available to fill important staff and command assignments, and the shortage of trained junior officers was severe.[25]

A U.S. Role in Training?

Lack of progress in organizing and training an effective Vietnamese National Army prompted many American officials to call for a more active U.S. role in the project. In April 1952 the three service secretaries, in a draft paper presented to the State Department, suggested a program of direct American training of the Vietnamese Army by an expanded Military Assistance Advisory Group. If Indochina was really "the key to Southeast Asia," said the secretaries, the United States should make greater efforts to establish an indigenous force capable at least of preserving internal security.[26] The head of the Economic Cooperation Administration in Vietnam, Robert Blum, agreed that the United States should "assume a direct influence commensurate with our contribution" in the formation of the National Army. Blum believed the United States had assumed great responsibilities and provided decisive aid in Indochina but had been accorded little say in military matters. Now was the time for the United States to assume a larger military role.[27] The State Department also felt a strong National Army would increase political stability (an idea which would later be emphasized by Secretary of State John Foster Dulles) and represent a highly visible symbol of the Bao Dai government's independence and sovereignty.[28]

General Brink and most of the Army members of the Military Assistance Advisory Group disagreed. They believed that training the Vietnamese should remain a French responsibility, for the French had "learned how to deal with the native soldier and how to teach him; they [have] also learned his limitations and have solved the problems caused by language difficulties."[29] General Brink also pointed out that an advisory group with training responsibility would require over 4,000 officers and enlisted men.[30]

Washington officials discounted those views, partly because of the dis-

[24]MDAP Monthly Rpt, Jan 52.

[25]Ibid., Aug 51, G–3 091 Indochina, RG 319.

[26]Memo, Secy of Army (Frank Pace), Secy of Air Force (Roswell Gilpatric), and Secy of Navy (Dan A. Kimball) for Secy of Defense, 8 Apr 52, RG 335.

[27]Ltr, Blum to State Dept, Dec 52, Incl to Harlan Cleveland to John H. Ohly, 5 Jan 52, OMA 091.3 Indochina, RG 330.

[28]Position Paper on Indochina for Discussion With French and British, 15 May 52, files of Office of Philippine and Southeast Asian Affairs, Lot 580207, records of Dept of State.

[29]Army Section, MDAP Monthly Rpt, Jun 52; Ltr, Brink to Maj Gen Reuben E. Jenkins, 12 May 52; Memo, Tyler Port (Under Secy of Army) for Secy of Army, 6 May 52, sub: Indochina. All in G–3 091 Indochina, RG 319.

[30]Memo, Port for Secy of Army, 6 May 52, sub: Indochina.

Ambassador Heath Greets General Trapnell *(left) on arrival in Vietnam, August 1952.*

couraging reports about the state of the Vietnamese Army submitted by the advisory group itself. Those reports described how Vietnamese units were often organized on paper for months before any men or supplies were actually assembled; "units are at least six months old before any progress other than the most basic training is made."[31] Although the French had requested large amounts of American weapons and equipment for the Vietnamese forces, the advisory group's Army section reported that native troops knew nothing about an item of American equipment until it actually arrived, and even then training aids or mock-ups of equipment were not used.[32]

Reports by the Navy section were even more pessimistic. Naval officers assigned to the advisory group reported that a French claim of having established a Vietnamese navy to which responsibilities could someday be transferred was "wholly without foundation." The so-called navy actually consisted of about 400 sailors serving in river forces under the command of French officers and noncommissioned officers. French plans for training additional sailors were very modest, and the naval training school at Nha Trang had yet to open.[33]

[31]MDAP Monthly Rpt, Jun 52.
[32]Ibid., May 52.
[33]Navy Section, MDAP Monthly Rpt, Jun 52, G–3 091 Indochina, RG 319.

Debate over American participation in training Vietnamese forces was continuing in July 1952 when General Brink, who for some time had been suffering from diabetes and arteriosclerosis, committed suicide while on a visit to Washington.[34] To succeed him, the Army named Brig. Gen. Thomas J. H. Trapnell, who at the time was commanding the 187th Airborne Regimental Combat Team, which had just completed the difficult and dangerous mission of putting down an uprising of North Korean prisoners of war at Koje-do prison camp in South Korea.[35]

Not yet fifty years old when he arrived in Vietnam in August 1952, General Trapnell brought vigor, enthusiasm, and a healthy skepticism to his new assignment. He quickly established friendly relations with senior Vietnamese officers, particularly General Nguyen Van Hinh, nominal commander of the Vietnamese National Army, who sometimes took the American general tiger hunting. Through such personal contacts General Trapnell was able to arrange on-the-spot visits to Vietnamese units without going through French intermediaries.[36] What Trapnell saw was disturbing. He quickly concluded that the French seemed to lack confidence in either the fighting ability or the political reliability of the Vietnamese soldiers and were making little use of them. Like numbers of other Americans, General Trapnell was soon convinced that the United States would have to play a more active role in the creation of the Vietnamese National Army.

Fall Offensives

General Trapnell was still learning details of his new post when the most serious crisis since the disasters at Cao Bang in 1950 developed. It began when three Viet Minh regiments supported by an artillery regiment attacked a French post in the Tai country, the heavily wooded region north and east of the Black River inhabited mainly by mountain tribesmen. The anchor of the French defenses there was the town of Nghia Lo, midway between the Red and Black Rivers. The Viet Minh attacked Nghia Lo in mid-October. The French fell back from weakly defended outposts around the town toward their main fortified positions, drawing the attackers with them. Paratroopers were then to drop behind the attacking forces to trap them. But bad weather prevented the use of paratroopers, and the Viet Minh attackers used a pincer movement to cut off the retreat of the French forces falling back on Nghia Lo. On 17 October the Viet Minh overwhelmed the town's last defenses; within a few days all of the Tai country east and north of the Black River was under Viet Minh control.[37]

[34]Ltr, Heath to Gen J. Lawton Collins, 1 Aug 52, CS 091 Indochina, RG 319.
[35]See Walter G. Hermes, *Truce Tent and Fighting Front*, United States Army in the Korean War (Washington, 1966), pp. 233–63.
[36]Interv, author with Lt Gen Thomas J. H. Trapnell, 5 Sep 74, Historians files, CMH.
[37]Memo, ACofS G–2, for CofSA, 4 Dec 52, sub: French Campaign, Indochina, G–3 091 Indochina, RG 319; Bernardo, The Franco–Viet Minh War, pp. 32–34.

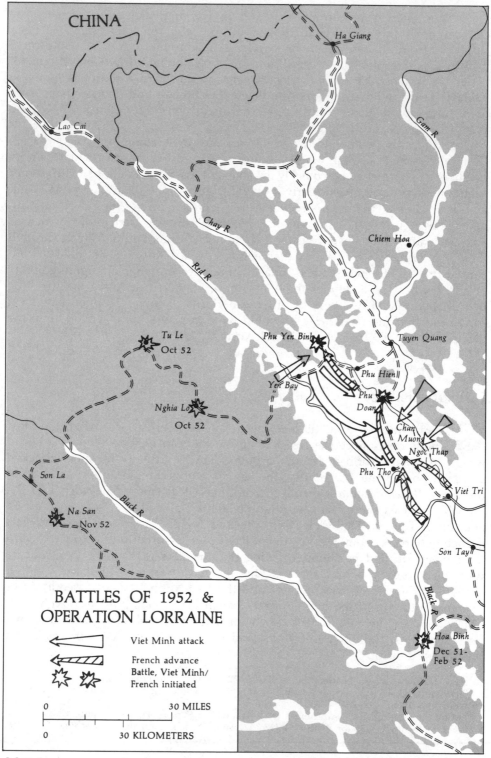

CHINA

Ha Giang

Lao Cai

Gam R

Chay R

Chiem Hoa

Red R

Tu Le
Oct 52

Phu Yen Binh

Tuyen Quang

Yen Bay

Phu Hien

Nghia Lo
Oct 52

Phu
Doan

Son La

Chan
Muong

Black R

Ngoc Thap

Na San
Nov 52

Phu Tho

Viet Tri

Son Tay

Black R

BATTLES OF 1952 &
OPERATION LORRAINE

Hoa Binh
Dec 51-
Feb 52

Viet Minh attack

French advance

Battle, Viet Minh/
French initiated

0   30 MILES

0   30 KILOMETERS

MAP 4

To divert the Viet Minh from the Black River, the French launched a strong offensive along the line of the Red and Clear Rivers northeast of Hanoi. This offensive, code named Operation LORRAINE, began at the end of October 1952 amid considerable fanfare and publicity. The largest operation ever attempted by the French in Vietnam, it involved over 30,000 men with large numbers of artillery, tanks, and planes. Advancing northwest, the French quickly seized the towns of Phu Doan and Phu Yen Binh, important Viet Minh supply centers where they found large stocks of weapons and ammunition. *(Map 4)* Then the attack bogged down, hampered by a long and precarious supply line. By mid-November Operation LORRAINE was in reverse gear, with French troops and supply columns withdrawing behind the de Lattre Line under constant harassment from Viet Minh troops and irregulars.

American observers were sharply disappointed, believing that the French had bungled a chance to inflict a decisive defeat on the enemy. They pointed out that the French had a two-and-a-half to one superiority in infantry and an overwhelming edge in artillery, tanks, and air support.[38] Yet to take advantage of their superiority, the French forces required large quantities of supplies that could be moved only by road, and the roads were particularly susceptible to Viet Minh infiltration and counterattack.

Only a few weeks later another major engagement developed along the Black River line at Na San, a strongpoint held by nine full-strength French battalions, supported by aircraft and five batteries of 105-mm. howitzers. Cut off from overland supply, Na San was a fortified area of about fifteen square kilometers with an airstrip on the floor of a valley. The French fortified the surrounding high ground and ran supplies to the beleaguered fortress by air.[39] Probably underestimating the strength of the defenders, the Viet Minh attacked Na San with two regiments. The major fighting occurred on 23 and 30 November. The Viet Minh attacked with skill and tenacity. Some French outposts received as many as five assaults in one night, but the defenses held. On the morning of 1 December the defenders counted almost 540 enemy dead on the field. Viet Minh losses probably totaled between six and seven thousand.

Although the French could count Na San as a victory, the intense fighting there and elsewhere during the autumn of 1952 severely taxed French resources, particularly those of the Air Force. Under pressure of battle, its maintenance facilities, never very efficient, had collapsed completely. At one airfield, for example, advisory group observers discovered only two men assigned to overhaul 20-mm. cannon, and they could handle only ten cannon a month, less than one-sixth the total requiring maintenance.[40]

The Viet Minh offensives led to new requests for additional American

[38]Memo, U.S. Army Attache (Col Leo W. H. Shaughnessey) for Heath, 24 Dec 52, sub: Request for Comments, records of ACSI.

[39]CINCPAC Study, Review of Autumn Campaign in Tonkin, Annex B to Incl 1 of Memo, Chief of Naval Operations for JCS, 18 Mar 53, sub: Staff Study (OP–30ZD3/jcr), CCS 092 Asia (6–25–58), sec. 42, BP pt. 9; Bernardo, The Franco–Viet Minh War, pp. 35–37. See also, O'Ballance, *The Indochina War, 1945–1954*, pp. 184–86.

[40]Air Force Section, MDAP Monthly Rpt, Aug 52.

Vietnamese Troops *of the French Expeditionary Corps ford a stream during Operation Lorraine.*

French Troops *view captured Viet Minh equipment.*

assistance. In December the French government formally asked that U.S. Air Force mechanics be sent to Vietnam for a month to perform routine maintenance checks on French C−47 aircraft. General Trapnell firmly supported the request, and in January 1953 twenty-eight Air Force mechanics on loan from the Far East Air Force arrived to perform the required maintenance and to train French ground crews in American techniques.[41]

In the meantime, to American officials in both the United States and Vietnam the fighting at Nghia Lo, Phu Doan, and Na San provided a graphic illustration of the bankruptcy of French military policy in Vietnam. Although the French called their successful defense of Na San an important victory, an evaluation team from the headquarters of the Commander in Chief, Pacific (CINCPAC), which had been at Na San during the engagement, assessed it as "an inconclusive battle in a mountain wilderness."[42] As the CINCPAC team saw it, the French command, with numerical superiority, interior lines of communications, and absolute command of the air, had chosen to wait passively until the enemy moved. After the Viet Minh offensive developed, the French, "instead of a vigorous counter-stroke at the enemy's lines of communication, laboriously transferred part of a division ahead of the enemy with the clear intent to establish a line of defense against which the enemy would break." When the French finally did attack two weeks after Operation LORRAINE had begun, they staged their attack "not as [a] decisive stroke but as a hit-and-run raid." Even if one accepted that the French had to fight a defensive battle, the American observers wrote, they would have done far better by holding Phu Doan with a reinforced LORRAINE task force. A powerful French force, firmly established across the enemy's lines of communications, would have been in an excellent position "to fight a decisive battle under conditions of French choosing."[43] French conduct of the entire campaign, the observers concluded, had been timid, unimaginative, and extremely defensive-minded.

General Trapnell agreed. He told General Collins that the French had been taken by surprise in the autumn campaign and that they had committed a major error by failing to make a stand at Phu Doan. "The enemy," Trapnell concluded, "retains the initiative."[44]

Though correct in many respects, these analyses tended to overemphasize the value of French numerical superiority. Intelligence officers on the U.S. Army staff, while noting that the French had more troops, remarked that this advantage was offset by the enemy's guerrilla tactics, which obliged the French to maintain a large proportion of their forces in static positions.[45]

[41]History of Indochina Incident, pp. 267−68.
[42]CINCPAC Study, Review of Autumn Campaign in Tonkin.
[43]Ibid.
[44]Ltr, Trapnell to CofSA, 20 Dec 52, CSA 091 Indochina, RG 319.
[45]Memo, ACofS G−2 for CofSA, 14 Dec 52, sub: Situation in Indochina, CSA 091 Indochina, RG 319.

French Colonial Troops *board aircraft at Na San.*

The Light Battalion Proposal

The outcome of the fighting in the fall of 1952 prompted American officials to renew their call for a genuinely effective Vietnamese Army. Since reinforcements from metropolitan France appeared unlikely (the French Assembly had forbidden use of draftees in Vietnam), increasing the number of Vietnamese troops seemed the only answer. In December 1952 General Trapnell urged that units for the Vietnamese Army "over and above those units already provided by the Joint Chiefs of Staff" should be formed on a priority basis. The forty to fifty additional units would be organized as "light battalions." First suggested by the French military adviser to Bao Dai, General Marcel Alessandri, the light battalion was envisaged as an infantry unit armed only with shoulder weapons, light machine guns, and mortars and able to find and destroy the enemy on his own terrain.[46] Each battalion would have a cadre of at least seven French officers and thirty French noncommissioned officers.

Although the French commander, General Raoul Salan, agreed to the plan, he maintained that the cost was too high for the French. Trapnell

[46]Ltr, Trapnell to CofSA, 20 Dec 52.

believed that the United States could provide the necessary equipment by substituting it for material already programmed in the fiscal year 1954 Mutual Defense Assistance Program, but such items as pay and rations would require additional funding. Yet Trapnell believed it would be money well spent. General Collins saw the proposal as an "excellent opportunity to persuade the French to grant more responsibility to the Associated States for participation in military matters," and strongly recommended acceptance.[47] Collins suggested that the French training system for the Vietnamese National Army should be restructured after a system of schools developed for training South Korean troops. Although the program would require additional

Vietnamese National Army Troops *with 81-mm. mortar.*

funds, General Collins believed that Congress would readily support a program along these lines.[48]

The only dissenting voice came from the State Department. After visiting Vietnam, the director of the Office of Philippine and Southeast Asian Affairs, Philip W. Bonsal, expressed doubts that the Vietnamese National Army would ever be able to cope with the Viet Minh unless the latter were seriously weakened by French military action. He also worried that large numbers of the newly armed Vietnamese recruits might defect to the Communists.[49]

Untroubled by these considerations, the Joint Chiefs of Staff endorsed the forty-battalion proposal, and the secretary of defense appointed an ad hoc committee to study the plan in detail. Visiting Washington at the end of January 1953, General Trapnell explained his ideas to representatives of the State Department and the Joint Staff and answered questions from the ad hoc committee. He emphasized that additional manpower was absolutely essential to achieve military success in Indochina. Since timing was also important, he hoped to have the new formations ready by the end of 1953, in time for the next campaigning season. He agreed with General Collins that the French should adopt the American training methods that had proven effective in South Korea and hoped to have senior French and Vietnamese officers visit

[47]Msg, Collins to Trapnell, 19 Jan 53, CSA 091 Indochina, RG 319.
[48]Memo, SGS for CofS, 14 Jan 53, sub: Forty Battalions, G–3 091 Indochina, RG 319.
[49]Memo, Bonsal for Chief, FE, 18 Nov 52, sub: Report on Visit to Indochina; Ltr, Bonsal to Donald Heath, 10 Dec 52. Both in files of Office of Philippine and Southeast Asian Affairs, Lot 580207, records of Dept of State.

South Korea to observe American training techniques. Because Trapnell believed the French would stubbornly resist a direct American role in training the Vietnamese, he made no such proposal. On 9 February the ad hoc committee reported favorably on the light battalion program and recommended that the United States raise the subject with the French in talks scheduled to begin later that month in Washington.[50]

The Unconventional Warfare Option

In the continuing search for something to change the pattern of events in Vietnam, a number of American officials came to believe that the best way for the French to deal with the unconventional warfare of the Viet Minh was to wage unconventional warfare themselves. During 1951 the CIA had suggested to General de Lattre that the French form "counterguerrilla" warfare groups to operate in rebel-controlled territory, but de Lattre had been uninterested. In the spring of 1952 Secretary of the Army Frank Pace, Jr., suggested that the United States again raise the question with the French during a visit to Washington by the French Minister for Indochina Jean Letourneau. On the theory that the "natives . . . resented French colonialism," Pace wanted to employ Vietnamese organized by American agents, a move which he believed would "materially reduce the psychological barrier" that existed between the French and the Vietnamese.[51]

When Pace asked the Army to report on the desirability of the project and whether the Army would be the appropriate agency to run it, the staff was less than enthusiastic. The plans and operations officer, Maj. Gen. Reuben E. Jenkins, reported that the staff saw numerous obstacles. The Viet Minh had established a firm police state in the areas under their control and had already conscripted most of the available manpower. General Jenkins also questioned whether political stability would really be increased by arming elements of the population of questionable loyalty. He doubted that U.S. control of the program would, in itself, remove the stigma of colonialism.[52]

That exchange of memos for a time ended official American discussion of forming unconventional warfare units. Along with the plan for Vietnamese light battalions, those discussions reflected an attempt to correct what American military observers saw as the two fundamental weaknesses in the French military position, a faulty strategy and a lack of manpower. The hope was that the light battalions would help to solve both problems at once. If the French would grant greater independence in military matters to the State of

---

[50]Prepared Questions for General Trapnell, 29 Jan 53, Annex C to Appendix A, Report of the Ad Hoc Committee to the Assistant Secretary Defense, International Security Affairs (ASD, ISA), 9 Feb 53, records of ASD, ISA, RG 330.

[51]Memo, Pace for CofSA, 13 Jun 52, sub: Unconventional Warfare Plan for Indochina, CSA 091 Indochina, RG 319.

[52]Memo, Maj Gen Reuben E. Jenkins, ACofS G–3, for Secy of Army, 14 Jun 52, sub: Unconventional Warfare in Indochina, CSA 091 Indochina, RG 319.

Vietnam, that concession would increase the prestige of the Bao Dai government in the eyes of the Vietnamese and make the people more willing to oppose the Viet Minh. The increased manpower would also make possible a more aggressive strategy for the Franco-Vietnamese forces.

In the end few of the hoped-for results were forthcoming. The plan for creating light battalions, like other plans for the Vietnamese National Army, was soon crippled by squabbles between Bao Dai and the French and by the continued indifference of the Vietnamese people. Concentrating on the manpower problem while assuming that the political and social problems would take care of themselves proved a failure. As long as

Letourneau and Bonnet *arrive in Washington.*

the underlying political problem—the unwillingness of France to grant meaningful independence to the State of Vietnam and the inability of the State of Vietnam to produce leaders who could command the respect and support of the people—remained unsolved, the French and their Vietnamese clients would never be able to attract the loyalty and support of any large segment of the population. And without the support of the people, forming an effective army, conventional or otherwise, was impossible. A new administration was about to enter office in Washington, but the pattern of simply tinkering with strategy, training techniques, and manpower policies was not over. Rather, it would continue on a far larger scale.

10

The Road to Dien Bien Phu

Dwight D. Eisenhower took office in January 1953 pledged to new initiatives in foreign policy, particularly in Asia. In his first State of the Union message, the new president characterized the Indochina War as part of a worldwide scheme of Communist aggression.[1] Secretary of State John Foster Dulles also left little doubt that he considered success in Vietnam vital to the defense of the free world. In March 1953 Dulles told French Foreign Minister Georges Bidault that he and the president believed Korea and Vietnam were parts of a single front and that Eisenhower was the first president publicly to recognize this.[2]

While the new American administration radiated purpose and resolution toward Vietnam, French nerves were rapidly wearing thin over a bloody conflict that continued to consume thousands of lives and millions of francs. Since 1952 an increasing number of French politicians had called for negotiations with the Viet Minh to stop the war, and by early 1953 prominent French leaders including newspaper publisher Jean-Jacques Servan-Schreiber and former Prime Minister Edouard Daladier had joined the ranks of those calling for an early end to hostilities. In May 1953 the American embassy in Paris reported that non-Communist newspapers were devoting increasing attention to the possibility of a negotiated settlement. A French officer in Saigon told the head of the U.S. Information Service that "most of the intelligent young French military men believed that a negotiated settlement was the only solution."[3] Marshal Alphonse Juin and other high-ranking French officers were reported to think that France no longer had interests in Indochina worth the costs of continuing the struggle there.[4]

At the time the Eisenhower administration took office, more than 137,000

---

[1]*Public Papers of the Presidents: Dwight D. Eisenhower, 1953* (Washington, 1960), p. 16.
[2]Hist Div, State Dept, Documentary History of U.S. Policy Toward Indochina, doc. D–4.
[3]Memo for Ambassador Heath, 9 Jan 53, Incl 1 to Am Embassy, Saigon, to State Dept, 23 Jan 53, 751G.00/1–2353, records of Dept of State.
[4]Statement of French Military Desires Regarding the Role of the United States in Indochina, Incl to USARMA to ACofS G–2, 13 Apr 53, S–49–52, records of ACSI.

long tons of American equipment had been delivered to the French, including some 900 combat vehicles, 15,000 other vehicles, almost 2,500 artillery pieces, 24,000 automatic weapons, 75,000 small arms, and nearly 9,000 radios. In addition, French air units had received 160 F – 6F and F – 8F fighter aircraft, 41 B – 26 light bombers, and 28 C – 47 transports plus 155 aircraft engines and 93,000 bombs.[5] Despite such massive assistance American leaders were still largely ignorant of future French plans and programs for Indochina. Washington was receiving a considerable amount of tactical intelligence on the military situation in Vietnam, but there was still no exchange of views with Paris on military strategy, no sharing of plans or evaluations.[6]

What Washington did know was discouraging. All American observers agreed that in operations during 1952 the French had, at best, achieved a stalemate. Military observers from Pacific headquarters believed that "decisive defeat of the Viet Minh military forces in Indochina is prevented by the current attitude of the French Union forces, which is strategically defensive in nature and which surrenders the initiative to the enemy."[7] That attitude persisted although, by Pacific headquarters reckoning, the French forces had 13 percent more men; greatly superior equipment, logistical support, and command and staff experience; and complete control of the air. The Viet Minh had won and retained the initiative despite the handicap of "heterogeneous equipment, long supply lines, and inadequate transport."[8]

While conceding that the French command "lacked the offensive spirit," the Military Assistance Advisory Group in Saigon argued that the French Expeditionary Corps lacked the numerical strength to mount an all-out offensive, a more realistic assessment of French resources than was usual among U.S. observers. Americans would normally total up the number of French battalions, as often as not including the relatively ineffective Vietnamese national forces, compare them with the estimated number of Viet Minh regular and regional units, and produce a neat comparison which seemed to suggest that the French with their greater mobility enjoyed a substantial advantage. Yet such calculation took no account of Viet Minh guerrillas and of the fact that the strength of the regular and regional Viet Minh forces was almost certainly underestimated. Nor did this reckoning consider the special nature of the war being waged by the Communists. When an American official touring Vietnam in March 1953 asked the French commander in Tonkin, Maj. Gen. Francois Gonzalez de Linares, why he did not take advantage of the French edge in firepower, armor, and air to "deliver a knockout blow," General de Linares replied that the opposing forces in

---

[5]U.S. Assistance Equipment Furnished up to February 1953, Appendix to Field Estimate of French Army Forces, 3 Feb 53, file 370.2, records of MAAG Indochina, RG 334.

[6]Memo, Chief, FE, for Secy of State, 28 Jan 53, sub: Discussions of Indochina Situation With M. Mayer and M. Letourneau, Lot 540190, records of Dept of State.

[7]Evaluation of Military Operations in Indochina, 18 Apr 53, CINCPAC serial 00043, CCS 092 Asia (6 – 25 – 48), sec. 42, BP pt. 9, JCS records.

[8]Field Estimate of Effectiveness of French Union Forces, 3 Feb 53, file 370.2, records of MAAG Indochina.

Tonkin were not really in balance. Although both sides had about ninety maneuver battalions, the Viet Minh had no posts or communication lines to guard. The French were obliged to employ more than two-thirds of their strength to protect their rear areas, leaving only twenty-five battalions for mobile operations.[9]

American observers also tended to err in assessing the French supply and transport system as superior to that of the Viet Minh. In fact, the reverse was true, for the road-bound French supply convoys, with hundreds of trucks constantly exposed to ambush, were far more vulnerable and less flexible than the primitive Viet Minh supply services. The Viet Minh also knew the terrain and had large numbers of laborers and porters who could operate along concealed routes. Despite their trucks, tanks, planes, and helicopters, the French were less mobile in a practical military sense than were the Viet Minh, who could shift entire divisions across vast areas unimpeded and often undetected by the French.

The principal hope for overcoming the deficiencies continued to rest with an indigenous Vietnamese National Army. In commenting on pessimistic reports by American military observers in Vietnam, the counselor of the embassy in Saigon, Robert McClintock, noted that such analyses failed to take into account the potential of that indigenous army. "If we are able to utilize native energies for the liberation of Vietnam," McClintock believed, the military situation would improve. "Once the new native battalions have been trained, we may look with ever-increasing confidence to good performance in the future."[10] But even though the United States in March 1953 formally notified the French government that it would underwrite the light battalion proposal first put forward by General Trapnell in December, conflict between the French and the Vietnamese continued to delay the project.[11] Emperor Bao Dai wanted the new battalions under his personal control, and the French were reluctant to sanction that step. The French in turn complained that the Vietnamese government was dragging its feet in recruiting for the new units. Neither the French nor the Vietnamese could agree on the amount or proper sharing of projected costs.[12] In May the Viet Minh provided a graphic demonstration of the inadequacies of the Vietnamese Army when three companies of Viet Minh troops attacked a training school for cadres at Nam Dinh and captured the entire 600-man student body and all the school weapons without incurring casualties.[13]

[9]Am Embassy, Saigon, to State Dept, 5 Mar 53, 751G.001/3–553, records of Dept of State.

[10]Ltr, McClintock to Frank C. Nash, 10 Apr 53, Incl of Counselor of State Dept (Douglas MacArthur II) to Secy of State, 24 Apr 53, 751G.00/4–2453, records of Dept of State. MacArthur "strongly recommended" that Secretary Dulles read McClintock's letter because it "cast a very interesting light on the way in which our military in Indochina are prone to report."

[11]MFR, R. G. Ferguson, sub: Forty Additional Battalions for Vietnam Army, G–3 091.3 Indochina, RG 319.

[12]Heath to State Dept, 4 Mar 53, 751G.00/3–453, and 9 May 53, 751G.00/5–953, both in records of Dept of State.

[13]Am Consul, Hanoi, to State Dept, 4 May 53, 751G.00/5–453, and 18 May 53, 751G.00/5–1853, both in records of Dept of State.

The Letourneau Plan

Against this backdrop of continued failure and frustration in Vietnam, the Eisenhower administration took up the search for a way out of the impasse. Committed to frugality in government yet also pledged to a vigorous anti-Communist policy in Asia while avoiding any more Korean-style involvements, the new administration could afford, even less than its predecessors, to underwrite a continued stalemate in Vietnam. What American policymakers now required of France was motion, progress, a plan.

They made that fact quite clear to the government of Premier Rene Mayer, which took office in January 1953. To the French government's request for still greater American financial and military aid in Vietnam, Secretary of State Dulles replied that the administration could obtain the additional funds from Congress "only if they were convinced that a sound strategic plan for Indochina existed and would be energetically carried out." The secretary explained that French officials would have to produce a program which would result in "the liquidation of the principal enemy forces within twenty-four months."[14] At the end of March, Mayer came to Washington with Minister for Indochina Jean Letourneau. In a conversation aboard the presidential yacht, *Williamsburg*, President Eisenhower told Mayer "in a very pointed manner" that before the United States could consider providing any additional aid, the French would have to produce a plan which "if it did not lead to complete victory, would, at least, give hope of an ultimate solution."[15]

That American insistence engendered the so-called Letourneau plan, a clever piece of improvisation produced by Letourneau and his staff on the spot in Washington. The plan was divided into three phases. In the first, French and Vietnamese forces would concentrate on securing rear areas, with the most rapid progress expected in central and southern Vietnam. The secure areas would then be occupied by the newly formed light battalions of the Vietnamese National Army. In a second phase, as the situation in the south stabilized, regular French forces would be increasingly concentrated in Tonkin. In the final phase, projected for spring 1955, Franco-Vietnamese forces would take the offensive against the Viet Minh main forces and destroy them. The plan depended on the creation of an effective Vietnamese army of over 120,000 men and on the absence of any devastating new Viet Minh offensives during the two years required to carry out the plan.[16]

A series of oral briefings rather than a formal document, the Letourneau plan was received with mixed feelings by American officials. Ambassador Heath pronounced the plan politically feasible and desirable and predicted that the Viet Minh propaganda advantage would be lost when Vietnamese

[14]Dulles to Am Embassy, Paris, 19 Mar 53, Hist Div, State Dept, Documentary History of U.S. Policy Toward Indochina, doc. D–5.

[15]Notes Made by Assistant Secretary Frank C. Nash of Initial Meeting With French Delegates, Frank C. Nash subject file, RG 330.

[16]Appendix to Incl 1 to JCS 1992/217, 22 Apr 53, Comments Concerning the Proposed French Strategic Plan for the Successful Conclusion of the War in Indochina, CCS 092 Asia, sec. 39, JCS records.

National Army troops finally conquered and controlled the southern region, but the chief of the Military Assistance Advisory Group, General Trapnell, expressed disappointment at the plan's timetable.[17] He believed the plan was too conservative and cautious but warned that the French high command would resist any pressure to modify it. General Trapnell preferred the plan, "slow and expensive" as it was, to the alternative of continued inaction.[18]

For want of anything better, Washington officials were also inclined to accept the Letourneau plan. While finding obvious political drawbacks and questioning whether the Viet Minh would obligingly remain static long enough for the Franco-Vietnamese forces to train and expand, the State Department was willing to go along on the political aspects if the Defense Department found the plan "militarily acceptable."[19] Echoing the objections of General Trapnell and the State Department, the Joint Chiefs of Staff observed that the plan relied excessively on small unit operations but pronounced it "workable." In the privacy of their meeting room the chiefs were considerably more pessimistic. Air Force Chief of Staff General Hoyt S. Vandenberg delivered a scathing critique of French military methods in Vietnam and of their failure to take the Vietnamese into their confidence. Army Chief J. Lawton Collins spoke at length on French shortsightedness in failing to use training methods proved in Korea. General Vandenberg called for "a 100 degree change in French political and military affairs in Indochina" and the dispatch of two additional French divisions to the area.[20]

The proposal to send large-scale French reinforcements to Vietnam, which would have entailed the assignment of conscripts as well as volunteers to duty there, was one long favored by some State Department officials.[21] The French government had considered such a course on at least half a dozen occasions since December 1950. In May 1952 Marshal Juin himself had requested that the Committee of National Defense take up the question. Yet no French government was inclined to face the political consequences of such a decision.[22] The Letourneau plan thus contained no mention of reinforcements.

Lest the French think that the American military was enthusiastic about the Letourneau plan, the Joint Chiefs cautioned the American embassy in Paris to point out that they accepted it only with great reservations.[23] Clearly no one in the American government was really satisfied with the Letourneau plan, and during talks in Paris in April Secretary Dulles told the French

---

[17]Heath to State Dept, 31 Mar 53, Incl to JCS 1992/215, CCS 092 Asia, sec. 39, JCS records.

[18]Views of General T. J. H. Trapnell on the Letourneau Plan, Incl B to JCS 1992/214, 31 Mar 53, CCS 092 Asia, sec. 39, JCS records.

[19]Dept Working Papers, 11 Apr 53, Incl to Philip W. Bonsal to Frank C. Nash, 13 Apr 53, Secy of Defense 091.3 Indochina, RG 330.

[20]Memo, FE Div for Mr. Matthews, 4 May 53, sub: Evaluation by the Joint Chiefs of Staff of the Letourneau Plan for Military Operations in Indochina, Lot 58D207, records of Dept of State.

[21]Memo, Philip W. Bonsal for Douglas MacArthur II, 20 Apr 53, Lot 58D207, records of Dept of State.

[22]Note d'information: Le recours au contingent, French Documents file, CMH.

[23]State Dept to Embassy, Paris, 24 Apr 53, records of Dept of State.

frankly that the Letourneau plan was not the type of dynamic program that would convince a skeptical Congress.[24]

A new sense of crisis developed in mid-April 1953 when three Viet Minh divisions invaded neighboring Laos, which until then had been a backwater in the war. By the end of the month the royal capital of Luang Prabang was partially surrounded, and French strongpoints at Muong Khoua and on the Plain of Jars were isolated. In early May the Viet Minh suddenly withdrew, leaving the French and Laotians badly shaken and Laotian Communist followers of Prince Souphanouvong encouraged and strengthened. The Laos invasion reinforced the American conviction that the French were foundering. The president's special assistant for National Security Affairs, Charles D. Jackson, told the National Security Council that until the invasion the president "had imagined that in due course, however slowly, the French would overcome their enemies. This confidence is now shattered." The president believed that if Laos were lost, the rest of Southeast Asia would follow and "the gateway to India would be opened."[25] Counselor Robert McClintock wrote from Saigon that the time had arrived to "tell our French friends very frankly what we think ought to be done by them if they are to receive the added aid they want. The new administration has every right . . . to demand that new conditions be met."[26] The administration was preparing to do precisely that. Eisenhower was convinced that "two and only two developments would really save the situation in French Indochina." The first was an official statement from the French government guaranteeing independence to the Associated States as soon as the fighting in Vietnam ended. The second was a dynamic new leader. Most of the French generals in Vietnam "struck the President as a poor lot."[27]

In early May 1953 Eisenhower addressed a frank letter to the American ambassador in France, C. Douglas Dillon, for delivery to Premier Mayer. Except for a word or two, the first portion of the letter could have been written by Dean Acheson. It repeated the same demand American officials had been making since early 1950: France must grant real independence to Vietnam. The president called on the French government to make a "clear and unequivocal public announcement . . . that France seeks self-rule for Indochina and that practical political freedom will be an accomplished fact as soon as victory against the communists is won." If the first portion of the president's letter held no surprise for the French, the second part may have caused some raised eyebrows. Eisenhower urged Mayer to appoint a new commander in chief for Indochina, a "forceful and inspirational leader" in the tradition of de Lattre. Eisenhower recommended either Lt. Gen. Jean E.

---

[24]First Session, Bipartite U.S.-French Conversations, 22 Apr 53, Hist Div, State Dept, Documentary History of U.S. Policy Toward Indochina, doc. D–13.

[25]Min, 141st Meeting of the National Security Council (NSC), 28 Apr 53, C. D. Jackson Papers, Eisenhower Library.

[26]Ltr, McClintock to Douglas MacArthur II, 21 Apr 53, 751G.00/4–2153, records of Dept of State.

[27]Min, 143d Meeting of the NSC, 3 May 53, Eisenhower-as-President Papers, Eisenhower Library.

Valluy, who had long experience in Indochina and was the officer responsible for the bloody bombardment of Haiphong in 1946, or General Augustin Guillaume, who had commanded French occupation troops in Germany and was then inspector of French forces in North Africa.[28]

Yet even as the president's message arrived in Paris, the French government was announcing the name of the new commander for Vietnam: Lt. Gen. Henri Navarre. Navarre was probably on no American list of candidates for the Indochina command— U.S. officers who had known him in NATO claimed that he was unaggressive, lacked organizational ability, and was inclined to vacillate. One general even believed that Navarre

General Navarre

had been appointed to give the French government a scapegoat for anticipated failures in Indochina.[29] A relatively junior lieutenant general, Navarre had been serving as chief of staff to Marshal Alphonse Juin, commander of NATO forces in Central Europe. He had never served in Vietnam, but Paris considered that "absence of prejudice toward operations in Indochina" as something of an asset.[30] Having spent a number of years in pacification campaigns in Morocco and Syria, he was considered an expert on counterguerrilla operations. While the choice of Navarre failed to impress American officials, there was a general feeling that any change would probably be for the better, and that the choice of a new commander was far less important than the adoption of an aggressive, systematic program to bring the war to a successful conclusion.

During the Eisenhower-Mayer talks in March, the latter had invited the United States to send a military mission to Indochina to look into the French requirements for additional aid. When the Joint Chiefs of Staff met in late May 1953 to discuss sending such a mission, they agreed that it should be headed by an Army general and selected Lt. Gen. John W. O'Daniel, then commander of the U.S. Army, Pacific, and a veteran of combat in North Africa, Italy, France, and Korea. The choice was particularly apt in that O'Daniel was recommended by the Commander in Chief, Pacific, Admiral Arthur W. Radford, whose headquarters would have to support the mission.

---

[28]Eisenhower to C. Douglas Dillon, 7 May 53, 751G.00/5–753, records of Dept of State.

[29]Memo, Acting ACofS G–2 for CofSA, 20 May 53, sub: Personality and Character Assessment of Lt Gen Henri Navarre, records of ACSI.

[30]Bernard B. Fall, *Hell in a Very Small Place: The Siege of Dien Bien Phu* (New York: J. B. Lippincott Co., 1967), p. 29.

Other members of the mission were to be named by the various services.[31]

The instructions drawn up for General O'Daniel clearly showed that the Joint Chiefs intended the mission as far more than a survey of French military requirements. O'Daniel was to gain "sufficient detailed knowledge of French military plans to acquaint U.S. leaders thoroughly with the plan of future conduct of the war in Indochina, the chances for ultimate victory," as well as the progress made in developing indigenous forces and strengthening the French Expeditionary Forces. He was to impress upon the French the necessity for "revision and aggressive implementation of [their] military plans for successfully concluding the war in Indochina," expanding and modernizing their training facilities, and accelerating the transfer of responsible military leadership to the Associated States.[32]

Essentially, the Joint Chiefs wanted General O'Daniel to make an overall judgment as to whether the French had a chance of succeeding in Vietnam. Although never explicitly stated, that requirement was reflected throughout the instructions. One paragraph, for example, requested the chief of mission's comments on whether the "scheduled build-up of Associated States forces during 1953 and 1954 . . . together with existing French forces [would] be sufficient to accomplish the decisive defeat of the Viet Minh by 1955."[33] There was no indication of what might happen should the mission return with a negative report.[34]

The O'Daniel mission arrived in Saigon on 20 June 1953, exactly a month after General Navarre had assumed command. Unlike O'Daniel, a hard-driving combat soldier whose nickname, "Iron Mike," testified to his toughness and tenacity in three wars, Navarre had made his reputation mainly as a staff officer. While O'Daniel was forthright and blunt (as military attache in Russia, he once told reporters that Moscow resembled "a vast slum"), Navarre was known for reticence and inscrutability.[35] A friendly writer noted that Navarre preferred to work alone and had "kept from the years he spent in intelligence the respect for secrecy and a taste for mystery."[36] A critic observed that "physically and morally he was a cat. . . . With him everything took place in the mind."[37] Yet for all the differences in temperament between O'Daniel and Navarre, the two almost immediately established a friendly relationship.

---

[31]MFR, Joint Secretariat, 29 May 53, CCS 092 Asia (6 – 25 – 48), sec. 42, JCS records. Lt. Gen. Robert C. Taber, at the time assistant Army attache in Saigon, observed: "I do not believe the choice was apt! They were sending an outstanding field soldier with no diplomatic or linguistic ability into a sophisticated arena where even the people immersed in the operation had a hard time understanding it." Marginal Comments by Gen Taber on Draft Manuscript, Incl to Ltr, Lt Gen Robert C. Taber to Chief of Military History, 10 Oct 79, Historians files, CMH.

[32]Proposed Terms of Reference for the Chief of the U.S. Military Mission to Indochina, 10 Jun 53, *U.S.-Vietnam Relations*, 9:61 – 62.

[33]Ibid., 9:66.

[34]Interv, author with John W. O'Daniel, 4 – 5 Feb 75, Historians files, CMH.

[35]John W. O'Daniel Obituary, *Washington Post*, 29 Mar 75.

[36]Max Olivier, "Portrait du General Navarre," *Indochine – Sud-Est Asiatique*, February 1954, p. 83.

[37]Jules Roy, *The Battle of Dien Bien Phu* (New York: Harper & Row, 1965), pp. 6 – 7.

At O'Daniel's urging and with his assistance Navarre prepared an aggressive new concept for the conduct of operations in Indochina, soon to become known as the Navarre plan. Navarre proposed "taking the initiative immediately" in local attacks, with a full-scale offensive to follow in September 1953. In the interim, rear-area units in static defensive positions were to be consolidated into a mobile striking force and maneuver battalions combined into regiments and divisions. The Vietnamese National Army was to be trained and equipped at an accelerated pace and given progressively greater responsibility in the conduct of operations.[38] As the American mission traveled throughout Vietnam, O'Daniel became convinced that Navarre and his principal commanders were determined "to see this war through to success at an early date." He detected an "increased aggressiveness in attitude" and a greater receptivity to American ideas and suggestions. O'Daniel returned home convinced that Navarre had "brought a new aggressive psychology to the war" and that the United States should "henceforth . . . think in terms of the 'Navarre concept' in association with the war in Indochina."[39]

Others were less optimistic. Throughout O'Daniel's visit the service attaches and CIA representatives attempted to correct what they believed to be the excessively favorable picture the French had been painting for his benefit. "You may ask why we didn't convince him," a former Army attache later wrote. "Naturally a three-star general is more inclined to believe a friendly nation's four-star [sic] general who is in the midst of fighting a war."[40] Although agreeing with O'Daniel that the Navarre concept of operations appeared sound and in keeping with French capabilities, Admiral Radford cautioned that only the test of actual performance would show whether the reported new aggressive attitude really existed. Radford nevertheless recommended that the United States give France "full and positive support."[41]

For the moment the outlook appeared unusually promising, for in late June 1953 a new French government headed by Premier Joseph Laniel took office pledged to prosecute the war to an early and successful conclusion. The new premier swept old hands from the government's Indochina agencies and embraced the Navarre plan as the official blueprint for victory. Laniel even agreed to send reinforcements from France to bolster Navarre's striking power. To the Associated States the French promised to "perfect their independence" within the French Union by giving them wider authority in military, political, financial, and legal affairs.[42]

[38]Report of U.S. Joint Mission to Indochina, Lt Gen John W. O'Daniel Thru CINCPAC to JCS, 14 Jul 53 (hereafter cited as O'Daniel Report), *U.S.-Vietnam Relations*, 9:69.
[39]Ibid., 9:96.
[40]Marginal Comments by Gen Taber on Draft Manuscript, Incl to Ltr, Taber to Chief of Military History, 10 Oct 79.
[41]Ltr, CINCPAC to JCS, 22 Jul 53, CCS 092 Asia, sec. 44, JCS records.
[42]Hammer, *The Struggle for Indochina*, pp. 301–02.

Financing the French

A merican leaders were finally dealing with a government that seemed to have the determination to fight the war to a decisive conclusion, a plan for doing so, and a commitment to real independence for the states of Indochina. The French reinforcements, the Navarre plan, and the accelerated buildup of the Vietnamese forces contemplated by the Laniel government, however, would all cost American money. At the end of July, Laniel told Ambassador Dillon that France would require an additional $400 million in aid for Indochina over the next year.[43]

Washington leaders felt they had no choice but to go along. As the State Department noted, the armistice just concluded in Korea would undoubtedly increase the pressure on the French government for a negotiated settlement in Vietnam, which, in the American view, "would mean the eventual loss to Communism not only of Indo-China but of the whole of Southeast Asia." A French withdrawal from Indochina would leave the United States with the unwelcome alternatives of either assuming the French burden or facing the certain loss of this critical area. The Laniel government was "almost certainly the *last* French government which would undertake to continue the war in Indo-China."[44] On 5 August 1953 the State Department recommended approval of the $400 million increase, and the next day the National Security Council endorsed the additional funds "providing the Department of State, the Foreign Operations Administration, and the Joint Chiefs of Staff were willing to affirm that the French program held promise of success and could be implemented."[45] The Joint Chiefs of Staff were inclined to concur. After expressing the usual cautions concerning past French performance and the need for close liaison "together with friendly but firm encouragement and advice," the Joint Chiefs declared that "if vigorously pursued militarily in Indochina and supported politically in France, the Navarre concept offers a promise of success sufficient to warrant appropriate additional U.S. aid."[46]

Secretary of Defense Charles E. Wilson was about to submit the views of the Joint Chiefs to the State Department when, near the end of August 1953, disquieting news arrived from Vietnam. General Trapnell and the three service attaches reported that the French apparently had no plans for implementing the large-scale autumn offensive called for in the Navarre plan. The reorganization of the French battalions into larger units was "still in the planning stages," and the reinforcements from France had amounted not to two divisions, as General O'Daniel had hoped, but to a few infantry battalions. There was also no sense of urgency in the training of senior Vietnamese commanders and staff officers, and no French military assistance advisory group had yet materialized.[47]

[43]Dillon to State Dept, 29 Jul 53, 751G.00/7 – 2953, records of Dept of State.
[44]Memo, Dept of State for National Security Council, 5 Aug 53, sub: Further United States Support for France and the Associated States of Indochina, *U.S.-Vietnam Relations,* 9:128.
[45]History of Indochina Incident, p. 284.
[46]Memo, Chairman, JCS, for Secy of Defense, 11 Aug 53, sub: The Navarre Concept for Operations in Indochina, *U.S.-Vietnam Relations,* 9:134 – 35.
[47]Msg, Trapnell to CINCPAC, DAIN 299535, 24 Aug 53, G – 3 091 Indochina, RG 319. General

Trapnell reported further that the French were showing as little enthusiasm as ever about adopting U.S. training methods. French officers and instructors had repeatedly visited American training schools in South Korea, where, the Americans believed, results were obvious. Still, they remained unconvinced that the Americans had anything to teach them in Vietnam. Although the chief of the French general staff, Marshal Juin, returned from South Korea with high praise for "the magnificent effort in training the ROK [Republic of Korea] divisions," he doubted that the school method was applicable in Vietnam since the Vietnamese could hardly hope to recruit and train troops on the scale of the United States in South Korea.[48] A joint American – South Korean team that visited the French training centers in Vietnam reported that the centers were operating at a very limited capacity by U.S. standards and that the basic training provided to the Vietnamese was insufficient. Because the classes were not staggered, the centers could take fewer students. Observing that the wars in Vietnam and in Korea had little in common, they noted that "Vietnamese political and military leaders have not yet developed the same intense desire to eradicate" the enemy as had the Koreans.[49]

Even as those disquieting reports were being received, new members were appointed to the Joint Chiefs of Staff, including General Matthew B. Ridgway as the chief of staff of the Army, Admiral Robert B. Carney as chief of naval operations, and Admiral Radford as chairman. Confronted with the reports from Vietnam and just returned from duty as Commander in Chief, Pacific, and United Nations commander in South Korea, respectively, Radford and Ridgway may have been more skeptical about the Navarre plan than were their predecessors. In any case, the new Joint Chiefs withdrew the earlier endorsement of the plan and submitted an even more cautious memorandum for forwarding to the State Department. They declared that military success in Indochina depended on "creating a political climate in the country which will provide the incentive for [the] natives to support the French and supply them with adequate intelligence." Noting French lassitude in implementing their plan as reported by General Trapnell, the Joint Chiefs recommended that additional U.S. support be made contingent upon actual French performance and French willingness to take and act upon American military advice.[50]

Yet the United States still had no acceptable alternative to supporting the French. If a negotiated settlement of the war was intolerable, then the only choice was to bankroll the Navarre plan and hope for the best. On 1 September the French government formally submitted its request for $385 million in additional aid, and a week later the National Security Council recommended

O'Daniel had particularly stressed the importance of divisions which "endowed with a divisional concept of teamwork, continuity, impetus, and employment of artillery could provide the military balance to assure an early victory. . . . I feel that any addition other than in divisional organization would be in error." O'Daniel Report, *U.S.-Vietnam Relations*, 9:76.

[48]Heath to State Dept, 4 Mar 53.

[49]Report of U.S.-ROK Training Mission to Indochina, 17 Apr 53, G – 3 091 Indochina, RG 319.

[50]Memo, Radford for Secy of Defense, 28 Aug 53, sub: The Navarre Concept for Operations in Indochina, *U.S.-Vietnam Relations*, 9:140 – 41.

Generals Hinh and Taylor *during Hinh's visit to observe U.S. training of Korean armed forces.*

to the president that the request be met, subject to a French promise to pursue the Navarre plan vigorously and to grant real independence to the Associated States.[51] At the end of the month the president approved the expenditure. Since Congress had already adjourned and a request for a supplemental appropriation seemed politically unwise, the administration shifted funds to Indochina from other foreign assistance programs.

The president's decision to divert funds to the new French assistance program touched off an immediate reaction by individual congressmen, many of whom expressed concern over the effect that this diversion would have on NATO military posture. Some congressional leaders doubted that the administration would be able to persuade Congress to appropriate the large amounts of money necessary to finance the Navarre plan in 1954 and 1955. Congressman John W. McCormack of Massachusetts, a Democratic leader in the House of Representatives, expressed concern that if the Navarre plan failed the United States might be obliged to deploy troops to Indochina. Although

---

[51]Further U.S. Support for Operations in Indochina, NSC 161st Meeting, 9 Sep 53, Item 2; Dulles to Am Embassy, Paris, 9 Sep 53. Both in *U.S.-Vietnam Relations*, 9:144–49 and 150, respectively.

McCormack agreed to back the plan in the House, he trusted the administration realized it was a calculated risk.[52]

Just how risky the commitment to the Navarre plan might be was revealed by another military setback in Vietnam during the autumn of 1953. The French had launched a special operation to clear Bui Chu in Tonkin in order to install a number of Vietnamese light battalions as regional security troops. They then turned over responsibility for the sector to the Vietnamese National Army. Soon afterward regular and regional Viet Minh forces from two neighboring provinces attacked. With little artillery support and no radio communications, the inexperienced Vietnamese battalions were badly mauled. By October the military situation had so deteriorated that the French were obliged to resume control of the province.[53] There were mutual recriminations. The Vietnamese Army commander, General Nguyen Van Van, maintained that the light battalions had been forced to stand up to regular Viet Minh units, something they had never been designed to do. In any case, the episode badly tarnished the reputation of the light battalions.

Political developments were also discouraging. The Vietnamese National Congress, apparently taking literally the French invitation to "perfect independence," in October refused to have any further dealings with France under the existing system and demanded that Vietnam be allowed to leave the French Union.[54] That action aroused widespread indignation in France, making it again apparent that, despite talk of protecting Vietnam from communism, the main French objective remained the preservation of French interests.

Yet if the American commitment to the Navarre plan was to make sense, that fact had to be resolutely denied. American leaders had to believe, as Dulles told the American Legion in September 1953, that Vietnam was "no longer a French colony but [a country] where complete independence is now in the making."[55] The refusal to acknowledge that France was in Vietnam to advance national ends rather than to stop communism led inevitably to a reluctance to accept that France would quit Indochina not when communism was vanquished but when the French had concluded that the sacrifices outweighed the gains.

The Second O'Daniel Visit

At the time of General O'Daniel's first visit to Vietnam, General Navarre and other French officers had repeatedly encouraged him to return in a few months "to witness the progress we will have made," and on 6 Novem-

---

[52]Memo, John H. Ohly for Director, FAO, 17 Sep 53, sub: Congressional Reaction to the Indochina Program, OMA Indochina file, RG 330.

[53]Am Consul, Hanoi (Paul J. Sturm), to State Dept, 14 Oct 53, 751G.00/10−1453, records of Dept of State.

[54]Ibid.

[55]Address by the Honorable John Foster Dulles, Secretary of State, Before the American Legion at Kiel Auditorium, St. Louis, Missouri, Wednesday, 2 September 1953, *U.S.-Vietnam Relations*, 9:142.

ber 1953 he arrived in Saigon for a second look.[56] Concluding that the Red River Delta was the vital battlefield, O'Daniel urged General Navarre to seal off the delta by establishing numerous small, mutually supporting posts along a perimeter, which would be completely wired in and controlled by fire from the posts.[57] Navarre replied that he had considered such a plan but had concluded that he had insufficient means to seal off the delta and at the same time take the offensive against the enemy's main forces.

Despite that negative response, General O'Daniel found reason for optimism. A mobile striking force was being formed in Tonkin, and activation of the light battalions was proceeding. The French, O'Daniel believed, "have established a far better situation than existed during the last dry season."[58] He was also pleased that General Navarre had agreed to accept four American officers on his staff. Since they would be working at the French operations center, O'Daniel hoped the Americans would be able to improve liaison with the French and to exert some influence on the staff.[59] Navarre also agreed to a small increase in the Military Assistance Advisory Group.

To provide the advisory group with a tactical intelligence capability to compensate for what the Americans considered unreliable French intelligence, Navarre allowed the group to bring in a combat intelligence detachment, a step for which General Trapnell had been seeking approval for several months.[60] Detachment P, 8533d Army Attache Unit (Special Foreign Assignment), arrived in Hanoi in December 1953. The unit consisted of 4 officers and 9 enlisted men, employed 7 Vietnamese, and operated directly under the Assistant Chief of Staff for Intelligence in Washington. Its mission was to obtain such data on Viet Minh forces as unit histories, prisoner of war interrogation reports, and logistical capabilities estimates, as well as information on any Chinese units or individuals operating with the Viet Minh.[61]

Although French concessions had been few, General O'Daniel returned to Washington with his basic faith in French leadership unimpaired. "We should fully support General Navarre, in whose success we have such a large stake," said O'Daniel.[62] Only later would O'Daniel conclude that his assessment was overoptimistic and that he had been misled by an impressive show of energy and activity probably staged for his benefit.[63] But by the fall of 1953 few other American military officials were willing to go along completely with such an optimistic report. The Commander in Chief, Pacific, Admiral Felix Stump, for example, "agreed in general" but warned that ultimate victory could not be achieved until sufficient Vietnamese forces were available to establish effective

[56]O'Daniel Report, *U.S.-Vietnam Relations*, 9:71.

[57]Progress Report on Military Situation in Indochina, 19 Nov 53, Appendix to Incl A, JCS 1992/260, CCS 092 Asia, sec. 52, JCS records.

[58]Ibid.

[59]Interv, author with O'Daniel, 4 Feb 75.

[60]Memo, N. E. Halaby for Under Secy of Army, 25 Apr 53, sub: Combat Intelligence Detachment to U.S. Army Attache, Indochina, OSA 340.09 Indochina, RG 319.

[61]Memo, Under Secy of Army (Earl D. Johnson) for ASD (ISA), sub: Combat Intelligence Section, G–3 091 Indochina, RG 319.

[62]Progress Report on Military Situation in Indochina, 19 Nov 53.

[63]Interv, author with O'Daniel, 4 Feb 75.

control of cleared areas and until "the native population has been won over by anti-communist psychological warfare." Admiral Stump also hoped that French and American political leaders would once again reaffirm their determination to prosecute the war to a successful conclusion.[64]

One U.S. Army observer, Brig. Gen. Paul W. Caraway, a member of the Joint Staff who accompanied Vice President Richard M. Nixon on a fact-finding tour to Southeast Asia soon after O'Daniel returned, would not accept even Admiral Stump's measured optimism. "Navarre talks," observed Caraway, "but there is nothing stirring at the grass roots." Caraway reported that the French had failed to free any appreciable number of battalions from static defense duties, that 60 percent of the Red River Delta was under Viet Minh control, and that the French were hard put even to maintain communications with outlying regions. "After dark," said Caraway, "the French hold only Hanoi and Haiphong." The only French operation of any size then under way had failed to make contact with major enemy units.[65] The sizable Vietnamese forces called for in the Navarre plan did not exist, and the competence of those operating with the French was so marginal as to pose a hazard to the French troops. "The French are not interested in producing indigenous forces," observed Caraway; their training system for the Vietnamese was unsatisfactory, yet they had no wish for the United States to exercise any responsibility for training.

The U.S. Army attache in Saigon, Col. Leo W. H. Shaughnessey, was as blunt as General Caraway, declaring that after six months of the Navarre plan the French were still on the defensive and appeared unlikely to change.[66] The assistant chief of staff for intelligence generally agreed with Shaughnessey's findings and pointed out that other high U.S. officials had also found the O'Daniel report too optimistic.[67]

When the Joint Strategic Plans Committee prepared an indorsement of the O'Daniel report for signature by the Joint Chiefs which noted "real military progress" in Vietnam and concluded that "prospects for victory are increasingly encouraging," General Ridgway opposed such unqualified acceptance. Reflecting the views of the Army staff, Ridgway objected to statements that the French Union forces had "wrested the initiative from the enemy" and wanted the Joint Chiefs to point out explicitly that the entire O'Daniel report was "overly optimistic." Although the Joint Chiefs declined to use that phrase, they agreed at Ridgway's insistence to state that military progress had been "limited" and that development of a large and effective indigenous force and a psychological warfare capability remained indispensable requirements for French victory.[68]

[64]Msg, CINCPAC to CNO, DAIN 25651, 2 Dec 53, CCS 092 Asia (6–25–48), sec. 5, BP pt. 10, JCS records.
[65]Ltr, Caraway to CofSA, 23 Nov 53, G–3 091 Indochina, RG 319.
[66]*U.S.-Vietnam Relations*, vol. 1, pt. II, sec. II.A.2, p. A–39.
[67]ACSI to CofSA, 17 Dec 53, sub: Critique of French Operations in Indochina, G–3 091 Indochina, RG 319.
[68]Memo, CofSA, 19 Dec 55, sub: O'Daniel Report, JSPC 148/1400, CCS 092 Asia, sec. 57, JCS records.

Dien Bien Phu

As American leaders debated progress under the Navarre plan, the ultimate fate of that plan and of the entire French campaign in Vietnam was
about to be decided. On 20 November 1953, 3,000 French paratroopers
descended upon a broad valley in the Tai country close to the Laotian frontier
near a village called Dien Bien Phu. The precise reasons behind the French
decision to occupy and hold Dien Bien Phu remain obscure. General Navarre
later justified the operation as necessary to defend northern Laos against a
renewed Viet Minh invasion, but the French commander in Tonkin, Maj.
Gen. Rene Cogny considered Dien Bien Phu useful only as a guerrilla base
for Tai partisans operating against the Viet Minh in northwestern Tonkin and
Laos.[69] French leaders sometimes spoke of Dien Bien Phu as bait to lure the
Viet Minh into a costly confrontation like the one at Na San in November
1952. General O'Daniel later observed that Navarre might have been influenced by the example of American "killer" operations in Korea, in which a
unit would be purposely exposed to attack in order to draw the enemy into
the range of American artillery. In the case of Dien Bien Phu, however,
O'Daniel saw the idea as entirely inappropriate.[70]

Reports of American observers reflected the French confusion about the
real purposes of the Dien Bien Phu operation. A day after the assault on the
valley, General Navarre assured Ambassador Heath that "there is no intention of establishing a new Na San at Dien Bien Phu" but rather a "base for
positive and offensive operations."[71] In December General Cogny confided to
the American consul at Hanoi that he would "be surprised" if the enemy
could maintain more than two divisions in the Tai country. In fact, during the
next two months the Viet Minh were to move four infantry divisions and an
artillery division into the country around Dien Bien Phu. Cogny confidently
asserted that the commander at Dien Bien Phu, Col. Christian de Castries,
could be counted on "to seize the initiative and not remain behind defensive
positions."[72]

The French consulted neither General Trapnell nor any other member of
the American advisory group before the operation. Nor was there at first any
particular American concern about the action—no one saw it as the beginning
of the decisive phase of the French struggle for Vietnam. The U.S. Army's
assistant chief of staff for intelligence, for example, considered it simply
another French operation designed to keep the enemy off balance while the
mobile striking force was being assembled in the Red River Delta.[73]

Yet by January 1954 the Military Assistance Advisory Group was becoming

---

[69]Fall, *Hell in a Very Small Place*, pp. 34–35; Rene Cogny, "La Libre Confession du General
Cogny," *L'Express*, 6 December 1963.

[70]Interv, author with O'Daniel, 3 Feb 75.

[71]Heath to State Dept, 23 Nov 53, 751G.00/11–2353, records of Dept of State.

[72]Am Consul, Hanoi (Sturm), to State Dept, 10 Dec 53, 751G.00/12–1053, records of Dept of
State.

[73]Memo, ACofS G–2 for CofSA, 17 Dec 53, sub: Critique of French Operations in Indochina,
G–3 091 Indochina, RG 319.

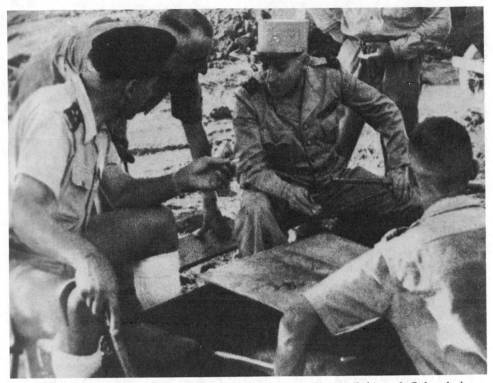

General Navarre *(right) confers with General Cogny (left) and Colonel de Castries (center).*

concerned. General Trapnell warned that the French at Dien Bien Phu were in serious danger. Since the French forces were "operating from an inferior defensive position, facing an enemy battle corps stronger by at least one division," and depending entirely upon "overtaxed air facilities" for resupply, he gave them only a fifty-fifty chance of surviving.[74] Trapnell was alarmed about the overall military situation as well. If the French saw their forces at Dien Bien Phu as a barrier to renewed invasion of Laos, they were mistaken, for in December 1953 the Viet Minh had returned to Laos, and General Trapnell considered that "the present situation bears a striking resemblance to last year's pattern in which the campaign season found the French in widely scattered defensive positions." They had again lost the initiative and were being seriously threatened not only at Dien Bien Phu but also in Laos and along the Red River.[75]

General Navarre meanwhile had begun to complain about delays in deliveries of American materiel and to charge that the Military Assistance Advisory Group had modified or reduced his requests for aid before forwarding them to Washington. "I cannot accept having my potential whittled away

[74]Msg, Trapnell to CINCPAC, Jan 54, G-3 091 Indochina, RG 319.
[75]Ltr, Trapnell to CINCPAC, 2 Jan 54, copy in Historians files, CMH.

in such a manner," protested Navarre in an indignant letter to General Trapnell.[76] American officials hastened to reassure Navarre and even arranged for certain items programmed for fiscal year 1954 to be delivered ahead of schedule. But they believed that Navarre was actually trying to document excuses for his probable failure to meet the goals of the Navarre plan during the coming year.[77]

Such skepticism about France's chances of success was not yet evident in Washington. NSC policy paper 177, United States Objectives and Courses of Action With Respect to Southeast Asia, which President Eisenhower approved on 16 January 1954, still reflected an essentially optimistic assessment of the overall military situation. "With continued U.S. economic and material assistance," the paper stated, "the Franco-Vietnamese forces are not in danger of being militarily defeated by the Viet Minh."[78] Eisenhower nevertheless remained markedly concerned about the situation in Vietnam. He told officials of the State and Defense Departments on 16 January 1954 that he saw no alternative to continued support for the Navarre plan; at the same time he emphasized the need to do everything possible to improve the French effort. The president ventured the opinion that if a distinguished American officer, such as General James A. Van Fleet, former United Nations commander in South Korea, could be sent to Vietnam in some capacity, it might enable the United States to exert more influence on French operations. In the end he appointed a Special Committee on Indochina, composed of CIA Director Allen W. Dulles, Under Secretary of State Walter Bedell Smith, Deputy Secretary of Defense Roger M. Kyes, Admiral Radford, and Special Assistant for National Security Charles D. Jackson.

Beginning deliberations at the end of January, the Special Committee produced a number of recommendations. It suggested forming a volunteer American air group to operate in Vietnam much as the "Flying Tigers" had served Chiang Kai-shek's government early in World War II, assigning more CIA operatives to Vietnam, and providing aid to the Associated States to help them develop an unconventional warfare capability.[79] The committee also recommended modifying and expanding the duties of the Military Assistance Advisory Group to include at least some involvement in training the Vietnamese and advising the French, and stationing General O'Daniel, then on a third inspection visit to Vietnam, in Saigon as a kind of informal strategic adviser to Navarre on matters of operations and training.[80] The French requests for additional military aid, the committee suggested, might be used to induce the French to agree to "maximum collaboration [with

[76]Msg, Trapnell to OSD for OMA, DAIN 27618, 19 Dec 53, G – 3 091 Indochina, RG 319.
[77]History of Indochina Incident, p. 327; Heath to State Dept, 27 Dec 53, 751G.00/12 – 2753, records of Dept of State.
[78]*U.S.-Vietnam Relations*, 9:225.
[79]Special Committee Rpt: Program for Securing Military Victory in Indochina Short of Overt Involvement of U.S. Combat Forces, NSC 1019a, no. 53, 10 Mar 54, copy in PSYWAR 091 Indochina.
[80]MFR, Brig Gen C. H. Bonesteel III, 30 Jan 54, sub: Meeting of President's Special Committee on Indochina, 29 Jan 54, *U.S.-Vietnam Relations*, 9:240 – 44.

O'Daniel] in training and strategy." The committee agreed that General O'Daniel's position should be reinforced "in every way possible . . . not only with the French in Indochina but also at the highest level in Paris."[81] To ensure that O'Daniel stay in Vietnam, the committee wanted him to succeed General Trapnell, who was due for rotation, as chief of the Military Assistance Advisory Group. Such a move would require no clearance by the French government.

Despite the evident resolve of American policymakers, this bid to use American aid to increase U.S. influence in Vietnam proved no more successful than earlier attempts to exercise leverage on the French. From Saigon General O'Daniel reported that Navarre had no interest in any permanent American "superadviser." At most, the French commander would agree to increase the number of American liaison officers at his headquarters from four to five and to allow periodic visits by O'Daniel. Soon afterward Navarre told Ambassador Heath that he "wanted it clearly understood" that he would accept O'Daniel only if "his attributes did not exceed those of Trapnell" and that his functions would be "limited to military assistance without any powers," advisory or otherwise, in the conduct and planning of operations or in the training of the Vietnamese National Army.[82] In addition, the French government let it be known that if O'Daniel were to be appointed chief of the advisory group, he would have to accept a reduction from lieutenant general to major general so as not to be the equal in rank of Navarre.

The President's Special Committee had consulted neither General Ridgway nor the other Joint Chiefs about O'Daniel's proposed assignment, and when Ridgway learned of the proposed reduction in rank, he objected strongly. He believed it would be "distinctly detrimental to prestige of the United States military services in general and to the United States Army in particular to demote a distinguished senior Army officer" merely to salve the pride of the French. Moreover, Ridgway pointed out, there was no indication that the French intended to accord to the Military Assistance Advisory Group the increased authority that the Special Committee contemplated.[83] Agreeing with General Ridgway, the Joint Chiefs of Staff urged that "the basic issue of increased responsibility of MAAG, Indochina, with respect to training be satisfactorily resolved" with the French.[84] But when the American embassy in Paris approached the French government concerning General O'Daniel's status, the French remained adamant.[85]

Thus the attempt to trade aid for increased influence in the person of General O'Daniel came to naught, as had all other attempts before it. But by early 1954 the political and military position of France was so delicate and changeable, the possibility that France might opt for a negotiated settlement

[81]Ibid., 9:242.

[82]Heath to State Dept, 21 Feb 54, 751G.00/2–2154, records of Dept of State.

[83]Memo, Ridgway for ACofS, 25 Feb 54, sub: Demotion of General O'Daniel, CSA 091 Indochina, RG 319.

[84]Memo, Radford for Secy of Defense, 5 Mar 54, sub: Reappraisal of General O'Daniel's Status With Respect to Indochina, *U.S.-Vietnam Relations*, 9:264–65.

[85]History of Indochina Incident, p. 358.

so likely, that American officials again decided they had no choice but to go along with whatever Navarre wanted. At a meeting in Berlin with Britain, France, and Russia, the United States reluctantly agreed to participate in a conference in Geneva at the end of April to discuss the two Koreas and Vietnam. Dulles and other officials feared that France might use that opportunity to end the burden of the Indochina War even by making a settlement favorable to the Communists.

Meanwhile, General O'Daniel, on his third visit to Vietnam, had received little information about Washington's plans and unsuccessful efforts to install him as a special adviser in Vietnam. O'Daniel considered that he was merely replacing General Trapnell as chief of the Military Assistance Advisory Group. Never a stickler for form, he graciously accepted his "demotion" as necessary to assuage French pride.[86] When General O'Daniel left Washington in mid-January it had seemed that he might not even be granted an audience with Navarre, who pled preoccupation with visitors from Paris and suggested that a trip by O'Daniel "was not advisable politically."[87] Still, O'Daniel had decided to proceed with the mission. During a stopover in the Philippines, O'Daniel received word from Trapnell that Navarre was still unwilling to meet with him. O'Daniel then dispatched a personal message to Navarre emphasizing the desirability of a meeting, but he had received no reply when he left the Philippines for Saigon. Only upon his arrival did Navarre send a letter agreeing to a meeting two days later.[88]

When O'Daniel met with Navarre at his Saigon headquarters on 28 January, Navarre was cordial and apologetic about the delays in arranging the meeting. He explained that having O'Daniel in Saigon except as chief of the advisory group would be too awkward politically, but he would be agreeable to having O'Daniel visit Saigon regularly, perhaps every four to six weeks. He reiterated his approval of the assignment of five Americans to his command as "special liaison officers," two with his training command and one each with headquarters of the French Army, Navy, and Air Force. General O'Daniel came away hopeful that the liaison officers might serve as "a means of influencing French conduct of the war."[89] O'Daniel also remained optimistic about the general military situation. The Viet Minh, he reported, had "been blocked in all their moves by General Navarre and do not have the strength for a sustained effort." The military situation was "well in hand and will improve rapidly."[90]

On the afternoon of 3 February, General O'Daniel visited Dien Bien Phu for a briefing by Colonel de Castries and his staff. O'Daniel accepted Navarre's explanation that Dien Bien Phu was a blocking base astride the main invasion route to Laos and that French forces in the base could maneu-

[86]Interv, author with O'Daniel, 4 Feb 75.
[87]Memo, O'Daniel for JCS, 5 Feb 54, sub: Report of U.S. Special Mission to Indochina, p. 1, O'Daniel Papers, CMH.
[88]Ibid., p. 5.
[89]Ibid., p. 7.
[90]Ibid., pp. 23–24.

ver at will to attack the invading forces.[91] In fact, the French were by that time completely surrounded and unable to move more than a few thousand yards from their base and surrounding strongpoints. Unknown to O'Daniel, two hours before his arrival the Viet Minh had fired 103 rounds at the base with 75-mm. guns they had captured from the French the year before at Hoa Binh. Although the French had replied with counterbattery fire, fighter planes, and light bombers, they had failed to hit anything.[92]

Several aspects of the French position did disturb O'Daniel. The French dugouts and bunkers did not appear particularly strong, and he was especially troubled by the fact that the French had failed to occupy the high ground around the Dien Bien Phu valley. "A force with two or three battalions of medium artillery," he warned, "could make the area untenable."[93] Despite those reservations, the general impression conveyed in O'Daniel's report to Washington was that there was no serious danger to Dien Bien Phu. O'Daniel believed the base could "withstand any kind of attack the Viet Minh are capable of launching" and summarized the military situation as one where "the French are in no danger of suffering a major military reverse. On the contrary they are gaining strength and confidence in their ability to fight the war to a successful conclusion."[94]

General Trapnell and his staff were disturbed by what they considered to be an excessively optimistic, even misleading, tone in O'Daniel's report. With Trapnell's encouragement, the acting U.S. Army attache, Lt. Col. Robert C. Taber, paid a number of visits to Dien Bien Phu. What he saw there confirmed the serious misgivings he already held about French conduct of the war. Early in February Taber reported to General Ridgway that Navarre was in reality conducting a "minimum casualty holding action in Indochina . . . with a view to eventual negotiations." Navarre had, as General O'Daniel reported, recovered a number of battalions from static defensive positions, but those units were dispersed throughout the country. The French had manifested little progress in such important fields as training and psychological warfare, and "their staff thinking and procedure is vintage 1935–39."[95]

Reaching Washington around the same time as O'Daniel's report, Taber's analysis created a considerable stir.[96] The unmistakable contrast in tone and substance between the reports prompted Secretary of State Dulles to ask the Defense Department to obtain General Trapnell's views on the conflicting analyses. Trapnell was pleased finally to have an opportunity to present his evaluation of the military situation to American policymakers.[97] In blunt language Trapnell emphasized that "despite the confidence reposed in

[91]Cf. ibid., p. 24.

[92]Roy, *Battle of Dien Bien Phu*, p. 127.

[93]Memo, O'Daniel for JCS, 5 Feb 54, sub: Report of U.S. Special Mission to Indochina, p. 27; cf. Fall, *Hell in a Very Small Place*, pp. 108, 295–96. Fall alleges incorrectly that O'Daniel gave unqualified endorsement to the French position.

[94]Memo, O'Daniel for JCS, 5 Feb 54, sub: Report of U.S. Special Mission to Indochina, p. 27.

[95]USARMA, Saigon, to CSUSA for G–2, Feb 54, CCS 092 Asia, sec. 57, JCS records.

[96]Ltr, Philip Bonsal to Donald Heath, 12 Feb 54, Lot 58D207, records of Dept of State.

[97]Interv, author with Trapnell, 10 Sep 74.

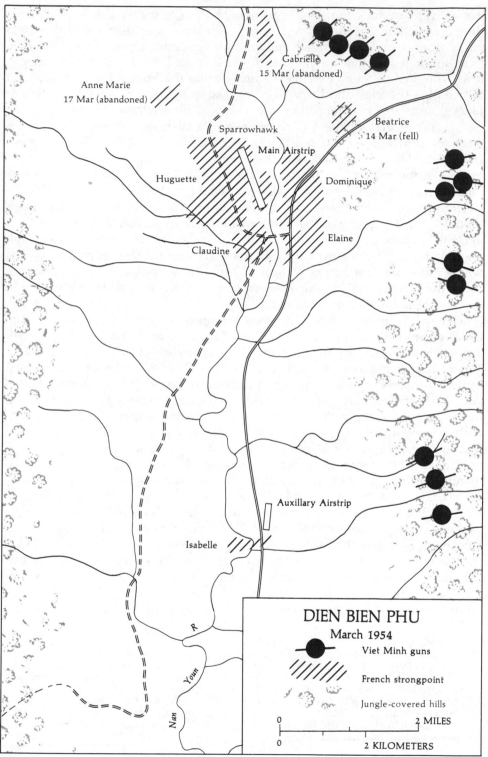

Anne Marie
17 Mar (abandoned)

Gabrielle
15 Mar (abandoned)

Sparrowhawk

Main Airstrip

Beatrice
14 Mar (fell)

Huguette

Dominique

Claudine

Elaine

Auxillary Airstrip

Isabelle

Nan Youn R

DIEN BIEN PHU

March 1954

Viet Minh guns

French strongpoint

Jungle-covered hills

0   2 MILES

0   2 KILOMETERS

MAP 5

Navarre and the French forces by visiting U.S. political notables and military missions, . . . the current campaign season has been dominated by the Viet Minh."[98] He endorsed Taber's conclusions in general and repeated criticisms of French strategy and techniques that he had outlined in previous reports.

At the Department of the Army, staff planners were equally concerned about the situation in Vietnam. The Operations and Plans Division warned that there was little evidence that the war in Indochina would be brought to a successful conclusion and pointed out that even a major French military success would not "in itself insure the attainment of U.S. objectives in the area," nor would American materiel support alone produce desirable results in the absence of "basic corrective actions." All the familiar problems remained: the absence of Vietnamese political motivation, French lethargy and negativism, deficiencies in military operations, lack of progress in creating a Vietnamese army. It was "imperative" that additional measures be taken to forestall further erosion of the French position.[99]

Taber's and Trapnell's warnings nevertheless failed to create any real sense of urgency at top levels in Washington. When questions were raised about the contrasts between O'Daniel's report and the reports from the attache and the advisory group, Admiral Radford explained that "our attaches tend to become frustrated as a result of continuously being on the scene. They tend to look at the situation from strictly a service point of view."[100] In testimony before the House and Senate on 16 and 18 February, both Under Secretary of State Walter Bedell Smith and Admiral Radford discounted "alarmist interpretations of recent military operations" in Vietnam.[101] Colonel Taber was summoned by Ambassador Heath and asked to stop sending messages questioning the French ability to win the war, a request he politely declined.[102]

By that time, close to 35,000 Viet Minh troops were deployed on the high ground around Dien Bien Phu. About a hundred 105-mm. and 75-mm. artillery pieces, together with another hundred heavy mortars and recoilless rifles, were sighted in on the French strongpoints in the valley below. *(Map 5)* At the beginning of February, Washington received the disquieting news from the U.S. Army attache that the French were doing no patrolling at Dien Bien Phu outside their perimeter and using no infrared equipment or scouting planes.[103] The French litany of assurances nevertheless continued. General Navarre confided to Ambassador Heath that he would be "disappointed" if a battle did not develop at Dien Bien Phu, because it was there that he saw the opportunity to "inflict a substantial, if not decisive, defeat."[104] Foreign Opera-

---

[98]Msg, Trapnell to Dept of Army, Feb 54, CCS 092 Asia, sec. 57, JCS records.
[99]Memo, G-3 Plans Div, Intel Br, 7 Feb 54, sub: Situation in Indochina, in JCS 1992/275, CCS 092 Asia, sec. 57, JCS records.
[100]Min, 184th Meeting of the NSC, 11 Feb 54, Eisenhower-as-President Papers, Eisenhower Library.
[101]State Dept to Saigon, 18 Feb 54, 751G.00/2-1854, records of Dept of State.
[102]Ltr, Taber to Chief of Military History, 10 Oct 79.
[103]Msg, ARMA, Saigon, to CofSA, 28 Jan 54, G-3 091 Indochina, RG 319.
[104]Heath to State Dept, 9 Feb 54, 751G.00/2-954, records of Dept of State.

tions Administration Director Harold E. Stassen returned from a visit to Vietnam to report that the French were confident they could crush any enemy attack and that General Navarre "continued to look forward to the opening of a big offensive in October."[105]

On the night of 13 March Viet Minh infantry, supported by heavy and accurate artillery fire, overran French strongpoint Beatrice on the northeast edge of Dien Bien Phu. During four more days of heavy fighting, the other northern strongpoints, Gabrielle and Anne Marie, were also lost. On the second day of the attack the French artillery commander, Col. Charles Piroth, committed suicide, reportedly out of despair over his inability to silence the Viet Minh batteries.[106] For the United States the "alarmist interpretation" of events in Vietnam had at last become inescapable reality.

---

[105]Min, 187th Meeting of the NSC, 4 Mar 54, Eisenhower-as-President Papers, Eisenhower Library.
[106]Fall, *Hell in a Very Small Place*, pp. 134 – 41; Roy, *Battle of Dien Bien Phu*, pp. 174 – 75.

11

The Question of Intervention

On Saturday morning 1 March 1954, the chief of the French armed forces staff, General Paul Ely, arrived in New York and immediately proceeded to Washington aboard Admiral Radford's personal plane. General Ely had come to Washington to inform the Americans of some unpalatable facts.[1] During the preceding month, Ely and the French service chiefs had accompanied Minister of National Defense Rene Pleven on an inspection tour of the Vietnam battlefields and had returned convinced that the best they could hope for was a military situation favorable enough to give France a tenable bargaining position during the forthcoming talks in Geneva.[2] That was far from the decisive military successes that the United States had expected from the Navarre plan and that the Joint Chiefs of Staff still believed essential for a satisfactory Vietnam settlement.

One week before General Ely's arrival in Vietnam, the Viet Minh had launched their powerful assault on Dien Bien Phu, and Ely brought to Washington a long list of additional military equipment and supplies that General Navarre required.[3] Moreover, the French were deeply concerned about the possibility of Chinese intervention, particularly aerial intervention. Since such action would radically alter the military balance in Vietnam, the French sought assurances that they could count upon effective American support to counter Chinese air power. Ely stressed the need for more aircraft and, in the event of Chinese intervention, for American air support.

On his first night in Washington Ely had a working dinner with Vice President Nixon, Admiral Radford, General Ridgway, and CIA Director Allen Dulles. Perceiving that American officials were even more pessimistic than his own government about the fate of Dien Bien Phu, he used the somber mood to press for more aid, particularly aircraft. General Ridgway pointed out that

[1]General Paul Ely, *L'Indochine dans la Tourmente* (Paris: Librarie Plon, 1964), pp. 25–37, passim.
[2]Extraits du Proces-Verbal du Comite de Defense Nationale du 6 Fevrier 1954, French Documents file, CMH.
[3]Memo, Secy of Defense for Dept of Army, 25 Mar 54, sub: Transfer of Additional Material to Indochina, CM–74–54, JCS records.

U.S. Air Force Technician *paints French insignia on C—119.*

in Korea the United States had had complete domination of the air and his experience in that conflict afforded no basis for believing that some additional air power in Indochina was going to give decisive results; nevertheless, General Ely persisted.[4] He told Secretary of State Dulles that a political settlement appeared to be the only way out, but that American air support might be required in the interim should the Chinese intervene. Dulles replied that before the United States committed any forces, it would want a greater degree of partnership with France and proof that the Associated States had achieved real independence and that both they and the French were resolved to fight on to final victory.[5]

In detailed conversations with Admiral Radford, Ely noted that French chances of holding Dien Bien Phu were no better than 50 percent and again requested prompt delivery of aircraft. When Radford suggested programs of psychological and guerrilla warfare, General Ely showed little interest, and

[4]Memo of Conversation, Ridgway, 22 Mar 54, Matthew B. Ridgway Papers, U.S. Army Military History Institute, Carlisle Barracks, Pennsylvania.
[5]Ely, *L'Indochine dans la Tourmente*, p. 61; Memo, Dulles for President, 23 Mar 54, sub: Indochina Situation, copy in Arthur W. Radford Papers, U.S. Naval Historical Center, Washington, D.C.

President Eisenhower, General Ely, and Admiral Radford *in Washington, March 1954.*

when Radford proposed expanding the Military Assistance Advisory Group so that American advisers could help in training the Vietnamese National Army, Ely responded that such a measure would have undesirable effects on the political situation in France and on French prestige in Vietnam.[6]

At Admiral Radford's suggestion, General Ely prolonged his stay an extra day so the two could discuss the problem of Dien Bien Phu in more detail. If the situation continued to deteriorate, said Radford, the United States would likely be willing to consider committing planes of the Far East Air Force and of the Seventh Fleet. Although Radford and Ely recognized the proposition as only a possibility that would require approval at the highest governmental levels of both nations, Ely came away with a strong impression that American consent would be readily forthcoming.[7] He based that conclusion on the talks with Radford and on the brief visit the two had with President Eisenhower, who, as General Ely recalled, "instructed the Admiral [Radford], without

[6]Memo, Radford for President's Special Committee on Indochina, 29 Mar 54, sub: Discussion With General Paul Ely, *The Senator Gravel Edition of the Pentagon Papers,* 4 vols. (Boston: Beacon Press, 1971), 1:455–57.

[7]Ely, *L'Indochine dans la Tourmente,* p. 63. In an interview Admiral Radford characterized General Ely's book as being "fairly accurate." Interv with Arthur W. Radford, Dulles Oral History Collection, Princeton University Library.

seeming to set limits, to furnish us with whatever we needed to save the entrenched camp."[8]

General Ely saw commitment of American aircraft as a onetime action to enable the French to "disengage the garrison" and "regain the initiative," after which the French would continue to prosecute the war as before.[9] But Admiral Radford was determined that "in case we did relieve Dien Bien Phu, we would have to have a voice in the command and in the planning of the war from then on." Radford had lost all confidence in French military leadership and would settle for nothing less than a total French effort aimed at victory.[10] The talks with Ely had convinced him that the French position in Vietnam was deteriorating rapidly. The United States, Radford advised the president, "had to be prepared to act promptly and in force to retrieve the situation."[11]

U.S. Strategic Options

American leaders were thus faced with a possibility which they had always dreaded: a French defeat or withdrawal in Vietnam. As early as June 1952 the National Security Council had agreed that "the loss of any single country [of Southeast Asia] would probably lead to relatively swift submission to or an alignment with communism by the remaining countries of this group."[12] A National Security Council paper (NSC 162/2), which was adopted in October 1953 and set forth the basic national security policy of the Eisenhower administration, had noted that certain countries, Indochina among them, were "of such strategic importance to the United States that an attack on them probably would compel the U.S. to react with military force either locally at the point of attack or against the military power of the aggressor."[13] American leaders thus seemed determined to fight for Indochina if necessary, but the question of what form American defense of Indochina might take continued to trouble them.

The Eisenhower administration was committed by its basic defense policy, popularly known as the New Look, to reduce defense spending through greater reliance on strategic nuclear air forces and less emphasis on large land and naval forces designed for conventional wars. Administration leaders also believed that the tactical use of smaller nuclear weapons in limited wars would greatly reduce the need for large conventional forces.[14] Consequently,

[8]Ely, *L'Indochine dans la Tourmente*, p. 32.
[9]Ibid., p. 38.
[10]Interv with Radford.
[11]Memo, Radford for President, 24 Mar 54, sub: Discussions With General Ely, CCS 092 Asia (6 – 25 – 48), sec. 60, JCS records.
[12]NSC 124/2, United States Objectives and Courses of Action With Respect to Southeast Asia, 25 Jun 52, *U.S.-Vietnam Relations*, 8:522.
[13]NSC 162/2, 30 Oct 53, *U.S.-Vietnam Relations*, 9:182.
[14]Glenn H. Snyder, "The 'New Look' of 1953," in Warner R. Schilling, Paul Y. Hammond, and

NSC 162/2 directed that in the event of hostilities brought about by Chinese or Russian aggression, "the United States will consider nuclear weapons to be as available for use as other munitions."[15]

Army strategists planning for the defense of Indochina were bothered by that statement. Did it mean, they wondered, that atomic weapons would be used in defense of Indochina? If they were employed would they be most effective against enemy troops in the field or against lines of communications or industrial and military installations in China itself? What would be the probable political and psychological effects at home and abroad of American use of atomic weapons against Communist forces in Southeast Asia? Army Chief of Staff Ridgway pressed for systematic studies of these questions by the Defense and State Departments, but with little success.[16]

Army leaders were convinced that with or without atomic weapons a successful U.S. defense of Indochina would be far more difficult than was generally realized. In two studies at the end of 1953 the Plans Division, G−3, of the Army staff had concluded that should the French decide to withdraw their forces from Indochina, it would take seven U.S. Army divisions plus a Marine division to replace them. The effects on the overall U.S. defense posture would be severe. Indochina operations would preclude further assistance by the United States in the buildup of NATO stockpiles, particularly ammunition, and prevent the Army from fulfilling its NATO commitments in the event of general war. Replacing the French in Vietnam would entail an extension within the U.S. Army of all terms of service by at least one year, a recall of individual reserve officers and technicians, an increase in the size of monthly draft calls, and a net increase of 500,000 men in the size of the Army.[17]

The planners estimated that U.S. forces could establish a secure base in the Red River Delta region in a few months but cautioned that successful military operations alone would not destroy the Viet Minh political organization. To accomplish this goal five to eight years of effective political and psychological measures like those being carried out by the British in Malaya would be required.[18] With these considerations in mind the G−3 Plans Division suggested that the United States reconsider "the importance of Indochina and Southeast Asia in relation to the possible cost of saving it."[19] At the same time, the CIA undertook a special intelligence estimate of the "probable consequences in non-communist Asia of possible developments in Indochina before mid-1954" and concluded that while a Communist victory in

Glenn H. Snyder, *Strategy, Politics, and Defense Budgets* (New York: Columbia University Press, 1962), p. 433.

[15]NSC 162/2, 30 Oct 53, *U.S.-Vietnam Relations*, 9:195.

[16]Memo for CofSA, 21 Dec 53, sub: National Estimates and Strategic Concepts Necessary to Defense Planning, file NSC 162, Tab 24, DCSOPS records.

[17]Memo, Chief, Plans Div, G−3 for ACofS G−1, ACofS G−2, ACofS G−4, 16 Feb 54, Inclosing two studies on Indochina prepared in Plans Div, copy in G−2 319.25 Indochina, records of ACSI.

[18]Ibid.

[19]*U.S.-Vietnam Relations*, vol. 1, pt. II. B.1, p. B−6.

Vietnam would expose the remaining countries of the region to greatly increased external and internal pressures from the Communists, it would not necessarily lead to the loss of all Southeast Asia.[20]

The Joint Chiefs of Staff, on the other hand, still felt strongly about the importance of Indochina. At the direction of the JCS Special Assistant for National Security Affairs, Air Force Maj. Gen. John K. Gerhart, the Joint Intelligence Committee prepared an estimate which predicted that "Communist control over Indochina would almost certainly result in the communization of all of Southeast Asia."[21] In subsequent discussions in the NSC Planning Board, General Gerhart convinced his colleagues of the critical importance of Indochina. As a result, the conclusions the National Security Council had drawn in June 1952 were largely reaffirmed in a new paper on Southeast Asia, NSC 177, completed at the end of December 1953.

NSC 177 recognized two principal threats to Southeast Asia: the deteriorating situation in Indochina, with the strong possibility that that country would succumb to Viet Minh domination, and the less probable danger of overt Chinese military attack against some part of Southeast Asia. In the event of Chinese Communist intervention in Indochina, the National Security Council called for the United States to provide "air and naval assistance for a resolute defense of Indochina itself; calling upon France and the Associated States to provide ground forces."[22] This provision bothered Army planners. If the proposed air and naval actions proved insufficient, they asked, was the United States then prepared to abandon Indochina? If so, what of the statements in other parts of NCS 177 that Indochina was vital to U.S. security interests? Yet the New Look budgetary ceilings, manpower limitations, and production cutbacks had left U.S. ground forces so reduced as to make abandonment of Indochina "the only feasible U.S. course under these conditions."[23]

These disparities in U.S. planning became even more apparent when the JCS Joint Strategic and Logistics Plans Committees undertook to explore the possible alternative courses of action open to the United States in two contingencies not discussed in NSC 177. The contingencies were a French decision to conclude the war in Indochina on unfavorable terms unless the United States agreed to military participation, or a French decision to pull out regardless of all offers of American assistance. In either case the United States would be confronted with the choice of doing nothing and accepting a Communist success in Indochina or committing its own service forces and, if necessary, combat troops to prevent a Viet Minh victory.[24] The committees recommended that the United States be prepared to use its own troops in Indochina and to provide such additional support to the forces of the Associ-

---

[20]SE – 52, 10 Nov 53, cited in History of Indochina Incident, p. 332.
[21]Ibid.; MFR of Interv, Samuel Tucker with Lt Col John Vogt, 4 Jan 55, JCS Historical Div files.
[22]NSC 177, 16 Jan 54, *U.S.-Vietnam Relations*, 9:234.
[23]Army Proposed JCS Comment to the Secretary of Defense on NSC 177, Tab B to Memo, ACofS G – 3 for VCofS, 5 Jan 54, sub: U.S. Objectives and Courses of Action With Respect to Southeast Asia, DCSOPS 1954 TS, DCSOPS records.
[24]Ibid.

ated States as seemed feasible. They also recommended that the United States inform Paris that a French decision to quit Indochina "under unsatisfactory conditions would necessitate a review of our overall strategy in regard to NATO on the assumption that France was no longer a full partner in the Free World coalition." At the strong insistence of the State Department the latter recommendation was dropped.[25]

Once again Army planners felt obliged to point out that action to meet these provisions would require manpower and other resources beyond those provided in the administration's New Look defense programs. The National Security Council Planning Board, however, incorporated the JCS report into a paper that was submitted to the National Security Council as a special annex to NSC 177.[26] At a meeting on 6 January, the Joint Chiefs of Staff quickly approved the adoption of the special annex, but when the Armed Forces Policy Council met the following day, Deputy Secretary of Defense Roger Kyes vigorously attacked the idea of U.S. participation in the Indochina War. Although Kyes ostensibly objected to inaccuracies in the logistical considerations in the annex, his real concern was with the effect of intervention on the defense budget.[27] The year 1954 was to inaugurate the Eisenhower administration's New Look in defense policy, and a major military commitment in Vietnam would almost certainly necessitate a sizable increase in the armed forces and in defense production and send the defense budget skyrocketing.

At the National Security Council meeting on 8 January, Kyes, representing the Defense Department, requested that the special annex to NSC 177 be withdrawn from consideration. The State Department representatives objected; the situation in Vietnam, they believed, was so serious that the United States had no choice but to use its own forces.[28] Admiral Radford suggested that if a French defeat at Dien Bien Phu appeared likely, the United States should be prepared to send an aircraft carrier; a single squadron of planes over Dien Bien Phu, he said, might in one afternoon save the situation.[29] The president's Special Assistant for National Security Affairs Robert Cutler and Treasury Secretary George M. Humphrey were strongly opposed to any intervention. "When we start putting our men into Indochina, how long will it be before we get into the war?" asked Humphrey. "And can we afford it?" President Eisenhower told the council "with great force" that he "could not imagine the United States putting ground forces anywhere in Southeast Asia except possibly in Malaya," and that a war in Vietnam "would absorb our troops by divisions." He nevertheless cautioned that the United States had vital interests in a non-Communist Indochina. The situation there was like "a leaky dike and with a leaky dike it's sometimes

[25]Memo, P. E. Bonsal for R. R. Bowie, 11 Dec 53, sub: NSC Special Annex, Lot 58D207, records of Dept of State.
[26]History of Indochina Incident, p. 338.
[27]MFR of Interv, Tucker with Vogt, 4 Jan 55.
[28]U.S.-Vietnam Relations, vol. 1, pt. II.B.1, p. B−7.
[29]Min, 179th Meeting of the NSC, 8 Jan 54, Eisenhower-as-President Papers, Eisenhower Library.

better to put a finger in than to let the whole thing be swept away."[30] Although the discussion of intervention proved inconclusive, by the end of the meeting Kyes convinced the council that the French could still endure and even "win by the spring of 1955," and it withdrew the special annex.[31] At the direction of the president, the annex was subsequently destroyed.

In the wake of these deliberations came an offer of help from an unexpected source. At the end of January 1954, South Korean President Syngman Rhee proposed to the Commander in Chief, Far East, General John E. Hull, that the Republic of Korea send a division to Indochina "to help in the Laos fighting." Rhee explained that he wanted to show his appreciation for United Nations help in the Korean War and to encourage anti-communism in Southeast Asia.[32] Reporting the offer to Washington, General Hull noted that, while the gesture was "the first instance of one anti-communist nation offering to come to the assistance of another" and might lead to closer cooperation and mutual support among Asian nations, it also had a number of disadvantages. The Korean division would have to serve under operational control of the French, airlift and air supply for the division would be difficult, and the American public might wonder why American troops had to remain in South Korea if the South Koreans could spare a division to serve in Indochina. The American ambassador to South Korea, Ellis O. Briggs, told the State Department that the offer was motivated by Rhee's "burning desire to mobilize an anti-communist front in Asia under his leadership and to court U.S. public opinion."[33]

At first the Army staff reacted favorably to the Rhee offer. A study by the Intelligence Division, submitted to the chief of staff on 12 February, pronounced the plan "feasible and desirable as a first step in the strategy of countering Communism in Asia with Asians with great psychological gain for the free world." In addition, the strengthening of French Union forces by an entire division might encourage the French to carry out more aggressive operations.[34] The Joint Chiefs of Staff, on the other hand, cited many of the same disadvantages mentioned by General Hull and recommended against accepting the proposal.[35] The South Korean offer was politely refused.

The Debate Over Intervention

By early March the worsening situation at Dien Bien Phu, the tone of the conversations with General Ely, and the approaching Geneva Conference

---

[30]Ibid.

[31]Ibid.

[32]HQ, FEC/UNC Command Rpt, Jan 54, 338 — 75 — 10009/35, FEC records.

[33]Ibid.

[34]ROK Division to Indochina, 9 Feb 54, Incl to Memo, Chief, Psy War, for Chief, Plans Div, 12 Feb 54, sub: Staff Study on ROK Offer of a Division to Indochina, G — 3 091 Indochina.

[35]Memo, JCS for Secy of Defense, 1 Mar 54, sub: Consideration of the ROK Offer to Send a Division to Indochina, *U.S.-Vietnam Relations*, 9:259 — 63.

had made it clear that a French defeat or a withdrawal under unfavorable conditions was a real possibility. On 11 March 1954 the Joint Chiefs of Staff again recommended that the National Security Council decide immediately whether the United States should commit its own armed forces to Vietnam if that step became necessary.[36] A few days later a special working group of the President's Special Committee on Indochina, headed by General Graves B. Erskine (U.S. Marine Corps, retired), concluded that "from the point of view of the U.S. strategic position in Asia . . . no solution to the Indochina problem short of victory is acceptable." The Erskine subcommittee recommended that if the French decided to accept a settlement that fell short of achieving real security and independence for the Associated States, the United States should disassociate itself from the agreement and "pursue, directly with the governments of the Associated States and with other Allies (notably the U.K.), ways and means of continuing the struggle." The subcommittee also recommended that the National Security Council consider committing air, naval, and ground forces "to the direct resolution of the war in Indochina with or without French support."[37] Secretary of Defense Wilson endorsed both the Joint Chiefs' recommendation and the Erskine report and forwarded them to the secretary of state.[38]

Convening on 25 March with President Eisenhower presiding, the National Security Council considered both items along with an urgent telegram from Ambassador Dillon in Paris emphasizing the necessity for an early decision on the question of intervention.[39] Secretary Dulles warned that the United States might soon be faced with a choice between abandoning its interests in Southeast Asia or assuming direct responsibility for the security of the region, but President Eisenhower told the council that he would agree to military intervention only if four conditions were met: the Associated States would have to request assistance, the United Nations would have to approve, other nations would have to participate, and Congress would have to sanction it.[40]

The president's remarks made it clear that the United States was not nearly as ready to enter the war as General Ely had assumed. None of the president's four conditions would be easy to meet, and obtaining congressional sanction could prove particularly difficult. At the end of January, Chairman of the Senate Armed Services Committee John Stennis had told Secretary of Defense Wilson that he would not approve sending American troops to Vietnam even in relatively small numbers.[41] The National Security Council nevertheless decided to direct its Planning Board to continue studies on the feasibility and consequences of intervention.[42]

At the Pentagon, planners were also studying the question. From at least

[36]Ibid., 11 Mar 54, JCS 1992/287, CCS 092 Asia (6–24–48), sec. 59, JCS records.

[37]Memo, Erskine for Special Committee, NSC, 17 Mar 54, sub: Military Implications of the U.S. Position on Indochina in Geneva, *U.S.-Vietnam Relations,* 9:271–75.

[38]Ltr, Wilson to Secy of State, 23 Mar 54, *U.S.-Vietnam Relations,* 9:276.

[39]Dillon to Secy of State, 11 Mar 54, records of Dept of State.

[40]NSC Record of Action, 1074–a, 25 Mar 54, cited in History of Indochina Incident, p. 377.

[41]Ltr, Stennis to Charles E. Wilson, 29 Jan 54, *U.S.-Vietnam Relations,* 9:239.

[42]NSC Action 1074, NSC Section, Plans Div, 25 Mar 54, G–3 Ops, DCSOPS records.

the latter part of March, the Army and Air Force staffs had been discussing the feasibility and desirability of employing atomic weapons in Indochina. While such a course was not specifically called for in the NSC 177 special annex, the New Look emphasis on early use of nuclear weapons on the battlefield caused many officers to believe that such weapons would likely be used in Indochina in the event of U.S. intervention.[43] In 1954 Air Force F–8F aircraft stationed in the Far East could deliver an implosion-type atomic bomb with a circular error probability of about 600 yards on targets in Indochina with a maximum of ten hours' preparation.[44] Navy AD–5, AD–6, F–2H, and F–2B aircraft operating from carriers or land bases were capable of delivering the same type of weapon. Carriers then in Far Eastern waters could reach launching points off the coast of Indochina in a minimum of four days.[45]

On 25 March officers of the G–3 Plans Division completed a study which concluded that atomic weapons could be used to relieve the beleaguered garrison at Dien Bien Phu in a number of ways, including bombing of the besieging Viet Minh, of areas intentionally abandoned to the Viet Minh, and of supply and base areas serving the Viet Minh forces around Dien Bien Phu.[46] Another study dated 8 April included a tentative operational plan for the use of one to six 31-kiloton atomic bombs to be delivered by Navy carrier aircraft during daylight against Viet Minh positions around Dien Bien Phu.[47] Both studies concluded that the use of atomic weapons in Indochina was technically and militarily feasible and could produce a major alteration in the military situation in favor of the French, turning "the entire course of events in Indochina to the advantage of the U.S. and the free world. If the act occurred before the Geneva Conference, that conference might never be held."[48] The authors of the two studies recognized that employment of atomic weapons risked retaliatory military action by the Soviet Union or China but argued that this risk could be minimized by disguising the U.S. role, for example by using aircraft with French markings. They also pointed out that *any* attempt by the United States to intervene decisively in the French–Viet Minh battle carried a risk of provoking Chinese or Russian counteraction.[49]

The chief of the Plans Division approved the G–3 studies and circulated them to the heads of the other staff sections, where they provoked sharp disagreement. The assistant chief of staff for intelligence questioned the use

---

[43]Interv, author with Lt Gen James Gavin, 1 Aug 80, Historians files, CMH.

[44]The circular error probability (CEP) was the radius of a circle within which half of the bombs could be expected to fall. Using a ground control team the CEP could be reduced to under 250 yards.

[45]Technical and Military Feasibility of Successfully Employing Atomic Weapons in Indochina, Tab B to Draft G–3 Study, 25 Mar 54, sub: Employment of Atomic Weapons in Indochina, G–3 091 Indochina TS, 8 Sep 54, DCSOPS records.

[46]Ibid.

[47]Proposed Tentative Operational Plan, Tab D to Draft G–3 Study, 8 Apr 54, sub: Employment of Atomic Weapons in Indochina, G–3 091 Indochina TS, 8 Sep 54, DCSOPS records; Ltr, J. I. Coffey to author, 5 Sep 80, Historians files, CMH.

[48]Draft G–3 Study, 8 Apr 54, sub: Employment of Atomic Weapons in Indochina.

[49]Ibid., and for 25 Mar 54.

of either tactical atomic weapons or saturation bombing with conventional bombs, arguing that the terrain around Dien Bien Phu, which offered excellent cover for the Viet Minh, and the widely dispersed nature of Viet Minh artillery emplacements would severely limit the effectiveness of this type of air attack.[50] Air Force intelligence analysts reached the same conclusion, noting that "Very few if any suitable targets would occur or could be induced if the target location were restricted to Indochina." In addition, the Air Force study cautioned that the use of atomic weapons in Southeast Asia "may involve the serious risk of initiating allout war."[51]

The G−3 Office of Psychological Warfare warned that the employment of atomic weapons in Indochina, while possibly resulting in an improvement in the local military situation, would also create resentment and distrust among U.S. allies who had not been consulted even "to the point of dangerously weakening existing collective security arrangements." It would also completely alienate Asian nations such as India, Burma, and Indonesia and furnish a rationale for overt Chinese intervention in Southeast Asia. The Psychological Warfare Office dismissed the idea that U.S. involvement could somehow be disguised. World opinion would certainly attribute a nuclear strike to the United States regardless of the cover plan employed. Communist propaganda would depict the United States as unstable, barbaric, and impatient. The chief of psychological warfare concluded that the damage to America's reputation arising from use of atomic weapons "would outweigh the psychological disadvantages which would follow the loss of Dien Bien Phu."[52]

The details of other discussions of the G−3 study within the Army staff have not been preserved, but the arguments of the Plans Division in favor of atomic weapons failed to convince either General Ridgway or his G−3, Maj. Gen. James M. Gavin, who ordered the studies shelved. Ridgway then directed the staff to conduct still another study of the consequences of intervention. This time the planners concluded that any form of military action by the United States in Vietnam would be ill-advised. Intervention with U.S. air and naval units operating from bases outside Indochina would probably lead to committing ground troops, would entail a diversion of American air resources in the Far East, might prompt retaliatory Chinese air attacks on American aircraft or even full-scale Chinese intervention, and would still not provide sufficient power to achieve a military victory over the Viet Minh. Using aircraft based inside Indochina would have the same disadvantages and would also require a substantial logistical buildup and commitment of U.S. ground forces to provide security for air bases. Intervention by ground troops, the staff noted, would necessitate calling nine National Guard divi-

[50]Incl 1, Tab A to G−2 DF, G−2 PREA to G−3, 29 Mar 54, sub: Request for Intelligence Targets in Indochina, records of ACSI.

[51]AIE−9−1, 5 Apr 54, sub: Opportunities for Air Action in Indochina, copy in OCE T−2068, Optimum Atomic Weapons for Defeating a Communist Assault on South Vietnam, 19 Oct 55, DCSOPS records.

[52]DF, OC/Psy War to ACofS G−3, 25 Mar 54, sub: Employment of Atomic Weapons in Indochina, PSYWAR 385−2 TS, DCSOPS records.

sions into federal service, extending terms of service for draftees, and resuming immediately war production of critical items. Until the newly mobilized divisions could become fully effective, a period of seven to nine months, the Army's strength and readiness in other areas of the Far East and in Europe would be seriously weakened.[53] Armed with these conclusions, General Ridgway continued resolutely to oppose any talk of military operations in Indochina.

On 31 March Admiral Radford convened a meeting of the Joint Chiefs to ascertain their views about recommending the commitment of U.S. naval air and Air Force units for the defense of Dien Bien Phu. General Ridgway's answer "was an emphatic No." He argued that any gain from "effective intervention in the Dien Bien Phu operation was altogether disproportionate to the liability it would incur" since the outcome of the Dien Bien Phu battle in itself would not decisively affect the military situation in Vietnam, although by intervening in Vietnam the United States would greatly increase the risk of general war. General Ridgway added that unless the question of intervention was put to the Joint Chiefs by proper authority, that body would be exceeding its authority by volunteering recommendations to the president and the cabinet.[54] The other service chiefs also recommended against such a course of action.[55]

In private conversations the next day Admiral Radford urged the service chiefs to reconsider their position. He reminded them that many times they had gone on record about the great importance of Indochina and the dire consequences of a French defeat.[56] On 2 April Radford reconvened the meeting of the Joint Chiefs of Staff and requested the chiefs to consider the question: "If proper authority asked the JCS for a statement of their recommended response to a French request for intervention, what would it be?" The discussion was apparently inconclusive, for the following morning Admiral Radford returned with a written request from the secretary of defense asking specifically for the recommendations of the Joint Chiefs. General Ridgway again recommended against intervening.[57] The Chief of Naval Operations, Admiral Robert B. Carney, took much the same position.[58] Marine Corps Commandant General Lemuel C. Shepherd, Jr., noted that the United States "could expect no significant military results from an improvised air offensive against guerrilla forces." The inevitable result of intervention, he said, would be either to accept a military failure or to intervene further.[59] Only the Air Force Chief of Staff, General Nathan F. Twining, was willing to

[53]Memo, ACofS G–3 (Maj Gen James M. Gavin) for CofS, Mar 54, Military Consequences of Various Courses of Action With Respect to Application of U.S. Military Forces in Indochina, G–3 091 Indochina, copy in Ridgway Papers.
[54]Memo, Ridgway for Radford, Twining, Carney, and Shepherd, 2 Apr 54, copy in Ridgway Papers.
[55]Memo, Radford for Secy of Defense, 31 Mar 54, sub: Indochina Situation, Radford Papers.
[56]Memo of Telephone Conversations, 1 Apr 54, Radford Papers.
[57]Ibid.
[58]Memo, Carney for Radford, Twining, Ridgway, and Shepherd, 2 Apr 54, sub: U.S. Intervention in Indochina, copy in Ridgway Papers.
[59]Memo, Shepherd for Radford, Twining, Ridgway, and Carney, 2 Apr 54, Ridgway Papers.

give even a qualified assent to the proposal, but his agreement was contingent upon French acceptance of "U.S. leadership in the training and employment of combat forces" and other conditions unlikely to be met.[60] Thus the answer of the Joint Chiefs of Staff was negative.

A few days later, the National Security Council again recommended that the United States "reach a decision whether or not to intervene [in Vietnam] with combat forces."[61] Once more the Army filed an emphatic dissent, taking the position that a military victory in Indochina could not be achieved with air and naval forces alone even if tactical nuclear weapons were employed. Army staff planners repeated their warning that the equivalent of seven U.S. Army divisions would be needed to replace the French in Vietnam even in the absence of Chinese intervention. If the Chinese were involved, no less than twelve divisions would be needed. Those divisions would require the support of "five hundred fighter-bomber sorties per day exclusive of interdiction and counter-air operations," a divisional airlift capability, and a division amphibious lift.[62] Finally, deploying sizable forces to Vietnam would seriously weaken American ground strength in Europe and in other parts of Asia.

Congress had already given an equally negative response on 3 April when Secretary of State Dulles had invited eight Democratic and Republican leaders of the House and Senate to a confidential meeting at the State Department. Also present were Admiral Radford, Under Secretary of Defense Kyes, Navy Secretary Robert B. Anderson, and Assistant Secretary of State Thruston B. Morton. Dulles had arranged the meeting to keep congressional leaders informed on developments in Indochina, and Radford and Dulles hoped to satisfy the conferees that "the particular job we want to do . . . can be done without sending manpower to Asia."[63] Admiral Radford presented a briefing which congressional leaders later told reporters included a plan for an air strike against Dien Bien Phu. The congressmen expressed concern and skepticism, particularly when Radford admitted he lacked the support of the other service chiefs. Senators Richard B. Russell and Lyndon B. Johnson clearly indicated that they would support no project that was undertaken without British and other allied participation. "It was the sense of the meeting," Dulles reported, "that the U.S. should not intervene alone but should attempt to secure the cooperation of other free nations."[64] In a telephone conversation with the president that day, the secretary expressed the belief that "Congress would be quite prepared to go along on some vigorous action" but only if "we were not doing it alone" and that "they want to be sure the people in the area are involved too." The president agreed. "You can't go in and win unless the people want you," he told Dulles. "The French could win in six months if the people were with them."[65]

[60]Memo, Twining for Radford, 2 Apr 54, sub: Indochina Situation, Ridgway Papers.
[61]NSC Action No. 1074–a, 5 Apr 54, *U.S.-Vietnam Relations*, 9:304.
[62]Army Position on NSC Action 1074–a, *U.S.-Vietnam Relations*, 9:332.
[63]Dulles Telecon with Admiral Radford, 1 Apr 54, Dulles Papers, Princeton University.
[64]*U.S.-Vietnam Relations*, vol. 1, pt. II.B.2, p. B–24.
[65]Dulles Telecon with President, 3 Apr 54, Dulles Papers.

The Joint Chiefs of Staff: *General Twining, Admiral Radford, General Ridgway, General Shepherd, and Admiral Carney.*

Operation VAUTOUR

Meanwhile, in Paris General Ely was proceeding on the assumption that American intervention was virtually assured. Although Ely found the French cabinet generally disposed to accept his plan for a short and decisive American aerial bombardment in support of Dien Bien Phu, the government was unwilling to make a final decision on the matter without consulting General Navarre in Vietnam. General Ely's aide, Col. Raymond Brohon, was dispatched to inform Navarre about the proposed American aerial intervention, code named VAUTOUR (VULTURE), and to solicit his opinion of its probable effectiveness.[66]

As Colonel Brohon was meeting on 2 and 3 April with Navarre in Hanoi, the defenders of Dien Bien Phu were fighting desperately to repel massive Viet Minh attacks. Portions of both the northeastern strongpoints, Eliane and Dominique, had already fallen to the enemy. General Navarre apparently first disapproved the air strike lest it provoke Chinese intervention, but on 4 April he radioed Paris his approval.[67]

[66]Ely, *L'Indochine dans la Tourmente*, p. 39.
[67]According to Ely, *L'Indochine dans la Tourmente*, p. 39, and Roy, *Battle of Dien Bien Phu*, p. 214.

Dien Bien Phu *under Viet Minh bombardment.*

A week later, when the commander of the Far East Air Force, General Earle E. Partridge, arrived in Vietnam on a routine liaison visit, General Navarre told him of the plan for Operation VAUTOUR, saying that the operation "had been cleared through diplomatic channels."[68] Although Partridge had received no indication from Washington that any operation was in the offing, he felt it was important to begin planning for the possibility of a large air strike. On the way home, Partridge radioed the commander of the Far East Air Force Bomber Command, Brig. Gen. Joseph D. C. Caldara, to meet him in Japan. Partridge briefed Caldara on his conversations with Navarre and, while making it plain that he had received no instructions from Washington, directed Caldara to confer with the French and prepare a contingency plan. Caldara had available about a hundred B−29 heavy bombers based in Japan and Okinawa. Partridge directed him to retain complete operational control over any aerial attack by the B−29's and specified that "the bomber force would be employed as a unit under mass-strike conditions."[69]

Bernard Fall, however, quotes Maj. Jean Pouget, Navarre's aide, to the effect that Navarre favored the operation from the start. See Fall, *Hell in a Very Small Place*, p. 299.
 [68]Robert F. Futrell, The U.S. Air Force in Southeast Asia, 1950−1965, p. 173, manuscript in Office of Air Force History.
 [69]Ibid.

Traveling in a B−17 to avoid attracting attention, Caldara and a small staff arrived in Saigon on 19 April 1954 and conferred with French officials. After inspecting the target areas around Dien Bien Phu from his B−17, Caldara concluded that there were "no true B−29 targets" in the area but that his aircraft, operating from Clark Air Force Base in the Philippines and escorted by carrier-based Navy fighters, could do the job if required. Because of the monsoon weather in the Dien Bien Phu region, he added, the bombers would require the aid of ground-based short-range navigational radar (SHORAN). This requirement posed an immediate problem, for Caldara and his staff learned, much to their consternation, that the French in Vietnam lacked that capability.[70]

The fate of Operation VAUTOUR, however, had already been decided in Paris, Washington, and London. Upon receiving Navarre's message of 4 April agreeing to VAUTOUR, General Ely had immediately met with Defense Minister Pleven and then with the cabinet and the chiefs of armed forces. Later in the evening Ambassador Dillon was summoned to join the meeting. The French told him that only "immediate armed intervention of U.S. carrier aircraft" could save Dien Bien Phu. Since the Chinese had been providing the Viet Minh with massive aid, including technical advisers, radar-controlled antiaircraft guns, communications systems, and supply trucks, the French government considered that the Chinese, in effect, had already intervened. It was therefore appropriate that the United States government initiate the actions Radford and Ely had discussed.[71]

The same evening Dulles and Radford had met in Washington with the president to assess the situation. Eisenhower had reaffirmed his determination not to become involved in the Vietnam fighting without congressional approval and without the support of the British and other nations. He also would require assurance from the French that they would not withdraw their own forces and would grant complete independence to the Associated States.[72] To satisfy the French request, said the president, "would be unconstitutional and indefensible." Dulles agreed, alluding to the insistence of congressional leaders two days before that the United States would not act alone. Referring to Admiral Radford's conversations with Ely in early March the secretary said he was sure Radford had made no commitment and recalled that he had made plain to Ely that "the political aspects needed to be attended to first. We can't lose our own prestige by going in and being defeated."[73] Under these circumstances, when the French request for immediate intervention arrived in Washington, Dulles simply replied that the United States was "doing everything possible . . . to prepare public, Congressional and Constitutional basis for united action" but that the United States could not commit acts of war in Indochina without a full political understanding

[70]Ibid.
[71]Telg, Dillon to Secy of State, 5 Apr 54, *U.S.-Vietnam Relations,* 9:296−97.
[72]Dwight D. Eisenhower, *The White House Years: Mandate for Change* (New York: Doubleday, 1963), p. 345.
[73]Dulles Telecon with President, 5 Apr 54, Dulles Papers.

with France, the active cooperation of Great Britain, and the consent of Congress.[74]

Foreign Minister Bidault replied that he "could well understand the position of the U.S. Government," but General Ely considered the American response tepid and disappointing. "The conditional answer made by the U.S. Government to our request for emergency intervention," wrote Ely to the French military attache in Washington, "causes me to fear that this intervention would be subject to a time lag which would be too long."[75] When the attache relayed this reaction to Radford, the admiral replied that he had made no commitment to Ely other than to promise "prompt and thorough consideration by the United States Government" of any French request; this was being done.[76]

These exchanges pointed up a fundamental misunderstanding between French and American officials about the nature of American intervention. The French wanted to limit U.S. intervention to a single military action, Operation VAUTOUR, to relieve Dien Bien Phu, but on the American side even Admiral Radford, the reputed author of Operation VAUTOUR, saw it as only the first step in American military involvement. As he later recalled, "I was not ready to support the French at Dien Bien Phu or anywhere unless we had proper arrangements with [the French]. In case we did relieve Dien Bien Phu, we would have to have a voice in the war, in the command, in the planning, from then on."[77] President Eisenhower told the National Security Council, "We are not prepared now to take action with respect to Dien Bien Phu in and by itself. But if we can put together a coalition program for Southeast Asia, we can assume that then the battle is 2/3 won."[78]

American consideration of military intervention thus did not end with the de facto rejection of the French plea for an attack at Dien Bien Phu. Throughout April the Joint Chiefs of Staff and the Department of Defense continued to plan for possible military action in Vietnam either unilaterally or in cooperation with the French. A plan worked out by the Joint Strategic Plans Committee in early April drew heavily on earlier planning by the Army staff. It called for "a coordinated attack in the northern part of Vietnam from the Tonkin Delta with the primary objective of destroying the organized Viet Minh forces" in the area.[79] That objective was to be accomplished in three phases. First, four infantry divisions and an airborne division with air support were to attack to secure the "major communications centers" of Yen Bay, Tuyen Quang, and Thai Nguyen, thereby interdicting the enemy's lines of communications and possibly trapping three Viet Minh divisions. Next, an infantry division was to seize and occupy an enemy base complex in the Hoa Binh

[74]Telg, Dulles to Am Embassy, Paris, 5 Apr 54, *U.S.-Vietnam Relations,* 9:359.
[75]Ely to Valluy for Radford, 7 Apr 54, cited in History of Indochina Incident, pp. 383–85.
[76]Ibid.
[77]Interv with Radford.
[78]192d Meeting of the NSC, 16 Apr 54, Eisenhower-as-President Papers.
[79]Report by the JSPC on Defense Implementation of Operations Coordinating Board Program for Indochina, Phase A, 1 Apr 54, JCS records; Outline Plan for Military Operations Indochina, Tab B of Memo, ACofS G–3 for CofSA, 24 Mar 54, CS 091 Indochina, DCSOPS records.

area, while a second division was to make an amphibious assault around Thanh Hoa and advance to seize the road junction at Hoi Xuan. The third phase, a reconnaissance in force to the Chinese border, was to reestablish frontier garrisons there. The planners believed that all three phases could be accomplished in about six months and saw the concept of the operation as valid "whether U.S. forces participated or not."

This plan—never implemented—appeared to take little cognizance of the underlying causes of French failures. As the French experience had demonstrated, capturing key bases and interdicting lines of communications usually had limited effect on an enemy who put little reliance on conventional road-bound supply and movement. The plan also largely ignored the underlying political and social conditions which contributed heavily to the effectiveness of the Viet Minh. Although the plan specified that "increased and full support for the indigenous peoples" and the "corresponding development of adequate responsible [Vietnamese] leadership" were essential to victory, it provided no mechanism for achieving those elusive aims.

At the same time, Army planners were alarmed at the Navy's insistence in the planning discussions that if U.S. operations were carried out in northern Vietnam, Hainan, a large island just east of the Gulf of Tonkin and a part of the People's Republic of China, would have to be attacked to neutralize the Chinese air bases there. Otherwise, those bases would pose an unacceptable threat to Seventh Fleet operations in Indochinese waters. As Lt. Gen. James M. Gavin, then Army Assistant Chief of Staff, G–3, recalls, the Army planners believed that an attack on Hainan would be considered

an act of war against the People's Republic of China. Based on our experience in Korea we believed that the PRC would enter the conflict. . . . We planned on dropping one airborne division in northern Vietnam. It would probably have been engaged with the Chinese at once. Further if we were intentionally going to war with China we could see no military objectives worthwhile seizing. It was obviously the wrong place to go to war with China. Much better would be seizing the war making capacity of Manchuria. So, as we thought the situation through it seemed to us to be utter folly to invade Southeast Asia.[80]

The Army Resists Intervention

Led by General Ridgway, the Army continued to protest most strongly against intervention. On 6 April, the Army chief warned that the use of American forces in Vietnam "aside from any local success they might achieve, would constitute a dangerous strategic diversion of limited U.S. military capabilities and would commit our armed forces in a non-decisive theatre to the attainment of non-decisive local objectives."[81] American commitment would also greatly increase the risk of general war and would play into the hands of the Chinese and Russians, who could stand aside while vital American military resources were dissipated in inconclusive fighting.

[80]Ltr, Gavin to Chief of Military History, 8 May 79, copy in Historians files, CMH.
[81]Memo, CofSA, 6 Apr 54, JCS 1992/296, CCS 092 Asia, sec. 62, JCS records.

Looking back on the period General Gavin recalls, "It was not an easy position for the Army to take. Washington was full of gossip about the combat readiness of the Army. After all the new look was based upon massive retaliation and many foresaw little need for an Army. The Army's attitude seemed to play into their hands . . . a well known columnist . . . told me that the gossip all over Washington was that the Army was splitting from the other services on the Vietnam issue because it was not combat-ready. So, as I say, it was a difficult position for the Army to take, but it seemed to be a commonsense one, so Ridgway and I stuck to our guns."[82]

If it was really vital to the United States to prevent the loss of Vietnam, the wisest course, in Ridgway's view, would be to strike directly at China, without whose aid the Viet Minh would be unable to persist. Yet that action should be taken only with the support of America's allies and after the start of a general mobilization to support the military effort. As General Ridgway later noted, he had no wish for a war with China or a preventive war with the Soviet Union but merely wished to point out, in the starkest terms, the magnitude of the decision confronting the country on the issue of intervention in Vietnam.[83]

The Joint Strategic Plans Committee was apparently surprised and upset by Ridgway's pronouncement. With the Army member dissenting, the committee declared that Ridgway's views were "inconsistent" with NSC 5405, which called for considering unilateral action, and with JCS 1992/262, which had concluded that Indochina could be "saved" by committing certain limited U.S. forces. "Direct action against Communist China . . . had . . . many advantages from the strictly military point of view," the committee declared, although conceding that it had "obvious political disadvantages."[84] But it was precisely those "obvious political disadvantages" and dangers of the entire movement toward involvement in Indochina that General Ridgway wanted to emphasize. At a meeting of the Joint Chiefs on 26 April he pressed his views and elicited an agreement to forward them in a memorandum to the secretary of defense.[85]

The British meanwhile were reacting in much the same way to an effort by Secretary Dulles to enlist them in a military coalition to save Vietnam. Arriving in Europe on 11 April with the avowed purpose of building a "united front to resist Communist aggression in Southeast Asia," Dulles found that Prime Minister Anthony Eden would engage in no discussion concerning a regional security arrangement until after the Geneva Conference had concluded.[86]

Many American leaders nevertheless continued to raise the prospect of

[82]Ltr, Gavin to Chief of Military History, 8 May 79.
[83]Memo, CofSA, 6 Apr 54.
[84]Memo, JSPC for JCS, 16 Apr 54, CCS 092 Asia (6 – 25 – 48), sec. 92, JCS records.
[85]Note, Secretaries to Holders of JCS 1992/296, 26 Apr 54, CCS 092 Asia (6 – 23 – 48), JCS records; MFR, Ridgway, 28 Apr 54, Ridgway Papers.
[86]Department of State *Bulletin,* 19 April 1954; History of Indochina Incident, p. 387; Anthony Eden, *The Memoirs of Anthony Eden: Full Circle* (Boston: Houghton Mifflin Co., 1960), p. 110; Townsend Hoopes, *The Devil and John Foster Dulles* (Boston: Little Brown Co., 1973), pp. 214 – 15.

doing something to "save" Indochina from the Communists. On 17 April, Vice President Nixon told a press conference that "The United States as a leader of the free world cannot afford further retreat in Asia"; if the French withdrew, the United States might have to "take the risk now by putting our boys in."[87] Although the vice president was speaking for himself, he knew that many administration leaders, including Secretary Dulles, shared his views.[88]

General Ridgway enlisted the aid of Army Secretary Robert Stevens in an effort to reverse the trend toward intervention. Directing the Army staff to prepare a special briefing on Vietnam, Ridgway recommended that Stevens "have the briefing at the earliest opportunity."[89] Following the briefing on 19 May, Stevens drafted a memorandum for Secretary of Defense Wilson summarizing the main points of the Army's case. Vietnam, Stevens told Wilson, was "devoid of local resources of use to the armed forces," and its monsoon climate made it extremely unhealthy for Western troops. Logistical facilities were totally inadequate to support a major military effort; the principal ports would require dredging, and even then considerable tonnage would have to be brought in over open beaches. Only three airfields were capable of handling heavy bombers; only eight could support C–119 supply aircraft, and almost all were unusable during the rainy season. The major logistic effort required would have to be protected by the Army, making the total number of ground forces needed for both local security and offensive operations "very large." During the next two weeks, General Ridgway personally presented the briefing both to Deputy Secretary of Defense Anderson and to President Eisenhower.[90]

While Ridgway sought to discourage intervention in Washington, the French government in Paris was making a desperate last-minute attempt to obtain Amerian military assistance at Dien Bien Phu. On 21 April, when Dulles arrived in Paris for pre-Geneva talks, he was met with new French pleas and suggestions. An American air attack at Dien Bien Phu, Premier Laniel told another American diplomat, "would galvanize the defenders and dramatically change the situation."[91] Foreign Minister Georges Bidault urged that the United States "give the most serious consideration to armed intervention promptly as the only way to save the situation." He predicted that a defeat at Dien Bien Phu would make the French public feel that further efforts in Indochina were futile. Dulles could only reiterate that the United States could not take military measures in Vietnam without the consent of Congress and the support of Britain. The British, however, had made their

---

[87]*New York Times*, 17 Apr 54.

[88]Interv with Richard M. Nixon, Dulles Oral History Collection.

[89]Memo, Ridgway for Secy of Army, 29 Apr 54, sub: Indochina. An outline of the briefing is attached to Memo, ACofS G–2 for SGS, 17 Apr 54, sub: Army Special Briefing. Both in CSA 091 Indochina, DCSOPS records.

[90]Memo, Stevens for Secy of Defense, 19 May 54, sub: Indochina; MFR, Ridgway, 17 May 54, Ridgway Papers.

[91]Ltr, Douglas MacArthur II to President, 24 Apr 54, Dwight D. Eisenhower Diaries, Eisenhower Library.

position quite clear when Prime Minister Winston S. Churchill stated publicly that Her Majesty's Government was "not prepared to give any undertaking now, in advance of the Geneva Conference, concerning United Kingdom military action in Indochina in advance of the results of Geneva."[92]

The situation at Dien Bien Phu was at that point so grim that most American military observers believed the stronghold would fall in a matter of days. From Hanoi General O'Daniel, who had assumed command of the U.S. Military Assistance Advisory Group on 31 March, reported that he had begun to lose faith in Navarre's ability to command. To O'Daniel and other Americans, Navarre appeared gloomy and increasingly unsure of himself. "I have supported him in the past based upon his statements and his intentions," wrote O'Daniel; "however, circumstances have led me to conclude that he fails to measure up to the ability to wage war here on a scale necessary to win."[93]

O'Daniel bombarded French headquarters with suggestions to break the siege at Dien Bien Phu by sending strong relief columns overland from Laos and the Red River Delta.[94] From Washington, Admiral Radford contributed a plan to support the garrison by using six Fairchild Packet transport planes, recently lent to the French. Since heavy equipment could be dropped from rear doors of the plane, Radford wanted to drop bulldozers for constructing an airstrip some fifty kilometers from Dien Bien Phu so that troops might be brought in by air to march overland and link with the besieged forces.[95] But those and other schemes for raising the siege of Dien Bien Phu all foundered on the same rock: lack of manpower. A large proportion of Navarre's mobile forces were tied down in defending Laos, while many of the remainder had been engaged in Operation ATLANTE, a large-scale sweep along the coastal area of central Vietnam which achieved little of military significance. On 1 May, when the Viet Minh opened a final offensive against Dien Bien Phu, the fortress was clearly doomed. Seven days later, as the Indochina phase of the Geneva Conference was about to begin, the last defenses at Dien Bien Phu collapsed.

The defeat at Dien Bien Phu signaled the failure of American policy toward Indochina, a policy that had consisted principally of bankrolling the Navarre plan in the hope that it would achieve significant military success on the battlefield and a strong, reliable Vietnamese army. Although responsibility for the debacle at Dien Bien Phu rested with the French, acceptance by too many American officials of faulty French estimates of the battlefield situation meant that Washington policymakers, accustomed to reports of "steady progress," had been unprepared for the crises of March and April 1954.

American delusions about Dien Bien Phu and the Navarre plan were merely the products of a larger delusion, a belief that military success alone would be sufficient to achieve American objectives in Vietnam and elsewhere

[92]Eden, *Full Circle*, p. 118.
[93]Msg, O'Daniel to CofSA, MG 1122A, 22 Apr 54, 751G.00/4–2254, records of Dept of State.
[94]Am Embassy to State Dept, 24 Apr 54, 751G.00/4–2454, records of Dept of State.
[95]Interv with Radford.

in Indochina. That belief ignored the fact that no lasting military success was possible without the active support of the majority of the Vietnamese people, support that could be achieved only by establishing a truly independent Vietnamese government.

Secretary Dulles put the best face possible on the situation, urging the French to "react vigorously to temporary setbacks and surmount them" and suggesting to the press that "Southeast Asia could be secured even without perhaps Vietnam, Laos and Cambodia."[96] Yet it was unrealistic to expect the French to carry on alone any longer. The Army attache in Saigon reported that the Viet Minh would be in a position to launch an all-out attack on the Red River Delta by 15 June, and the chief of French intelligence in Vietnam confided to a CIA official that "internal security in Saigon was in a critical state." Vietnamese officials were described as "almost hypnotized by the Geneva conference" and unable to maintain order.[97] By the end of May Maj. Gen. Rene Cogny, the French commander in Tonkin, was "speaking frankly of the probable necessity to evacuate Hanoi" and General Navarre was calling for an early cease-fire.[98]

Under those circumstances, the United States could intervene with American forces or accept whatever settlement the war-weary French could achieve at Geneva. As for a settlement, the National Security Council with the endorsement of President Eisenhower declared on 8 May that the United States would "not associate itself with any proposal . . . directed toward a cease-fire in advance of an acceptable armistice agreement, including international controls."[99] The State Department, the Joint Chiefs of Staff, and the National Security Council all agreed that "no satisfactory settlement was possible without a substantial improvement" in the French military position.[100]

Echoing this last point, on 10 May Premier Laniel told Ambassador Dillon in Paris that "the strength with which the French could oppose Chinese propositions at Geneva would have a direct connection with the amount of support they received from the other Western powers, particularly the U.S."[101] Describing the situation in northern Vietnam as critical, Laniel declared that it was vitally important for him to know what, if any, military action the United States might be prepared to take. Washington responded to Laniel's request with a list of six conditions that would have to be met before the president would agree to ask Congress for authority to commit American forces:

1. A formal French request for U.S. military participation.

---

[96]Dulles to Acting Secy of State, 23 Apr 54, records of Dept of State; Dulles Press Conference, 11 May 54, *U.S.-Vietnam Relations*, vol. 1, pt. II.B.2, p. B–30.

[97]Am Embassy, Saigon, to State Dept, 26 May 54, 751G.00/5–2654, and 20 May 54, 751G.00/5–2054, both in records of Dept of State.

[98]Msg, USARMA to Dept of Army, June 54; McClintock to Secy of State, 6 May 54, both in records of Dept of State.

[99]*U.S.-Vietnam Relations*, vol. 1, pt. III.A.1, p. A–10.

[100]History of Indochina Incident, p. 402.

[101]Telg, Dillon to Secy of State, 10 May 54, *U.S.-Vietnam Relations*, 9:447.

2. Similar invitations to Thailand, the Philippines, Australia, New Zealand, and Britain, with an understanding that the first two would accept at once, that the next two would probably accept, and that Britain would either participate or be acquiescent.

3. Immediate presentation of some aspect of the matter to the United Nations.

4. French guarantee to the Associated States of complete independence, including an unqualified option to withdraw from the French Union.

5. No withdrawal of French military forces from Indochina during the period of united action in order to assure that American forces—principally air and sea forces—and others would supplement French forces, not substitute for them.

6. An agreement on training native troops and on a satisfactory command structure for united action.[102] Although President Eisenhower had specified similar conditions for intervention during the Dien Bien Phu crisis, there were now two important differences. The proviso that Britain had to be one of the participating nations was dropped, and the demand that the Associated States be accorded real independence was made much more specific by the provision of a right to withdraw from the French Union.

With intervention again under consideration, the acting secretary of defense asked the Joint Chiefs of Staff to prepare contingency plans for submission to the National Security Council. Still strongly opposed to intervention, General Ridgway had apparently made some headway in bringing his fellow service chiefs to his point of view, for the Joint Chiefs now recognized, as they put it in a memorandum to the secretary of defense, that Vietnam was "devoid of decisive military objectives" and that to commit more than token forces would be a misallocation of limited American military resources.[103] The major emphasis, the chiefs suggested, should be on development of an effective Vietnamese army. American commitment should be limited to a carrier task force and selected units of the Far East Air Force.[104]

In any case, the question of intervention was becoming academic, for French and American political leaders were unable to agree on the conditions for American military involvement, particularly in regard to independence for the Associated States. The French government maintained that guaranteeing

[102]Telg, State Dept to Am Embassy, Paris, 11 May 54, *U.S.-Vietnam Relations*, 9:452–53.

[103]Alarmed by renewed talk of intervention, General Ridgway decided to send a special reconnaissance team to Vietnam to examine logistical and topographical conditions there. In strict secrecy a team of five officers was formed under the command of Col. David W. Heiman and dispatched to Vietnam in the guise of inspecting the Military Assistance Advisory Group. Heiman's team arrived in Vietnam on 27 May 1954 and remained about three weeks. The team's report, received on 22 June, provided the chief of staff with additional ammunition. See Memo, Lt Gen L. L. Lemnitzer for ACofS G–3, 10 May 54, sub: Engineer Reconnaissance in Indochina; Memo, ACofS G–2 for CofSA, 29 Jul 54, sub: Award for Col David W. Heiman, CSUSA 201.2. Both in RG 319.

[104]Interv, author with General Matthew B. Ridgway, 15 Apr 76, Historians files, CMH; Memos, JCS for Secy of Defense, 20 May 54, sub: U.S. Military Participation in Indochina, and 26 May 54, sub: Studies With Respect to Possible U.S. Action Regarding Indochina, both in *U.S.-Vietnam Relations*, 9:477–79, 487–93, respectively.

the Associated States the right to withdraw from the French Union, a right they had never requested, was a gratuitous insult to French good faith and would have an adverse effect on French public opinion. American leaders contended that without that explicit evidence of Vietnam's real independence, the participation of such countries as Thailand and the Philippines would be impossible.

By late June, it had become obvious that the French would not request American intervention until all possibility of a negotiated settlement had been exhausted. The Americans for their part had come to believe that military intervention of the type envisaged by the French could have no decisive effect on the situation in Vietnam. That intervention had not taken place was in large measure attributable to differences between the Americans, the French, and the British, but it was also attributable in part to General Ridgway and the Army staff, whose skeptical view of prospects in Vietnam had prevailed, at least for the moment. A negotiated settlement of the war, so long dreaded by American policymakers, appeared at that point inevitable, even though a number of American leaders still hoped to find some means to "save" Indochina. In the end they found a way.

General O'Daniel Bids Farewell to Generals Vy and Don

PART THREE
Going It Alone

12

"Political Considerations Are Overriding" The Decision on Training

Most American officials regarded the Geneva Agreements as a major defeat for United States policy in Southeast Asia. Under terms of a separate military agreement between the French and the Viet Minh, Vietnam was partitioned along the 17th Parallel.[1] Armed forces of the Viet Minh were to regroup north of the parallel, French forces to the south. No new equipment or troops were to be introduced into Vietnam except as replacements, a proviso to be supervised by an International Control Commission (ICC) composed of representatives of India, Poland, and Canada.

On 21 July 1954 a majority of the governments participating in the conference—the Soviet Union, the People's Republic of China, France, the United Kingdom, Cambodia, Laos, and the Viet Minh—adopted a final declaration confirming the military agreements and adding a provision that general elections were to be held in July 1956 under the supervision of the commission. Neither the United States nor the Bao Dai government (known as the State of Vietnam) concurred in the final declaration, although the United States pledged to "refrain from the threat or the use of force to disturb" the agreements while warning that "it would view any renewal of aggression in violation of the . . . agreements with grave concern and as seriously threatening international peace and security."[2]

Although American officials adopted a public attitude of guarded optimism toward the agreements, private assessments were gloomy. The G–3 Plans Division of the Army staff observed that American prestige and influence in Southeast Asia had been seriously lowered and Communist influence correspondingly increased by the Geneva Agreements. As a result the achievement of U.S. objectives in Southeast Asia had become "far more difficult and

---

[1]France concluded similar agreements with Laos and Cambodia.

[2]A convenient reproduction of the agreements and the final declaration is in Dept of State, *American Foreign Policy, 1950–1955: Basic Documents*, Department of State Publication 6446, 2 vols. (Washington, 1957), 1:750–67. Quotes from page 788, same volume.

Delegates of the Great Powers, *Geneva, 1954.*

costly."[3] The National Security Council was even more pessimistic, pointing out that the Communists had secured an "advance salient" from which to mount operations against neighboring countries. The council's Operations Coordinating Board declared that the Geneva Agreements represented "a drastic defeat of key [American] policies . . . the psychological and political effects of which will be felt throughout the Far East and around the globe."[4] "I think this is going to be looked back on as a great mistake," predicted Admiral Radford to Vice President Nixon. "It is a black day for us," the vice president agreed.[5]

Until Dien Bien Phu the two principal goals of the Army, and of other American agencies, had been to foster a genuinely independent State of Vietnam with its own army and to have a strong voice in forming and training that army. Ironically, both of those objectives were substantially achieved only after Dien Bien Phu and the Geneva settlement had rendered them irrelevant for Vietnam as a whole. Independence was largely attained on 3 June 1954 with the initialing by France and the Bao Dai government of

[3]Rpt, G–3 Plans Div, Military Implications of the Cease-Fire Agreements, 22 Jul 54, CS 091 Indochina, RG 319.
[4]Cited in *U.S.-Vietnam Relations*, vol. 1, pt. III.D.2, p. D–15.
[5]Radford Telecon, 21 Jul 54, Radford Papers.

two treaties which recognized Vietnam as "a fully independent and sovereign state invested with all the competence recognized by international law." Yet those treaties, while ostensibly applying to all of Vietnam, were concluded less than seven weeks before the agreement at Geneva effectively created two separate countries, a Democratic Republic of Vietnam (North Vietnam) and a State of Vietnam (South Vietnam). Only the latter was in any meaningful way under the jurisdiction of the Bao Dai government.

Reorganizing the Vietnamese Army

The United States now also achieved its other aim, a role in training a Vietnamese Army. Although the French had long resisted any such American role, as their military position had grown more precarious in the spring of 1954 they had become more amenable. By early May General Ely had consented to allow Americans to participate in training the Vietnamese Army as well as to place U.S. advisers with Vietnamese units. The French command would, however, retain operational control.

By that time American officials were beginning to reconsider the French offer. From Saigon, Charge d'Affaires Robert McClintock observed that "the complete apathy of the Vietnamese populace . . . the absolute breakdown of the mobilization plan, internecine rivalries between the few men capable of showing leadership and the lack of leadership from Bao Dai and his ministries" all made the task of increasing the effectiveness of the Vietnamese Army in a relatively short time extremely difficult, if not impossible.[6] Army Chief of Staff Ridgway, commenting on what he called Ely's "ironic offer," warned that the assumption of responsibility by the United States for training and leading Vietnamese forces "while the French still retained overall control would put the U.S. in an invidious position, where we would be blamed for failures even though these failures were beyond our control and authority."[7]

General O'Daniel, however, was anxious to proceed. On 13 May he urged that the United States act quickly before the end of the Geneva Conference to expand the Military Assistance Advisory Group and to reorganize the Vietnamese Army into 9 divisions.[8] O'Daniel wanted 4 light and 5 medium divisions, each to consist of 3 regiments of 3 battalions. The light divisions would have only shoulder weapons and light mortars; the medium divisions, some artillery and heavy mortars.[9]

Despite the disaster at Dien Bien Phu, General O'Daniel believed that the war in Indochina could still be won.[10] Since early March he and his staff had

---

[6]McClintock to State Dept, 9 May 54, 751G.00/5–954, records of Dept of State.
[7]Memo, Brig Gen F. W. Moorman for ACofS G–3, 11 May 54, sub: Gen Ridgway's Comments on French Offer, G–3 091 Indochina, RG 319.
[8]Msg, Ch, MAAG, to DA, 13 May 54, G–3 091 Indochina, RG 319.
[9]Interv, author with O'Daniel, 3 Feb 75.
[10]Msg, Ch, MAAG, to DA, 13 May 54.

been developing a plan for a general offensive against the Viet Minh, code named REDLAND and based on a plan developed in 1949 by General James A. Van Fleet for the Greek Army in its war against indigenous Communist guerrillas. O'Daniel wanted to consolidate the eighty-odd battalions of the Vietnamese Army into nine divisions while keeping eight light battalions as a reserve to occupy areas won from the enemy. He intended the French to provide air and naval support; the United States would supply additional military assistance and division-level advisers.[11]

A three-phase operation, REDLAND was to be completed within two years. First, three Vietnamese divisions were to clear the Cochin peninsula and the Mekong Delta. In phase two an amphibious task force was to seize Bong Son and Vinh in central Vietnam, joining with a larger force from the south. In the final phase the Vietnamese divisions, having gained experience and confidence in the earlier actions, were to join with French Union forces to destroy the Viet Minh in the Red River Delta.[12] "The whole idea," O'Daniel later recalled, "was to create enthusiasm and increasing momentum as we went along."[13] The operation was to be accompanied "by an intense psychological warfare campaign to convince the people that the Associated States' armies symbolized the independence" of the states and that "the powerful Vietnamese army [was] piling up victory after victory for the security of all."[14] To provide the troops for the operation, General O'Daniel hoped to expand and strengthen the Vietnamese training program, using American methods and concepts. More training facilities, including a command and general staff college, an amphibious training center, and a specialist training center, were to be established and Vietnamese officers and noncommissioned officers sent to training schools in the United States.[15]

Since General Van Fleet had devised the original plan, O'Daniel and a special assistant, Lt. Col. William R. Rosson, took advantage of a visit by Van Fleet to Hong Kong to present their plan to him; Van Fleet promptly endorsed it. General Ely, on the other hand, was unimpressed. He found the plan too complex and believed it to be "unrealistic [because] it gave priority to operations in the south while the principal and immediate threat [was] in the north."[16]

Ely was nevertheless becoming ever more interested in American training of the Vietnamese Army. At the beginning of June 1954, he formally requested that O'Daniel and the United States join France in organizing and training the Army of Vietnam.[17] O'Daniel told General Ridgway that his first priority would be to reorganize the Vietnamese Army into regiment- and division-size units. Because most Vietnamese battalions were committed to static defensive operations and General Navarre was reluctant to pull them

---

[11]Campaign Plan REDLAND, 5 Mar 54, p. 2, 350.09, records of MAAG Indochina, RG 370.
[12]Ibid., pp. 2–3.
[13]Interv, author with O'Daniel.
[14]Campaign Plan REDLAND, Annex F, 24 Mar 54.
[15]Training Plan REDLAND, 23 Mar 54, 350.09, records of MAAG Indochina, RG 370.
[16]Telg, U.S. Embassy, Paris, to State Dept, 27 May 54, *U.S.-Vietnam Relations,* 9:496.
[17]Msg, Ch, MAAG, to DA for CSUSA, DAIN 64188, 9 Jun 54, G–3 091 Indochina, RG 319.

out for reorganization and training, O'Daniel suggested withdrawing a few officers and noncommissioned officers from each battalion to form cadres for new battalions and regiments. Again the French were unenthusiastic. "Navarre did state," noted O'Daniel, "that if the Vietnamese could furnish the men and the U.S. the equipment he would have no objections. He may have felt this was a safe statement. I sure would like to call him on it."[18]

By that time Washington was becoming wary of all French proposals. Secretary of State Dulles suspected that Ely's request might be part of a French scheme "to draw the U.S. into [the Vietnam] conflict without having U.S. conditions on intervention met." Other American officials feared that the military situation had already degenerated to such a point that a training program, no matter how well conceived, would have no chance of influencing the outcome.[19]

O'Daniel protested any delay in undertaking a training program.[20] He believed that a liberal reading of the Military Assistance Advisory Group's directive to perform "end use checks of American equipment" could be rationalized as a cover to begin reorganizing the Vietnamese Army.[21] When his intentions became known in Washington, General Ridgway issued explicit instructions that O'Daniel was to "make no commitments whatsoever in regard to training."[22] A few days later, however, Secretary Dulles directed that O'Daniel might "assist by advising in the training activities of the Vietnam National Army" and approved augmenting the Military Assistance Advisory Group by ninety spaces. The key word was apparently "advising," for the sanction was "not to be construed as U.S. approval of a MAAG Training Mission."[23]

Even after the Geneva Conference, General O'Daniel continued his appeals for authority to form a training mission. Vietnam, O'Daniel believed, would prove a testing ground for determining the ability of the United States "to combat the kind of warfare Communist troops would hope to employ everywhere, including the United States."[24]

For most American leaders, however, the reluctance to assume responsibility for training had grown even stronger. On 2 August 1954 General Ridgway, who had long opposed American intervention in Indochina, recommended that "before the United States assumes responsibility for training the forces of any of the Associated States" four essential conditions should be met. The conditions, which would consititute the position of the Joint Chiefs of Staff for the next five months, were:

[18]Ltr, O'Daniel to CofSA, 2 Jun 54, Attachment to ACofS Summary Sheet for CofSA, 28 Jun 54, CS 091 Indochina, RG 319.

[19]Dulles to Am Embassy, Paris, 12 Jun 54, 751G.00/6–1254. See also Telg, State Dept (Murphy) to Am Embassy, Paris, 10 Jun 54, *U.S.-Vietnam Relations*, 9:553–54.

[20]Msg, Ch, MAAG, to CSUSA, DAIN 65099, Jun 54, CSA 091 Indochina, RG 319.

[21]Am Embassy, Saigon, to State, 15 Jun 54, 751G.00/6–1554, records of Dept of State.

[22]Ibid., 12 Jun 54, 751G.00/6–1254, records of Dept of State.

[23]Msg, Joint State-Defense to Saigon, 26 Jun 54, 751G.00/6–2654, records of Dept of State.

[24]Msg, Ch, MAAG, to DA, 27 Jul 54, 751G.00/7–2754, records of Dept of State. Ambassador Heath concurred in General O'Daniel's recommendations.

(1) A reasonably strong, stable, civil government in control. It is hopeless to expect a U.S. military training mission to achieve success unless the nation concerned is able to effectively perform [its] governmental functions.

(2) The government of the Associated States should formally request that the United States assume responsibility for training its forces.

(3) Arrangements should be made with the French . . . providing for the phased orderly withdrawal of French forces, French officials and French advisors from Indochina. The United States from the beginning should insist on dealing directly with the governments of the respective Associated States.

(4) The size and composition of the forces of each of the Associated States should be dictated by the local military requirements and the overall U.S. interests.[25]

Diem Comes to Power

In the summer of 1954 those conditions appeared unlikely to be fulfilled. In South Vietnam a strong and stable civil government seemed especially far from realization. A government with Ngo Dinh Diem as prime minister, which had taken office in Saigon on 7 July 1954, talked bravely of achieving real independence and victory over communism, but in fact it was in a precarious position. Although Diem had a reputation for incorruptible honesty and uncompromising nationalism, he was also inexperienced, shy, dogmatic, and relatively unknown outside his native Annam. Bao Dai offered him little support, the French were suspicious of his ultranationalism, and most other South Vietnamese leaders, unwilling to be associated with a government that might well collapse, held themselves aloof. The government as instituted consisted primarily of Diem's relatives.

Born in 1901 in Hue, the new prime minister came from a Catholic mandarin family. After attending the French school of administration in Hue, Diem rose rapidly in the mandarinate. In 1933 he resigned his post as minister of the interior, the most important position in the emperor's government, to protest the French refusal to allow more Vietnamese participation in governing the country. For the next twenty years he held no office. The Japanese offered him a position in their puppet regime after their March 1945 coup, and Ho Chi Minh personally invited him to join the Viet Minh government in 1946, but Diem refused both offers. He left Vietnam in 1950 and spent two years at Maryknoll seminaries in the United States before settling in Europe in 1953. On 7 June 1954 Bao Dai invited Diem to become prime minister. The emperor had little choice—there was simply no other non-Communist leader of Diem's stature who was not tainted by close association with the French.

"Tell me about Diem," an American journalist asked a Vietnamese friend, observing that the prime minister reminded him of a priest. "Not a priest,"

---

[25]Memo, CofSA for JCS, 2 Aug 54, sub: U.S. Assumption of Training Responsibilities in Indochina, JCS 1992/367, 4 Aug 54, JCS records.

replied the Vietnamese. "A priest at least learns of the world through the confessional. Diem is a monk living behind stone walls. He knows nothing."[26]

The Geneva settlement had denied Diem the heavily Catholic districts of the North, which would have been a basic source of his support. Large areas of South Vietnam were still ruled by Viet Minh shadow governments in rural villages and districts; other regions were under the firm control of two politico-religious sects, the Cao Dai and the Hoa Hao, which had their own private armies subsidized by the French.[27] Not even in Saigon was the Diem government in complete command, for a gangster organization, the Binh Xuyen, controlled the city's police. Neither the sects nor the Binh Xuyen were represented in the Diem government.

The National Army of Vietnam had, in the opinion of U.S. observers, experienced "a complete breakdown of combat capabilities since the cease-fire and the stopping of supplies from the United States."[28] On paper the army numbered about 150,000 men plus 35,000 auxiliaries, all organized into some 125 battalions. Many of the battalions were considerably understrength through desertion and defections to the Viet Minh, and all lacked adequate combat support and combat service support units. The best units were the Vietnamese paratroopers, some of whom had fought in the final battles of 1954, but they were few in number. In fact, the army's weakness probably benefited the Diem regime since Chief of Staff Hinh, the son of former Premier Nguyen Van Tam, was Diem's avowed enemy. Counting the French Expeditionary Corps, the armies of the sects and the Binh Xuyen, and Hinh's forces, there were five separate and competing armies in South Vietnam, none fully supporting the Diem government.[29] Facing the Vietnamese and the dwindling French forces were approximately 230,000 veteran Viet Minh regulars organized into nine infantry and two artillery divisions backed by more than 100,000 "Armed People's Militia."[30]

The Refugee Operation

In addition to its military problems, the new regime had to transport and resettle approximately 800,000 refugees from North Vietnam who wanted to move to South Vietnam. Article 14(d) of the Geneva Agreements had set aside a period of approximately ten months during which "any civilians residing in a district controlled by one party who wish to go and live

[26]Denis Warner, *The Last Confucian* (New York: Macmillan, 1963), p. 71.

[27]NIE 63–5–54, Post-Geneva Outlook in Indochina, 3 Aug 54, *U.S.-Vietnam Relations*, 10:696.

[28]MAAG Monthly Activities Report No. 21 for Aug 54, 751G.5–MSP/9–2254, records of Dept of State.

[29]Collins to Am Embassy, Paris, 4 Feb 55, 751G.00/2–455, records of Dept of State; Interv with J. Lawton Collins, Dulles Oral History Collection.

[30]Memo, ACSI for CofSA, 31 Aug 54, sub: Visit to Pacific Areas; Rpt, Maj T. J. Hanifen, Staff Visit to Far East and Southeast Asia, 15 Sep–19 Nov 54. Both in records of ACSI. Memo, K. T. Young for Under Secy of State, 4 Jan 55, Lot 58D207, records of Dept of State.

Vietnamese Refugees *board U.S. Navy LST at Haiphong.*

in the zone assigned to the other party shall be permitted . . . to do so."[31] Many of the refugees were Catholics from the Red River Delta who had strongly opposed the Viet Minh during the war. They were joined by other Vietnamese who had been functionaries or servants of the French or who had served in the French Army. During August 1954 these people began to flee in large numbers to Hanoi and Haiphong, seeking passage south. Although the French government promised to evacuate all persons who wished to leave the North, the French appeared unequal to the gigantic task of moving almost one million civilians in a few months' time.

On 7 August the South Vietnamese government formally requested assistance from the United States in dealing with the refugee problem. Designated as coordinator of all U.S. activities in support of the evacuation, General O'Daniel established an Evacuation Staff Group with headquarters at 461 Rue Gallieni in Saigon. The United States Navy formed a special group—Task Force 90—under Rear Adm. Lorenzo S. Sabin to evacuate the French and Vietnamese from the North; with 28 ships, which included 15 attack transports, and 5 attack cargo ships, the task force began embarking refugees at Haiphong on 16 August.[32] Liaison detachments from the Military Assistance

[31]Dept of State, *American Foreign Policy, 1950 – 1955: Basic Documents,* 1:755.
[32]MAAG Rpt 21 for Aug 54. A detailed discussion of the evacuation may be found in Edwin Bickford Hooper, Dean C. Allard, and Oscar P. Fitzgerald, *The United States Navy and the Vietnam*

Catholic Refugees *on their way south.*

Advisory Group operated in the Haiphong area to coordinate embarkation. Civilian refugees were transferred by lighter to the ships of Task Force 90 anchored in Henrietta Pass at the mouth of the Red River. The first ship to depart, the U.S.S. *Menard*, left Haiphong on 17 August with 2,000 refugees aboard, and by the end of the month nearly 50,000 people, 133 vehicles, and 117 tons of military equipment had been transported south.[33] The evacuation continued through May 1955; of the more than 800,000 people transported to South Vietnam, Task Force 90 moved 311,000.

The United States and the State of Vietnam reaped enormous propaganda benefits from the mass exodus. The spectacle of hundreds of thousands of refugees, approximately one-thirteenth of Vietnam's population, fleeing to the South, was a striking indictment of the Viet Minh regime. Ruthless and brutal actions by the Democratic Republic of Vietnam to try to prevent the migration lent credence to Diem's claim that his government, and not that of the Viet Minh, was the true representative of democracy and freedom. Even so, resettling the refugees and integrating them into the population of South Vietnam was an enormously complex and costly job serving to tax still further the slender resources of the Diem regime.

Conflict, vol. 1, *The Setting of the Stage to 1959* (Washington: Naval History Division, 1976), pp. 273–98.

[33]MAAG Rpt 21 for Aug 54; Interv, author with O'Daniel, 3 Feb 75.

The Decision on Training

Viewing South Vietnam in late summer of 1954—a country burdened with refugees, rent by the power struggles of the sects, and threatened by a formidable Viet Minh presence in the provinces—the U.S. Joint Chiefs of Staff were reluctant to begin a long-term military training program unless the four conditions set out by General Ridgway could be met. Secretary of State Dulles reasoned differently. Conceding that the Diem government was "far from strong or stable," Dulles believed that "one of the most efficient means of enabling the [South] Vietnamese Government to become strong is to assist it in reorganizing the National Army and in training that army." He suggested that training could be undertaken as one of a number of political and economic measures to strenghen the Vietnamese government.[34] In an informal conversation with Army staff planners Dulles explained that the sole purpose of the reorganized South Vietnamese Army would be to maintain internal security; any external threat would be met by a new regional defense organization for Southeast Asia that was then being discussed in Manila by representatives of the United States, France, Britain, Australia, and various Asian nations. Given the limited mission of the South Vietnamese Army, a force of about 50,000 would be adequate; since that mission was to defend against political subversion, "guidance as to the size and nature of the forces should come from the State Department rather than the Joint Chiefs of Staff." The important thing, Dulles told Deputy Defense Secretary Robert B. Anderson, was "to start training rather than worry about the specific number of people we are prepared to train."[35]

Anderson agreed, as did the other members of the National Security Council and the president, who, on 12 August, approved NSC 5429/1 providing for U.S. assistance, "working through the French only insofar as necessary," in the creation of indigenous military forces for internal security.[36]

The State Department on 18 August notified the French government that the United States intended to assign a training mission to its Military Assistance Advisory Group in Vietnam.[37] Two days later President Eisenhower approved a new policy statement on Southeast Asia, NSC 5429/2, which called upon the United States to "make every possible effort, not openly inconsistent with the U.S. position as to the [Geneva] armistice agreements, to defeat Communist subversion and influence and to maintain and support friendly non-Communist governments" in Indochina and reaffirmed the decision to assist the non-Communist states economically and militarily.[38]

[34]Ltr, Dulles to Charles E. Wilson, 18 Aug 54, *U.S.-Vietnam Relations*, 10:728.

[35]Memo, ACofS G–3 for G–3 Plans Div, International Branch, 10 Nov 54, sub: Views of Secy of State on Strategy and Force Levels in Indochina, PSYWAR 091 Indochina; Record of Telecon, Dulles to Anderson, 9 Jul 54, Dulles Papers, Princeton University.

[36]The Joint Chiefs of Staff and the War in Vietnam, 1954–1959, p. 61, manuscript in JCS Historical Div files.

[37]State Dept to Am Embassy, Paris, 18 Aug 54, 751G.00/8–1854, records of Dept of State.

[38]NSC 5429/2, Review of U.S. Policy in the Far East, 20 Aug 54, *U.S.-Vietnam Relations*, 10:731–41.

On 8 September representatives of Britain, France, the United States, New Zealand, Australia, Pakistan, the Philippines, and Thailand signed the Southeast Asia Collective Defense Treaty, which established a loose regional defense organization, the Southeast Asia Treaty Organization (SEATO). Its members pledged to "act to meet the common danger" in the event of aggression against any of the signatories.[39] Unlike NATO, SEATO would have no standing military forces, and the members made no specific pledge of military action. A separate protocol of the treaty extended its security provisions to Laos, Cambodia, and the "free territory under the jurisdiction of the State of Vietnam" should those nations request assistance.[40]

The Joint Chiefs of Staff, meanwhile, continued a rearguard action against assuming training responsibilities. When the State Department was drafting its letter of 18 August to the French government, the Joint Chiefs objected to the wording on the grounds that the French might interpret it to mean that the United States was prepared to furnish training assistance regardless of French compliance with the American conditions.[41] On 22 September the Joint Chiefs declared that the provisions of the Geneva cease-fire agreement would present a major obstacle to introducing a sufficient number of American training personnel and additional arms and equipment.[42]

But by mid-October 1954 the Joint Chiefs had acceded. While still strongly opposed to a Vietnamese training program, "from a military point of view," they agreed to go along "if it is considered that political considerations are overriding."[43] In fact, the Joint Chiefs were well aware that Dulles, the State Department, and most members of the National Security Council considered precisely those conditions overriding. The outspoken desire of such powerful officials as Secretary Dulles and presidential assistant Robert Cutler to see the training program undertaken may have contributed to their capitulation, and they may also have been aware that President Eisenhower himself wanted it. Only three days after the Joint Chiefs acquiesced, the president told the National Security Council that "in the land of the blind, the one-eyed men are kings. What we want is a Vietnamese force which will support Diem . . . the obvious thing to do is simply to authorize O'Daniel to use up to X millions of dollars to produce the maximum number of Vietnamese units which Prime Minister Diem can depend on to sustain himself in power."[44]

Read literally, the Joint Chiefs' position was quite illogical. Their paper said that the creation of an effective Vietnamese Army under existing conditions was impossible, but they were nevertheless prepared to undertake the task because of political considerations. In other words, they would agree to

[39]Dept of State, *American Foreign Policy, 1950–1955: Basic Documents*, 1:913.
[40]Ibid., 1:916.
[41]Memo, JCS for Secy of Defense, 12 Aug 54, sub: Message to the French Prime Minister, *U.S.-Vietnam Relations*, 10:715.
[42]*U.S.-Vietnam Relations*, vol. 1, pt. IV.A.3, p. 9.
[43]Memo, JCS for Secy of Defense, 19 Oct 54, sub: Development and Training of Indigenous Forces in Indochina, *U.S.-Vietnam Relations*, 10:773–74.
[44]Min, 218th Meeting of the NSC, 22 Oct 54, Eisenhower-as-President Papers, Eisenhower Library.

do that which they had just declared to be unwise and impossible. Actually, the Joint Chiefs designed their statement as a bureaucratic compromise, to put on record the military's objections to the training program and thereby shift responsibility to the political leaders while at the same time allowing the program to proceed.

The Joint Chiefs of Staff, and particularly the Army staff, had recently succeeded in preventing the commitment of American combat forces in Vietnam. Having risked much, fought hard, and won the fight, Army leaders thought it foolish to quarrel over the relatively minor issue of American training assistance. As the Assistant Chief of Staff for Operations, Lt. Gen. James M. Gavin, recalled, "we in the Army were so relieved that we had blocked the decision to commit ground troops to Vietnam that we were in no mood to quibble."[45] Whatever the motives, the Joint Chiefs of Staff had agreed to a proposal that set in motion a chain of events that would soon prove irreversible.

---

[45]James M. Gavin, *Crisis Now* (New York: Random House, 1968), p. 49.

13

The Collins Mission

By the time the Joint Chiefs approved training of the Vietnamese Army, the Operations Control Board of the National Security Council had already been working for several days on a program for Indochina which included training of "minimum Vietnamese security forces."[1] When the State Department incorporated that provision into a draft message for the American embassy in Saigon, the stipulation was so general that Admiral Radford feared that Ambassador Heath and General O'Daniel would interpret it as a signal to implement their long-awaited, full-scale training program (which indeed they did). Radford directed the Joint Chiefs of Staff to draw up a more precisely worded directive; but before the staff could act, the National Security Council met and authorized sending the original message.[2] On 22 October 1954, the State Department instructed the Saigon mission immediately to develop and to initiate with the Vietnamese government a "program for training that number of Vietnamese armed forces necessary to carry out internal security missions."[3]

In addition to the military training effort, the new program included measures by the State Department and the CIA to help the Diem government cope with the refugee problem and win the support of the Vietnamese people. To provide impetus to the program, Admiral Felix Stump, Commander in Chief, Pacific, suggested that the United States appoint a single individual with overall authority to control the entire American effort in Vietnam. Such an individual would need great personal prestige and proven executive ability to break the "long history of U.S. officials in Indochina being duped by the French." French foot-dragging, said the admiral, "must be ruthlessly overcome."[4] Apparently impressed with Stump's suggestion, Secre-

---

[1]Item 4, Indochina, NSC 218th Meeting, 22 Oct 54, *U.S.-Vietnam Relations*, 10:789–90.
[2]*The Joint Chiefs of Staff and the War in Vietnam*, p. 63. Col. Alfred E. Stevens of the Army staff, who was present at the meeting of the Operations Control Board, reported that the Defense Department representatives on the board felt the message "reflected the best terms obtainable" from the State Department. Stevens' Notes of OCB Meeting, 28 Oct 54, PSYWAR 337.
[3]State Dept to Am Embassy, Saigon, 21 Oct 54, *U.S.-Vietnam Relations*, 10:784.
[4]Msg, Stump to CNO, 300402F, Oct 54, copy in Collins Papers, National Archives.

tary of State Dulles asked the president's military adviser, Col. Andrew J. Goodpaster, to suggest "any fairly senior military man that might be sent out to assess [the situation] and see whether a viable military position could be created."[5] Goodpaster recommended the man who had been Army chief of staff during the Korean War, retired General J. Lawton Collins.

Dulles discussed the proposed mission with the president and received his approval. General Collins was to go to Vietnam as the president's special representative with wide authority and the personal rank of ambassador. In a letter of instruction, Eisenhower gave Collins "broad authority to direct, utilize and control all agencies and resources of the U.S.

General Collins

government with respect to Vietnam." The immediate and urgent requirement was to assist in stabilizing and strengthening the government of Prime Minister Diem.[6] Secretary Dulles explained to Collins that the most pressing need was to decide on the size and scope of the U.S. effort in Vietnam, "in view of the slim chances of great accomplishments." How much, for example, should the United States spend to support the French Expeditionary Corps, the Vietnamese Army, and the Vietnamese economy, and for how long?[7] The secretary rated the chances for success in Vietnam as "only one in ten."[8]

While General Collins did, in fact, quickly become the coordinator and director of U.S. activity in Indochina, his original concept of his mission was less ambitious. "The idea was that I would go down on a brief mission, make a survey, some recommendations and come back and make a report and that would be that," Collins later recalled.[9] Yet unlike earlier short and usually fruitless fact-finding missions, the Collins mission would last for an extended period and profoundly affect U.S. policy in South Vietnam.

Preventing a Coup

Although General Collins had considerable experience in Asia and had visited Vietnam in 1951, he was amazed and appalled at the situa-

---

[5]Interv with Andrew J. Goodpaster, Dulles Oral History Collection.
[6]Eisenhower to Collins, 2 Nov 54, 120.25G/11–254; Dulles to Am Embassy, Saigon, 1 Nov 54, 120.25G/11–154; both in records of Dept of State.
[7]Indochina Briefing Papers, 1 Nov 54, Collins Papers.
[8]General J. Lawton Collins, *Lightning Joe: An Autobiography* (Baton Rouge: Louisiana State University Press, 1979), p. 379.
[9]Interv with Collins.

tion that greeted him as he arrived in Saigon on 8 November 1954.[10] Chief of Staff General Nguyen Van Hinh had concentrated tanks a few blocks from the presidential palace where Diem was "guarded" by police under the control of the Binh Xuyen. It was obvious to Collins that until this crisis could be resolved, no effective reorganization and development of the South Vietnamese Army could be undertaken. Collins found that General O'Daniel and Ambassador Heath differed on how to deal with the situation. Having worked closely with Hinh on planning for training and reorganizing the army, O'Daniel believed that the general was basically honest and patriotic and could be persuaded to cooperate with Prime Minister Diem. Ambassador Heath, on the other hand, thought that O'Daniel's view of Hinh was naive and that the Diem government's difficulties could not be solved unless Hinh was removed.[11] As an officer in the U.S. mission recalls, "Nguyen Van Hinh was not only a French citizen with a French wife but was a regular or career officer in the French Air Force and thus supposedly under French military discipline. . . . To most Vietnamese in the army he was French; his political ascendancy would have been a mockery of Vietnam's 'independence.' "[12]

By late August Hinh was freely admitting to members of the Military Assistance Advisory Group that he had been consulting with leaders of the Cao Dai and Hoa Hao sects on forming a government to succeed Diem.[13] Alarmed by that development, on 27 August Ambassador Heath had met with General Ely, "stated very firmly to him that Diem must be given another chance," and two days later had warned General Hinh that any attempt to overthrow the Diem government by force "would cause a very unfavorable impression in the U.S."[14] Heath worked to get General Hinh out of the country, but Hinh had refused to leave. On 11 September, when President Diem directed Hinh to make a six-week "study tour" in France, Hinh had openly defied the order.

Because of the delicacy of the situation, Ambassador Heath had instructed all members of the American mission to have no contact with Hinh. But General O'Daniel had become convinced by the afternoon of the 12th that Hinh was about to launch a coup and that he should talk with Hinh and try to dissuade him from acting. Unable to contact either Ambassador Heath or Counselor Randolph A. Kidder (it was a Sunday), O'Daniel had seen no recourse but to take action on his own. Accompanied by his special assistant, Colonel Rosson, O'Daniel had called on Hinh at his home, where in a two-hour conversation Hinh had protested his loyalty and his willingness to cooperate with Diem. O'Daniel always believed that his visit to Hinh was instrumental in averting a coup.

The incident nevertheless worsened relations between O'Daniel and Ambassador Heath. Reporting to the State Department, Heath said that he

[10]Ibid.
[11]Heath to State Dept, 26 Aug 54, 751G.00/8–2654, records of Dept of State.
[12]Ltr, Maj Gen Edward Lansdale to Chief of Military History, 6 Jun 79, CMH files.
[13]Heath to State Dept, 27 Aug 54, 751G.00/8–2754, records of Dept of State.
[14]Ibid., and 29 Aug 54, 751G.00/8–2954, records of Dept of State.

General Hinh With Prime Minister Diem *in Saigon.*

had explicitly told O'Daniel not to see Hinh and that his action was "in direct contravention of my instructions, indulging his tendency to take matters into his own hands and to mix into political situations without proper clearance from the Chief of Mission." When confronted, O'Daniel "insisted that he had not heard my instructions." Heath also said O'Daniel told him that he preferred "Hinh to Diem should he have to make a choice between the two men."[15] General O'Daniel later denied making either statement but said he was so convinced that something had to be done immediately that, when unable to reach Heath or the embassy's counselor, he had acted on his own.[16]

As the situation continued tense with recurring rumors of plots, Ambassador Heath, General O'Daniel, and other members of the U.S. mission all made clear to Hinh that in the event of a coup, American aid would almost certainly be cut off. When Hinh told O'Daniel's aide, Maj. Frank Gorman, in late September that he would attempt a takeover if his terms were not met,

[15]Ltr, Heath to State Dept, 16 Sep 54, in *U.S.-Vietnam Relations*, 10:753–55.

[16]See Intervs, author with O'Daniel, 2 Feb 75, and Charles V. P. von Luttichau and Charles B. MacDonald with O'Daniel, 9 Mar 70. Hinh's chief of staff, General Tran Van Don, believed that "Hinh had the military clout to overthrow Diem but instead preferred to bluff and play around." Don recalled only one occasion, at the end of September, when Hinh seriously considered staging a takeover but was dissuaded by General Ely. MFR, Conversation Between Author and General Don, 6 Dec 76. All in Historians files, CMH.

Heath "reminded Hinh that the bulk of the Vietnamese defense budget was defrayed by the United States . . . any *coup de force* by the Army would be fatal to the future of the Army of Vietnam. It would be disastrous for Hinh personally."[17] Although by early October General O'Daniel thought he had persuaded Hinh to issue a statement to the army affirming his loyalty to the Diem government and warning against violent action, Hinh at the last moment began to quibble over the wording.

Hinh's reluctance to issue the statement may have come from an awareness that his position was steadily deteriorating, for the Diem government had begun to receive powerful psychological support from the United States. In mid-October Washington authorized Heath and O'Daniel to

state without equivocation that no long range support to the Vietnamese armed force will be programed or extended by the U.S. as long as there is the slightest doubt as to the loyalty of the Chief of Staff or other high officers. Should you determine that it is not practical to work with the existing armed forces organization you are authorized to approach the Prime Minister to say that the U.S. is willing to commence immediately the organization of a national police or other force separate from the armed forces.[18]

On 15 October an influential Democratic member of the Foreign Relations Committee, Senator Mike Mansfield, submitted a report on a visit to Vietnam in which he strongly endorsed Diem as the only possible leader for a non-Communist South Vietnam. If the Diem government fell, said Mansfield, the United States should consider suspending all aid to South Vietnam since it was improbable that any other suitable leader could be found. President Eisenhower voiced his support for Diem in a letter, made public on 25 October, in which he told the Vietnamese prime minister that the American ambassador to South Vietnam had been instructed "to examine with you . . . how an intelligent program of American aid given directly to your Government can serve to assist Viet Nam in its present hour of trial."[19]

Although the Eisenhower letter and the Mansfield report delighted Diem, they surprised and irritated the French. Premier Pierre Mendes-France objected that the Eisenhower letter went far beyond his understanding of agreed Franco-American policy in regard to Diem.[20] Ambassador Henri Bonnet in Washington complained to Secretary Dulles that "the President's letter had given Diem full rein without requiring of him . . . that he should first succeed in forming a strong and stable government."[21] The French regarded the Eisenhower letter as only the most glaring example of a dangerous and irresponsible anti-French policy pursued by the United States in South Vietnam. The French Deputy High Commissioner in Indochina, Jean Dariden, told an American diplomat that "while Heath was doing his best to

---

[17]Heath to State Dept, 29 Sep 54, 751G.00/9–2954, and 10 Oct 54, 751G.00/10–1054, both in records of Dept of State.

[18]Dept of State to Saigon 1679, 15 Oct 54, copy in Collins Papers.

[19]*Public Papers of the Presidents: Dwight D. Eisenhower, 1954* (Washington, 1960), Item 306, p. 949.

[20]C. Douglas Dillon to State Dept, 24 Oct 54, 751G.00/10–2454, records of Dept of State.

[21]Memorandum of Conversation, Dept of State, 26 Oct 54, sub: Indochina, *U.S.-Vietnam Relations*, 10:799.

set things straight, the American intelligence services, STEM, and MAAG were going off on separate tangents. One often gets the impression that their principal aim is to remove all French influence and prestige."[22] An article in *Le Monde* entitled "M. Diem, Marionette Americaine," declared that "the young turks of the American embassy and the American services tear each other apart in their rivalry. . . . They see in Mr. Diem only what they consider his 'qualities.' "[23]

Just as the French saw in U.S. actions a concerted effort to undermine their interests and prestige, so many Americans in Saigon were convinced that because of Diem's outspoken anti-French attitude, some elements among the French were scheming to overthrow him. The State Department observed that the Vietnamese factions and individuals most opposed to Diem were also those most susceptible to French influence and speculated that the knowledge that many French groups had never accepted Diem must have encouraged General Hinh and his followers. French officials sometimes spoke as if they were "hankering to reestablish a puppet regime similar to the Cochinchina Republic of 1946."[24] The CIA reported persistent rumors of French-backed plots to overthrow Diem.[25] General Ely noted later that he was, in fact, often "hindered by elements that were sometimes difficult to identify but were sentimentally hostile to the Diem government as well as to the Americans."[26]

Also worrisome to many Americans was a special mission under Jean Sainteny which the French had established in Hanoi after the Geneva Conference to look after their interests in North Vietnam. This action suggested to American officials that the French were hedging their bets and preparing to make a deal with the Viet Minh at the expense of Diem to preserve their interests in Vietnam.[27] Rumors circulating in Paris that the French had given up hope of holding South Vietnam and were keeping in the south a force just large enough to fight its way out added to these misgivings.[28]

In that atmosphere of mutual suspicion General Collins' arrival served at first to heighten French nervousness. General Ely believed that the United States was replacing Ambassador Heath "because his realism had caused him to oppose the State Department in defending positions which were very close

[22]Memorandum of Conversation, 30 Nov 54, Incl to W. M. Gibson to Livingston Merchant, 3 Dec 54, 751G.00/12–354, records of Dept of State.
[23]Ibid., see copy of article attached.
[24]State Dept to Am Embassy, Saigon, 21 Oct 54, 751G.00/10–2154, records of Dept of State.
[25]Ibid.
[26]Ely, *L'Indochine dans la Tourmente*, p. 64. Maj. Gen. Edward G. Lansdale observed: "I respect General Paul Ely as a man of great decency. When I tried to carry out a project jointly for him and General Collins in 1955 I discovered some of Ely's staff up to shenanigans unknown to him. Apparently they considered him to be a novice in the problems of 'their' Vietnam." Ltr, Lansdale to Chief of Military History, 6 Jun 79.
[27]Memo, K. T. Young for Acting Secy of State, 21 Sep 54, Lot 58D207, records of Dept of State; Collins, *Lightning Joe*, p. 395. Minister Sainteny, in a conversation with the author in 1975, firmly denied that there was any contradiction between France's professed support of Diem and his mission to Hanoi. Interv, author with Jean Sainteny, Paris, France, Nov 75, Historians files, CMH.
[28]Memo, K. T. Young for Asst Secy, FE, 4 Dec 54, sub: Principal Points for Discussion Regarding Associated States, Lot 58D207, records of Dept of State.

to ours." Ely predicted that the Collins visit would create a very unfavorable impression in France where it "would be taken as meaning that the U.S. was going to take over in Indochina." He strongly hinted to Ambassador Heath that he did not care to remain in Vietnam under such conditions.[29] General Ely did not come to Saigon for General Collins' arrival, remaining instead at his villa in the highland resort of Dalat. The next day Collins flew to Dalat to see Ely, with whom he had worked on the NATO Standing Group. Collins' tact and candor, and perhaps also his excellent command of French, soon won Ely's confidence; by the end of the first day the two were calling "each other by the first names and exchanging hearty pats on the back."[30]

Ely and Collins agreed that the feud between Diem and Hinh had to be ended and that there should be no support for the armed militias of the Binh Xuyen and the sects, which posed a threat to the development of an effective national army. General Ely also explained that even with the Vietnamese Army, a sizable French Expeditionary Corps would have to remain in Vietnam both to guard against Viet Minh aggression and to protect French Nationals. Little reliance, in his view, could be placed on assistance from the Southeast Asia Treaty Organization. Collins agreed to recommend continued U.S. support of the French Expeditionary Corps, at least until the elections scheduled under the Geneva Agreements, but cautioned that Congress would probably cut funding somewhat. He also pointed out that even with the Expeditionary Corps at full strength and backed by the Vietnamese National Army, Vietnam would still have to rely on the SEATO pact as the major deterrent to aggression.[31]

Four days after General Collins arrived in Saigon, the crisis engendered by General Hinh's intransigence was at last resolved. On 12 November, under considerable French and American pressure, Emperor Bao Dai ordered Hinh to report to him in France; two weeks later Hinh reluctantly complied. His departure left General Collins free to proceed with the program directed by the National Security Council. Collins and his staff had developed a seven-point program of measures to strengthen the Vietnamese government, including U.S. support for refugee resettlement, land reform, creation of a national assembly, economic development aid, and a program to train Vietnamese for public administration.[32] Collins also planned to extend his mission until mid-January when he would assess its chances of success.

The most important aspect of the seven-point program was the revitalization of the Vietnamese Army. By mid-November Collins had drawn up a proposal to form a smaller but well-equipped and well-trained army. Under its terms, the existing force of about 170,000 men was to be reduced by July 1955 to some 77,000. Entirely under Vietnamese command and control, the

---

[29]Ely, *L'Indochine dans la Tourmente*, p. 168; Heath to State Dept, 3 Nov 54, 120.2510/11–354, records of Dept of State.

[30]Ely, *L'Indochine dans la Tourmente*, p. 168.

[31]MFR, Col John Kelly, 15 Nov 54, sub: Discussions Between Ambassador Collins and General Ely, Collins Papers.

[32]Memo, Chairman, OCB Working Committee on Indochina, for Chairman, OCB, 8 Dec 54, sub: Brief Status Rpt, Lot 58D207, records of Dept of State.

revamped army was to have 6 divisions—3 full field divisions capable of at least delaying an invasion from North Vietnam and 3 territorial divisions organized around existing regional commands to provide internal security and, if necessary, to reinforce the field divisions.[33] Quickly approved by the Joint Chiefs of Staff and the State Department, Collins' proposal would form the basis for American planning over the next six months.

There remained the problem of obtaining French agreement and cooperation, an unlikely prospect, for American and French objectives in Vietnam were by that time far apart. The French resented what they saw as American attempts to assume the control of economic and military assistance to Vietnam while expecting France to bolster South Vietnam militarily. The French had asked for, and believed they deserved, American financial support of $330 million as a first-year outlay to maintain their Expeditionary Corps in Vietnam at a time when French troops were badly needed in North Africa. Washington, as General Collins had predicted, was unenthusiastic about bankrolling the Corps Expeditionaire although American leaders insisted that France cooperate in making South Vietnam militarily secure. Many American officials believed that the French forces were potentially more a source of trouble than of protection for the Diem government.[34] Even General Collins, who believed a premature withdrawal of French forces would be disastrous militarily, was not inclined to support the huge sum the French asked.[35] The outcome was predictable. When the United States agreed to provide only $100 million for the first year's support of the French Expeditionary Corps, France immediately accelerated the withdrawal of its troops so that by the end of 1955 only about 40,000 French troops would be left in South Vietnam.

Establishing a Training Mission

U nder those circumstances, it was imperative to implement the program for improving the effectiveness of the South Vietnamese Army as soon as possible. To General Ely, Collins proposed that the French agree to grant full autonomy—that is, actual command of all Vietnamese Army units by Vietnamese officers—by July 1955 and full American control of the training program under Ely's general direction with a gradual phasing out of all French instructors and advisers.[36]

Meeting with Secretary Dulles in Washington in November, Premier Mendes-France objected to all aspects of the Collins proposal. He doubted that the South Vietnamese Army could be ready for autonomy by July 1955

---

[33]Memo, John Foster Dulles for President, 17 Nov 54, sub: General Collins' Recommendations Regarding Force Levels, 751G.00/11 – 1754, records of Dept of State.

[34]*U.S.-Vietnam Relations*, vol. 1, pt. IV.A.3, p. 6; The Joint Chiefs of Staff and the War in Vietnam, p. 67.

[35]Memo, Dulles for President, 17 Nov 54, sub: General Collins' Recommendations Regarding Force Levels.

[36]The Joint Chiefs of Staff and the War in Vietnam, p. 69.

and pointed out that a U.S. advisory group large enough to take over training would violate the limitations imposed at Geneva on stationing foreign troops in Vietnam. Replacing French instructors and advisers with Americans would represent an intolerable loss of prestige to France and would damage the morale of the French Expeditionary Corps.

After prolonged discussion Dulles and Mendes-France agreed to let Collins and Ely settle the matter. On 13 December 1954, after three weeks of negotiations, Collins and Ely initialed a draft minute of understanding. The agreement specified a force structure of around 88,000 men for the South Vietnamese Army, slightly more than Collins had recommended in November. That figure was to be attained by reducing the existing Vietnamese armed forces. The French were to grant full autonomy to the South Vietnamese Army by July 1955. General O'Daniel was to have full responsibility for assisting the government of Vietnam in organizing and training its armed forces, working under the French Commander in Chief, Indochina, who was specifically recognized as possessing "overall authority in all matters pertaining to the strategic direction of French and Vietnamese armed forces and to the security of Vietnam against external aggression and internal subversion."[37]

Since the understanding embodied essentially what Collins had earlier asked, it was hardly likely to be well received in Paris; Mendes-France announced that it would have to be studied closely for possible conflicts with the Geneva Agreements.[38] Specifically objecting to the wording of the agreement, the French submitted a revised draft which made no mention of General O'Daniel's authority in matters of training. A month of bickering followed before the United States and France agreed on a compromise. The French formally presented their version of the agreement to the Diem government; an exchange of letters spelled out the promise of autonomy for South Vietnamese forces and the grant of authority to General O'Daniel. On 12 February 1955, almost ten months after first proposing to train Vietnamese forces, O'Daniel assumed responsibility for the organization and training of the South Vietnamese Army. The signing of the Collins-Ely agreement marked the achievement of a long-sought American goal, seemingly without sacrificing French goodwill and cooperation, as indicated by the arrangement for joint Franco-American training under the overall authority of General Ely but the direct command of General O'Daniel.

On 3 December 1954, even before the formal adoption of the Collins-Ely agreement by the French and American governments, Collins and Ely directed General O'Daniel to establish a skeleton staff for the new binational training organization, tentatively designated the Advisory Training and Organization Mission.[39] Three days later a skeleton staff of five French and five American

---

[37]Am Embassy, Saigon, to State Dept, 13 Dec 54, 751G.00/12–1354, records of Dept of State.
[38]The Joint Chiefs of Staff and the War in Vietnam, p. 71.
[39]Monthly Rpt of TRIM Activities, Rpt No. 1, 3 Dec 54 Through 28 Feb 55, Attachment to MAAG Monthly Activities Rpt No. 27 for Feb 55, 15 Mar 55, 370.2, records of MAAG Indochina, RG 334.

officers reported to South Vietnamese general staff headquarters. Over the next few weeks as the staff grew, the mission established offices at the headquarters of the Military Assistance Advisory Group. The name of the training organization was changed to the Military Support Mission and finally to the Training Relations and Instruction Mission (TRIM).[40]

General O'Daniel was formally designated chief of the training mission on 12 February 1955, and all American and French advisory and training personnel attached to South Vietnamese units were assigned to his command. The French contingent consisted of about 200 officers who had previously served as advisers or officer cadre. Although the table of distribution for the training mission called for 217 American officers, in March 1955 only 68 were available. By July the total had increased to 121, but the goal of 217 was not to be reached during 1955.[41] In the directive specifying the mission's duties, General Ely said the South Vietnamese Army should be trained to establish order and governmental authority in all areas of South Vietnam, to conduct counter-guerrilla activities in the event of a new insurrection, and to wage conventional warfare against a Viet Minh invasion of South Vietnam. Deficient leadership at all levels, Ely believed, was the principal problem facing the South Vietnamese.[42]

General O'Daniel organized the training mission in two parts: a staff echelon at the level of the South Vietnamese armed forces headquarters and a field and school echelon assigned to specific units and agencies of the South Vietnamese Army. Commanded by Col. Andre Masse of the French Army, the staff echelon was responsible for plans, operations, and intelligence. It consisted of four divisions, with air force, army, and navy sections responsible for the training, organization, and logistics of their respective services. The fourth, national security, division was led by Air Force Col. Edward G. Lansdale. Nominally the assistant U.S. air attache, Lansdale actually headed the Saigon Military Mission, a special Central Intelligence Agency team separate from the regular CIA organization in Vietnam.

Lansdale was a colorful and controversial figure who had served as an adviser to President Ramon Magsaysay in the anti-Huk campaign in the Philippines.[43] His specialty was political and psychological warfare, his objective to help the Diem government use the army to win the loyalty and cooperation of the rural population, particularly in areas formerly controlled by the Viet Minh, and to ferret out and destroy the Viet Minh underground

---

[40]Col. Victor J. Croizat, U.S. Marine Corps, recalled that because the acronym for the Advisory Training and Organization Mission (ATOM) had "unfortunate connotations . . . a little group gathered in O'Daniel's office to choose a new name. After seeing how ATOM was functioning, I suggested we redesignate it Supreme Headquarters Instruction and Training. . . . General O'Daniel didn't think that was very funny, but some staff officers thought it quite appropriate." Oral History Interv with Croizat, U.S. Marine Corps Historical Center.

[41]U.S. Army Command and General Staff College (USACGSC), Staff Study on Army Aspects of the Military Assistance Program in Vietnam, 10 June 1960, p. D – 4, copy in Historians files, CMH.

[42]Ely, General Directives Concerning the Training of the Vietnamese Army, 26 Feb 55, Incl O to Monthly Rpt of TRIM Activities, Rpt No. 1.

[43]Edward Geary Lansdale, *In the Midst of Wars* (New York: Harper & Row, 1972), pp. 32 – 125.

network. Lansdale enjoyed the confidence of Prime Minister Diem and had been active in efforts to resolve the problem of General Hinh.

At the field and school echelon of the training mission, adviser groups consisting of a senior adviser and several associate advisers were assigned to subordinate headquarters, units, schools, and training centers. The French assumed primary responsibility for officer and specialist training schools at Dalat, Thu Duc, and Camp Chanson; the Americans were responsible for other schools, basic training centers, and field forces.

The Training Relations and Instruction Mission was thoroughly binational in structure. American division chiefs had French deputies and vice versa, while at the field and school echelon senior and associate advisers were of different nationality. Despite that binational composition, the training mission was primarily an American enterprise, and French cooperation was sometimes slow and grudging. Differences between French and American training concepts, standards of efficiency, and supply procedures made friction between the officers of the two countries almost unavoidable, and the South Vietnamese complained that French instructors often ridiculed the South Vietnamese soldiers and the new American training methods. At one point the army's chief of staff asked the Americans not to discuss the shortcomings and errors of South Vietnamese units in the presence of the French during the monthly senior advisers' conferences.[44]

With precipitate withdrawal of the French Expeditionary Corps and renewal of hostilities by North Vietnam both considered likely, the American officers in the training mission felt they were working against a desperately short timetable. In an attempt to improve the South Vietnamese units rapidly, they employed on-the-job training, orientation courses, and mobile and technical training teams. A program to provide 6,300 specialists by the end of 1955 was instituted in which students were to receive only the minimum training needed to perform their functions.[45] A demonstration battalion was established to "show the Vietnamese how a battalion ought to look, how it ought to function, how it ought to be organized."[46] A division course was instituted for commanders of the light divisions and a six-week civil guard course for militiamen. Yet until adequate numbers of South Vietnamese could be trained as instructors, no fundamental reorganization of the training program or school system could take place.

A basic problem was language. Few Americans spoke Vietnamese, nor were there nearly enough South Vietnamese interpreters and translators. All forms of training aids and literature had to be translated from French or English into Vietnamese, a job complicated by the fact that there were no expressions in the Vietnamese language for most American military terms and

[44]Ltr, Lt Gen Samuel T. Williams to Adm Felt, 20 Feb 59, Samuel T. Williams Papers, Folder 54, CMH.

[45]Briefing for Lt Gen Bruce C. Clarke, CGUSARPAC, Incl to Rpt of Visit of Lt Gen Bruce C. Clarke to Western Pacific and Southeast Asia, 6–29 Sep 55, vol. III, CCS 092 Asia (6–25–48), BP pt. 5, JCS records.

[46]Interv, author with O'Daniel, 3 Feb 75.

phrases.[47] With the help of the United States Information Service, the advisory group opened an English-language school in Saigon in June 1955, but it was many months before enough translators and interpreters were available to meet the needs of the training program.

Although the basic aims of the Training Relations and Instruction Mission were to train and develop the efficiency of the South Vietnamese armed forces, most of its activities during the first three months were devoted to aiding Diem in asserting the authority of the South Vietnamese government over areas which had formerly been under Viet Minh control. Of particular concern were the Ca Mau peninsula at the southern tip of South Vietnam and the central coastal provinces of Binh Dinh and Quang Ngai, areas designated by the Geneva Convention as regroupment zones for Viet Minh military forces. Since the Viet Minh were scheduled to evacuate Ca Mau on 8 February 1955 and Quang Ngai and Binh Dinh Provinces in April, the government had to be prepared to move in quickly to fill the vacuum. American officers in Colonel Lansdale's National Security Division, many of them specialists in psychological warfare, began an accelerated program to prepare the South Vietnamese for those moves. They helped the South Vietnamese to set up a civil affairs organization, to create specialized task forces, and to draft appropriate directives.[48] American advisers were convinced that areas that had been under firm Viet Minh control had to be occupied by the army, for whatever the shortcomings of the military leaders, they were more experienced than civilian officials and they controlled fairly efficient transport and communications systems.[49]

On 31 December 1954 President Diem issued a national security action directive, which established three classifications for the areas to be occupied. Provinces in a first category—national security—would require troops to establish governmental authority; those areas were to be placed under a military commander with both civil and military power. Provinces in a second category—transition—were those in which the transfer from military to civilian jurisdiction might be started, with a civilian deputy province chief who was to be granted progressively wider responsibilities as the province became more stabilized. Provinces in the third, civil, category were considered sufficiently under control to be run by a civilian province chief.[50]

Occupying the Ca Mau peninsula was clearly an assignment for the South Vietnamese Army. In planning for the occupation—called Operation LIBERTY—American advisers were particularly concerned lest the troops indulge their usual penchant for intimidating, abusing, and robbing the population (in November 300 officers and men had combined to rob the treasury of the town of Phan Rang).[51] Thus the advisers stressed training for civic action:

[47]Briefing for Clarke.
[48]Interv, author with Rufus Phillips, formerly of National Security Div, TRIM, 24 Mar 76; Memo, Lansdale for Ambassador Ellsworth Bunker, 18 May 67, sub: Historical Notes; copy of both in Historians files, CMH.
[49]Lansdale, *In the Midst of Wars*, pp. 229 – 30.
[50]Monthly Rpt of TRIM Activities, Rpt No. 1, sec. III, National Security, pp. 52 – 53.
[51]Min, Conf at MAAG, 29 Nov 54, O'Daniel Papers.

psychological warfare, food distribution, and medical care. At the same time, troop information teams staged plays and demonstrations to emphasize the need for soldiers to behave considerately toward the civilian population.[52] With virtually no active opposition from the Viet Minh, the operation proceeded smoothly, and the training mission was soon able to cite impressive statistics: 1,300 patients a day treated by medical civic action teams during the first weeks, 250,000 propaganda leaflets dropped. But the long-range impact on the population was minimal: the Viet Minh had left behind an underground governmental structure and cadres of guerrillas upon which the occupation had little apparent effect.[53]

Operation GIAI PHONG in Binh Dinh and Quang Ngai Provinces in April produced similar results. The training mission's report cited "enthusiastic demonstrations everywhere . . . dispensaries established . . . 1,020 tons of rice moved to the area, roads improved."[54] Yet those accomplishments also produced no lasting effect, for the political and social conditions which had long generated support for the Viet Minh remained virtually unchanged.

Confrontations With the Sects

The problems of civic action were soon overshadowed by the complexities of South Vietnamese politics. On 3 March 1955 leaders of the Cao Dai and Hoa Hao sects joined with the Binh Xuyen to form a United Front of Nationalist Forces; three weeks later they issued an ultimatum to President Diem demanding formation of a new national government. The dissatisfaction of the sects focused on plans for the Vietnamese National Army, which called for relatively small numbers of sect troops to be integrated into new army units and the rest to be disbanded. The sects had also been angered when, in February, the French had abruptly terminated subsidies paid the sect forces. The sect leaders, whose political power rested largely in their troops, demanded that their private armies be integrated intact into the South Vietnamese Army and stationed in their home territories and that the government provide financial assistance to any of their soldiers who might be forced to leave the military.

As early as January 1955, the American embassy in Saigon had warned that the problem of the integration of the sects and splinter group armies into the Vietnamese armed forces could prove a highly explosive issue.[55] In March General O'Daniel had met with leaders of the sects and explained that the

---

[52]Lansdale, *In the Midst of Wars*, pp. 232–33. General Lansdale observed: "Civic action was essentially the brotherly behavior of troops along lines taught by Mao and Giap to their troops. Admittedly the Americans never succeeded in teaching this to the Vietnamese Army. Up to the very end of the Vietnam war the army was still stealing from the population. We sure tried though." Ltr, Lansdale to Chief of Military History, 6 Jun 79.

[53]USACGSC, Staff Study on Army Aspects of Military Assistance, p. F–9; Lansdale, *In the Midst of Wars*, p. 236.

[54]TRIM Rpt No. 4, sec. III, National Security, Incl to MAAG Rpt No. 30 for May 55, 370.2, records of MAAG Indochina, RG 334.

[55]Charge, Saigon (Randolph Kidder), to State Dept, 26 Jan 55, 751G.00/1–2655, records of Dept of State.

Vietnamese Army Troops *fight the Binh Xuyen in Saigon.*

training mission planned to integrate some 20,000 of their troops into the Vietnamese National Army, but the leaders were not reassured.[56] Their basic concern, it developed, was that President Diem was trying to isolate them politically and to destroy the basis of their power.

The Binh Xuyen had most to lose. Having fought with the Viet Minh after the British and French reoccupied Saigon in 1945, the Binh Xuyen had rallied to the Bao Dai government in June 1948. With their leader, Bay Vien, appointed a colonel in the Vietnamese National Army, Binh Xuyen bands took over responsibility for local military operations in some sectors. By 1952 Bay Vien, then a brigadier general, had obtained a lease on all gambling operations in the Cholon section of Saigon, including the Grand Monde casino, the largest in the city. Three years later, the Binh Xuyen controlled virtually all of Cholon as well as the Saigon police force (reportedly sold to them by Bao Dai to pay his gambling debts).[57] These were gains not to be lightly surrendered.

After the French stopped their subsidies in February Diem began to put pressure on the Binh Xuyen and win factions of the sect forces to his

---

[56]John W. O'Daniel, Footsteps to Freedom, ch. 2, p. 6, manuscript of chapter in O'Daniel Papers.

[57]Binh Xuyen, Attachment to USARMA to ACSI, 8 Aug 53 (5–18–53) OARMA, records of ACSI.

Cao Dai Troops *parade in Saigon.*

side through bribery and persuasion. Cao Dai Generals Trinh Minh The, Nguyen Thanh Phuong, and Tran Van Soai and Hoa Hao General Nguyen Giac Ngo were all richly rewarded for "rallying" to the government with their troops.[58] (Diem complained to Lansdale that he had to pay "millions" to General The alone.)[59] These bribes could prove a double-edged sword, however, since the sect generals sometimes used part of their subsidies to suborn government troops.[60] Diem also moved against the Binh Xuyen by refusing to renew their license to operate the Grand Monde gambling casino. The Binh Xuyen responded by forming the United Front of Nationalist Forces. At first even the sect leaders who had previously rallied to Diem joined the United Front, but under pressure from Lansdale and Collins Generals Phuong and The publicly broke with the front when it issued the manifesto and reaffirmed their loyalty to Diem.[61]

[58]Ltr, Lt Joseph J. Redick to Lansdale, 19 Mar 55, Collins Papers; Collins, *Lightning Joe*, p. 397.
[59]Memo, Lansdale for Ambassador Collins and General O'Daniel, 21 Mar 55, sub: Highlights on Sect Problems, Collins Papers.
[60]Ltr, Redick to Lansdale, 19 Mar 55. General Lansdale commented: "I neither offered nor gave money or other favors, but did explain the realities of the situation to the [sect] leaders and urged them to make a choice." Ltr, Lansdale to Chief of Military History, 6 Jun 79.
[61]Memo, Lansdale for Ambassador Collins and General O'Daniel, 23 Mar 55, sub: Meeting With Ngo Dinh Diem; ibid. for Collins, 29 Mar 55, sub: Cao Dai Division in Sect United Front; both in Collins Papers. Lansdale, *In the Midst of Wars*, pp. 252–54.

President Diem With General Ely

In the weeks following the formation of the front General Collins worked to head off a confrontation between Diem and the sects. A joint French-American team of twenty officers was hastily formed to study the sect problem. Brig. Gen. Fernand Gambiez, who headed the French part of the team, argued that the sects did not trust Diem and could not be expected to give up their arms as long as Diem was head of government. Gambiez insisted that the French were using their influence to placate the sects and that most individual Frenchmen who had been supplying arms to the sects had been identified and stopped. He believed the sect problem could be brought under control only after the integration or resettlement of the sect soldiers had been completed. Until then it was unrealistic to expect the sect leaders to give up their arms and recognize the Vietnamese National Army as the sole legitimate armed force.[62]

Diem was in no mood to wait patiently as Gambiez suggested. He replied to the sects' ultimatum with an offer to negotiate, but he refused to resign and moved army units from Tonkin, loyal to him, into the city.[63] On 29 March he ordered the replacement of the Binh Xuyen chief of the National

---

[62]Memo, Counselor of Embassy for Ambassador, 16 Mar 55, sub: Discussion With General Gambiez, Collins Papers.
[63]Collins, *Lightning Joe*, p. 398.

Police, Lai Van Sang, by one of his own appointees. That night a band of about eighty Binh Xuyen attacked the police headquarters in Cholon which had been occupied earlier by Vietnamese National Army troops. Other Binh Xuyen units attacked army headquarters in Cholon and shelled the presidential palace. The attacks were repulsed, and General Ely arranged a shaky truce the following day.

In the clash in Saigon, General O'Daniel was "convinced that the Vietnamese military were fired on first by the enemy [the Binh Xuyen] and that the Vietnamese military had conducted itself in a creditable manner," and Colonel Lansdale would later call the action a Binh Xuyen ambush.[64] O'Daniel, Lansdale, and their staffs were outraged that the troops they were painstakingly training to combat the Viet Minh should be obliged to battle it out in the streets of Saigon with the gangsters of the Binh Xuyen.[65] When General Ely moved quickly with French troops to halt the fighting, O'Daniel and Lansdale concluded that the French had acted to protect the Binh Xuyen. They suspected that the French were supporting the Binh Xuyen and the sects in an attempt to sabotage the Diem government's efforts to establish its authority, possibly even with the goal of bringing it down.[66]

Although General Ely had little faith in Diem, he would later maintain that his only concern was to prevent bloodshed in the capital and to protect the lives and property of French colonials. Ely assumed that Diem could defeat the Binh Xuyen in Saigon, but thought that he would be unable to defeat them and the forces of the sects outside the city. Civil war might ensue and "throw Viet Nam into chaos . . . playing into the hands of the Viet Minh, who were only waiting for this to happen to send their revolutionary forces into action."[67]

Meanwhile, after a period of uncertainty, General Collins had concluded that Diem should be replaced. He had first become concerned in December 1954 when Diem refused, despite recommendations from Collins, Ely, Lansdale, and the visiting Senator Mansfield, to appoint as minister of defense a respected politician, Dr. Phan Huy Quat. This action led Collins to believe "that Diem does not have the capacity to unify the divided factions in Vietnam."[68] Yet a month later Collins had come to a more optimistic view, observing that Diem's "strong nationalism, tenacity, and spiritual qualities

---

[64]Msg, O'Daniel to CINCPAC, 30 Mar 55, records of MAAG Indochina, RG 334; Lansdale, *In the Midst of Wars*, p. 263.

[65]Lansdale, *In the Midst of Wars*, pp. 263–64.

[66]O'Daniel, Footsteps to Freedom, ch. 2, p. 3; Lansdale, *In the Midst of Wars*, p. 264.

[67]Ely, *L'Indochine dans la Tourmente*, p. 171. A high-ranking Communist defector told Jeffrey Race that the party made a serious error by not taking advantage of the Binh Xuyen crisis. "We should have supplied men and provided support. . . . But the responsible cadres failed to seize the opportunity and take full advantage of the situation. . . . If we had done so the armed conflict between the Binh Xuyen and the Diem regime would have been expanded and prolonged and so produced great benefit for the Party. . . . the cadres who were responsible were reprimanded for their 'mechanical interpretation' of the provisions of the Geneva Accords forbidding military activity." Jeffrey Race, *War Comes to Long An: Revolutionary Conflict in a Vietnamese Province* (Berkeley: University of California Press, 1971), p. 36.

[68]Collins to Defense Dept, 16 Dec 54, 751G.00/12–1654, records of Dept of State.

render him the best available Prime Minister to lead Vietnam in its struggle against Communism."[69]

The trouble with the sects again changed General Collins' mind. By early April he was urging the State Department to think in terms of alternatives to Diem. "The major portion of responsibility for the critical situation in which Diem now finds himself," noted Collins, "must, in all fairness, be laid at Diem's door." He had had "a fair chance to establish an effective government" but had "produced little, if anything, constructive."[70] Collins proposed replacing Diem with a coalition government under Foreign Minister Tran Van Do.

In Washington the Defense Department agreed that "alternatives to the Diem government should be given adequate consideration." Some advisers within the Office of the Assistant Secretary of Defense for International Security Affairs even went so far as to suggest that the withdrawal of U.S. support from South Vietnam "should not be stated as a clearcut negative" and suggested courses of action which the United States might take to "minimize the effects of a Communist take over in South Viet-Nam."[71]

Long under pressure from the French government to consider alternatives to Diem, Secretary of State Dulles had consistently refused to set a deadline for replacing Diem or even to discuss possible replacements.[72] Dulles admired Diem personally and after a visit to South Vietnam in late February had advised President Eisenhower that Diem was "much more of a personality than I had anticipated. He is not without defects but his merits seemed greater than I had thought."[73] Even had Dulles been inclined to dispense with Diem, he might have hesitated, for influential Democratic leaders, particularly Senator Mansfield, had made clear that they would not agree to support any other regime in Vietnam.[74] Dulles cautioned Collins that any change in the government might be for the worse. The Diem government, he said, had a right to assert its authority against "a gang which exploits its privileges to protect vice on a vastly profitable scale," even if that required the use of force.[75]

Collins remained adamant; Diem had to go.[76] While reluctantly agreeing to consider replacing Diem, Dulles insisted that Collins return to Washington to confer with the president and the National Security Council on future plans

[69]Collins, Rpt on Vietnam for the National Security Council, 20 Jan 55, *U.S.-Vietnam Relations,* 10:866.

[70]Collins to State Dept, 31 Mar 55, 751G.00/3 – 3155, records of Dept of State; Telg, Collins to Secy of State, 9 Apr 55, *U.S.-Vietnam Relations,* 10:894 – 96.

[71]Programs for the Implementation of U.S. Policy Towards South Viet-Nam, Incl to Ltr, H. Struve Hensel to Walter S. Robertson, 22 Apr 55, *U.S.-Vietnam Relations,* 10:931.

[72]Dulles to Am Embassy, Paris, 18 Apr 55, 751G.00/4 – 1855; State Dept Briefing Paper, 19 Jan 55, 751G.00/1 – 1955; Ltr, Douglas MacArthur II to Theodore Achilles, 20 Jan 55, 751G.00/1 – 2055. All in records of Dept of State.

[73]Interv with John W. Hanes, Dulles Oral History Collection; quote from Dulles to Acting Secy of State for President, 1 Mar 55, 751G.00/3 – 155, records of Dept of State.

[74]Memo of Conversation, Kenneth T. Young with Mike Mansfield, 8 Apr 55, 751G.00/4 – 855, records of Dept of State.

[75]Dulles to Am Embassy, Saigon, 9 Apr 55, *U.S.-Vietnam Relations,* 10:908.

[76]Telg, Collins to State Dept, 20 Apr 55, *U.S.-Vietnam Relations,* 10:918 – 22.

for Vietnam.[77] In a conversation with his brother, CIA Director Allen Dulles, the secretary unhappily observed that "it looks like the rug is coming out from under the fellow in Southeast Asia." In that event, the brothers agreed, "the gangsters will have won."[78]

Arriving in Washington on 21 April, General Collins repeated his oft-voiced objections to Diem: the prime minister lacked good judgment, was unable to work with other men of ability, and was isolated politically.[79] Two days later, he bluntly told President Eisenhower that no solution was possible in South Vietnam "as long as Diem remains."[80] When the president later expressed the view that it was essential for the South Vietnamese Army to destroy the power of the Binh Xuyen or no government could exist, General Collins replied that to attempt to destroy the Binh Xuyen and the sects would produce a civil war, that the Binh Xuyen might become guerrillas and "raise hell for years."[81] By late April it seemed apparent in Washington that Diem's days were numbered. Secretary Dulles informed Ambassador Dillon in Paris that "after full consultation here with General Collins, it appears that some change in political arrangements in Vietnam may be inevitable."[82]

But by then, a change in political arrangements quite different from anything envisioned in Washington was already under way in Saigon. On 28 April fighting again erupted between the Binh Xuyen and South Vietnamese troops, with the Binh Xuyen shelling the presidential palace. By that time the sect front had broken up after most of the Cao Dai forces, a portion of the Hoa Hao, and even some Binh Xuyen troops came over to Diem. When French forces failed to intervene, the Vietnamese Army troops in a few hours routed the Binh Xuyen forces and drove them into Cholon.

Now Bao Dai attempted to step in, summoning Diem to Paris for "consultations" and placing command of the army in the hands of a known enemy of the Diem regime, General Nguyen Van Vy. Diem and his brother Nhu countered by organizing representatives of defunct political parties, government functionaries, and sect leaders friendly to Diem in a General Assembly of the Democratic and Revolutionary Forces of the Nation. Stage-managed by Nhu, the assembly called for Bao Dai's abdication and a new government under Diem's leadership.[83] Army forces in the Saigon area under Colonels Tran Van Don and Duong Van Minh (who soon became generals) backed Diem, and General Vy fled to Dalat. By 2 May the South Vietnamese Army had driven the Binh Xuyen from the capital.[84]

[77]Dulles to Collins, 16 Apr 55, 751G.00/4–1655, records of Dept of State.

[78]John Foster Dulles Telecon with Allen Dulles, 11 Apr 55, Dulles Papers.

[79]Memo for ASD (ISA), 25 Apr 55, sub: Department of State Debriefing of General Collins, *U.S.-Vietnam Relations*, 10:937–40.

[80]Memo, William J. Sebald for Secy of State, 23 Apr 55, sub: President's Conversation With General Collins, 751G.00/4–2355, records of Dept of State.

[81]Min, 246th Meeting of the NSC, 28 Apr 55, Eisenhower-as-President Papers, Eisenhower Library.

[82]Dulles to Am Embassy, Paris, 27 Apr 55, 751G.00/4–2755, records of Dept of State.

[83]Buttinger, *Vietnam: A Dragon Embattled*, 2:880–83.

[84]Ibid., 2:883–85.

The French Withdraw

The crisis days of late April and early May served to exacerbate further the animosity and suspicion of the Americans in Saigon toward their French counterparts. Returning to Saigon at the beginning of May, General Collins was "shocked at the strong anti-French feeling among . . . staff officers as a result of the incidents of the past week."[85] Americans in Saigon believed that the French were deliberately hindering Diem's attempts to crush the Binh Xuyen, whose troops were permitted to take refuge in French Army "security zones" in the capital. The South Vietnamese Army also claimed to have captured French officers serving as advisers to the Binh Xuyen and to have discovered a French ambulance carrying concealed arms to them.[86] When General Ely complained that Charge d'Affaires Kidder, Colonel Lansdale, and other Americans had "failed to restrain Diem and even encouraged him," Counselor Kidder, who never conceived it as part of his mission to restrain Diem, replied that Ely's "almost hysterical" dislike of Diem had rendered him incapable of evaluating the situation objectively.[87] To the Americans it seemed that "some elements among the French had undertaken a deliberate anti-U.S. campaign." When someone planted bombs in several embassy vehicles and tossed a thermite grenade through the open window of an American officer's car, many Americans suspected the French.[88]

Echoes of the Franco-American disputes in Saigon found their way into American-British-French talks which opened in Paris on 8 May 1955. Secretary Dulles entered the talks buoyed by Diem's surprising success against the Binh Xuyen and convinced, as he told General Collins, that there was no longer a question of replacing Diem, for recent events had made Diem "in the U.S. and the world at large . . . a symbol of Viet nationalism struggling against colonialism and backward elements."[89] The French, on the contrary, saw the Binh Xuyen affair as demonstrating that Diem was "not only incapable but mad."[90] At the talks French Foreign Minister Edgar Faure predicted that a continuation of the Diem regime would widen the breach between the United States and France and result in a Viet Minh victory. Under those circumstances, he said, France could not continue in Vietnam. "What would you say," asked Faure, "if we were to retire entirely from Indochina and call back the FEC [French Expeditionary Corps] as soon as possible?"[91] Calling for a brief recess to consider the French proposal, Dulles told Washington that Faure had, in effect, issued an ultimatum. If convinced that replacing Diem was no longer admissible, the United States faced the choice of withdrawing

---

[85]Collins to Dept of State, 3 May 55, 751G.00/5 – 355, records of Dept of State.
[86]Buttinger, *Vietnam: A Dragon Embattled*, 2:886.
[87]C. Douglas Dillon to State Dept, 2 May 55, 751G.00/5 – 255, and Kidder to State Dept, 28 Apr 55, 751G.00/4 – 2855, both in records of Dept of State.
[88]O'Daniel, Footsteps to Freedom, ch. 2, pp. 4 – 5.
[89]Dulles to Am Embassy, Saigon, 3 May 55, 751G.00/5 – 355, records of Dept of State.
[90]Telg, Paris to Secy of State, 8 May 55, *U.S.-Vietnam Relations*, 10:963.
[91]Ibid., 10:964.

from Vietnam or of precipitating a French withdrawal by continuing to support him.[92]

The Joint Chiefs of Staff commented that, while continued support for Diem was a matter of policy to be decided by the president, in their view Diem's government showed "the greatest promise of achieving the internal stability essential for the future security of Vietnam." Although a precipitate withdrawal of the French Expeditionary Corps would make South Vietnam less stable, they suggested that "possible United States actions under the Southeast Asia Collective Defense Treaty could ultimately afford security to South Vietnam equal to that provided by the continued presence of the French Expeditionary Corps."[93] The National Security Council Planning Board had even fewer doubts. A French withdrawal, the planners believed, would remove the United States from the "taint of Colonialism" and end the danger that the French might make a deal with the Viet Minh.[94]

Americans in Saigon viewed the prospect of a sudden French withdrawal with no such equanimity. Counselor Kidder had already advised Washington that "saving this country from Communism . . . will require wholehearted agreement and coordination between Vietnamese, Americans and French. . . . If this tripartite approach is not secure, we should withdraw from Vietnam."[95] General Collins pointed out that a French withdrawal would have devastating effects on the logistical and training support programs for the South Vietnamese armed forces.[96]

Secretary Dulles apparently found the arguments of the National Security Council's Planning Board more convincing. Meeting with Faure again on 11 May, he observed that the problem in South Vietnam "did not lend itself to a contractual agreement." It would be best if the United States and France were to proceed independently while keeping each other fully informed of what they were doing.[97] Although face-saving agreements and formulas followed, the trilateral talks in reality marked the end of Franco-American collaboration in Vietnam and the end of American support for the French presence there.

The decision of the French and American governments to go their separate ways made the tasks of the Training Relations and Instruction Mission and the Military Assistance Advisory Group more difficult. Following the engagements in April and May between South Vietnamese troops and the Binh Xuyen, the French ceased to take any active part in the training mission; in Lansdale's National Security Division some French officers never appeared at their desks.[98] As the French accelerated their withdrawal, they cut drastically the number of officers assigned to the training mission. By fall 1955, French

[92]*U.S.-Vietnam Relations,* 10:974.
[93]Memo, JCS for Secy of Defense, 9 May 55, sub: Indochina (Vietnam), *U.S.-Vietnam Relations,* 10:971−73.
[94]Memo, C. H. Bonesteel III for Dulles, sub: Possible French Withdrawal From Vietnam, *U.S.-Vietnam Relations,* 10:975.
[95]Saigon to Secy of State, 5 May 55, *U.S.-Vietnam Relations,* 10:970.
[96]Collins to State Dept, 9 May 55, 751G.00/5−955, records of Dept of State.
[97]*The Joint Chiefs of Staff and the War in Vietnam,* pp. 120−21.
[98]Interv, author with Phillips, 24 Mar 76.

General O'Daniel Confers With President Diem

strength was reduced by more than 70 percent while American strength remained almost static until March of the next year.[99]

Diem's determination to destroy completely the power of the Binh Xuyen and to eliminate the private armies of the Cao Dai and Hoa Hao sects delayed the training of many South Vietnamese Army units. Over the next year, Diem used the army to rout the remnants of the Binh Xuyen from the swamps south of Saigon, to crush hostile factions of the Cao Dai, and to defeat the Hoa Hao during the winter and spring of 1955–56.[100] The campaigns against

[99]The following table shows TRIM strength from March 1955 to March 1956.

Date	U.S. Officers	French Officers
March 1955	68	209
May 1955	121	225
July 1955	124	108
September 1955	125	66
November 1955	142	58
January 1956	149	53
March 1956	189	0

Source: USACGSC, Staff Study on Army Aspects of Military Assistance, p. D–4.

[100]The Joint Chiefs of Staff and the War in Vietnam, pp. 134–35; Buttinger, *Vietnam: A Dragon Embattled*, 2:888–89.

the sects also prevented officers from attending staff or specialist schools and delayed a planned deployment of units to various parts of the country and their concentration into divisional formations.[101] Although O'Daniel protested that "it would be a mistake to allow a few bandits to hold large numbers of troops away from training," Diem was more concerned with eliminating the last vestiges of sect opposition than with training schedules and redeployments.[102]

O'Daniel had no more success in persuading Diem to ease his relentless pressure for a speedy and complete withdrawal of the French Expeditionary Corps from South Vietnam. Should a major Viet Minh attack develop, O'Daniel said, "two or three French divisions would look mighty good."[103] An early French pullout would leave a military vacuum which the South Vietnamese Army could not hope to fill before 1956. Diem replied that the French were not to be counted upon in a major battle; they "would be more of a hindrance than a help," and the Viet Minh were exploiting their stay for propaganda purposes.[104] O'Daniel countered by suggesting that the French remain in Vietnam under the auspices of the Southeast Asia Treaty Organization, making them subject to the SEATO high command. Yet Diem clung stubbornly to his decision. In early June when talks opened in Paris between the French and Diem's representative, Nguyen Puu Chau, he told the French that if they wanted to keep any military forces or installations in South Vietnam, they would have to submit to South Vietnamese command.[105] That kind of arrangement obviously had no appeal for the French, but since the negotiations also involved the nature of future political and economic relations between France and the Republic of Vietnam, they dragged on through the summer. Diem finally cut them off by terminating unilaterally the special economic and financial agreements that had been signed with France in 1954 and by withdrawing South Vietnam from the French Union. The following October in a national referendum in which the ballots cast exceeded the number of names on the electoral rolls, the citizens of South Vietnam voted to abolish the monarchy and elected Diem president of a Republic of Vietnam, officially established on 26 October 1955.[106]

Throughout that period the size of the French military in Vietnam had

[101]Memo for General O'Daniel, 28 Aug 55, sub: Record of Conversation at Meeting with President Diem; Memo, O'Daniel for Ambassador Reinhardt, 7 Sep 55, sub: Meeting With General Ty and General Minh, 5 Sep 55; ibid., 10 Sep 55, sub: Meeting With President Diem on 9 Sep 55. All in O'Daniel Papers.

[102]Memo, O'Daniel for Ambassador Reinhardt, 10 Sep 55, sub: Meeting With President Diem on 9 Sep 55. Lansdale's civic action specialists, on the other hand, considered that the war against the sects at least had the advantages of keeping the army in the countryside and in touch with the people. Interv, author with Phillips, 24 Mar 76.

[103]Memo, Lt Col Rolland W. Hamelin for O'Daniel, 13 Jul 55, sub: Conference With Mr. Tran Trung Dung, Deputy Minister of Defense; Memo, John M. Finn for Ambassador Reinhardt, 1 Aug 55, sub: Record of Conversations, President Diem and General O'Daniel; both in O'Daniel Papers.

[104]Ibid.; quote from Memo, Finn for Ambassador Reinhardt, 11 Jul 55, sub: Meeting With President Diem, O'Daniel Papers.

[105]Memo, Finn for Ambassador Reinhardt, 11 Jul 55, sub: Meeting With President Diem.

[106]Buttinger, *Vietnam: A Political History*, pp. 414–15.

continued to shrink. Even had the French been inclined to submit their forces to South Vietnamese command, they needed all available troops to put down insurrection in North Africa. By February 1956 only 15,000 French troops remained in South Vietnam, and on 26 April 1956 the French high command for Indochina was officially abolished. The Franco-American partnership in developing the South Vietnamese armed forces had lasted just over a year.

Long before the last French soldiers sailed, the authors of that partnership had gone. General Collins left Saigon on 14 May 1955, to be replaced by a new ambassador, G. Frederick Reinhardt, and two weeks later General Ely also ended his long and often stormy tour of duty in Vietnam. The experiment of creating a South Vietnamese Army had become an entirely American enterprise.

14

Picking Up the Pieces, 1955–1956

American leaders had begun 1955 confident that France would at last cooper-ate with the United States (on American terms) in building a stable govern-ment and an effective military establishment in South Vietnam. The sect crisis and Diem's subsequent triumph over the forces of the Binh Xuyen and the sects had dashed those expectations. Diem's open hostility to a continued French presence in South Vietnam and his unswerving insistence on removal of the last vestiges of the French Expeditionary Corps would have made continued Franco-American military collaboration virtually impossible even had France been inclined to continue it. In fact, France had no such inclina-tion. General Pierre Jacquot, who succeeded General Ely in May 1955 to oversee the French withdrawal, found that in Paris "no one wanted to hear about it [Vietnam]." The French considered it a lost cause and preferred to discuss means of salvaging their interests in North Africa.[1] They were bitter and disillusioned over what they considered Diem's treachery and irresponsi-bility toward them and angry at what they saw as the ill-concealed eagerness of many American technical and military advisers to shoulder them aside. The South Vietnamese Army's abrupt adoption of American-type uniforms and the American salute and a ceremonial burning by South Vietnamese officers of their French-style insignia of rank were galling to French pride and indicative of the mood of the Diem regime.[2]

In Washington the U.S. Army staff took a complacent view of the immi-nent French withdrawal, noting that exclusive American responsibility for training the South Vietnamese would make that training more effective and efficient, "not only because of the superiority of U.S. methods but also because of differences in French and American doctrine."[3] General O'Daniel

[1]Notes of Conference With Pierre Jacquot, 14 Dec 55, and Memo of Conversation, Capt Judson C. Spence with Gen Jacquot, 24 Feb 56, both in Folder 3, Williams Papers.
[2]Record of Conversation, Lt Gen Samuel T. Williams with Gen Pierre Jacquot, 11 Jan 56, in Folder 3, Williams Papers.
[3]Memo, DCSOPS for CofSA, 14 May 56, sub: U.S. Policy Toward Vietnam, CS 091 Vietnam, RG 319.

was less assured. He knew that at its existing strength his Military Assistance Advisory Group was woefully inadequate to assume the entire burden of training. The group could be expanded beyond the 342 officers and enlisted men in Vietnam at the time of the signing of the Geneva Agreement only if some way could be found to circumvent its restrictive terms. To provide some reinforcement, O'Daniel asked that neither personnel not physically present (on leave or otherwise), nor replacements whose tours overlapped with the men they were relieving, nor personnel assigned on temporary duty be counted against the advisory group's ceiling. He specifically wanted to bring in fifty-one mobile training teams for temporary duty tours of three to six months.[4]

General Williams

Ambassador Reinhardt and the Commander in Chief, Pacific, Admiral Felix Stump, endorsed O'Daniel's proposals, as did the Defense Department.[5] But the State Department demurred, insisting on strict adherence to the agreement's provisions. Although Defense Department legal experts advanced many arguments as to why Article 16 of the cease-fire agreement was not intended to apply to U.S. personnel, the State Department remained firm. A few months later the International Control Commission informed the United States that its members interpreted "military personnel" to mean all those subject to military law regardless of their status or function in South Vietnam.[6]

The issue of reinforcing the advisory group was still under discussion when General O'Daniel left South Vietnam, succeeded on 24 October 1955 by Lt. Gen. Samuel T. Williams. Since a separate advisory group had been established for Cambodia, on 1 November Williams' group dropped Indochina from its name and became the Military Assistance Advisory Group, Vietnam.

---

[4]Ltr, O'Daniel to CINCPAC, 23 May 55, sub: Guide Lines Relating to Space Ceiling for MAAG Indochina, I – 139915, records of ISA, RG 330.
[5]Memo, Director, Mil Asst Programs (Brig Gen J. K. Wilson), for ASD (ISA), 22 Aug 55, sub: Personnel Policy, MAAG Indochina, I – 14578/5, records of ISA, RG 330.
[6]Memo, Director, Office of Foreign Mil Affairs, for ASD (ISA), 6 Dec 55, sub: Personnel Ceiling, MAAG Vietnam, I – 16399/5, records of ISA, RG 330.

U.S. Tanks, Trucks, and Gun Carriages *abandoned by the French, 1955.*

The Temporary Equipment Recovery Mission

At the time of Williams' arrival, the need to expand the advisory group took on new urgency as the French withdrawal precipitated a major logistical crisis. During the four years that the United States had supported the French military effort, immense quantities of military equipment—from tanks and aircraft to small arms, ammunition, and spare parts—had poured into Vietnam. Under the terms of the Pentalateral Agreement of 23 December 1950 between the United States, France, and the Associated States, title to that equipment, valued at more than $1.2 billion, was to revert at the conclusion of hostilities to the United States.[7] Despite that requirement, American officials had made no plans or preparations for return of the equipment, and during the war the understrength advisory group had kept no accurate records or inventories of material delivered to the French. There was thus no recourse but to rely on the French for that information. The lack of records also made it impossible to determine which items of American equip-

---

[7]ASD (ISA) to Secy of Defense, 25 Jan 56, I—12377/6, *U.S.-Vietnam Relations*, 10:1045. The following discussion is based, in part, on Vincent H. Demma, *The Turnover in South Vietnam After the Indochina War*, CMH Monograph, 1969.

Axles and Engines *in outdoor storage.*

ment the French had purchased and which had been supplied under the Mutual Defense Assistance Program.

The Collins-Ely agreement of December 1954 provided that the United States and France would jointly survey military equipment of American origin in South Vietnam to determine which items would be returned to the United States, transferred to the South Vietnamese, or retained by the French. American inspectors were to be allowed to examine French depots and embarkation points, and losses incurred in combat or through wear were to be charged off equally to French- and American-owned equipment. Faced with a growing military crisis in North Africa, the French proceeded to implement those provisos so as to allow them to retain the best equipment of whatever origin. French officials sometimes refused to permit American inspection of their depots, and members of the advisory group reported that the French tried to remove assistance program markings from equipment they wanted to take with them.[8]

However disturbing that policy for the American taxpayer, the consequences for the South Vietnamese were catastrophic. Created originally as a kind of combat auxiliary to the French Expeditionary Corps, the South Viet-

[8]Demma, *Turnover*, p. 10; see also USACGSC, Staff Study on Army Aspects of Military Assistance, p. D–7; MFR, Gen M. O. Perry, 1 Feb 56, Folder 3, Williams Papers.

namese Army had almost no logistical capability and was singularly unprepared to cope with huge amounts of deteriorating and inoperable equipment. Yet the French "literally dumped mountains of equipment" upon the South Vietnamese.[9] At the central maintenance depot near Saigon, thousands of tons of equipment lay scattered in disorder over thirty-two acres of open fields; at the Chi Hoa salvage yard, American advisers found vehicles with rotted tires and vital parts missing; at Go Vap collecting point, vehicles the French described as in good condition had fenders, sides, or roofs dented in and parts removed.[10] Throughout the country, stores of American ammunition had been abandoned during the final months of the war—the French had found it easier to have ammunition shipped directly from the United States to combat zones than to move if from place to place within Vietnam.

The lack of spare parts made the situation even more intractable. On their unilateral inventory of equipment, not completed until March 1955, the French failed to list spare parts. To make an equal division of spare parts possible, the deputy chief of the advisory group, Brig. Gen. Miller O. Perry, pressed the French to sanction a joint inventory; they agreed only in February 1956. By that time most records had been removed "or were virtually useless for inventory purposes."[11]

The South Vietnamese received quantities of weapons and equipment far beyond the needs of the modest, 100,000-man army that the United States had agreed to support. In spite of the deluge, Diem and his army commanders, anticipating further trouble from the sects or a possible invasion by North Vietnam, were reluctant to part with any of it. That reluctance placed still further strains on the army's inadequate logistical system.

The 342 members of the advisory group, already trying to train and advise the South Vietnamese, had little hope even of coping with an estimated $100 million worth of equipment returned directly to U.S. control by the French. By the end of 1955 most American officials in South Vietnam and elsewhere had concluded that the logistical crisis had made an increase in the advisory group essential, whatever the political risks involved. Admiral Stump argued that the United States should be able to replace departing French troops with Americans, for the Geneva Agreements specified only that there would be no increase in *foreign* troops.[12] Both the Joint Chiefs and Secretary of Defense Wilson agreed that it would be more realistic to interpret the provisions of the Geneva Agreements to permit replacement of French military personnel by U.S. military personnel.[13]

---

[9]USACGSC, Staff Study on Army Aspects of Military Assistance, p. D–8.

[10]Memo, Capt J. M. Schultz for Gen Williams, 23 Mar 56, sub: Report of Visits to Local Depots, Folder 3, Williams Papers.

[11]Ltr, Ch, MAAG, Vietnam, to Ch, MAAG, France, 28 May 56, sub: Disposal of MDAP Excess, Attachment to Brig Gen D. S. Campbell to Secy of Defense, 30 Jul 56, I–650116, records of ISA; MFR, Perry, 1 Feb 56.

[12]CINCPAC to CNO, 2 Nov 55, CCS 092 Asia (6–25–48) (2), sec. 15, JCS records.

[13]Memo, JCS for Secy of Defense, 9 Dec 55, sub: Raising U.S. Military Personnel Ceiling of MAAG Vietnam, CCS 092 Asia (6–25–48) (2), sec. 16, JCS records; Ltr, Secy of Defense to Secy of State, 3 Dec 55, records of Dept of State.

Two interagency survey missions to South Vietnam in late 1955 had also recommended augmenting the advisory group with additional logistics personnel. The missions found an estimated $500 million worth of U.S. equipment, nominally in the custody of the Vietnamese but actually in unprotected dumps without proper maintenance. Most of this equipment was unidentifiable because of the inadequate inventory method the French and Vietnamese had employed. The surveyors reported that if the United States could regain accounting control of this property an estimated $150 million or more might be saved. The immediate need was for U.S. assistance to Vietnam in the identification, storage, and repair of equipment and the proper training of the Vietnamese in American supply management procedures. Unless the State and Defense Departments acted promptly tens of millions of dollars of U.S. property would be lost.[14]

The prospect of such a loss had a prevailing influence on the deliberations in Washington. Lt. Col. Robert Evans, an officer from the advisory group sent to plead the case for more logistics personnel, noted that the Department of Defense had "built a considerable fire under the problem of protecting U.S. equipment in Vietnam" and that nobody in the State Department wanted "to be responsible for the loss of 700 [sic] million dollars worth of equipment passing into Vietnam hands."[15] Secretary of Defense Wilson assured Secretary of State Dulles that the immediate dispatch of a team of 150 to 200 Americans skilled in supply and logistics would save the United States not less than $100 million worth of material.[16]

The State and Defense Departments discussed various courses of action. The United States rejected a French offer to leave some 1,000 logistics personnel in Vietnam for about one year, probably because the French also wished to keep their high command there for the same length of time and because, in American eyes, French supply management left much to be desired. President Eisenhower suggested that the Defense Department investigate using civilian contractors to recover its equipment; this idea was rejected because military personnel would be needed to identify the equipment.[17]

In the meantime Secretary Dulles had broached with Britain and France the sending of a temporary U.S. mission to recover the equipment. Both countries vigorously objected that sending additional American troops under whatever guise would violate the Geneva Agreements. Only after determining that two of the three members of the International Control Commission— Canada and India—would have no objection did they acquiesce.

With Dulles' approval, in early February 1956 the State and Defense Departments jointly developed a plan for a temporary U.S. mission to super-

---

[14]ASD (ISA) to Secy of Defense, 25 Jan 56, *U.S.-Vietnam Relations*, 10:1045; Staff Study: U.S. Policy Toward Vietnam, 25 Apr 56, ACSI 092 Vietnam, records of ACSI; Memo, Director of Opns, DCSOPS (Brig Gen David W. Gray), for DCSOPS, 1 Mar 56, sub: Utilization of Additional U.S. Military Personnel for Vietnam, G—3 091 Vietnam, RG 319.

[15]MFR, Lt Col Robert Evans, 21 Feb 56, Folder 3, Williams Papers.

[16]The Joint Chiefs of Staff and the War in Vietnam, p. 196.

[17]MFR, Col W. H. Brucker, 3 Mar 56, sub: U.S. Personnel Requirements for Vietnam, G—3 091 Indochina, RG 319.

U.S. Military Assistance Advisory Group Headquarters

vise recovery and shipment of excess equipment and to assist the South Vietnamese Army in improving its logistical capability.[18] Although the Army staff wanted its component of the mission to consist of standard technical units—ordnance, engineer, signal—that plan would have required a minimum of 2,800 men, a figure far in excess of what the State Department had in mind.[19]

The plan finally agreed upon was one submitted by Colonel Evans on behalf of the Military Assistance Advisory Group in Vietnam and the Commander in Chief, Pacific. It called for the Temporary Equipment Recovery Mission, known by the acronym TERM, to have 350 officers and enlisted men, who were to arrive in increments over a 120-day period. In addition to the members of the mission, which was to be separate from but subordinate to the Military Assistance Advisory Group, the advisory group was to gain 48 spaces to allow for personnel in transit, on leave, or otherwise temporarily out of South Vietnam. Of the total of 740 spaces in both groups, 535 were allotted to the U.S. Army.[20] To allow a reasonable time for the International

[18]Dulles to Saigon, 9 Feb 56, 320.3, records of MAAG Indochina.
[19]Memo, DCSOPS for CofSA, 14 May 56, sub: U.S. Policy Toward Vietnam; Memo, Director of Opns, DCSOPS, for DCSOPS, 1 Mar 56, sub: Utilization of Additional U.S. Military Personnel for Vietnam.
[20]Msg, State Dept to Saigon, 12 Apr 56, as quoted in Williams to ACSI for Secy of Army, 19 Jan 60, Folder 71, Williams Papers.

Control Commission to approve the recovery mission, none of the members was to arrive before the end of May. Although the State Department through the South Vietnamese government informed the commission on 20 May 1956 of plans for the recovery mission, it had received no reply when the first officers and men began to arrive in early June. In the event, neither approval nor disapproval was ever received from the International Control Commission.

The State Department specified that even though the mission would have to perform some training functions in connection with recovery and shipment of equipment, "training should in no case be allowed to become the single or even the primary duty" of the mission. In addition, a substantial amount of equipment would have to be actually recovered and shipped out of the country "so as to implement in good faith the promises made to other governments whose benevolent acquiescence to the operation we have obtained."[21]

Yet from the first the Military Assistance Advisory Group viewed the equipment recovery mission as a means of fleshing out its very limited training capability. Members of the mission were regularly assigned as advisers on logistical matters to South Vietnamese Army units and all major South Vietnamese logistical installations, and training courses were established for South Vietnamese logistics personnel. Despite the admonitions of the State Department, logistical training soon became the recovery mission's major activity, freeing members of the advisory group for operational and staff training. By the end of 1957, only 7 of the 350 personnel assigned to the equipment recovery mission were working full time on the recovery and disposition of American equipment.

As a clandestine reinforcement for the advisory group, the equipment recovery mission nevertheless had certain disadvantages. Few officers and men assigned to the mission had previous advisory experience, nor were they graduates of the Military Assistance Institute. Since their tour of duty lasted only eleven to twenty-three months, officers and noncommissioned officers of the mission barely had time to develop a feel for the country and for the peculiar problems of their assignments before they were replaced with other novices. To maintain the subterfuge that its primary mission was different from that of the advisory group, the equipment recovery mission operated as a quasi-separate organization with its own staff, which caused wasteful duplication and administrative problems for both organizations. Despite those shortcomings the mission was reasonably effective as a logistics training agency until eventually absorbed by the advisory group in 1959.

South Vietnamese Force Structure

Although the logistics crisis was the most critical and most visible result of the rapid French withdrawal, there were other far-reaching effects. The

---

[21]Ltr, Robert D. Murphy to Secy of Defense, 1 May 56, *U.S.-Vietnam Relations*, 10:1058

entire force plan for the South Vietnamese Army was now called into question. Generals Collins and Ely had planned for an army of some 100,000 men by the end of 1955. They had arrived at this figure based on the limited financial support the United States was willing to furnish and on the assumptions that France would continue to retain a sizable force in South Vietnam and that the South Vietnamese Army's primary role would be to preserve internal security.[22] The 100,000-man figure had disturbed South Vietnamese officials from the start, for they saw their army primarily as an instrument of defense against external aggression.[23] Minister of Defense Nguyen Van Vy had declared that his government could see no reason to cut the size of its army at the same time that the North Vietnamese were increasing theirs.[24]

Many American observers doubted that the 100,000-man figure could ever be reached given the total lack of proper administrative machinery to demobilize efficiently and the manifest opposition of Vietnamese politicians and sect leaders to any further reductions. There was also a well-founded fear of the economic consequences of forcing large numbers of former soldiers onto the already strained civilian economy. The French withdrawal gave considerable force to these objections, as did reports of the continued expansion and improvement of the Viet Minh Army to the north.[25]

By May 1955 Washington leaders had recognized that a larger force was unavoidable, and the Department of Defense asked the advisory group to devise a more realistic force structure for the Vietnamese Army without primary reference to cost restrictions. General O'Daniel responded with a recommendation for a new force level of 150,000 men. He suggested some 6,000 additional support troops, with the remaining increase almost equally divided between infantry and territorial, that is, internal security, troops and 1,000 added men each for the Air Force and the Navy. Washington approved these recommendations in August. (*Table 1*)

Contrary to the views of Washington officials, General O'Daniel from the first had wanted a South Vietnamese Army that could both maintain internal security and resist a North Vietnamese invasion.[26] With the withdrawal of the French Expeditionary Corps, the development of some capability to resist external attack became an obvious necessity, and the organization of the army came to reflect O'Daniel's concept of its dual mission. He planned to set up 4 field divisions and 6 light divisions with 13 territorial regiments for regional security. The territorial regiments were to be capable of consolidation into 3 or more light divisions if necessary.

O'Daniel designed both the field and light divisions to meet the peculiar needs of warfare in Indochina. About one-third the size of a standard U.S. infantry division, the light division was conceived as a small "mobile striking

[22]Rpt of Visit of Clarke to Western Pacific and Southeast Asia, vol. III, p. 6.
[23]Msg, O'Daniel to CG, USARPAC, 10 Aug 55, records of MAAG Indochina.
[24]Min, Conference at MAAG, 29 Nov 54.
[25]Ltr, O'Daniel to CINCPAC, 9 Aug 55, records of MAAG Indochina; The Joint Chiefs of Staff and the War in Vietnam, p. 143; Rpt of Visit of Clarke to Western Pacific and Southeast Asia, vol. III, pp. 6–7.
[26]Rpt of Visit of Clarke to Western Pacific and Southeast Asia.

TABLE 1—SOUTH VIETNAMESE ARMY FORCE BASIS AS PROPOSED
BY O'DANIEL, MAY 1955

Categories	Existing Strength	Proposed Strength
Army		
Central command	2,500	2,400
Field divisions	25,000	34,000
Light divisions	15,675	31,350
Airborne brigade	4,000	4,000
Support troops	13,275	19,700
Territorial commands	4,600	4,800
Territorial regiments	0	21,125
Territorial support troops	8,450	9,000
Schools and camps	6,000	6,000
Pipeline	4,000	9,625
Reduced pay trainees	10,000	0
Total, Army	94,000ª	142,000
Navy	3,000	4,000
Air Force	3,000	4,000
Total, armed forces	100,000	150,000

ªActually 93,500; figure used rounded off by MAAG to 94,000.

Source: Rpt of Visit of Clarke to Western Pacific and Southeast Asia, vol. III, pp. 7, 18.

force unencumbered by unnecessary equipment but with considerable fire-power for close-in fighting." Designed for "action in the jungles, paddies and mountains where roads were non-existent," it had over 30 percent more light machine guns than an American division, 10 percent more Browning automatic rifles, and the same number of 60- and 81-mm. mortars. At the same time it had no organic artillery, ordnance, and quartermaster units and only a fraction of the transportation equipment of an American division. The field divisions were about one-half the size of a U.S. Army division but had 50 percent more automatic rifles and one-third more 81-mm. mortars. Unlike the light division, the field division had company-size signal, engineer, transportation, ordnance, quartermaster, intelligence, and medical support units.[27] (*Charts 1 and 2*)

Throughout most of 1955 these divisional formations existed on paper only. The Vietnamese Army was still the heterogeneous collection of units, battalion size or smaller, which it had been at the end of the Geneva Conference. Although many of these small units would be inactivated as the divisions were formed, other logistical and service units which did not yet exist would have to be created. None of this could be accomplished while

[27]Ibid., pp. 21–22. From the perspective of the 1970s, General O'Daniel still believed this was an appropriate type of combat force for Vietnam. "Some people had the idea that armor and other heavy stuff would be needed in Vietnam, but I never did." Interv, author with O'Daniel, 3 Feb 75.

General O'Daniel *visits Vietnamese National Army Training Center.*

Vietnamese Army units were scattered throughout the country on security duties or campaigns against the sects.[28]

O'Daniel repeatedly urged President Diem to concentrate the scattered battalions into regiments and then into divisions so that proper training could commence and the divisions could deploy to locations where they would be of greatest strategic benefit. The president and his advisers, however, viewed such steps with anxiety, frequently complaining that if troops were pulled out of certain areas people who supported the government would be exposed to intimidation by the remnants of the sects and the Viet Minh. Diem repeatedly reminded O'Daniel of the need for the army to guarantee internal security. The general responded that the regroupment would, in the long run, provide better internal security as well as the capability to meet external aggression.[29] By the fall of 1955 concentration of the troops had begun, and a four-week orientation course for division commanders, staff, and regimental commanders

[28]Memo, Gen O'Daniel for Ambassador Reinhardt, 29 Jun 55, sub: Meeting With President Diem on 28 Jun 55, O'Daniel Papers.

[29]Memo, Col John M. Finn for Gen O'Daniel, 5 Aug 55, sub: Minutes of Meeting With Minister of Defense on 4 Aug 55; Memo, Gen O'Daniel for Ambassador Reinhardt, 26 Aug 55, sub: Meeting With President Diem on 24 Aug 55; ibid., 10 Sep 55, same sub, 9 Sep 55; ibid., 30 Sep 55, same sub, 28 Sep 55. All in O'Daniel Papers.

CHART 1—SOUTH VIETNAMESE ARMY LIGHT DIVISION, 1956

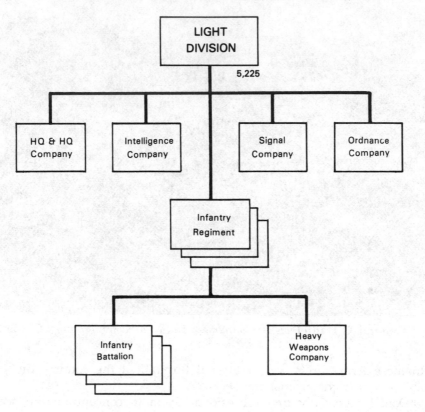

CHART 2—SOUTH VIETNAMESE ARMY FIELD DIVISION, 1956

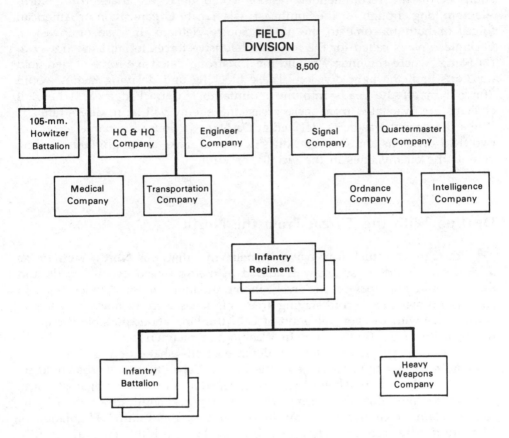

had been instituted. Still, it was to be many months before the divisional formations were fully manned and equipped.

O'Daniel believed that a well-trained Vietnamese force organized and equipped in the recommended fashion could delay an attack from North Vietnam long enough for the Southeast Asia Treaty Organization or American forces or both to come to the aid of South Vietnam. In case of invasion, O'Daniel's plans called for the forward defensive forces to fall back slowly to Da Nang, where the enemy would meet a strong defensive force of two field divisions and one light division. These blocking and delaying tactics would "force him off the roads into the mountainous untracked areas where, if civilians are evacuated from these areas, the enemy will be in dire straits."[30] While the enemy was being delayed at Da Nang, a South Vietnamese force of two field divisions and one light division would make an amphibious landing behind the enemy lines in the vicinity of Vinh.

Dealing With the Threat From the North

Although O'Daniel was naive in believing that the North Vietnamese Army would be seriously hindered by being forced off the roads and that it could not operate effectively in mountainous jungle (which was, in fact, its normal supply and staging area), his ideas were in many respects in consonance with the general trend of U.S. thinking about possible threats to the security of South Vietnam. In Washington planners were taking a long second look at possibilities for the defense of the shaky young Vietnamese republic now that the assistance of the French Expeditionary Corps could no longer be relied upon. They generally agreed that an offensive against South Vietnam would follow three primary routes of attack: south down the narrow coastal plain of central Vietnam; south through the Central Highlands of Vietnam and eastern Laos along the so-called Ho Chi Minh Trail; and southwest from Vinh through Laos to Thakhek and Savannakhet, thence south through the Mekong River valley to Saigon.[31] (*Map 6*) Although opinions varied as to which of these routes would be used or which would prove most important, there was little doubt that South Vietnam would be hard pressed to defend itself against such thrusts.

In August 1955 the National Security Council Planning Board asked the Joint Chiefs of Staff to determine what U.S. military operations would be required, with and without atomic weapons, in the event of a renewal of aggression in Vietnam. The Joint Chiefs were to decide what operations would be needed to "repulse and punish overt Viet Minh aggression" and to

[30]Memo, O'Daniel for Ambassador Reinhardt, 1 Aug 55, sub: Conversation With President Diem, O'Daniel Papers; O'Daniel, An Estimate of the Situation, 16 Nov 55, Folder 6, Williams Papers.
[31]HQ, Far East Command, Rpt of Joint Intelligence Conference, 17–20 Apr 56, p. 4; Intelligence Estimate to Limited War Capabilities Study, 12 Jun 57, ACSI 381; both in records of ACSI.

CHINA

NORTH VIETNAM

CHINA

BURMA

Red R

Red
River
Delta

HANOI

Haiphong

LAOS

Mekong R

Thanh
Hoa

Vinh

HAINAN

VIENTIANE

Thakhek

Savannakhet

17th Parallel
Quang Tri

Hue

THAILAND

Du Nang

SOUTH

Kontum Qui
Pleiku Nhon

BANGKOK

CAMBODIA

Mekong R

VIETNAM

Ban Me Thuot

Nha Trang

PHNOM PENH

SAIGON

My Tho

PHU
QUOC

Can Tho

Mekong Delta

PROBABLE ATTACK ROUTES

1956

0   200 MILES

0   200 KILOMETERS

MAP 6

"destroy the Viet Minh forces and take control of North Vietnam." Since the Commander in Chief, Pacific, and other unified and specified commanders had not yet developed plans to meet these contingencies, the Joint Chiefs assigned the study to an ad hoc committee in which the Army participated.[32]

The committee concluded that the armed forces of South Vietnam would be capable of only limited resistance to a North Vietnamese attack. Unless warning of such an attack came early enough to allow the United States to take effective countermeasures, a portion of South Vietnam would probably be overrun and part of the South Vietnamese Army destroyed. The committee plan called for initial reliance on Vietnamese ground forces to slow the enemy advance, immediate air and naval strikes against the North Vietnamese forces, and "early movement forward of mobile U.S. Forces for joint operations" with the South Vietnamese as well as increased logistical support. Forces required included two to four army divisions and supporting air elements. To destroy the North Vietnamese Army and defeat the Democratic Republic of Vietnam would require up to 8 U.S. divisions and 2 to 3 tactical air wings, a carrier task force, a Marine landing force, and additional Vietnamese forces, and a major local security campaign. Like O'Daniel the ad hoc committee called for an amphibious attack against North Vietnam to cut the enemy supply lines and seize major bases. O'Daniel's attack was aimed at Vinh, but the committee preferred to target the Red River Delta.[33]

The chances for success in such operations would depend on the military effectiveness of the South Vietnamese, the degree of warning, and the nature of the restrictions placed on U.S. military operations by Washington. Merely to check aggression and push the invaders back to the 17th Parallel would take up to a year—longer if atomic weapons were not used. A prohibition on the use of atomic weapons would also prevent "the most effective employment of U.S. armed forces and require greater forces than justified from the overall point of view."[34]

In the following weeks the Army staff continued to examine the feasibility of the second option of the ad hoc committee's study: an assault on North Vietnam and the destruction of the North Vietnamese Army. The Army staff's Campaign Plan—North Vietnam assumed that U.S. and Vietnamese forces had pushed the invaders back to the armistice line by the end of the first twelve months and developed bases adequate to support U.S. and allied forces. During the thirteenth month, six U.S. and five Vietnamese divisions would cross the demarcation line in conjunction with an amphibious landing at the town of Thanh Hoa on the coast of the South China Sea due south of Hanoi. The amphibious attack force of two reinforced divisions would then link up with the main U.S.-Vietnamese force coming north from the 17th

---

[32]U.S. Policy in Event of Renewal of Aggression in Vietnam, JCS 1992/479, Incl to Memo, JCS for Secy of Defense, 9 Sep 55, CCS 092 Asia (6 – 25 – 48) (2), JCS records, RG 218; Memo for CofSA, 26 Mar 56, sub: U.S. Policy in Event of Renewal of Aggression in Vietnam, G – 3 091 Vietnam, RG 319.

[33]U.S. Policy in Event of Renewal of Aggression in Vietnam, JCS 1992/479.
[34]Ibid.

Parallel. Together they would attack and seize Haiphong and then take the Red River Delta with another amphibious assault in the vicinity of Haiphong. These last two tasks would take about three months, with another eight months to clear the rest of North Vietnam. If atomic weapons were not employed, the campaign would be longer and require larger forces.[35]

The Army staff developed the Campaign Plan—North Vietnam primarily to provide a concept of operations against which military planners could evaluate the feasibility of and requirements for successful operations by American forces in defense of South Vietnam.[36] To the Army the implications of these plans were clear. Any effective response to aggression in Vietnam would require large numbers of ground troops and an effort comparable in size and scope to the Korean War.

Yet such a commitment of ground forces was precisely what the Eisenhower administration and its New Look policy aimed to avoid. Thus, in June 1956 JCS Chairman Radford presented to the National Security Council an alternative concept for U.S. action in the event of aggression in Southeast Asia. Radford abandoned the idea of subduing North Vietnam in the event of a Communist attack and concentrated on stopping the attack south of the 17th Parallel. Operations into North Vietnam would be undertaken only if it appeared that with U.S. naval, air, and limited U.S. Army combat and logistical support, the Vietnamese had the capability of retaking North Vietnam.[37] He also assumed that Chinese Communist military forces would not intervene except to provide supplies and advisers to the North Vietnamese. Radford theorized that if the North Vietnamese launched a surprise attack across the 17th Parallel, "The Vietnamese Army . . . will carry the main burden of the defeat of the aggression" supported by U.S. air and naval forces. The U.S. Army support would be limited to assistance in the defense of a few vital areas and the provision of advisers. A hard fight was anticipated around Quang Tri after which the South Vietnamese were expected to fall back to Da Nang. Like O'Daniel, Radford saw defense of the Da Nang area as the centerpiece of the campaign, but he provided for no amphibious strike behind North Vietnamese lines. Instead U.S. forces, equipped with atomic weapons, would be airlifted from Japan or Korea to Da Nang to assist in its defense. "If concentration of Viet Minh troops provide atomic targets the use of such weapons might end the aggression very rapidly."[38] By limiting U.S. objectives to the defense of South Vietnam, by assuming that China would fail to intervene, and by specifying the early use of atomic weapons, Radford was able to justify the reduction of the ground force requirements from the 2 to 4 U.S. Army divisions called for in the earlier plans to 1 or 2 regimental combat teams.

---

[35]Memo, Chief, Psy War Plans Br, for Chief, Plans Div, 26 Sep 55, sub: Campaign Plan—North Vietnam, PSYWAR 091 Vietnam, RG 319.

[36]Min, Staff Conference Held on 28 Oct 55, PSYWAR 337 Staff Conf (1955), RG 319.

[37]Plan for U.S. Participation in Event of Viet Minh Aggression in Vietnam, Appendix to Memo, JCS for CINCPAC, 11 Jul 56, sub: Development of a Contingency Plan for U.S. Military Participation in Event of Viet Minh Aggression in Vietnam, CCS 092 Asia (6 – 25 – 48), sec. 24, RG 218.

[38]Ibid.

The National Security Council discussed and generally approved Radford's approach to dealing with local aggression in Vietnam. President Eisenhower, who was present at the meeting, also directed that the appropriate U.S. military authorities encourage Vietnamese leaders to plan for defense against aggression along lines consistent with American concepts and policies.[39] A few weeks later the Joint Chiefs of Staff furnished copies of Admiral Radford's plan to the commanders of the Pacific, Far East, and Strategic Air Commands and directed them to supplement their plans with a contingency plan for Vietnam incorporating the main features of the Radford concept.[40] Pacific Command responded with Operation Plan 46–56, which closely followed Radford's outline.

Army planners found little of value in Radford's ideas as embodied in Operation Plan 46–56. They considered it unrealistic to assume that China would not intervene and that North Vietnamese aggression could be defeated merely by holding at the 17th Parallel. Moreover, the plan failed to consider the near certainty that the North Vietnamese would attack through Laos and Cambodia as well as frontally through central Vietnam. The plan also overestimated the capabilities of the South Vietnamese Army and of American air and naval forces, with the result that insufficient U.S. Army ground forces were allocated to accomplish the tasks called for.[41]

Although the Army, the Joint Chiefs, and Pacific Command planners differed about how to meet a threat of North Vietnamese invasion, all agreed that this was not the most immediate danger. In their September 1955 study of U.S. courses of action in the event of a North Vietnamese attack, the Joint Chiefs of Staff emphasized that "at this time the major threat [to South Vietnam] continues to be that of subversion."[42] The National Security Council Planning Board had reiterated that view when Radford presented his outline plan, and estimates by the Central Intelligence Agency in the fall of 1955 provided added support.[43] The CIA predicted that "should the Viet Minh initiate large-scale guerrilla operations supported by substantial infiltration from the north, the South Vietnamese government would be hard pressed. . . . If the operation were prolonged, the government probably could not survive without military assistance from outside."[44]

Yet General O'Daniel and his successor continued to make preparation for a conventional military attack by North Vietnam the cornerstone of their advisory effort. Their reasons were many. O'Daniel believed that an army organized and equipped in the manner he prescribed would also be capable

[39]Note by Secy to the JCS on Capability to Deal With Local Aggression, Incl to JCS 1992/555, CCS 092 Asia (6–25–48) (2), sec. 24, RG 218.

[40]Memo, JCS for CINCPAC, 11 Jul 56, sub: Development of a Contingency Plan, CCS 092 Asia (6–25–48) (2), sec. 24, RG 218.

[41]DF, Col R. L. Kolb, 23 Nov 56, sub: CINCPAC Operation Plan 46–56, ACSI 381.01 Pacific Area, records of ACSI.

[42]U.S. Policy in Event of Renewal of Aggression in Vietnam, JCS 1992/479, sec. 11.

[43]Draft Statement of Policy by NSC Planning Board, 11 Jul 56, sub: U.S. Policy in Mainland Southeast Asia, CCS 092 Asia (6–25–48) (2), RG 218.

[44]NIE 63.1–3–55, 11 Oct 55, *U.S.-Vietnam Relations*, vol. 2, pt. IV.A.5, Tab 4, p. 9.

of performing internal security duties. The territorial regiments, he believed, were well equipped to suppress any uprising in their areas, and the light divisions could serve as a general reserve to reinforce them when necessary. The field divisions would not generally engage in internal security operations but would act as a strategic force, ready to combat any possible aggression.[45] General Williams on the other hand believed strongly that internal security functions were best left to specially trained paramilitary organizations. Both men were probably influenced by the fact that many of the measures for combating Communist subversion were political and economic in nature and consequently the primary concern of civilian agencies. Finally, neither general believed, in the mid-1950s, that the Communists were capable of organizing an insurgency so formidable as to threaten the existence of South Vietnam. As General Williams wrote, "Communist guerrillas have been destroyed in Greece, Korea, the Philippines and Iran. They can be destroyed in Vietnam."[46]

Williams' views on the problem of combating guerrillas were fairly representative of Army thinking in the 1950s. Counterinsurgency (the term itself was almost unknown at that time) was little studied or understood.[47] Army training and doctrine in the area of counterguerrilla warfare were primarily oriented toward preventing or defeating enemy raids behind the lines or enemy infiltration. The guerrillas were usually envisioned as troops of the enemy's regular forces who had been cut off or had infiltrated or been inserted behind friendly lines.[48] Few officers or enlisted men had had any practical experience in actual counterguerrilla operations. Whereas the conduct of guerrilla warfare was a specialized skill restricted to U.S. Army Special Forces units, the Army considered counterguerrilla training to be adequately covered in the four hours of instruction provided for all troops.[49]

It was understandable then that General Williams should continue O'Daniel's emphasis on preparation to meet a conventional North Vietnamese attack. As an officer in the advisory group recalled, General Williams "was certain that that was the way that the war was going to go . . . and that was the way he trained and organized the Vietnamese forces. . . . I don't recall anybody ever trying to talk him out of it because that was one of those things you just didn't do with General Williams."[50] Williams saw insurgency within South Vietnam as a problem principally because it might divert the army from

[45]Rpt of Visit of Clarke to Western Pacific and Southeast Asia.

[46]Notes Handed to President Diem by Gen Williams, 28 Dec 55, Williams Papers.

[47]Ltr, Lt Col Jack Shannon to Lt Gen James A. Gavin, 22 Nov 57, sub: Army Special Warfare Capabilities, CS 370.64, records of CSA, RG 319.

[48]Army Subject Schedule No. 21–16, Anti-infiltration and Antiguerrilla Warfare Training, 29 Sep 55; ibid. No. 33–11, same title, 22 Jun 56; USCONARC Memo No. 22, Preparation of Army Training Programs, 3 Jul 58. All in Tab F to Incl 6 of Memo, SGS (Brig Gen C. H. Bonesteel III) for DCSOPS, 10 Jul 58, sub: U.S. Army Guerrilla Warfare Activities, CS 370.64, records of CSA, RG 319. Department of Army Field Manual 31–15, *Operations Against Airborne Attack, Guerrilla Action, and Infiltration*, ch. 6; ibid. 31–21, *Guerrilla Warfare*, ch. 5, 6.

[49]Ltr, Shannon to Gavin, 22 Nov 57, sub: Army Special Warfare Capabilities; Summary Sheet, U.S. Army Guerrilla Warfare Activities, 31 Jul 58, CS 370.64, records of CSA, RG 319.

[50]Interv, author with Col James M. Muir, U.S. Army (retired), Hilton Head, S.C., 27 Aug 79, Historians files, CMH.

undertaking the dispositions and preparations necessary to repel an invasion. As he explained to President Diem:

Communist guerrilla strategy is simple. By using a small amount of arms and equipment and a few good military leaders, they force [their opponents] to utilize relatively large military forces in a campaign that is costly in money and men. In Korea in 1950, the South Koreans were using three divisions to fight less than 7,000 guerrillas in the Southeast. When the North Koreans attacked, the South Korean Army suffered from this diversion as their army was not strategically or tactically deployed to meet the North Korean attack.[51]

Guided by such beliefs Williams prepared to embark upon the difficult task of creating an effective South Vietnamese Army.

[51]Notes Handed to President Diem by Gen Williams, 28 Dec 55.

15

Building a Vietnamese Army, 1956–1959

A veteran of both world wars, Lt. Gen. Samuel T. Williams had risen from the ranks after enlisting as a private in the Texas National Guard and had commanded a division during the last year of the Korean War. He had built a reputation for working well with Korean troops and had served for a time as deputy commander of the II Republic of Korea Corps. Between the wars he had acquired the nickname "Hanging Sam" because of his insistence on stern punishment for a child rapist in a regiment he commanded. It was an appropriate nickname in another sense as well, for Williams was a disciplinarian, outspokenly intolerant of slackness, incompetence, or boodling. Williams was a man who inspired strong feelings in all who knew him—in some, of deep admiration, in others, of intense dislike. "He believed you were there to put out and that was it," recalled one of his associates. "In that sense he was a wonderful commander."[1]

Despite a fiery personal style and plain-spoken manner when he disagreed with one of Diem's policies or decisions, Williams quickly established a close relationship with the president, who came to trust and to confide in Williams to an unusual degree. He was equally successful in winning the confidence of senior South Vietnamese officers, who often went so far as to discuss their intimate personal and family problems with him.[2]

The president's conversations with Williams often lasted several hours, with the president doing most of the talking. "Sometimes the general was able to get in some important points but most of the time it was a case of General Williams making small talk while the president just plain rambled." Diem always received Williams at a small table in the richly furnished protocol office of the palace. General Williams and his interpreter sat on the president's right, opposite the table which was laid with a tea service and a tray of Vietnamese cigarettes. During the meeting the president would pick up one cigarette after another—the interpreter would light them—take a puff

[1]Interv, author with Maj Gen John F. Ruggles, 24–25 Feb 77, Historians files, CMH.
[2]Interv, Charles B. MacDonald and Charles V. P. von Luttichau with Lt Gen Samuel T. Williams, San Antonio, Tex., 13 Nov 70; Interv, author with Col Nathaniel P. Ward, 16 Aug 79; both in Historians files, CMH.

or two, and immediately take up another brand, while the harried interpreter attempted to take notes, translate, and keep his lighter handy.[3]

In addition to the embassy, the advisory group, and the equipment recovery mission, the U.S. mission in South Vietnam included the U.S. Information Agency, the Central Intelligence Agency—known euphemistically as the Office of the Special Assistant to the Ambassador—and the U.S. Operations Mission, a field agency of the International Cooperation Administration. Together with the deputy chief of mission, the heads of the various agencies constituted a country team headed by the ambassador. Although Ambassador

Ambassador Durbrow

Reinhardt was the nominal coordinator and director of all these American agencies and activities, he chose to exercise little detailed supervision. Accordingly, the agencies tended to proceed with their programs in their own way and to maintain their own channels of communication with their parent agencies in Washington.

General Williams justified his personal relationship with President Diem on the theory that since Diem acted as his own minister of defense he had close day-to-day involvement with the military assistance program.[4] That relationship and Williams' tendency to run the advisory group with little reference to the embassy caused trouble when Reinhardt was succeeded in March 1957 by Elbridge Durbrow, who was more inclined to assert his authority as head of the mission. "There was never any doubt in my mind that the ambassador was the head of the country team," recalled one officer, "but Williams sure didn't believe it, didn't like it, and wouldn't put up with it anymore than he had to."[5] The situation was further exacerbated by a personality clash between Williams and Durbrow. There were "frequent shouting matches" between the two at country team meetings.[6] According to one of Williams' principal deputies, "Relations with the ambassador were about as poor as they could be."[7]

[3]Interv, author with Lt Col Edward M. Dannemiller, U.S. Army (Retired), Augusta, Ga., 10 Mar 80, Historians files, CMH.

[4]MFR, Williams, 10 Dec 59, Incl 3, Country Team Coordination for (Senator Albert) Gore and (Senator Gale) McGee Hearings, Williams Papers.

[5]Interv, author with Muir, 27 Aug 79.

[6]Ibid.

[7]Interv, author with Lt Gen Samuel L. Myers, 22–23 Feb 77; confirmed in Interv, author with Elbridge Durbrow, 9 Dec 76; both in Historians files, CMH.

Relations between the Military Assistance Advisory Group and the service attaches were often little better. General Williams professed to see no value in having attaches in countries which also had advisory groups. He believed that he would be compromising his special position of trust with the Vietnamese government and armed forces if he passed information he received to the Army attaches who might, in turn, share it with their British or French counterparts. Well aware of their chief's attitude, other advisory group officers were reluctant to share information or even to associate with the service attaches.[8]

Bureaucratic rivalries and suspicions within the country team intensified this thinly veiled hostility. Members of the Military Assistance Advisory Group complained that the country team was "loaded against the military"; they believed that although the military assistance program was by far the most important and expensive American project in South Vietnam, those responsible were given "only one voice out of five."[9]

Many officers considered Durbrow a poor administrator and worried that his lack of understanding of even elementary military matters impeded their efforts.[10] Others in the country team were just as unhappy with the advisory group, believing that General Williams was maneuvering to get a larger military mission and that the military in general were keeping important information from the other agencies. By the end of Durbrow's first year, some members of the country team were barely on speaking terms with General Williams.[11]

A single individual or organization in Washington charged with issuing guidance to the field might have helped, but there was no one authority—other than the president himself—responsible for overall direction of the American effort in South Vietnam. The National Security Council's Operations Control Board was supposed to provide the necessary coordination, but the studies it produced were vague and general. As a result, the State and Defense Departments were left to compete for authority over programs while the U.S. Information Agency, the Central Intelligence Agency, and the U.S. Operations Mission maintained their own counsel in their more restricted fields. Even within the Defense Department, both the Office of the Assistant Secretary of Defense for International Security Affairs and the Joint Chiefs of Staff had responsibilities for South Vietnam. The interdepartmental Foreign Military Assistance Coordinating Committee, chaired by the secretary of state,

---

[8]Ltr, Col L. B. Woodbury to ACSI, 11 Sep 57, sub: Study of MAAG Role in the Worldwide Collection Efforts, 5–31–57, OARMA 350.09, records of ACSI. See also Intervs, author with Brig Gen Charles A. Symroski, U.S. Army (Retired), Williamsburg, Va., 16 Aug 79, and with Col Richard H. Comstock, Ithaca, N.Y., 14 Sep 78, copies in Historians files, CMH. Colonel Comstock believed "Williams was jealous that he didn't command the attache office and that the attaches came, in protocol, somewhat above MAAG. Also he didn't want anybody sending adverse information to Washington." Comstock Interv.

[9]Interv, author with Myers, 22–23 Feb 77.

[10]Ibid. with Col Ernest P. Lasche, U.S. Army (Retired), Marianna, Fla., 30 Aug 79, Historians files, CMH.

[11]Ibid. with Leland Barrows (AID), 27 Jul 76, and with former CIA Station Chief, Saigon, 30 Jul 76, both in Historians files, CMH.

still presided over the collection of rival interests but had no real authority to impose order. Thus neither in Washington nor in Saigon was there much unified direction of American policy toward South Vietnam.

The State of the Vietnamese Army

General Williams inherited the mission of advising an army that was far from capable of effective military operations of any type. The army suffered from an acute shortage of officers, particularly those qualified for higher command, and after his experiences with General Hinh and the sects, President Diem tended to value political reliability in senior officers far more than military expertise. The officer corps was riddled with favoritism and corruption. Officers who had failed to manifest personal loyalty to the president often fell victim to secret denunciations by jealous or ambitious rivals.[12]

At the beginning of 1956 the South Vietnamese Army was "essentially a heterogeneous collection of separate battalions." Many of its divisions existed largely on paper; even those which had begun to function lacked their full complement of men and material. Virtually all the divisional and regimental commanders were new to their units and did not know their men or their subordinate officers. Few had ever commanded anything larger than a battalion. All lacked experience in the use of artillery and other supporting arms.[13]

The continued dispersion of small units in mopping-up operations against the sects and other dissidents created the most serious difficulties. These operations often achieved only minimal results, but their cost to unit training and general readiness was enormous. The division commander and his staff had no opportunity to practice command or even to get to know their component units. Training schedules were disrupted, and even simple target practice had to be postponed.[14]

The 1st Field Division, the only division with a full complement of troops and equipment, had never trained as a unit or even reached its assigned station area. The Vietnamese Army staff described two other field divisions as virtually "paralyzed" because of dispersal for local operations and lack of equipment. In the 12th Light Division morale was "too low for the unit to have any value." The army staff was obliged to "admit in all sincerity that we do not have all the necessary elements to contain [the enemy] much less defeat him."[15]

[12]Ltr, Col James Evans to ACSI, 22 May 56, sub: Politics in the Army of the Republic of Vietnam, 5 – 6 – 56, OARMA 350.05, records of ACSI.

[13]Ibid., 11 Apr 56, sub: Vietnamese Document Entitled "Reorganization of the Battle Corps to Meet the Threat of Invasion," 5 – 4 – 56, OARMA 350.05, records of ACSI.

[14]Ibid. See also Annex C to Quarterly Rpt of 4th Field Div Advisory Gp, Incl to Ltr, Col L. B. Woodbury to ACSI, 21 Feb 57, OARMA 350.05, records of ACSI.

[15]Ltr, Evans to ACSI, 11 Apr 56, sub: Vietnamese Document Entitled "Reorganization of the Battle Corps to Meet the Threat of Invasion."

With his brothers, Ngo Dinh Nhu, the president's confidential adviser, and Ngo Dinh Can, the political boss of central Vietnam, Diem controlled a network of Catholic refugees, government officials, and relatives called the Can Lao Nhan Vi Cach Mang Dang, or Can Lao, a secret political party which dominated most government operations.[16] Within the Defense Ministry, for example, the director of personnel, the director of military security, and the director general of the Office of Accounting, Budget, and Control, as well as a number of division and corps commanders, were all Can Lao members hand-picked by Ngo Dinh Can.[17] Cells or committees of the Can Lao existed at all echelons of the army, frequently without the knowledge of the unit commanders. The staffs of senior commanders were so riddled with Can Lao operatives and informers that some generals like Duong Van Minh hesitated to plan any real operations with their staffs. Minh kept his large G sections busy with training lessons and exercises while he actually carried out operational planning in the privacy of the general's quarters or on drives in his jeep with only his American adviser and a trusted aide present.[18]

During the elections for the National Assembly of South Vietnam in early 1956, the Vietnamese Army officially permitted and tacitly encouraged its soldiers to participate in political meetings and rallies, although officers were prohibited from becoming candidates.[19] "Whenever we saw them [Can Lao] misusing our vehicles for political purposes I'd push the minister of defense until he went to the president," recalled one adviser. The minister always returned to report that Diem flew into a rage at his complaint and there was nothing more to be done.[20]

The command structure in the South Vietnamese forces accurately mirrored the president's obsession with controlling the army. The Department of National Defense appeared designed primarily to increase confusion with "conflicting, duplicating chains of command and communication and . . . various major agencies . . . installed in widely separated areas so as to hamper coordination, rapid staff action and decision making."[21] The result was an administrative situation in which a general commanding a division had to obtain written authorization from the army chief of staff to requisition a jeep.[22] In the field, a battalion commander often received orders from both the commander of his regiment or division and the commander of the military region in which he was operating. President Diem not infrequently sent orders directly to battalions and regiments over his own radio net, bypass-

---

[16]Dennis J. Duncanson, *Government and Revolution in Vietnam* (New York: Oxford University Press, 1968), pp. 217–18; Am Embassy, Saigon, to State Dept, 2 Mar 59, 751G.00/3–259, records of Dept of State.

[17]Memo, Col James Muir for Chief, MAAG, 19 Mar 59, sub: Appointments of Vietnamese Personnel, Folder 68, Williams Papers.

[18]Interv, author with Lt Gen George Forsythe, U.S. Army (Retired), Beaufort, S.C., 20 Apr 80, Historians files, CMH.

[19]Ltr, Evans to ACSI, 22 May 56, sub: Politics in the Army of the Republic of Vietnam.

[20]Interv, author with Lasche, 30 Aug 79.

[21]USACGSC, Staff Study on Army Aspects of Military Assistance, p. C–20.

[22]Interv, MacDonald and Luttichau with Williams, 13 Nov 70.

ing the Department of National Defense, the general staff, and the field commanders.

In an early meeting with Diem, General Williams was amazed to learn that the president intended to select a permanent chief of staff and general staff only "after war had begun." Williams explained to Diem that this idea was "not militarily feasible," and the president reluctantly agreed to appoint General Le Van Ty as permanent chief of staff.[23]

General Ty, who had spent some thirty years in the French Army and had risen to the rank of captain before transferring to the Vietnamese Army in 1948, "spoke better French than Vietnamese and preferred to drink champagne over anything else." Cautious and unimaginative, he was exactly the type of safe personality the Ngos desired. One senior American adviser thought that "Ty would have made a real good sergeant."[24] The chief of staff's performance was also conditioned, at least in part, by his recognition that exercising strong control over his commanders had less chance of achieving the results he sought than of "causing him difficulty with the President."[25]

American advisers were also concerned by the South Vietnamese Army's lack of national feeling. Many senior officers, such as Tran Van Don, Le Van Kim, Duong Van Minh, and Le Van Ty, had fought in the French forces in the first Indochina War and some had even been French citizens. There were virtually no senior officers in Diem's army identified with resistance to French colonialism, the principle upon which the Diem regime was supposedly founded. General Ty was "certain that many of our units would disappear into the countryside at the very start of the reopening of hostilities."[26] Insubordination was rampant; orders were freely disobeyed, and senior officers were reluctant to punish subordinates who might have powerful political connections.[27]

A former adviser recalled, "One day I went to the Minister of Defense and said 'Look, I just passed one of your sentry towers and I saw a couple of feet sticking up there and a guitar. Obviously that sentry's asleep. Let's go out and get my jeep and we'll straighten it out.'" The minister demurred, explaining that all he could do was to go to the chief of the Joint General Staff who would go to the chief of staff of the army who would go to the corps commander and so forth until the appropriate noncommissioned officer might be found to discipline the drowsy sentry.[28]

Many officers and noncommissioned officers regarded their service in the

[23]MFR, Lt Col Vincent Usera, 14 Jul 56, sub: Conversations Between President Diem and Chief, MAAG, Folder 4, Williams Papers.

[24]Intervs, author with Ruggles, 24–25 Feb 77, and with General Tran Van Don, 20 Dec 76, Historians files, CMH; Croizat Interv.

[25]Memo, Liaison Officer, DOD, for Chief, MAAG, 12 Nov 59, sub: Personal Views Expressed by Dr. Dieu, Folder 68, Williams Papers. See also Interv, author with Don, 20 Dec 76, and Croizat Interv.

[26]Maj Gen Le Van Ty, Evaluation of the Vietnamese Army, 19 Mar 56, Folder 10, Williams Papers.

[27]Ibid.

[28]Interv, author with Lasche, 30 Aug 79.

army as an opportunity to enrich themselves. By Asian standards, the pay of the South Vietnamese armed forces was extraordinarily high. A master sergeant in the South Vietnamese Army, for example, received $161.00 a month compared to $14.00 a month for a master sergeant in the Army of the Republic of Korea; a South Vietnamese second lieutenant received $208.00 a month compared to $18.00 for his South Korean counterpart. The pay system was a legacy of the French era when many French officers and noncommissioned officers had been transferred to the Vietnamese National Army. To induce them to serve, it had been necessary to pay them at the same rate as that of the French Expeditionary Corps, so that the pay of the Vietnamese had also been increased. South Vietnamese officers and officials nevertheless appealed frequently to their American sponsors for even higher pay and allowances. In the summer of 1955, Minister of Defense Tran Trung Dung had asked General O'Daniel to try to secure a pay raise for enlisted personnel "to cut down on desertions," a rationale that O'Daniel must have found strange, since, as he pointed out, the South Vietnamese Army was approximately 50,000 men overstrength and desertion hardly a pressing problem.[29] In 1958, when the South Vietnamese Navy requested an increase in the amount of money allocated for sea pay, it became apparent that the "sea pay" was to go to everyone, whether or not they were actually assigned to sea duty. According to the transcript of the meeting, "General Williams said he thought navy officers stayed in the navy because of love of the sea and for service to their country, just as other officers do. . . . The Chief of Staff said those officers unfortunately are a minority. That when Vietnam was mobilized, students tried to get in the navy as a refuge from fighting in the army. . . . That it was not love of the sea but desire for a superior position."[30]

Many senior officers routinely supplemented their income by selling on the black market, embezzling official funds, exploiting prostitution, and dealing in drugs. The lower ranks committed extortion and sometimes even outright robbery against the local population, particularly in outlying districts.[31] In those remoter areas, regional commanders occasionally attempted to establish themselves as local warlords, in some instances even trying to collect taxes.[32]

In Saigon contractors doing business with the Defense Ministry were routinely assessed 5 to 10 percent of the contract price as a "contribution" to the Can Lao Party.[33] "Few business transactions occur in Vietnam," reported the American embassy in 1959, "without some benefit to the Can Lao."[34]

For long General Williams remained unaware of or unconcerned about the

---

[29]Memo of Meeting Between General O'Daniel and Defense Minister Dung, 4 Aug 55, O'Daniel Papers.
[30]Gen Williams – President Diem Conversation, 8 Jan 58, Williams Papers.
[31]Min, USARPAC-FARELF (Far East Land Forces) Intelligence Conference, 16–20 May 60, p. 5, USARPAC records.
[32]Interv, author with Myers, 22–23 Feb 77.
[33]Memo, Col E. W. Taylor for Chief, MAAG, 26 Mar 59, sub: Discussions of 24 Mar 59, Folder 68, Williams Papers; Interv, author with Lasche, 30 Aug 79.
[34]Am Embassy, Saigon, to State Dept, 2 Mar 59.

fundamental economic, social, and political conditions underlying most of the South Vietnamese Army's problems. He appeared to look upon the South Vietnamese Army as simply a less sophisticated and less experienced version of the U.S. Army and refused to take seriously the existence of political cliques in the army, comparing the feuds between factions with the rivalry between the U.S. Marines and the Army or between the Navy and the Air Force. Nor did he appear to appreciate the central role that the generals played in South Vietnamese politics.[35]

Schools and Training

The "greater majority of Americans in Vietnam," observed a French journalist based in Saigon, "very sincerely believe that in transplanting their institutions, they will immunize South Vietnam against Communism."[36] That was particularly true of the advisory group. Like his predecessors, General Williams believed that exposure to American training schools and methods would solve many of the problems of the South Vietnamese Army.[37] He wanted a maximum number of South Vietnamese officers to attend U.S. military schools and courses in the Philippines, Japan, and the United States. During the first half of 1956, for example, over three hundred South Vietnamese officers and enlisted men completed courses at those schools.[38] Senior generals such as Duong Van Minh and Le Van Kim, attended the U.S. Army Command and General Staff College at Fort Leavenworth.

It is difficult to assess the net effect of the overseas training effort. Some of the senior officers selected by Diem for training in the United States were incompetent or marginal performers who spent most of their time shopping, sightseeing, and socializing.[39] A problem for even the most conscientious Vietnamese student was the language barrier. All instruction at Leavenworth was, of course, in English. With sufficient time potential students could be given accelerated English courses, but sufficient time was seldom available. Diem did not select the officers to attend the Leavenworth short course commencing in January 1957, for example, until late November 1956.[40]

Although company grade officers were in general better performers, once they had undergone advanced training they were in such demand that they

[35]Memo, Williams for Ambassador Durbrow, 5 Mar 58, sub: Conversation With President Diem, Williams Papers. General Williams listed as one of his major problems the "failure to wean Vietnamese officers from French political habits." Interv, MacDonald and Luttichau with Williams, 13 Nov 70.

[36]Mende Tibor, "les Deux Vietnams," *Esprit*, 6 June 1957.

[37]First Draft Report of the Draper Study Committee, 17 Feb 59, Folder 102, p. 44, Williams Papers.

[38]Memo, Chief, TERM, for Chief, MAAG, 27 Sep 56, sub: Review and Analysis of MAAG Programs, Williams Papers.

[39]Memo, Muir for Chief, MAAG, 19 Mar 59, sub: Appointments of Vietnamese Personnel; Interv, author with Myers, 22–23 Feb 77.

[40]Interv, author with Dannemiller, 10 Mar 80.

Recruits *at Quang Trung Basic Training Center.*

Cadets *at Dalat Military Academy.*

Vietnamese Army Trainees *on obstacle course, Nha Trang Commando School.*

2d Division Gunners *fire 105-mm. howitzer.*

were often absorbed into headquarters staff work or administration in Saigon rather than being returned to field commands.[41] Many company grade officers also appeared to believe that what they had learned in the United States could not easily be applied in Vietnam. As an American adviser recalled,

One day during practice in firing the 60 mm. mortar I was rather appalled at the complete lack of organization of the class. For example there would be ladies, in their large straw conical hats, out selling bowls of soup and other things to nibble on right in among the class . . . that type of thing. The lieutenant in charge had a 45 automatic stuck in his back pocket, no belt, no holster or anything of that nature. And finally at the conclusion of the day I went to this lieutenant and asked him, "You're just back from Fort Benning aren't you?" and he said, "Yes, sir." "You had mortar instruction at Fort Benning?" "Yes, sir." And I said, "Well, what do you think? How do you compare the instruction you just finished giving with that which you received at Fort Benning?" and his answer was "Oh, it was much better at Fort Benning." So I said, "Why?" and he said, "Well, sir, that was Fort Benning and this is Vietnam."[42]

By the end of 1956, there were four major school systems in operation within South Vietnam. The army's basic training center at Quang Trung, near Saigon, was then capable of handling over 9,000 recruits in its standard sixteen-week course, and there was also an eight-week course for reservists.[43] The school for senior officers, the Military College in Saigon, offered a "staff course" for junior officers and a "command course" for field grade officers, while the Dalat Military Academy provided basic officer training for about 800 students.

The Thu Duc School Center, a few miles northeast of Saigon, housed the major branch schools: armor, infantry, transportation, signal, administration, engineer, ordnance, artillery, and quartermaster. All together they were capable of training about 1,700 officers and senior noncommissioned officers in their respective specialties. In addition to reorganizing and expanding that major training complex, the advisory group established a physical training and ranger school at the coastal town of Nha Trang for 75 to 100 students and an intelligence and psychological warfare school in Saigon.[44]

The school system was sound in concept, but its actual effectiveness varied according to the ability of the instructors and students assigned, the resources available, and the capacity of the school. The commanding general of the Quang Trung Training Center, for example, was described by the U.S. Army attache as a "pompous, fat, stupid man . . . who will do anything to increase his personal fortune." He was reportedly financing a brothel run by his mistress, an act that allegedly scandalized the general's fellow officers "not so much because of his interest in a business venture but because he

[41]Interv, author with Ruggles, 24–25 Feb 79.
[42]Interv, author with Dannemiller, 10 Mar 80.
[43]Briefing by Brig Gen Tran Van Don for Australian Parliamentary Delegation, 6 Dec 56, Folder 5, Williams Papers.
[44]Ibid.; Training Directorate, HQUSMACV, History of the U.S. Training Effort: Development of the Training Directorate, May 1970, pp. 18–20, copy in Historians files, CMH.

was personally interested in the madam."[45] In the case of the Military College, a well-run, well-staffed institution, many of the students simply lacked the capacity to absorb the material offered in the command and general staff course because they had never been exposed to officer training courses dealing with the more basic aspects of command.[46] Some schools, such as the Artillery School at Thu Duc, did a satisfactory job in teaching students to maintain, clean, load, and aim their weapons but provided little information about the practical employment of artillery in modern, combined arms warfare. Although most advisers considered the Ranger School at Nha Trang first class, its capacity was limited to little more than a hundred students.[47] The small size of the advisory group limited its ability to influence the school system. In general only one or two advisers could be assigned to each school, and often their time was taken up in selecting suitable material from American training manuals and overseeing its translation.[48]

The prevalent American view of the Vietnamese as primitive and uneducated may have had some effect on training. Americans routinely referred to the South Vietnamese as "the natives" until the term was officially banned in 1957. In studying the military assistance program, the U.S. Army's Command and General Staff College attributed the deficiencies of the South Vietnamese Army to "the long-standing nature of the Vietnamese people: passive, submissive, fatalistic, accustomed to being led . . . pastoral and non-mechanical."[49]

The Language Barrier

A lack of advisory personnel with Vietnamese language skills clearly had an effect. While thousands of South Vietnamese took English language courses between 1956 and 1959, the Military Assistance Advisory Group averaged less than a dozen officers and enlisted men possessing any facility in Vietnamese. Few were ever assigned advisory or training duties; instead, they were usually retained in Saigon in a translator pool.[50] General Cao Van Vien, later chief of the Joint General Staff, could recall no instance "in which a U.S. adviser effectively discussed professional matters with his counterpart in Vietnamese."[51]

That the language barrier could create unexpected problems was illustrated by the experience of one American instructor who was attempting to teach basic facing movements to a group of recruits.

[45]Ltr, Lt Col L. B. Woodbury to ACSI, 1 Mar 58, sub: ARVN Key Personnel Changes, 5 – 8 – 58, ACSI 350.09, records of ACSI.

[46]Interv, author with Myers, 22 – 23 Feb 77.

[47]Ibid.

[48]Ltr, OARMA to ACSI, 28 Feb 57, ACSI 350.09, records of ACSI.

[49]USACGSC, Staff Study on Army Aspects of Military Assistance, p. C – 19.

[50]Memo, Williams for Ambassador Durbrow, 7 Apr 59, sub: Personnel of MAAG-TERM Who Speak Vietnamese, Williams Papers.

[51]General Cao Van Vien et al., *The U.S. Adviser*, Indochina Monographs Series (Washington: U.S. Army Center of Military History, 1980), pp. 31 – 32.

15th Light Division Cantonment *near Duc My*.

U.S. Advisory Detachment Buildings *at Ban Me Thuot*.

He instructed the interpreter to tell the men "About Face!" The interpreter looked at the major rather quizzically, then spoke rapidly to one of the trainees. The man broke from the ranks, went over to a pail of water, washed his face and then returned to the formation. Each time the advisor would attempt to teach this facing movement the same act would be repeated. Finally after the third attempt the trooper broke down. He told the major that there was nothing wrong with his face, that it was clean because he had washed it three times.[52]

At the end of General O'Daniel's tour of duty, he had recommended that the U.S. Army train some officers in Vietnamese before sending them to Saigon, but the Army had no Vietnamese language school at the time, and the staff considered that, in view of the number of officers in the advisory group, "such a program would be extremely expensive."[53]

The shortage of Vietnamese-trained officers was in part a reflection of a larger, Army-wide problem with language training. During the 1950s no single individual or agency had responsibility for the Army language program. The deputy chief of staff for military operations was responsible for training most military linguists; the deputy chief of staff for personnel selected, tested, and assigned officers to language training; and the assistant chief of staff for intelligence conducted his own Foreign Area Specialist Program. Officers in the agencies involved often had other duties, and the language program tended to take a backseat to more pressing concerns.[54] As a result of such inattention and divided responsibility, sizable numbers of individuals were trained in languages without subsequently being assigned to jobs that called for their use. This problem was all the more serious because during the late 1950s the Army as a whole remained about 20 percent short of its requirements for language-trained officers.[55]

Vietnamese-trained officers were rare items even in the defense attache's offices until the end of the 1950s. In Saigon, however, many officers assigned to government agencies found that facility in French was far more useful in dealing with the highly Westernized elite of the government and army whose own knowledge of colloquial Vietnamese was sometimes rudimentary. When the first Vietnamese-speaking Army attache was presented to General Ty, he attempted to carry on a discussion in Vietnamese. The general smiled and nodded his way through the attache's fluent exposition in Vietnamese, then privately requested that the embassy send him a French-speaking officer.[56]

Officers and enlisted men newly assigned to the Military Assistance Advisory Group received little orientation in Vietnamese culture either before or

[52]Short History of MACV Advisory Teams, 1971, 228–OP, Organizational History files, MACV records.

[53]Memo, Brig Gen David W. Grey, DCSOPS for CofSA, 5 Mar 56, sub: Contents and Disposition of a Report by Lt Gen J. W. O'Daniel Relating to Situation in Indochina, G–3 091 Indochina.

[54]Memo, Maj Gen Robert A. Schow for CofSA, 31 Oct 58, sub: Comments on the Intelligence Activities of the U.S. Army, 020 ACSI, records of ACSI.

[55]Ibid.

[56]Interv, author with Comstock, 14 Sep 78. Few officers spoke French either. In 1957 there were four officers in the advisory group with "good knowledge of military French." Interv, author with Dannemiller, 10 Mar 80.

after arrival. Through 1960 all incoming officers received a standard four-hour briefing on some dozen subjects, none touching directly on the government, politics, or recent history of South Vietnam.[57] The Army frequently "expressed concern about officers going 'Asiatic,' losing their professional ethos, and conceivably their personal morals when immersed in the culture of Southeast Asia for prolonged periods."[58]

In addition to these handicaps the Military Assistance Advisory Group in Vietnam labored under a number of rigid restrictions imposed by Washington. The number of advisers was strictly limited, and no serious thought was given to raising the limitation until the end of the 1950s. The size of the Vietnamese armed forces and the availability of equipment were likewise circumscribed by the level of aid agreed upon in 1956. The sort of open-ended support for Vietnam made available by the Kennedy and Johnson administrations was quite unknown during General Williams' day, when every dollar spent had to be painstakingly justified and cuts in aid levels seemed far more likely than increases.[59]

The heart of the American advisory effort was the Combat Arms Training Organization (CATO), formed after the demise of the Training Relations and Instruction Mission in April 1956.[60] The Combat Arms Training Organization functioned as a kind of operations staff for the chief of the Military Assistance Advisory Group and also controlled all the MAAG field detachments assigned to Vietnamese schools and commands. The chief of the Combat Arms Training Organization was the rating officer for all advisers except those senior to him, a somewhat unusual arrangement since, as a staff officer, the CATO chief had only infrequent opportunities to observe the advisory detachments in the field.[61]

There were, until 1960, four major advisory commands serving with South Vietnamese units in the five military regions. They included I Corps and 2d Military Region with headquarters at Da Nang, a command which also comprised the advisory detachments assigned to the 1st Field Division at Da Nang and the 2d Field Division at Hue. The II Corps and the 4th Military Region, with headquarters at Ban Me Thuot in the Central Highlands, and the 3d Military Region headquartered at Pleiku included the advisory detachments with the 12th Light Division at Kontum, the 14th Light Division at Qui Nhon, the 15th Light Division at Duc My, the 3d Field Division at Song Mao, and miscellaneous units stationed in the region. The 1st and Capital Military Regions included detachments with the 4th Field Division at Bien Hoa and

[57]Briefing Orientation—MAAG, Vietnam, Incl to Ltr, Williams to Brig Gen Henry G. Newton, 6 Jan 60, Folder 73, Williams Papers.

[58]Ltr, Maj Gen Paul Gorman to Chief of Military History, 1975, sub: Comments on Proposed Monograph: the U.S. Adviser, copy in Historians files, CMH. "I would have loved to have had an orientation in Vietnamese history," one former adviser stated. "I have no doubt that many people could have been far more effective had they had this background training." Interv, author with Lasche, 30 Aug 79.

[59]Interv, author with Forsythe, 20 Apr 80.

[60]Training Directorate, HQUSMACV, History of the U.S. Training Effort, pp. 17–18.

[61]Interv, author with Symroski, 16 Aug 79.

LAOS

THAILAND

Hue
2d Field Division

MR II

Da Nang
I Corps Hq
2d MR Hq
1st Field Divison

MR III

Kontum
12th Light Division

Pleiku
3d MR Hq

Qui Nhon
14th Light Division

MR IV

CAMBODIA

Ban Me Thuot
II Corps Hq
4th MR Hq

Duc My
15th Light Division

Nha Trang

MR I

Tay Ninh
11th & 13th Light Divisions

Song Mao
3d Field Division

Bien Hoa
4th Field Division

SAIGON
CAPITAL MR
CAPITAL-I MR Hq

MR V   *My Tho*
5th MR Hq
16th Light Division

Can Tho

ADVISORY COMMANDS
(BEFORE 1960)

0 _____ 100 MILES

0 _____ 100 KILOMETERS

Note: Different units were rotated into MR V to perform
assigned missions. Miscellaneous units were assigned in all MR's.

MAP 7

the two or three light divisions stationed at Tay Ninh. The 5th Military Region in the Mekong Delta, with headquarters at the town of My Tho, usually included the 16th Light Division and frequently one or two other light divisions drawn from the II and, later, the III Corps areas. (*Map 7*)

The light divisions each had a lieutenant colonel of infantry or artillery assigned as senior adviser; an infantry major assisted by two noncommissioned officers served as adviser to each of the three infantry regiments of the division. The field divisions had a colonel of infantry as senior adviser, three infantry majors as regimental advisers, and an artillery major as artillery adviser; they were assisted by two or three noncommissioned officers.

Advisory detachments at the I and II Corps headquarters consisted of about a dozen officers and enlisted men with a colonel of infantry as senior corps adviser, and two lieutenant colonels to advise the corps engineer, armor, ordnance, and signal units. The other military regions each had an armor, artillery, or infantry colonel as senior adviser and a varying number of other advisers, usually less than half a dozen, depending on the number and size of units operating in the region.[62]

Other advisory detachments assigned to the various schools and training centers reported to the Combined Arms Training Organization through its Operations and Training Division, while those at the technical service schools and depots reported to the chief of the Temporary Equipment Recovery Mission.[63] In Saigon advisers were also assigned to various sections of the Vietnamese Ministry of Defense and the general staff.

The Adviser's Role

Approximately forty U.S. military personnel of all ranks and services were permitted to have their families accompany them to Vietnam on a two-year tour of duty. The remaining 700-odd members of the advisory group served for one year, the maximum time which the Department of the Army thought reasonable for an unaccompanied tour in an unhealthful and distant country. Their actual tour as advisers seldom exceeded eleven months.[64]

Military Assistance Advisory Group personnel in Saigon lived in comfortable bachelor officer or enlisted quarters with good common messing facilities and the entertainment and recreational opportunities of Saigon close at hand. In the field advisers occupied more primitive, although seldom uncomfortable, quarters with few diversions except for a nightly movie in the mess hall. They also suffered fewer distractions and demands for paperwork than their

[62]The foregoing information is based upon a short paper entitled "Some Recollections of the U.S. Advisory Program of MAAG-Vietnam" that was prepared especially for the Center of Military History by Col. Nathaniel P. Ward III, U.S. Army (Retired), former Senior Adviser, II U.S. Corps, and later (1959) Chief of Staff, MAAG, Vietnam. Copy in Historians files, CMH.

[63]Training Directorate, HQUSMACV, History of the U.S. Training Effort, p. 19.

[64]Intervs, author with Lasche, 10 Aug 79, with Ward, 16 Aug 79, and with Symroski, 16 Aug 79.

General Williams *receives briefing on amphibious exercise.*

counterparts in the capital. The Vietnamese Army provided quarters, offices, vehicles, guards, and drivers; most advisers hired and paid their own cooks and orderlies.

As a general rule the lower the rank of the adviser and the farther from the capital, the closer his relationship to his unit and his counterpart.[65] The regimental, division, or corps adviser spent a good deal of his time consulting with his Vietnamese opposites and observing and inspecting the components of his unit, either alone or with the unit commander. Nor did the field adviser completely escape the demands of paperwork. His immediate superiors and advisory group headquarters required frequent periodic reports, and the U.S. adviser often had to aid his counterpart in dealing with Vietnamese paperwork. The adviser was also likely to spend a good deal of his time traveling since the area assigned to his division or regiment was frequently large and its subordinate units scattered. One officer spent almost all of his time in travel. He was the deputy chief of the Military Assistance Advisory Group, a major general, who regularly visited and inspected all units in the field to keep General Williams informed and to ensure at least some uniformity in the training effort.

[65]Ward, "Some Recollections of the U.S. Advisory Program"; Interv, author with Ward, 16 Aug 79.

A good deal of the adviser's effort was directed toward persuading his counterpart of the wisdom of certain policies, procedures, or assignments he wished the Vietnamese to adopt. Aided by an informal system of communications, advisers at the higher echelons would pass the word on what measures had been applied and in some cases aid the lower ranking adviser by persuading their Vietnamese opposites to direct their subordinates to take the desired action. Yet in an army where orders of superiors were frequently ignored or evaded, such methods were far from completely effective.[66]

At the higher policy levels the advisory group was also able to exert leverage through the budget review committee. Chaired by the deputy chief of the Military Assistance Advisory Group, the committee included the chief of the Combat Arms Training Organization, the heads of the advisory group's air force and navy sections, a representative of the ambassador, and the chief of the Temporary Equipment Recovery Mission. It conducted an annual review of the Vietnamese military budget in concert with Vietnamese officials. This process consumed several weeks and was sometimes used as a means of influencing the armed forces to adopt policies favored by the advisory groups.[67]

There was, one senior adviser recalled, much speculation over advisory styles.

One of the major issues was the degree of intimacy which should exist between the advised and the adviser. One school of thought held that the American should seek to cultivate as warm and as personal a friendship with his counterpart as their respective personalities permitted. Another school of thought, usually articulated unofficially, held that the adviser should keep some maneuver distance between himself and his counterpart so that he could exercise leverage when the Vietnamese seemed reluctant to take action, or move in the proper direction. Obviously, such interpersonal distance was also useful when the American had reason to believe that his counterpart was involved in some shady transaction or other. Those who have argued the latter view, point out that an American pursuit of intimacy might lead to disrespect—achieve exactly the opposite of the effect intended, by causing the Vietnamese to regard his counterpart as less than wholly serious, or in some other sense, not to be taken seriously.[68]

The eleven-month tours tended to militate against adviser effectiveness. As one officer recalled, "A Vietnamese division commander would have an adviser for eleven months, and then he'd get a new one. The new one would have to start from the zero point again. [The Vietnamese commander] had heard everything before and he knew that the adviser didn't understand the language and that the adviser couldn't be everywhere all the time to see what was going on. . . . He knew all about how to handle advisers."[69]

Because the short tour separated an officer from his family, advisers often

---

[66]Interv, author with Symroski, 16 Aug 79.
[67]Ibid.
[68]Ltr, Gorman to Chief of Military History, 1975, sub: Comments on Proposed Monograph: The U.S. Adviser.
[69]Interv, author with Symroski, 16 Aug 79.

Vietnamese and U.S. Instructors *on rifle range, Nha Trang Training Center.*

considered it a hardship and a nuisance. "One consequence of the short tour was that we had a number of people who merely wanted to get through," observed one former senior adviser. "They'd spend three months getting oriented into their jobs and the last three months getting ready to leave."[70]

General Williams' principal means of evaluating and controlling the advisory effort was the Senior Advisers' Conference. This quarterly (later bimonthly) meeting brought together all senior advisers down through the division level and all school advisers. The officers sat in a U-shaped arrangement with General Williams and his deputies at the open end. Beside the deputy chief of the advisory group sat the Vietnamese chief of staff. An agenda was published in advance, and the meeting proceeded logically. The I Corps adviser reported first, followed by the division advisers in the corps, then the II Corps adviser followed by his division advisers, and on down the list with General Williams frequently interrupting to ask questions or share information.[71]

A former chief of the Combat Arms Training Organization observed of these meetings: "Looking back, I have the feeling there was a tendency to report things optimistically. I believe that, in a number of cases, people held

[70]Ibid. with Lasche, 30 Aug 79.
[71]Ibid. with Symroski, 16 Aug 79.

back a little bit in reporting anything wrong because they feared that it would reflect on them adversely."[72] Another former adviser recalled that at his first visit to a Senior Advisers' Conference in late 1959 he was

shocked to hear some advisers reporting on a world I had never seen. A man from Mars listening to it would have believed that everything was going quite well. When it came Col. Miner's [Col. Russell M. Miner, senior adviser to I Corps, 2d Military Region] turn to report, I had drafted his report and in substance we reported that while the unit we were working with was probably as good or better than comparable units, it couldn't really punch its way out of a paper bag. . . . Col. Miner's report blew the lid off, General Williams was absolutely incensed. And his reason, I feel, was that since he had been there from the very beginning he felt any criticism was a failure on his part. . . . People were scared to death of General Williams. . . . People were afraid to speak.[73]

A more serious obstacle to obtaining an accurate picture of the Vietnamese Army's progress was the lack of any standard method for rating the morale and combat effectiveness of Vietnamese units. Each reporting officer used his own descriptive adjectives in evaluating his unit's effectiveness. In periodic reports the words excellent, exceptionally high, very high, high, good to excellent, fair to good, poor, fair to poor, low, lower, and average all appeared. No attempt was made to establish the relationship between the words, their order of ranking, or their precise meaning. Was satisfactory better than average? Was fair to poor worse than somewhat low? To complicate matters still further each adviser defined his unit differently for rating purposes. Some attempted to rate the unit as a whole, while others rated each of the component commands separately.[74]

The Army Reorganizes

The advisory group under General Williams continued to try to organize the scattered units of the South Vietnamese Army into division-size units so that divisional training and field exercises could get under way. Yet few divisions were able to complete the entire MAAG training cycle, for the demands of security operations, warfare against the sects, and guard duty frequently intervened.[75] General Williams was even less tolerant than O'Daniel of those distractions, but there was little he could do about them.

Williams saw the organization of the South Vietnamese Army as "weak and inadequate" for the tasks it would have to perform. An inexperienced South Vietnamese general staff was attempting to control directly all separate

[72]Ibid.
[73]Ibid. with Lt Col Bergen B. Hovell, 22 Apr 80, Historians files, CMH.
[74]Ltr, Col L. B. Woodbury to ACSI, 12 Sep 57, sub: Morale and Combat Effectiveness of Vietnamese Army, OARMA 350.09, records of ACSI.
[75]Memo, Chief, TERM, for Chief, MAAG, 27 Sep 56, sub: Review and Analysis of MAAG Programs.

battalions and regiments and all ten divisions, for there were no intermediate headquarters. Dividing the country into military regions, each under an army officer as regional commander, merely increased the confusion, for in addition to commanding military forces assigned to the regions, the regional commanders often attempted to assume control of other units temporarily operating in their areas.[76]

General Williams also disliked the structure of the divisions as devised by his predecessors. In particular, he wanted to do away with the territorial regiments and light divisions, which Generals Trapnell and O'Daniel had seen as valuable for maintaining internal security. Because they lacked artillery and had exceedingly austere combat service support, Williams saw no possibility of quickly upgrading them for a regular combat role should the North Vietnamese launch a conventional invasion.[77]

A start on reorganization was made in the fall of 1956. The primary objective was to increase the effectiveness of the logistical and support elements while leaving the 150,000-man force level unchanged. To this end most of the territorial regiments were dissolved, and an ordnance company was added to each of the light divisions. Two corps headquarters were also created and the number of military regions increased from three to five. A 155-mm. howitzer battalion was formed to provide corps artillery for the two corps areas. The remaining spaces released by the abolition of the territorial regiments were used to strengthen the combat support units and to provide small increases for the navy and the air force.[78]

By early 1957 the advisory group was conducting studies to determine the most feasible type of division organization. Diem, to whom larger and more heavily armed units had always appealed, encouraged the advisory group to think in terms of heavier U.S.-type formations. Ignoring the role played by Trapnell and O'Daniel in creating light divisions, he declared that the French had been the sole influence behind their introduction "with a view toward making the Vietnamese military effort seem insignificant."[79]

Although Diem wanted to reorganize the army immediately into divisions of a single type of about 10,000 men each, General Williams insisted on first conducting extensive studies and field tests to determine the optimum size and organization for a standard division. Actual reorganization of the South Vietnamese Army, which began in early 1959, was not completed until the following year. Both the light and field divisions and most of the territorial regiments were abolished. In their place seven standard infantry divisions of 10,450 men were formed, each consisting of three infantry regiments, two artillery battalions (one with 4.2-inch mortars), and a number of combat support and combat service support units. *(Chart 3)*

---

[76]Ltr, Williams to Adm Felix Stump, 23 Aug 57, Folder 16, Williams Papers.

[77]Ibid. Lt Gen Arthur G. Trudeau, 25 Jul 57, Williams Papers.

[78]Ltr, Lt Col L. B. Woodbury to ACSI, 25 Sep 56, sub: Proposed Reorganization of the Vietnamese Army, 5–10–56, OARMA 350.09, records of ACSI.

[79]Memo of Conversation Between President Diem and Gen Williams, 19 Jan 57, Williams Papers.

CHART 3—REORGANIZED SOUTH VIETNAMESE ARMY INFANTRY DIVISION, 1959

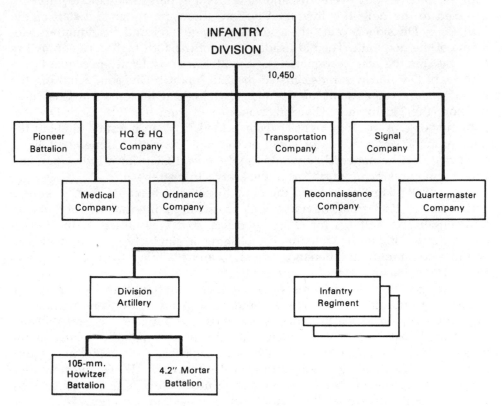

Source: Information compiled from USACGSC, Staff Study on Army Aspects of Military Assistance.

In the reorganization the 1st and 2d Field Divisions became the 1st and 2d Infantry Divisions, the 3d Field Division became the 5th Infantry Division, and the 4th Field Division became the 7th Infantry Division. The 11th and 13th Light Divisions were disbanded and their personnel and equipment assigned to the new 21st Infantry Division; the commander and staff of the 11th Light Division became the commanding general and headquarters elements of the new unit. The old headquarters of the 13th Light Division in Tay Ninh became the rear headquarters of the 21st Infantry Division. Similarly the 14th Light Division was redesignated the 22d Infantry Division, acquiring the personnel and equipment of the old 12th Light Division. The final new division, the 23d Infantry Division, was formed from the 15th Light Division with elements of the 16th Light Division added.[80] When questioned about the high numeric designations of some of the new divisions, General Williams explained that he hoped they would "fool General Giap for a little while and keep them guessing up north" as to the army's true strength.[81]

General Williams considered the new divisions to be capable of resisting a conventional attack from the north while maintaining internal security, able to fight either conventional forces or guerrillas, and well suited to the terrain and weather of South Vietnam. Establishing a single type of combat unit would also simplify maintenance, logistics, and planning for operations and for future military assistance requirements.[82]

Although the new divisions were specifically designed to be superior in firepower to the units of the North Vietnamese Army, they were intended to fight primarily on foot in mountains, swamps, and jungles. General Williams maintained that "contrary to much fallacious reasoning," the soldier of the division had "the same foot mobility" as a guerrilla. "His individual equipment is light, extremely durable, and most effective."[83] While the new divisions possessed a number of trucks and prime movers, those vehicles were intended for the divisional "tail," not for employment in operations.[84]

To assertions that the new division was a carbon copy of an American infantry division, General Williams reacted with annoyance, denying any significant similarity.[85] Because the American infantry division during the late 1950s was also undergoing testing and reorganization, it would be difficult to make a precise comparison. The very nature of a division and the requirements for accomplishing its combat mission foreordained certain similarities. Thus all the technical services (engineer, signal, medical, ordnance, quartermaster) were represented in both the American and the South Vietnamese

---

[80]Short Historical Sketches of the Eleven Infantry Divisions, the Airborne Division, and the Marine Division, Incl to Msg, Am Embassy, Saigon, to CINCPAC, 6 Feb 73, copy in Historians files, CMH.

[81]Marginal comments by Col Nathaniel P. Ward on draft manuscript of this volume.

[82]Ltr, Williams to U.S. Ambassador, 1 Jun 60, sub: Training of the Republic of Vietnam Armed Forces, Folder 77, Williams Papers.

[83]Ibid.

[84]Ibid. See also Interv, author with Myers, 22–23 Feb 77.

[85]Cf. *U.S.-Vietnam Relations*, vol. 2, pt. IV.A.4, p. 26. The authors concluded that "there were more similarities than differences."

divisions, although in less strength in the latter. The American division had 2,672 more men, and although the overall strength of the basic maneuver units in both divisions was almost identical, they were organized differently. The South Vietnamese division had three regiments of 2,450 men each, while the American division had five battle groups (roughly reinforced battalions) of 1,420 men each. The South Vietnamese regiment contained three battalions of four companies each. There was no American battalion, but the battle group also had four companies. American artillery strength was considerably larger: the U.S. division had a total of seventy 4.2-inch mortars and 105-mm. howitzers as well as twelve 155-mm. howitzers. The South Vietnamese division had only twenty-four 4.2-inch mortars and 105-mm. howitzers. Unlike the South Vietnamese division, the American division had two reconnaissance troops (light armored vehicles), an aviation company (helicopter), two transportation companies with fifty armored personnel carriers each, and a medium tank battalion.

Whatever the similarities or differences, the inescapable fact was that the new Vietnamese Army, like the old French Expeditionary Corps, remained a road-bound force. The soldiers themselves moved on foot, as General Williams emphasized, but their artillery could not; and as time passed Vietnamese commanders became less and less inclined to operate beyond supporting range of their 4.2-inch mortars and 105-mm. howitzers.[86]

In addition to seven infantry divisions, the reorganized South Vietnamese Army had four separate armored battalions, an airborne brigade, a marine group, and a helicopter squadron. The South Vietnamese Air Force had a fighter-bomber squadron, two C – 47 transport squadrons, and two light aircraft observation squadrons. The South Vietnamese Navy comprised 7 subchasers, 3 minesweepers, and 18 amphibious craft.

The logistical support system of the army, also reorganized, corresponded closely to the U.S. general staff system with the logistics section exercising general supervision over the technical services in matters of logistics. The six technical services—engineer, medical, ordnance, quartermaster, signal, and transportation—were generally similar to their American counterparts in function and organization but often had additional responsibilities and restrictions unusual to their branch of service. For example, the Quartermaster Corps had responsibilities for financial management; the Transportation Corps handled only highway transport and had no role in overall planning and coordination, tasks often neglected entirely.[87]

In the area of logistics, members of the equipment recovery mission were able to bring considerable improvement in the near chaotic conditions prevailing in the wake of the French withdrawal. By late 1957, the amount of materiel in outside storage had been reduced to a minimum, consolidation and rewarehousing had been completed, shipping and receiving procedures along American lines had been introduced, and the spare parts and tools

[86]Intervs, author with Dannemiller, 10 Mar 80, and with Forsythe, 20 Apr 80.
[87]USMAAG, Vietnam, Country Statement for Vietnam as of 30 Jun 57, records of MAAG Vietnam.

received from the French had been identified and inventoried. Yet at the beginning of 1958 American advisers still considered the South Vietnamese Army's logistical system "incapable of supporting the Vietnamese armed forces." Maintenance of equipment at all levels was below minimum U.S. standards, regulations were not enforced, and inspections were infrequent. Both officers and enlisted men lacked necessary technical training.[88] Advisers considered the Transportation Corps poorest of all because its organization and mission precluded centralized control of transportation means. The other technical services were considered generally adequate for peacetime, but their lack of trained personnel made their wartime effectiveness questionable.[89]

As part of the reorganization the two corps headquarters were given operational control of most of the divisions, removing them from the direct control of the general staff. Headquarters of the I Corps, responsible for the area from Da Nang on the coast north to the 17th Parallel, had been activated on 1 June 1957, and headquarters of the II Corps, responsible for the Central Highlands and the coastal region from southern Quang Nam Province south to the town of Phan Thiet, the following October. The II Corps headquarters, originally at Ban Me Thuot, was moved to the town of Pleiku in the summer of 1959. A third provisional corps headquarters was being formed for southern Vietnam and would be activated as the III Corps in September 1959. Between the general staff and the corps was a field command consisting of a commander and a small staff.[90]

Williams hoped the reorganization would alleviate some of the command and control problems that had plagued the South Vietnamese Army from the start. Yet many South Vietnamese commanders and officials simply ignored the new chain of command as they had the old. Superiors continued to bypass subordinates; subordinates continued to go over the heads of superiors; and all commanders continued to issue orders to units not under their control.[91]

The new divisional organization reflected the advisory group's view that the most likely threat to South Vietnam was a North Vietnamese invasion. Pacific Command's Operation Plan 46 – 56 provided that the chief of the Military Assistance Advisory Group would, in the event of such an invasion, assume command of a new unified command, the Vietnam Defense Command, under the Commander in Chief, Pacific.[92] As a subordinate commander, General Williams had prepared a supporting plan detailing measures for the defense of South Vietnam. Williams' plan, called CINCPAC Operation Plan 46A, differed from the parent plan mainly in emphasizing the importance of the high plateau in the vicinity of Kontum, Pleiku, and Ban Me Thuot. The Pacific Command plan called for an all-out defense of Da Nang

---

[88]Country Statement Report, 22 Jan 58, p. 19, records of MAAG Indochina.
[89]USMAAG, Vietnam, Country Statement for Vietnam as of 30 Jun 57.
[90]First Draft Report of the Draper Study Committee, 17 Feb 59, Folder 107, p. 36, Williams Papers; Interv, author with Ward, 16 Aug 79.
[91]USACGSC, Staff Study on Army Aspects of Military Assistance, p. C – 20.
[92]See ch. 14, p. 272.

but Williams, supported by other Pacific Army commanders, argued that while the Da Nang area should be held as long as possible, its defense should not jeopardize the high plateau area. This difference became academic in 1959 when the 46-series plans were superseded by others, yet throughout his tenure General Williams advised stationing plans for Vietnamese Army units which would provide the best dispositions to implement his concept for defense of the highlands.[93]

As for the Vietnamese, the reorganization and redispositions of 1956 through 1959 had long since made their single war plan of August 1956 obsolete, but they produced no other despite the urgings of American advisers.[94] President Diem's principal concern in the war planning was to provide for an amphibious counterattack against North Vietnam. Diem insisted the assault be carried out by South Vietnamese troops with allied forces in supporting roles. Foreign troops in North Vietnam, he said, would only "alienate the population."[95]

Diem's interest in an attack on North Vietnam was more political than military. His plan called for South Vietnamese airborne troops to seize a position on the North Vietnamese coast to disrupt the enemy's advance but, more importantly, to "hold on long enough to permit the withdrawal of some two or three million" people into South Vietnam. He thus hoped to reenact his political and propaganda triumph of 1954 when large numbers of North Vietnamese had moved south. He was confident that the people of North Vietnam were eager to be liberated, and "in this way the Viet Minh regime will lose human resources which will surely affect the morale of the population."[96]

Even after reorganization, the South Vietnamese Army still suffered from rampant politicization and corruption in the officer corps. "All too frequently," General Williams observed, "officers who are performing their duties efficiently are relieved and transferred to other duties . . . the general impression is that the officer has incurred the ill-will of some high official." Such practices contributed to lack of stability in key assignments throughout the army, lowered morale, and gave rise "to the opinion that one must have friends or influence in high places in order to succeed."[97]

Although the readiness and effectiveness of South Vietnamese units were much improved over 1954, some were still unsatisfactory. After an inspection of the 16th Light Division in 1958, for example, an American officer reported

---

[93]Memo, Col R. P. Davidson for ACSI, 15 Nov 57, sub: CINCPAC Operation Plan No. 46A – 57, 381 CINCPAC – OP – 46 – A – 57, records of ACSI; PACOM MAP Country Inspection Trips, Vietnam, Incl 22A to HQ, USARPAC, ACofS G – 3, Quarterly Historical Summary, Oct-Dec 58, copy in Historians files, CMH.

[94]Ltr, Woodbury to ACSI, 25 Sep 56, sub: Proposed Reorganization of the Vietnamese Army; Interv, author with Lasche, 30 Aug 79.

[95]Record of Conversations, Ambassador Durbrow and Gen Williams with President Diem, 26 Oct 57, Williams Papers.

[96]Memo of Conversation Between President Diem and Gen Williams, 15 Jan 57, Williams Papers.

[97]Memo, Williams for Tran Trung Dung, Asst Secy of State for National Defense, 31 Jul 58, sub: Long-Range Military Planning, Folder 35, Williams Papers.

that the division was 21 percent understrength and lacked half of its medical personnel. Leadership ability of the key command and staff officers was "relatively low." The status of training was "unsatisfactory," and only 40 percent of the division's radio equipment was operational.[98] In the 13th Light Division "half the division strength is on TDY [temporary duty] or ineffective, overage etc." The enlisted men "wore tattered uniforms, needed hair cuts, lacked military bearing even when marching, and many of their weapons were rusty inside and out."[99]

Despite these continued problems almost all American observers were nevertheless convinced by the late 1950s that the effort to create an effective South Vietnamese Army had succeeded. Reporter Jim G. Lucas of the Scripps-Howard newspapers described the army as "a crack, combat-ready force" with "top military schools, a small navy and air force and a tiny but rough Marine Corps."[100] A study by the U.S. Army Command and General Staff College in 1960 commended the advisory group for "profiting from the lessons of 1946–1954" and "emphasizing aggressive, hard-hitting mobile divisions with high fire-power organized to ensure close mutual support."[101] An investigation in 1959 of the aid program in South Vietnam by the Senate Foreign Relations Committee's Subcommittee on State Department Organization and Public Affairs blasted the American mission as "the weakest country team that we have met" but singled out the advisory group for special praise.[102] It was possible, declared the *Army Times*, that General Williams' advisory group was "the finest there is."[103]

Yet within a year American leaders were to be confronted with irrefutable evidence of the inability of the South Vietnamese Army to assure the internal security of South Vietnam and a clear demonstration that it was not a reliable instrument of the Diem government.

[98]Ltr, Col Rolin B. Durbin to Williams, 14 Feb 58, Folder 34, Williams Papers.

[99]Ltr, Maj Gen Samuel L. Myers to Williams, 10 Sep 57, Incl to Williams to Gen Ly Van Ty, 10 Sep 57, Williams Papers.

[100]Scripps-Howard Dispatch, 14 Dec 59, Clipping file, Williams Papers.

[101]USACGSC, Staff Study on Army Aspects of Military Assistance, pp. 6–7.

[102]U.S. Congress, Senate, Committee on Foreign Relations, Subcommittee on State Department Organization and Public Affairs, *Situation in Vietnam, Hearings, 30 July 1959* (Washington, 1959). Williams' deputy, Maj. Gen. Samuel L. Myers, told the committee the South Vietnamese Army was "now able to maintain internal security and . . . should there be renewed aggression from the north they can give a really good account of themselves." Ibid., p. 171.

[103]"Congress Praises Army Job," *Army Times*, 23 Apr 60.

16

Roots of a New War, 1957—1959

By 1957 the United States appeared well on the way to achieving its aims in South Vietnam. The government of Ngo Dinh Diem had vanquished the armies of the sects and the Binh Xuyen and had successfully defied North Vietnam on the issue of national elections. In July 1955 Diem had refused even to consult with the Democratic Republic of Vietnam on the subject. The Republic of Vietnam, said Diem, was in no way bound by the Geneva Agreements. His government had declined to adhere to them and, while eager for a "reunification in freedom," would consider no proposals from a regime which subordinated the national interest to the interests of communism.[1]

The United States had never had much enthusiasm for the elections, believing that North Vietnam would never permit a really free expression of political views.[2] Privately, many American officials also acknowledged that even a relatively "fair" election would almost certainly result in a lopsided victory for North Vietnam. Its larger population and superior political organization and control would weigh heavily in favor of the North, as would the personal prestige of Ho Chi Minh and a continuing popular identification of the Viet Minh with nationalism.[3] As a State Department expert on Vietnam observed, the Diem government would "be campaigning against the massive fact of Viet Minh victory, against ubiquitous Viet Minh infiltration, and against the knowledge, shared even by illiterate coolies, that there would be no such independence as now exists had it not been for the Viet Minh."[4]

---

[1]*The Senator Gravel Edition of the Pentagon Papers*, 1:287.

[2]Secy of State to Am Embassy, Saigon, 6 Apr 55, 751G.00/4–655, records of Dept of State.

[3]Memo, Edmund Gullion, 15 Feb 55, sub: What Next in Indochina?, Attachment to Memo, Jacob Beam for Livingston Merchant, 17 Feb 55, same sub; Memo, Richard M. Scammon for Douglas MacArthur II, 21 Apr 55, sub: All-Viet Nam Elections. Copies of all in Collins Papers.

[4]Memo, Gullion, 15 Feb 55, sub: What Next in Indochina? Other contemporary observers confirmed Gullion's view. AP Correspondent William L. Ryan estimated that Ho would get 75 percent of the votes if elections were held. The French expert Philippe Devillers put the figure at 80 percent. Franklin B. Weinstein, *Vietnam's Unheld Elections*, Data Paper no. 60 (Ithaca, N.Y.: Department of Asian Studies, Cornell University, 1966), pp. 13–14.

Nevertheless, the United States could hardly oppose or openly obstruct the holding of nationwide elections. To do so would contradict the traditional American stand that nations divided against their will, such as Germany and Korea, should be reunited through free elections supervised by the United Nations. This position had been reiterated by the American representative at Geneva, Walter Bedell Smith. There was also the possibility that the Communists might again resort to arms if elections were denied or postponed.[5]

Eisenhower and his advisers never adopted a firm policy on the question of elections. In general, Washington leaders saw them as something to be delayed rather than eliminated. They counseled Diem to consult about elections, as required by the Geneva Agreements, but then to stall by insisting that elections be held only when, as the agreements specified, "all necessary conditions obtain for a free expression of national will." In the meantime the Diem government would presumably build up the popular support necessary to win the elections, should they take place.[6] When Diem instead opted simply to have nothing to do with elections, the United States, impressed with his recent successes, went along with little protest. Although the Democratic Republic of Vietnam appealed to the cochairmen of the Geneva Conference—Britain and the Soviet Union—and hinted at renewed military action if the elections were not held, the July 1956 deadline for opening consultations passed without incident.[7]

Early in 1957 Diem came to the United States aboard President Eisenhower's personal plane to be hailed everywhere as the savior of Southeast Asia. The South Vietnamese president addressed a joint session of Congress and paid a ceremonial visit to New York, where Mayor Robert F. Wagner pronounced him "a man history may yet adjudge as one of the great figures of the twentieth century." Senator John F. Kennedy referred to South Vietnam as "the cornerstone of the Free World in Southeast Asia, the keystone to the arch, the finger in the dike."[8] The *Saturday Evening Post* called Diem the "mandarin in a sharkskin suit who's upsetting the Red timetable."[9]

Yet even while Diem was receiving those accolades in the United States, members of the country team in Saigon were reaching different conclusions about the achievements of the South Vietnamese government. During the fall of 1957 Ambassador Durbrow, U.S. Operations Mission Chief Leland Barrows, Embassy Counselor Thomas D. Bowie, and Economic Affairs Officer Wesley Haroldson prepared a report sharply critical of the character and policies of the Diem regime. They described Diem as a man unable to delegate responsibility: "He overrides most of his Ministers, reduces their

---

[5]Ibid.

[6]NSC 5519, U.S. Policy on All Vietnam Elections, 17 May 55, records of National Security Council, National Archives; Memo, Brig Gen William C. Westmoreland to Gen Maxwell Taylor, 16 May 56, sub: U.S. Policy Toward Vietnam, CS 091 Indochina, RG 319.

[7]Weinstein, *Vietnam's Unheld Elections*, pp. 31 – 33.

[8]Both as quoted in Frances FitzGerald, *Fire in the Lake: The Vietnamese and the Americans in Vietnam* (Boston: Little, Brown and Co., 1972), pp. 73 and 84, respectively.

[9]"The Bright Spot in Asia," *Saturday Evening Post*, 15 September 1956, p. 4.

authority, and assumes personal responsibility for the smallest details of government. He is inclined to be suspicious of others; he lacks an understanding of basic economic principles."[10] Economic development and agrarian reform had been neglected while the president concentrated on pet projects related to security. In the countryside, discontent with the government was increasing, and internal security was expected to decline. In the more sophisticated urban areas, there was considerable resentment and fear of Diem's covert Can Lao Party, which, the officials noted, had managed to infiltrate almost all political, social welfare, journalistic, cultural, and other public activities.[11]

Other members of the country team including the CIA station chief and the Army, Navy, and Air Force attaches endorsed the report in general, but Williams dissented. He believed that in order to retain Diem's confidence and cooperation it was imperative to avoid associating with his critics and enemies. "Otherwise we would go the way of the French."[12] General Williams also doubted that the situation was as serious as the report indicated. "The receipt [in Washington] of the proposed dispatch," he warned Ambassador Durbrow, "would unquestionably cause alarm and unnecessary concern . . . the reports I have seen do not indicate a state of considerable concern regarding internal security, the economic situation, or the executive ability of the government of Viet Nam."[13] In a lengthy and heated discussion with other members of the country team, Williams insisted that he was unable to "subscribe to the idea that the president was on the way to failure." Even after persuading the foreign service officers to moderate the tone of their report, he refused to concur in its conclusion.[14]

The months to come were to show that the country team had been, if anything, too mild in its criticism of the Diem government. From observing Diem on numerous trips and inspection tours, General Williams had become convinced that the president was extraordinarily popular, but that popularity turned out to be largely a sham.[15] The American consul at Hue, for example, observed that the villagers who were often paraded out to participate in ceremonies honoring Diem and to make appropriate responses to slogans "have virtually no concept of what they are doing."[16] As a British journalist noted, "Diem holds the fort through the Army and the police force provided by U.S. [money]. It is not that the communists have done nothing because Diem is in power, rather Diem has remained in power because the communists have done nothing."[17]

[10]Country Team Report, 8 Jan 58, Williams Papers.
[11]Ibid.
[12]Interv, MacDonald and Luttichau with Williams, 13 Nov 70.
[13]Ltr, Williams to Ambassador Durbrow, 9 Oct 57, Folder 16, Williams Papers.
[14]Ibid. to Adm George W. Anderson, 9 Dec 57, Folder 16, Williams Papers.
[15]Interv, MacDonald and Luttichau with Williams, 13 Nov 70.
[16]Am Consul, Hue, to State Dept, 6 May 58, 751G.00/5 – 658, records of Dept of State.
[17]David Hotham, "South Vietnam, Shaky Bastion," *New Republic*, 25 November 1957.

Vietnamese Army Convoy *in the Central Highlands.*

The Uses of American Aid

By the late 1950s, South Vietnam was receiving about $190 million annually in American aid, more per capita than any other country in South and Southeast Asia except Laos.[18] Recently torn by war and with a primitive, mainly agrarian economy, Vietnam was incapable of financing any substantial military program. Expenditures of the size specified in the U.S.-approved force levels would have constituted about 9 percent of the total gross national product.[19] In 1955 the Vietnamese government collected revenues amounting to only one-third of its expenditures. Even without defense spending the Vietnamese budget would have been in deficit; with it's massive amounts of foreign aid were required. Of the total of $207 million projected for the 1957 defense budget, $187 million would have to come from the United States. In 1958, 84 percent of the military and 44 percent of the nonmilitary expenditures of the Diem government were paid for by some form of American aid.[20] Over 80 percent of the total aid funds went into a "commodity-import pro-

[18]Some Facts About American Aid, 1958, Incl to Memo, Chester H. Opul for Gen Williams, 10 Sep 58, sub: USIS-USOM Material, Folder 37, Williams Papers; Robert Scigliano, *South Vietnam: Nation Under Stress* (Boston: Houghton Mifflin Co., 1963), p. 112.

[19]Report by the Interdepartmental Committee on Certain U.S. Aid Programs, 3 Aug 56, copy in ODCSOPS 091 Vietnam, DCSOPS records.

[20]Some Facts About American Aid.

gram" whose purpose was to prevent that aid from having an inflationary effect on the South Vietnamese economy. Under this program the United States purchased various foreign commodities for South Vietnamese importers, using dollars or other foreign currencies. The importers paid for the goods in piasters, which were deposited in a "counterpart fund" and used to support governmental programs. More than three-quarters of all the aid received from the United States was allocated directly to the military and security forces.[21] Almost 70 percent was needed simply to pay the inflated salaries of the South Vietnamese armed forces.[22] Of the nonmilitary aid, agricultural improvement and land reform projects received only 17 percent; health, education, and industrial development received about 7 percent each; and social welfare and housing received 3 percent.

The bulk of the nonmilitary aid was devoted to two of Diem's favorite projects: developing South Vietnamese settlements in the Central Highlands and building a secondary road system to connect the highlands with the more populous coastal areas and the cities of central Vietnam with those in the south. Diem believed that roads in the highlands would open remote areas to development, which in itself might deter guerrillas from establishing base areas in the region, but which would also facilitate his own military operations against guerrilla forces. He was especially interested in linking the town of Kontum in the highlands with the town of Pakse in Laos and connecting Kontum with Da Nang and Hue along the coast, thereby opening up areas where residual elements of the Viet Minh were thought to be active. South Vietnamese Army engineers were almost continuously occupied in the road-building projects throughout the late 1950s.[23]

General Williams supported the road-building program into the highlands because it fit American military contingency plans. Operation Plan 46A envisioned the Mekong valley as the main enemy route of invasion and the Central Highlands as the critical theater of war.[24] Pakse and the Plateau des Bolovans inside Laos, Williams noted, constituted a "stopper that controls the whole Mekong Valley." In the event of a war between North and South Vietnam, holding that area would be a first step in preventing movement down the Mekong.[25] Williams also felt that road construction provided valuable training for the army's engineer unit.

Members of the U.S. Operations Mission were skeptical of the value of Diem's "bunch of low-grade military roads into the bush." Viewing the question from the perspective of economic rather than military requirements, the Operations Mission wanted to concentrate on rebuilding Route 1, the main north-south coastal highway, and particularly on providing it with first-class bridges.[26] The road-building program thus became another source

---

[21]Scigliano, *South Vietnam*, pp. 112–13.
[22]First Draft Report of the Draper Study Committee, 17 Feb 59, Folder 107, Williams Papers.
[23]Memo, Acting Chief, MAAG (Maj Gen S. L. Myers), for Leland Barrows, 30 Jan 58, sub: Conference With the President, Folder 37, Williams Papers.
[24]See ch. 12.
[25]First Draft Report of the Draper Study Committee, 17 Feb 59.
[26]Interv, author with Barrows, 27 Jul 76.

of controversy between the Military Assistance Advisory Group and other elements of the country team, a controversy complicated by the fact that the members of the advisory group felt constrained for security reasons not to discuss the military implications of the road system with their colleagues.

Diem's second project, settling lowland South Vietnamese in the Central Highlands bordering on Cambodia and Laos, was also motivated in part by considerations of national security. He hoped to develop a network of fortified villages or "development centers" along the border to bar guerrilla infiltration from Laos and Cambodia. At the same time he expected the highland settlements to provide opportunities for landless peasants from the lowlands and refugees from North Vietnam to become small proprietors. Diem even had visions of the settlements raising a cash crop, such as rubber, for export. By the end of 1959 about 210,000 people had been resettled in 147 centers scattered throughout the Central Highlands.[27]

While Diem was intensely interested in the highlands, he cared little about the native highlanders, ethnically distinct tribes who had long inhabited the region. Called Montagnards by the French, the tribal peoples were to the lowland Vietnamese little better than savages (*moi*). (Diem confided to General Williams that "mountain people are very lazy and don't like to work.")[28] The Montagnards in turn felt a strong animosity toward the Vietnamese. Except in such towns as Kontum, Pleiku, and Ban Me Thuot, few ethnic Vietnamese had ever lived in the highlands; when they began to arrive under Diem's program, the Montagnards strongly resented the incursion. Aside from what the Montagnards saw as Vietnamese condescension and heavy-handed attempts to "civilize" them, they objected to large-scale land-grabs by the South Vietnamese government to provide land for the settlers. By late 1958 the CIA was reporting "mounting discontent among tribal groups in the highlands."[29] The Vietnamese settlers were almost as unhappy. They often found that the land granted them was infertile or difficult to cultivate, and they suffered severely from an especially virulent form of malaria, *falciparum*, which was prevalent in the highlands and against which the lowlanders had built up no immunity.[30]

Land Reform

Although Amerian civilian officials were critical of both the road-building and resettlement projects, they pointed with pride to another South Vietnamese program: land reform. In the summer of 1959, for example, Ambassador Durbrow told a U.S. Senate subcommittee that the South Viet-

[27]Scigliano, *South Vietnam*, p. 105.
[28]Williams, Memorandum of Conversations With President Diem, 11 Oct 58, Williams Papers; Interv, author with Gerald C. Hickey, former member of Michigan State University Advisory Team, 21 Apr 76, Historians files, CMH.
[29]Current Intelligence Weekly Summary, 16 Oct 58, pt. 2, p. 12, copy in CMH; Ward, marginal comments on draft manuscript.
[30]Bernard B. Fall, "South Vietnam's Internal Problems," *Pacific Affairs*, February 1958, p. 252; Interv, author with Hickey, 21 Apr 76.

namese government was carrying out "the largest land reform program in Asia."[31]

Land reform was clearly a subject of importance in a country where 75 to 80 percent of the population lived in rural areas and large landholdings by absentee landlords were commonplace. The problem was most acute in the Mekong Delta region, where a majority of the rural population owned no land and a small but extremely wealthy class of absentee landlords held much of the fertile land. Most peasants rented land on a sharecropping basis, with the drawbacks attendant to such a system. To a landlord who provided no credit, seed, or fertilizer, the peasant paid one-third to one-half of the expected yield; in the event of crop failure, the landlord still had the right to demand his share of the normal yield.[32]

During the long war against the French, the Viet Minh had driven away or killed many landlords and turned over their land to the poorer peasants. Instead of accepting that situation, the Diem government restored land to the landlords and then tried to regulate the extent of their landholdings and the landlord-tenant relationship.[33] In 1955 the Diem government passed an ordinance setting a maximum of 15 to 25 percent of a crop as the lawful rent, and the following year limited individual landholdings to 247 acres. Acreage exceeding that maximum was to be purchased by the government and sold in small parcels to tenants, laborers, and other landless persons. Whether or not this constituted "the largest land reform program in Asia," it was certainly one of the most conservative. Landlords were allowed to select the lands to be retained, and the 247-acre limit was far greater than that allowed in Japan or Korea. In many provinces peasants were granted the right to purchase land that they had already been given by the Viet Minh. Although the government established loans to enable penniless peasants to buy land, its rigorous enforcement of repayment provisions often resulted in hardship. In Kien Phong Province, for example, farmers were forced to sell their rice at slump prices to meet loan payments. One farmer was reportedly "placed in a cage too small to stand up in and had to remain there until his wife sold their oxen" to pay the loan.[34]

The implementation of the land reform program was so ensnarled in red tape and legalisms that in many areas relatively little land actually changed hands. In one province in the Mekong Delta, the first land redistribution took place only in 1958, almost two years after the land reform law was established.[35] A 1960 census showed that only 23 percent of the farmers in the

---

[31]Testimony of Elbridge Durbrow, Senate, Committee on Foreign Relations, Subcommittee on State Department Organization and Public Affairs, *Situation in Vietnam, Hearings, 30 – 31 Jul 59,* p. 7.

[32]Roy F. Prosterman, "Land Reform in Vietnam," *Current History* 57 (December 1969):330 – 31; Jeffrey Race, *War Comes to Long An: Revolutionary Conflict in a Vietnamese Province* (Berkeley: University of California Press, 1972), p. 7.

[33]Prosterman, "Land Reform," p. 332.

[34]CIA Field Intel Rpt, CS 3/405,784, 22 Jul 56, sub: Security Situation in Kien Phuong Province, copy in CMH.

[35]Race, *War Comes to Long An,* p. 59.

Mekong Delta owned any land at all, and about 56 percent of those lived on two-acre farms, one acre of which was rented.[36]

Communist Strategy After Geneva

Aside from the government's failure in land reform, rural residents were also affected adversely by a strongly promoted "anti-Communist campaign" mounted during 1955 and 1956 against known and suspected members and ex-members of the Viet Minh. The Viet Minh leaders had left Geneva confident that Vietnam would soon be unified under their control either through the scheduled elections or through the precipitate collapse of the South Vietnamese government.[37] Following the Geneva Conference the Communist leadership began actively to prepare for a campaign of political agitation and propagandizing in the South. They summoned many former Viet Minh soldiers and cadres to regroup in North Vietnam while those who remained behind, an estimated 10,000 active agents, began to agitate for elections and reunion with the North. Mass meetings in the villages were organized by Communist cadres who harangued the crowds about "the victory of Geneva." In many villages in the south and southwest, photos of Ho Chi Minh and copies of the Geneva Agreements appeared on the wall of every house. In Saigon and other large cities the insurgents made a determined effort to win over non-Communist leftists, students, and intellectuals through such ostensibly patriotic organizations as the Saigon-Cholon Peace Movement.[38]

The Diem government responded with the Anti-Communist Denunciation Campaign and with armed action against Viet Minh–led organizations and demonstrations. Although the campaign did considerable damage to the Viet Minh's civilian infrastructure, it was conducted in such a brutal, corrupt, and capricious manner that it alienated large segments of the population.[39] Even

[36]Prosterman, "Land Reform," p. 131.

[37]Carlyle A. Thayer, "Southern Vietnamese Revolutionary Organizations and the Vietnam Workers' Party: Continuity and Change, 1954–1974," in Joseph J. Zasloff and McAlister Brown, *Communism in Indochina* (Lexington, Mass.: D. C. Heath, 1975); Weinstein, *Vietnam's Unheld Elections*, pp. 17–18. P. J. Honey believed that the Vietnamese Communist leadership never expected elections to occur and were "bitterly disappointed at the outcome of the Geneva Conference" but later asserted that the Communist leaders "based their hopes for national reunification upon the collapse of the Ngo Dinh Diem regime." "North Vietnam's Model of Strategy and Tactics for Revolution," in George Pisnenny and Alexei Akimenbro, eds., *Studies on the Soviet Union, 1966,* vol. 6, no. 2, p. 10. All agreed that neither the North Vietnamese nor any of the other conferees at Geneva foresaw the emergence of a relatively strong, stable, and unified government in the south so soon after the close of the conference.

[38]Situation in Quang Tri, Thua Thien, and Quang Nam Provinces, 20 Sep 54, ibid. in Thua Thien and Quang Nam Provinces, 16 Oct 54, and Vietminh Implantations and Administration in South Vietnam, 17 Dec 54, all in OARMA to ACSI, 28 May 55, 5–6–55, records of ACSI; *New York Times,* 29 Sep 54 and 13 Mar 55; Experiences of the South Vietnam Revolutionary Movement During the Past Several Years (document captured by U.S. 1st Inf Div, Jan 66), copy in Historians files, CMH, pp. 1–4; Thayer, "Southern Vietnamese Revolutionary Organizations," pp. 34–36.

[39]David Hotham estimated that over 14,000 persons were arrested in a single year in the central provinces "without evidence and without trial." Hotham, "South Vietnam, Shaky Bastion."

former members of the Communist Party who were inactive or no longer loyal to the Viet Minh and former Viet Minh who had never been Communists were harassed, arrested, and in some cases executed. In some areas, families with sons who had gone to North Vietnam following the Geneva Agreements or who had relatives involved in insurgent activities were also affected. "Not only were local officials and police agents frequently incompetent at singling out the active Viet Minh agents, but many were also arrogant and venal in the execution of their tasks and by their offensive behavior generated sympathy for the Viet Minh."[40] In one province, villagers could be jailed simply for having been in a rebel district. The people especially resented a curfew, which hampered fishermen and farmers, and a compulsory unpaid labor program to improve roads and perform other public works.[41]

Despite the disruption to Communist Party organizations in many hamlets and districts, party cadres and innocent victims of the purges could often make their way to jungle, swamp, or mountain areas where they easily evaded government forces.[42] By alienating large numbers of non-Communist and neutral peasants, the heavy-handed campaign also made it easy for the Viet Minh to rebuild their organizations and recruit new members.

Nevertheless, the campaign's short-run impact on the Communist apparatus in South Vietnam was severe. By early 1955 most Viet Minh cadres who had escaped arrest had been driven underground, and Communist-organized demonstrations had become infrequent.[43] With many of its military forces regrouped in the North the party was in a poor position to meet the vigorous onslaught of the South Vietnamese government.

Pressure from the Diem government, combined with disappointment at the cancellation of the hoped-for elections, probably led to a decline in membership and morale in the party. At a meeting of top party leaders in the South in March 1956 Le Duan, Secretary of the Central Committee's Directorate for South Vietnam, expressed strong dissatisfaction with the North Vietnamese government's policy, which emphasized political agitation in the South and diplomatic pressure on the former Geneva conferees. The only way to achieve reunification, said Le Duan, was to wage armed struggle against the Diem regime.[44]

Yet in 1956 many North Vietnamese leaders were reluctant to become

---

[40]J. J. Zasloff, *Origins of the Insurgency in South Vietnam, 1954–1960: The Role of the Southern Cadres,* Rand Memorandum, RM 5163/Z-ISA/ARPA (Santa Monica: Rand, 1968), pp. 9–10.

[41]CIA Field Intel Rpt, CS 3/405,784, 22 Jul 56, sub: Security Situation in Kien Phuong Province, copy in CMH.

[42]Ibid., p. 17; Race, *War Comes to Long An,* p. 41.

[43]Situation in Quang Tri, Thua Thien, and Quang Nam Provinces, 8 Jan 55, Incl to OARMA to ACSI, 28 May 55, 5–6–55, records of ACSI; Thayer, "Southern Vietnamese Revolutionary Organizations," p. 36.

[44]Thayer, "Southern Vietnamese Revolutionary Organizations," p. 37; U.S. Department of State, Working Paper on the North Vietnamese Role in the War in South Vietnam, item 18: Interrogation of a Former Viet Minh Cadre, and item 19: Translation of a Document Found on the Person of a Political Officer With the Communist Forces in Zone 9, copies in Historians files, CMH.

involved in a renewed war, wanting first to "build socialism" in North Vietnam. War would retard development and would carry with it a risk of American intervention. Communist leaders in South Vietnam continued to object to that policy, preferring to proceed with overthrowing the Diem regime before Diem became fully established.[45]

Finally Le Duan offered a compromise. In a pamphlet entitled *On the Revolution in South Vietnam* he argued for a long-term approach to the problem of South Vietnam which, while continuing political agitation and subversion, would also lay the groundwork for a future armed uprising against Diem. Le Duan's arguments were favorably received at the Eleventh Plenum of the Central Committee in December 1956.[46]

By 1957, when Le Duan was recalled to fill a senior party position in North Vietnam, a campaign of terrorism and subversion had begun in the South without direct support from the North. During much of this time, Communist units consciously avoided contact with government forces, concentrating instead upon *tru gian* ("the extermination of traitors"), a systematic program of assassination of government officials and anyone considered an obstacle to the movement.[47] In some provinces special assassination squads of about half a dozen men were formed solely for this purpose.[48] Any village official or government functionary was considered a legitimate target for *tru gian*. "In principle,"explained a former party leader in Dinh Tuong Province, "the Party tried to kill any [government] official who enjoyed the people's sympathy and left the bad officials unharmed in order to wage propaganda and sow hatred against the government."[49] At times the insurgents terrorized or executed even persons known to be innocent of any pro-government activity to encourage anxiety and distrust among the villages.[50]

In many regions *tru gian* took the form of a three-phase campaign. First, village notables and officials would be subjected to propaganda attacks and warned to cease "oppressing the people" (that is, obey the party). Those who proved recalcitrant would then be kidnapped or intimidated, while those judged most dangerous were murdered.[51] In some areas threats or a single

[45]CIA Intel Rpt, No. 0487/70, 2 Feb 70, sub: Hanoi's Leaders and the Divisions Over War Policy, 1956–1968, copy in CMH.

[46]Experiences of the South Vietnam Revolutionary Movement, pp. 4–5. William J. Duiker, *The Communist Road to Power in Vietnam* (Boulder, Colo.: Westview Press, 1981), pp. 177–80. Duiker believes that Le Duan's pamphlet was intended not only to convince members of the Central Committee in the North but also some segments of the southern leadership who still believed in "the validity of the line of peaceful struggle and the possibility of reunification elections." See page 180.

[47]Race, *War Comes to Long An*, pp. 81–84.

[48]ARVN Intel Rpt, 3 Apr 57, Attachment to Ltr, OARMA to ACSI, 23 Jun 59, records of ACSI.

[49]William R. Andrews, *The Village War: Vietnam Communist Revolutionary Activities in Dinh Tuong Province, 1960–1964* (Columbia: University of Missouri Press, 1973), p. 59.

[50]Ibid., pp. 57–58; Russell H. Bates, *Viet Cong Village Control* (Cambridge: MIT Press, 1969), pp. 25–26; W. P. Davison, *Some Observations on Viet Cong Operations in the Villages*, Rand Memorandum, RMS 267/2–5A (Santa Monica: Rand, 1968), pp. 24–37.

[51]Ltr, OARMA to ACSI, 30 Mar 57, sub: ARVN Intel Rpts, Feb-Mar 57, 5–12–57, OARMA 350.09, records of ACSI.

murder was sufficient to bring villages under party control. In others the party ruthlessly murdered entire families to achieve its aims.[52]

Along with assassination and intimidation went continued political organization and agitation. The party set up all-embracing groups such as the Farmers' Liberation Organization, the Vietnam-Cambodian Buddhist Association, the Association of Ten Year Combatants, and various youth movements to spread propaganda and act as a cover for its activities.[53] The Communists also attempted to subvert or neutralize the government's military and paramilitary forces. Antidraft demonstrations were organized, false rumors circulated, and new recruits encouraged to desert. Occasionally entire squads or platoons of local militia went over to the Communist side, bringing their weapons with them.[54]

In keeping with Le Duan's policy the party emphasized rebuilding and consolidating its political and military apparatus in preparation for a future showdown with Diem. In the interim much of the actual fighting was undertaken by armed remnants of the sects.[55] Some of these bands had long since surrendered or come over to the government, but the remainder had been effectively infiltrated by the Communists who reportedly assigned scores of cadres to rearm, resupply, and retrain the sect forces.[56] Although they continued to operate under their old names, most sect units were effectively under Communist control by early 1957.[57] In Tay Ninh Province, for example, several hundred former Cao Dai and Binh Xuyen armed partisans had been formed into a force called Binh Doan ("Inter-Army"), ostensibly led by a Binh Xuyen chieftain but actually controlled by the chieftain's "political adviser," a Communist.[58] In An Xuyen Province an uncooperative Hoa Hao battalion commander was reportedly assassinated by the Communists.[59] By May 1958 Vietnamese Army intelligence analysts considered all remaining armed sects to be Communist led.[60]

During 1957 and 1958 the sect bands were among the most aggressive Communist forces. In July a Hoa Hao battalion became involved in a battle with contingents of a South Vietnamese division, and later in the month a Hoa Hao band raided the town of Chau Duc, killing seventeen persons in the ensuing skirmish.[61] Other clashes occurred in Ha Tien Province and in Binh Hoa, where a Binh Xuyen battalion of about a hundred men raided an

[52]Andrews, *The Village War*, pp. 56–57.
[53]Ibid.; USMAAG, Vietnam, Country Statement for Vietnam, 30 Jun 57.
[54]ARVN Intel Rpt for Jan-Feb 57, Attachment to OARMA to ACSI, 28 Feb 57, 5–6–57, OARMA 350.09; ibid. for Mar 57, Attachment to Ltr, OARMA to ACSI, 30 Mar 57, sub: ARVN Intel Rpts, Feb-Mar 57, 5–12–57, OARMA 350.09. Both in records of ACSI.
[55]Thayer, "Southern Vietnamese Revolutionary Organizations," p. 35.
[56]ARVN Intel Rpt for Jan-Feb 57, Attachment to OARMA to ACSI, 28 Feb 57, 5–6–57, OARMA 350.09, records of ACSI.
[57]Ibid.; Race, *War Comes to Long An*, p. 36.
[58]CIA Field Intel Rpt, CS 3/380,436, 11 Dec 58, sub: Armed Communists and Dissidents in Tay Ninh, copy in CMH.
[59]Msg, USARMA, Saigon, to Dept of Army, 071038z Mar 58, records of ACSI.
[60]Ibid., 091040z Mar 58, records of ACSI.
[61]Memo of Conversation, Williams with President Diem, 15 Nov 57, Williams Papers.

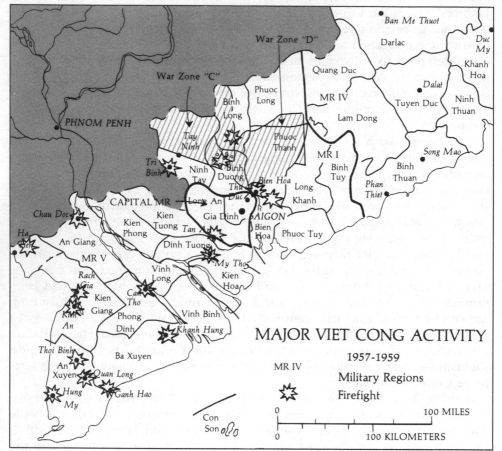

Ban Me Thuot

Darlac

Duc
My

War Zone "D"

Quang Duc

Khanh
Hoa

War Zone "C"

MR IV

Dalat

Binh
Long

Phuoc
Long

Lam Dong

Ninh
Thuan

Tuyen Duc

PHNOM PENH

Tay
Ninh

Phuoc
Thanh

MR I

Song Mao

Tri
Binh

Ninh
Tay

Binh
Duong

Binh
Tuy

Binh
Thuan

Bien Hoa

Thu
Duc

Long
Khanh

Phan
Thiet

CAPITAL MR

Long An

SAIGON

Chau Doc

Kien
Tuong

Tan An

Gia Dinh

Bien
Hoa

Phuoc Tuy

Ha
Tien

Kien
Phong

An Giang

Dinh Tuong

MR V

My Tho

Vinh
Long

Kien
Hoa

Rach
Gia

Can
Tho

Kien
Giang

Phong
Dinh

Vinh Binh

Kien
An

Khanh Hung

Thoi Binh

Ba Xuyen

An
Xuyen

Quan Long

Hung
My

Ganh Hao

Con
Son

MAJOR VIET CONG ACTIVITY

1957-1959

MR IV   Military Regions

Firefight

0   100 MILES

0   100 KILOMETERS

MAP 8

agricultural center and captured some small arms with little resistance from government forces. Another Binh Xuyen battalion with over 300 uniformed, well-armed men raided the Minh Thanh Rubber Plantation in southern Binh Long Province, causing the government to divert two entire army divisions to operations against it.[62] (*Map 8*)

The most spectacular military action of the period occurred on the night of 10 August 1958, when a force of about 400 men raided the large Michelin Rubber Plantation north of Saigon. The site was defended by local security forces and a company of Vietnamese Army troops—over 200 men. Nevertheless the raiders, led by a Binh Xuyen commander with Communist advisers, achieved complete surprise and made off with over a hundred weapons and 5 million piasters (some $143,000) from the plantation's safes. Subsequent investigation revealed that the army company had failed to take even the most elementary security precautions and had been unable to call for reinforcements because between 2200 and 0600 the radio net was inoperative.[63] The Communists also achieved a significant psychological success by paying their own visit to a plantation the president had inspected less than a week before and struck a heavy blow at the government's efforts to step up rubber production. The president was reported to be "deeply perturbed" over the raid.[64]

Incidents involving insurgents increased throughout 1957 and into 1958. During January 1957, Communist guerrillas clashed with South Vietnamese Army troops seven times in the Mekong Delta provinces. The following month a Viet Cong force of about thirty men attacked a government civic action team in the village of Tri Binh, fifteen miles south of Tay Ninh; the entire team was killed or wounded, and the local government militia force took no action against the raiders.[65] During a single month in the autumn of 1957, 22 village notables and other local government officials were killed or wounded by the Viet Cong, 6 village chiefs were killed, and 11 members of local militia were killed and 14 kidnapped.[66] During the last quarter of 1957 some 140 armed attacks and terrorist acts were reported throughout the country in addition to more than 50 skirmishes initiated by government troops or security forces. Terrorists wounded, assassinated, or killed at least 74 persons, including 20 government officials and 31 police and security personnel.[67]

The Communists concentrated their armed activities in the southern provinces, mainly in the more rugged and inaccessible region along the Cambo-

[62]ARVN Intel Rpt for Feb 57, Attachment to OARMA to ACSI, 28 Feb 57, 5–6–57, OARMA 350.09; Msg, USARMA, Saigon, to Dept of Army, 100921z Feb 58; ibid., 120316z May 58. All in records of ACSI.

[63]Ltr, Williams to Col Elisha Peckham, 28 Aug 58, Folder 35, Williams Papers; Am Embassy, Saigon, to Secy of State, 13 Aug 58, copy in records of ACSI.

[64]Am Embassy, Saigon, to Secy of State, 14 Aug 58, records of Dept of State.

[65]Msg, Chief, MAAG, to CINCPAC, 28 Feb 57, Williams Papers; Ltr, OARMA to ACSI, 28 Feb 57, 5–6–57, OARMA 350.09, records of ACSI.

[66]Memo of Conversation, Williams with President Diem, 15 Nov 57, Williams Papers.

[67]National Intelligence Survey, South Vietnam, NIS 430, sec. 57, pp. 11–12, copy in Historians files, CMH.

dian border where the terrain favored concealment and ambush. Toward late 1957 and early 1958 an increasing number of incidents were also reported on the outskirts of medium-sized towns such as Tan An, Can Tho, My Tho, Soc Trang, Rach Gia, and Ca Mau.[68] Although the insurgents were either new recruits to or veterans of the Viet Minh, the Diem government for propaganda purposes renamed them Viet Cong, a derogatory term meaning Vietnamese Communists. By mid-1957 the name had come into general use.

Problems of Intelligence

Despite those developments and other signs that the tempo of insurgent activity was quickening, General Williams saw no reason for alarm. "There are no indications of a resumption of large-scale guerrilla warfare at this date," he told Ambassador Durbrow at the end of 1957. "They [the Viet Cong] lack sufficient strength, do not have a popular base and are faced with a central government whose efficiency to deal with the subversion threat has gradually improved since its inception." He estimated the Viet Cong's combat strength in the central provinces at no more than 1,000 including sect forces, plus around 200 political and propaganda cadres.[69] Williams made this assessment of the situation based on the limited information available to him. The Military Assistance Advisory Group had no intelligence unit, so that in the main General Williams had to depend on South Vietnamese sources for information about the insurgents.[70]

The whole matter of intelligence in Vietnam was a complicated and vexing one and, like so many other problems, was closely related to bureaucratic rivalries within the country team and to the peculiarities of the Diem regime. As in other areas of Vietnamese government activity, intelligence functions were divided among a number of agencies. The Central Intelligence Agency identified six major and several lesser intelligence-collecting groups within the Diem government "competing, duplicating, thrusting and nullifying each other's efforts through lack of centralized co-ordination."[71] Within the Vietnamese military, regional and division commanders frequently operated their intelligence systems with little or no operational coordination or control by the army general staff or Ministry of Defense. American advisers suspected that some of these numerous intelligence networks were actually exploiting the same informants, but since the Vietnamese lacked an informant control system it was impossible to be sure.[72]

---

[68]Ibid., p. 12.
[69]Ltr, Williams to Ambassador Durbrow, 10 Dec 57, Folder 18, Williams Papers.
[70]Interv, MacDonald and Luttichau with Williams, 13 Nov 70.
[71]Deputy Director of CIA to ACSI, 23 Jun 60, sub: Coordination of U.S Army Plans for Vietnam, ACSI 6249VN, records of ACSI.
[72]Memo for CO, U.S. Army Assistance Group, 22 Sep 60, sub: Intelligence Community in South Vietnam, Incl 2 to CO, 902d CFC Gp, to Chief, Security Div, OACSI, 29 Sep 60, sub: After-Action Rpt, Vietnamese Army Training, ACSI 6249VN, records of ACSI.

The National Security Act of 1947 had given the newly created Central Intelligence Agency responsibility for coordination of all U.S. clandestine intelligence activities abroad. During the 1950s the National Security Council progressively strengthened CIA control over clandestine operations until, by 1958, the agency had "primary responsibility for U.S. clandestine activities abroad." Other departments were permitted to conduct "supplementary" operations as required but only subject to coordination by the CIA.[73]

Army commanders in the Far East, at all levels, were unhappy with this state of affairs. They believed that the Central Intelligence Agency was not providing the detailed military information about their potential antagonists that they needed to carry out their mission.[74] Pacific Command contingency planning called for General Williams to head a unified command in Vietnam in the event of war. He was therefore eager to obtain accurate and timely information on the armed forces of the Democratic Republic of Vietnam, such as detailed orders of battle, tables of organization and equipment of divisions, and data on training methods, logistics, and key personalities. These intelligence requirements had been levied on the CIA's Saigon station, but General Williams complained that the station was failing to furnish him with the desired information.[75]

Since 1954 CIA attempts to conduct effective clandestine intelligence operations against the Democratic Republic of Vietnam had met with only indifferent success. North Vietnamese security forces had quickly neutralized the "stay behind" agents planted after the Geneva Agreements and had thwarted a high percentage of penetration efforts directed against North Vietnamese targets. The lack of any legal trade or travel between the two Vietnams severely limited the opportunities to put agents in the North. The preoccupation of South Vietnamese intelligence agencies with local Communists and dissidents also militated against penetrating North Vietnam.[76]

While General Williams' complaints were focused on the lack of information about North Vietnam, the CIA's lack of success in this regard also hindered efforts to acquire an accurate picture of Communist insurgent operations. General Isaac D. White, Commander in Chief, U.S. Army, Pacific, described CIA intelligence on Viet Cong forces in South Vietnam as "inadequate in almost all areas of command interest" particularly in regard to strength, dispositions, leadership, equipment, and tactics.[77] Generals Williams and White were also concerned about the need to provide the Vietnamese general staff G–2 with a capability to conduct clandestine intelligence opera-

[73]Memo for ACSI, 6 Feb 60, sub: Centralization of Clandestine Intelligence, ACSI 570, records of ACSI.
[74]Msg, CINCUSARPAC to ACSI, 102225z Aug 60, Vietnam Training file, records of ACSI.
[75]Memo, Ch, MAAG, for CINCPAC, 1 Oct 59, sub: Field Operations Intelligence Training for ARVN G – 2 Personnel, ACSI, 6249VN, records of ACSI.
[76]MFR, Maj J. Buffkin, 11 Aug 59, sub: Discussions With CIA Representatives Regarding Vietnam; MFR, Lt Col W.G. Silva, 10 Jul 58, sub: Conference With CAS Representatives, Incl to Memo, ACAS G – 2, USARPAC (Brig Gen Paul H. Draper), for ACSI, 23 Jul 58, sub: USACRAPAC-CIA Coordination on Vietnam Intelligence Training. All in ACSI 6249VN, records of ACSI.
[77]Msg, CINCUSARPAC to ACSI 102225z Aug 60.

tions in wartime. Personnel had to be trained for those operations, usually called field operations intelligence, during peacetime.[78]

As early as 1956 the assistant chief of staff for intelligence had been aware of the need to improve intelligence capabilities in countries adjacent to the Communist nations. His solution was to establish intelligence training teams in these countries to provide planning assistance, training, and operational guidance to the host country's armed forces in the conduct of clandestine intelligence activities. Army intelligence planners had proposed such a program for Vietnam in December 1956 and even sent General Williams a sample letter that the government of Vietnam might use in requesting such assistance. But General Williams was unsuccessful in persuading President Diem to sign the letter, and efforts to broach the subject with the Vietnamese head of state during his 1957 visit to Washington also had failed.[79]

The matter was not raised again until January 1958 when the problem of providing better intelligence coverage for Vietnam was discussed at a U.S. Army, Pacific, Commander's Conference. General Williams and other conferees agreed that sending a U.S. Army field operations intelligence team to Saigon would be the best way to meet that requirement. Such a team could function in two capacities, training the Vietnamese Army in clandestine intelligence and improving the intelligence "take" for both the Military Assistance Advisory Group and the U.S. Army, Pacific. General Williams intended to provide three to five personnel spaces for a field operations intelligence team within the advisory group's already existing Combat Intelligence Training Unit. If President Diem agreed to the program, the U.S. Army would train selected Vietnamese Army intelligence personnel in clandestine operations in Okinawa, Hawaii, or Japan.[80]

As a start Williams suggested that Diem send two key South Vietnamese Army intelligence officers to Japan for a ten-day orientation on plans to develop the army's clandestine intelligence capability. The president appeared receptive to this idea, and in late April two Vietnamese officers arrived in Japan for discussions and orientation in the functioning of a field operations intelligence unit.[81] While the Vietnamese officers were in Japan plans proceeded for establishment of a U.S. field operations intelligence team in Vietnam. But these plans came to an abrupt halt when Central Intelligence Agency officers in Vietnam and Japan protested that clandestine intelligence training was a CIA responsibility and that Williams' invitation to the two officers had disrupted their own efforts in Saigon.

---

[78]Ibid.; to COUSACRAPAC, 080010z Nov 59, ACSI 6249VN, records of ACSI.

[79]Memo, Brig Gen William R. Frederick for Ch, MAAG, 19 Dec 56, inclosing Draft Copy of Letter Presented to President Diem, ACSI 6249VN; Msg, USARMA, Saigon, to Dept of Army for ACSI, 070248z Dec 56, ACSI 6231 Indonesia; Memo, Maj Gen R. A. Schow for Acting ACSI, 13 May 57, sub: Intelligence Training for Vietnam Armed Forces, ACSI 6231 Indonesia. All in records of ACSI.

[80]Msg, CINCUSARPAC to Dept of Army for ACSI, 220259z Feb 58, ACSI 6249VN, records of ACSI.

[81]Ibid.; same to ACSI, 231902z Apr 58, ACSI 6249VN, and to Dept of Army, 010036z May 58, ACSI 6231 Indonesia, both in records of ACSI.

The CIA claimed that it had been negotiating for a number of months with the Vietnamese government about the establishment of a clandestine training program for the Vietnamese Army. The main point of dispute concerned control of covert operations, with the Vietnamese desiring to direct their own operations and the CIA insisting on joint control. Just when it appeared to the CIA that the Vietnamese were willing to compromise, the U.S. Army, by its proposal for intelligence training, had offered the Vietnamese the opportunity to bargain and to play off one U.S. agency against another.[82] The Central Intelligence Agency had no objection to a field operations intelligence training team in the Military Assistance Advisory Group, provided that any actual operations were coordinated in detail with the CIA Saigon station.[83]

General Williams and U.S. Army, Pacific, intelligence officers doubted that the CIA had really had an alternative training program near fruition; they expressed annoyance that the CIA station chief had failed to contact the advisory group before the two Vietnamese officers departed for Japan even though he had been fully aware of their plans. They noted that Vietnamese officers complained that CIA intelligence advisers spent most of their time operating rather than instructing and pointed out that, as designated area commander, General Williams had a right to try to ensure that the Vietnamese Army had the resources to carry out its assigned wartime mission.[84]

Whatever the merits of the case, a request from President Diem for Army field operations intelligence training failed to materialize, and in August 1958 the CIA station chief informed General Williams that he had concluded a satisfactory arrangement with the Vietnamese government for clandestine training and operations. Yet for many months Generals Williams and White continued to express dissatisfaction with the quality and quantity of intelligence they were receiving from the CIA.[85]

By mid-1959 General Williams had concluded that the CIA could not fulfill his requirements for intelligence. He was therefore prepared to reopen the subject of clandestine intelligence training with President Diem, but only if "action has been taken at the national level to preclude repercussions from the CIA."[86] That September Chief of Staff Le Van Ty formally requested that the advisory group provide training for the South Vietnamese Army's intelligence staff in clandestine collection of strategic and tactical military intelligence in enemy territory. After more months of negotiation between the Army and the Central Intelligence Agency, this time at the Washington level,

[82]MFR, Col Silva, 10 Jul 58, sub: Conference With CAS Representatives, Incl to Memo, ACAS G – 2, USARPAC, for ACSI, 23 Jul 58, sub: USACRAPAC-CIA Coordination on Vietnam Intelligence Training.

[83]Msg, CINCUSARPAC to ACSI, 061840z Jun 58, ACSI 6249VN, records of ACSI.

[84]Ibid.; Memo, ACofS G – 2, USARPAC, for ACSI, 18 Aug 58, sub: USACRAPAC-CIA Coordination of Vietnam Intelligence Training, ACSI 353VN, records of ACSI.

[85]Memo, ACofS G – 2, USARPAC, for ACSI, 18 Aug 58, sub: USACRAPAC-CIA Coordination; Memo, Ch, MAAG, for CINCPAC, 1 Oct 59, sub: Field Operations Intelligence Training.

[86]Memo, ACofS G – 2, USARPAC, for ACSI, 9 Sep 59, sub: Intelligence Training for Vietnamese Army, ACSI 6249VN, records of ACSI.

in October 1960 the CIA finally agreed to the establishment of an Army combat intelligence and counterintelligence team in South Vietnam trained and equipped to conduct clandestine operations.[87] Yet this concession came far too late to aid General Williams or the advisory group on charting the course of the ballooning Viet Cong insurgency during the critical period from 1957 through 1959. With the intelligence then available, it was easy to underestimate the strength of the insurgents and to dismiss the murders as isolated acts of terrorism or banditry.

Forces for Internal Security

Above all, General Williams' misreading of the nature and seriousness of the Viet Cong threat was due to his persistent belief that guerrilla warfare was merely a diversionary tactic to degrade the South Vietnamese Army's readiness to fight a conventional war. Williams observed that the increase in Viet Cong activity raised the "possibility that military units will again have to be diverted to this primarily police-type task thus depriving them of the opportunity of continuing orthodox military training. This will in turn delay the Vietnamese government in its endeavor to develop a deterrent well-trained armed force in being."[88] President Diem largely agreed with Williams' analysis of Viet Cong activities. In December 1957 he told a group of American visitors that the "terrorism that the communists are now waging is essentially directed against the Army's training program. . . . They want to get the Army dispersed on security missions to prevent training."[89]

While insisting that the South Vietnamese Army not be diverted to local security duties, General Williams was nevertheless conscious of the need for internal security, especially in the more remote areas of the Mekong Delta and the Central Highlands. The advisory group's proffered solution was to create efficient and well-equipped forces which could relieve the army of the burden of local security duties.

There were a number of police and paramilitary organizations in South Vietnam in the mid-fifties, many a legacy of the French period. A survey in May 1957 had revealed that there were 54,000 men enrolled in the paramilitary Civil Guard; 7,000 in the municipal police; 3,500 in the Vietnamese Bureau of Investigation, or *Surete;* an undetermined number in the *Gendarmerie;* and about 50,000 in the Self-Defense (militia) Corps. Impressive in size only, these forces generally were poorly equipped, ill-trained, and poorly disciplined. The Self-Defense Corps was particularly weak, with approximately two weapons for every three corpsmen. Those weapons were mostly obsolete French rifles for which the ammunition was limited and so

---

[87]Memo, Deputy Director (Plans), CIA, for ACSI, sub: Coordination of U.S. Army Plans for Vietnam, copy in CMH.
[88]Ltr, Williams to Ambassador Durbrow, 10 Dec 57.
[89]Record of Conversations, Gen Williams and President Diem, 13 Dec 57, Williams Papers.

old that only about one round in seven was likely actually to fire.[90] A survey by American police experts found that corpsmen usually came from the lower levels of village society, had scant education, and received little or no training. The experts estimated that "the capability of the SDC [Self-Defense Corps] to withstand assaults by armed and organized Viet-Cong units is virtually nil." The advisory group believed that in most areas of the South the Self-Defense Corps was thoroughly infiltrated by the Communists; in some provinces it even reportedly "covers up more information than it furnishes."[91]

The most important organizations from the point of view of regional security and counterguerrilla operations were the Civil Guard and the Self-Defense Corps. A static, part-time, militia force, the Self-Defense Corps was intended to protect villages "against the subversive activities of dissident elements."[92] The Civil Guard was a more mobile unit organized to patrol the rural districts and was composed of armed, uniformed, full-time personnel responsible for maintaining law and order and collecting intelligence.

Since May 1955 a group of police and public administration specialists from Michigan State University under contract to the U.S. Operations Mission had been working on a number of projects to improve the training and operations of the security forces. The group established a six-week basic training course, which had trained 14,000 Civil Guardsmen by mid-1957, and also set up a national police academy. The Michigan State University advisers saw the Civil Guard as a civilian police force similar to the Pennsylvania State Police or the Texas Rangers.

President Diem had different ideas about the guard. Since the entire South Vietnamese Army would be needed in the event of invasion to defend along the 17th Parallel, he maintained that a strong internal security organization was crucial to control the high plateau region and the Mekong Delta. Thus the Civil Guard should be "capable of assisting the army in rear areas in time of war."[93] The president wanted the Ministry of Defense to assume responsibility for training, disciplining, and supplying the guard, but in peacetime it would remain under the operational control of the interior minister.[94] He wanted the Civil Guard's officers to be graduates of the military academy and to have an additional year of training in jurisprudence and traffic control. Since Diem saw the Civil Guard as a kind of second-line army, he wanted it to be unusually well armed and equipped with helicopters and armored cars.

While Diem spoke of internal security and military defense, his real interest in the Civil Guard was political. Most members of the guard were

[90]Michigan State University (MSU) Advisory Group Rpt, Civil Police Administration, May 57, copy in CMH; Msg, Williams to CINCPAC, 29 Nov 57, Williams Papers; MAAG Country Statement, 22 Jan 58, p. 16, records of MAAG Indochina; Michigan State University Vietnam Advisory Group, Review of Self-Defense Corps, 31 Oct 57, p. 3, copy in CMH.
[91]Ibid., pp. 10–11; MAAG, Vietnam, Country Statement on MAP, Non-NATO Countries, 22 Jan 58, p. 16, records of MAAG Vietnam.
[92]MSU Advisory Group Rpt, Civil Police Administration.
[93]Msg, MAAG to CINCPAC, 140755z Oct 57, Williams Papers.
[94]Notes of Protocol Visit of General I. D. White, CGUSARPAC, to President Diem, 16 Jan 58, Williams Papers.

former militiamen from the Catholic regions of North Vietnam who had fled south after the Viet Minh victory in 1954 and were among Diem's most loyal supporters.[95] The president wanted to develop the Civil Guard into a strong force to counter the power of a possibly disloyal army. When the advisers from Michigan State University insisted that a lightly armed but well-trained territorial police force was more appropriate to the needs of South Vietnam, Diem was contemptuous. "This is not Brazil, Argentina, France, or Michigan," he told General Williams. "They do not know the country or the language and are at the mercy of their interpreters."[96]

Although General Williams was aware that Catholics and northerners were heavily represented in the Civil Guard, he was less interested in the political dimensions of Diem's proposal than in the fact that an upgraded Civil Guard would "release the Army from guard and pacification duties and enable them to concentrate on training under their division commanders."[97] General Williams saw the advisers from the Michigan State University group as "police types who don't see the big picture."[98] He also viewed Diem's concept of transferring responsibility for the training, discipline, and supply of the Civil Guard to the defense minister as logical and efficient, although slightly unorthodox. He explained that the Defense Ministry was "an up-and-coming organization which is becoming more efficient every month" and was thus in a better position than the Interior Ministry to supply and administer the Civil Guard. In addition, the Defense Ministry's "control of promotions would ensure that incompetents, grafters, etc., would be weeded out."[99] Both President Diem and General Williams knew that as long as the Civil Guard and the Self-Defense Corps remained under the control of the Ministry of the Interior, they would continue to receive arms and equipment from the Michigan State University advisory group working through the U.S. Operations Mission rather than from the military assistance program. The Operations Mission's resources were more limited than those of the Military Assistance Advisory Group and its array of military hardware far less opulent. It was unlikely that the Operations Mission would ever be able to obtain funding for rearming the Civil Guard and Self-Defense Corps on the scale that Diem envisioned.

Most of the other country team members were dubious about Diem's plans for the Civil Guard. Ambassador Durbrow and Operations Mission Chief Barrows insisted that the Civil Guard was a civilian police force, not a paramilitary body, and thus ought to remain fully under control of the Ministry of the Interior. Its work in peacetime would normally be closely linked with other police agencies regulated by that ministry. In addition, Congress had already appropriated certain American aid funds for the Civil Guard under the assumption that it was part of the regular civil police

[95]First Draft Report of the Draper Study Committee, 17 Feb 59, p. 33.
[96]Memo of Conversations, President Diem with Gen Williams, 8 Oct 57, Williams Papers.
[97]Msg, Chief, MAAG, to CINCPAC, 14 Mar 57, Williams Papers.
[98]Memo of Conversations, Williams with Diem, 3 Dec 57, Williams Papers.
[99]Ltr, Williams to Brig Gen Edward Lansdale, 1 Mar 58, Folder 34, Williams Papers.

establishment; it would be hard to justify use of those funds to support a large military force.[100] Durbrow also believed that Washington would probably view a heavily armed, 50,000-man Civil Guard as an attempt to circumvent the 150,000-man ceiling on the South Vietnamese armed forces.[101] Indeed, both Durbrow and Barrows believed that the Military Assistance Advisory Group had always wanted a larger army and that Williams, with Diem's encouragement, was simply using the Civil Guard issue as a device for covertly expanding the size of the armed forces. The U.S. Operations Mission and officials of the Michigan State University advisory group argued that, however important a larger

Director Barrows

army might be, it would be a mistake to ruin the country's rural police system—the Civil Guard—in order to get it.[102]

General Williams and other American officials were even farther apart on the question of the Self-Defense Corps. So notoriously ineffective and so heavily infiltrated by Communists was that organization that many members of the country team, including Ambassador Durbrow, favored dropping it entirely from the U.S. aid program. Others such as Barrows favored a support program for a reduced corps of not more than 30,000 men. Those differences in late 1957 produced a lively debate on the future of the Self-Defense Corps. General Williams argued forcefully for U.S. support of a Self-Defense Corps of at least 43,500 men. With strong support from Admiral Felt, he was eventually able to obtain country team approval for funding an expanded Self-Defense Corps if a "clearly defined chain of command" could be established for the corps, an effective training program could be undertaken, and Viet Cong infiltrators could be weeded out through fingerprinting and improved background checks. The Military Assistance Advisory Group would be the agency advising the corps.[103]

Despite continued bankrolling, the Self-Defense Corps over the next three years improved little. In the fall of 1958, General Williams complained to the South Vietnamese Defense Ministry that training of the Self-Defense Corps

[100]Ltr, Durbrow to Diem, 26 Feb 58, copy in Folder 36, Williams Papers.

[101]Memo of Conversations, Ambassador Durbrow, Gen Williams, President Diem, 27 Feb 58, Williams Papers.

[102]Interv, author with Barrows, 27 Jul 76.

[103]Msg, Williams to CINCPAC, 29 Nov 57; Memo of Conversations, Williams with President Diem, 23 Sep 58; Ltr, Williams to Lansdale, 1 Mar 58. All in Williams Papers.

could proceed smoothly only if numerous "faults which handicap training" could be corrected. Those included inadequate firing ranges, deficient training aids, unserviceable ammunition, and inadequate housing. He urged officials of the Self-Defense Corps to borrow training aids and equipment from the army and offered to make available American advisers to assist training camp commanders.[104] Yet the officials apparently failed to avail themselves of those opportunities.

The status of the Civil Guard, meanwhile, continued to divide the advisory group and the U.S. Operations Mission. At the beginning of 1958 the Operations Mission had available about $3.5 million for equipping the guard, which, Williams estimated, was sufficient to arm about 10,000 men with M1's, carbines, Browning automatic rifles, and submachine guns. Yet Barrows refused to release those funds as long as Diem insisted on transferring any functions of the guard to the Defense Ministry.[105] The debate continued for weeks. General Williams urged the country team to adopt a pragmatic approach and begin immediately to use the available funds to arm and equip the Civil Guard without worrying over the "academic" questions of its ultimate size and mission.[106] Although Barrows agreed at that point that funds on hand could be used, he and Ambassador Durbrow insisted that requests for future funds would have to be based on a firm and definite plan for the Civil Guard's development.

These deliberations were still under way when the South Vietnamese government presented a startling proposal for the organization and equipment of the Civil Guard. The plan called for a force of 55,000 men organized into companies: 225 light infantry, 15 armored, 21 horse, 26 riverine, and 13 mobile infantry. They were to be armed with artillery, light tanks, scout cars, half-tracks, and helicopters.[107]

General Williams was appalled at those figures. "Whoever sold Diem this idea was nuts!" he wrote to a friend in Washington.[108] Incredulous, Williams asked the president whether he really believed he needed such weapons as tanks and helicopters. Diem replied complacently that he needed them for "subduing riots," that he "just wants tanks to disperse a mob."[109] General Williams later learned that a Vietnamese Army general officer had been assigned to draw up a table of organization and equipment for the guard. That unfortunate general, finding himself completely overwhelmed, had attempted to "come up with something that looked professional by copying sheet after sheet out of the U.S. Army armored division tables."[110] But the

---

[104]Ltr, Williams to Nguyen Dinh Thuan, 19 Sep 58, Williams Papers.

[105]Ltr, Williams to Lansdale, 1 Mar 58; Memo of Conversations, Williams, Barrows, President Diem, 3 Dec 57, Williams Papers.

[106]Comments by Gen Samuel T. Williams at Meeting at U.S. Embassy, 3 Mar 58, Williams Papers.

[107]Ltr, Williams to Lansdale, 1 Mar 58.

[108]Ibid.

[109]Memo of Conversations, President Diem, Ambassador Durbrow, Barrows, Gen Williams, Chan, 5 Mar 58, Williams Papers.

[110]Ltr, Lt Gen Samuel T. Williams to Chief of Military History, 26 Apr 79, copy in Historians files, CMH.

damage had been done. The fantastic proposal confirmed the suspicions of the Operations Mission that Diem simply intended to use the Civil Guard as a private army.

Although General Williams advised the South Vietnamese Defense Ministry to withdraw the ambitious plan and submit a more reasonable proposal, the impasse over the Civil Guard continued. Not until January 1959 was there a possibility of a solution when Diem agreed to allow a newly formed Public Safety Division of the U.S. Operations Mission to assume responsibility for training the Civil Guard.[111] But General Williams, who doubted that Americans with police rather than military backgrounds could successfully reorganize and train the Civil Guard, continued to advocate training by the Defense Ministry with advisers from the Military Assistance Advisory Group.[112]

The Situation Deteriorates

While Americans and Vietnamese in Saigon argued over the question of paramilitary forces, the security situation in the countryside continued to deteriorate. Because travel through most parts of South Vietnam was safe and because Viet Cong units continued to avoid South Vietnamese Army units and fortified government positions of any strength, American officials long failed to detect the full extent of the deterioration. Yet signs were there. Early in 1958 South Vietnamese officials notified the advisory group that there were extensive Viet Cong supply trails in the western parts of the northern provinces of Quang Nam and Thua Thien, and along the Laotian border.[113] During a single week in February in An Xuyen Province at the southern tip of South Vietnam, a Viet Cong company of about a hundred men attacked a government post in the town of Thoi Binh; a force of equal size attacked the town of Hung My; and a small South Vietnamese Army patrol was wiped out in an ambush near the town of Ganh Hao.[114] The American embassy observed that "in many remote areas the central government has no effective control."[115]

The Viet Cong were reportedly most active in the region of the Plain of Reeds adjoining the Cambodian border, which included portions of Kien Phong and Kien Tuong Provinces; the old sect strongholds of Tay Ninh, Binh Long, Phuoc Long, Bien Hoa, Binh Duong, Long Khanh, and Phuoc Tuy Provinces; and the Ca Mau peninsula at the southern tip of the country. The CIA estimated that, together with the remnants of the sect forces, the Viet Cong by early 1958 had an armed strength of some 1,700 men.[116] By the

[111]*U.S.-Vietnam Relations*, vol. 2, pt. IV.A.4, p. 23.
[112]Ltr, Williams to Diem, 3 Jul 59, Williams Papers.
[113]Memo of Conversation, Gen Williams and President Diem, 16 Feb 58, Williams Papers.
[114]CIA Field Intel Rpt, CS 3/350,691, 3 Apr 58, sub: Activities of Communists in Ca Mau Area, copy in CMH.
[115]Am Embassy to State, 25 Jul 58, 751G.00/7 – 2558, records of Dept of State.
[116]CIA Field Intel Rpt, CS 3/352,788, 30 Apr 58, sub: Activities of the Communists in South Vietnam, copy in CMH.

spring there were reports of Viet Cong units operating out of small posts in heavily wooded areas north of Saigon. In June a Viet Cong force of from twenty to fifty men attacked a government detention center at Pleiku in the Central Highlands, releasing some fifty prisoners, many of them "known communists," while incurring no casualties. Diem attributed the failure to the fact that many of the prison guards were Montagnard tribesmen.[117]

Although General Williams could hardly have been unaware of increasing Viet Cong pressure, he remained convinced that countering insurgency was not the primary business of the South Vietnamese Army. "A division on pacification duty goes to pieces fast," he observed. "The guerrillas go underground and soon the troops start sitting around on bridges and in market places and go to pot."[118] When Vice President Nguyen Ngoc Tho warned Diem that the wave of terrorism and assassination was demoralizing the country, Williams insisted that using army units for security operations "is exactly what the communists want us to do." With division maneuvers scheduled to begin in the early spring of 1958, he observed: "If I were Giap, the first thing I would try to do would be to try to prevent these division maneuvers."[119]

Despite Williams' misgivings the South Vietnamese government responded to the increased Viet Cong activity with a major military effort. For the first time Vietnamese Army units penetrated traditional Communist base areas in the Plain of Reeds, in the Ca Mau peninsula, and in War Zone D, the area northeast of Saigon. Many of these operations were slow and ponderous. In the Ca Mau peninsula a battalion of Vietnamese marines was able to capture some Viet Cong suspects and locate hidden caches of food but soon discovered that the Viet Cong had withdrawn to a strongpoint in the vast swamp and salt marsh immediately behind the western tip of the peninsula. The attackers could approach the enemy strongpoint only by a water route that would lead them directly along the line of fire of the defending Viet Cong. At that point the operation ground to a halt while the battalion commander negotiated with the military region commander and the South Vietnamese Air Force for air strikes.[120]

Although slow and indecisive, the government's operations certainly dealt a heavy blow to the Viet Cong. Party membership in the South, which had stood at some 5,000 in mid-1957, fell to about one-third that level by the end of the year.[121] Official party histories refer to the period of late 1958−early 1959 as "the darkest period" of the struggle in the South, a period when "the enemy . . . truly and efficiently destroyed our Party. . . . The political struggle movement of the masses although not defeated was encountering increas-

---

[117]Memo of Conversations, Gen Williams and President Diem, 24 May 58 and 12 Jun 58, Williams Papers.

[118]Ltr, Williams to Brig Gen Philip H. Draper, Jr., 18 Aug 58, Folder 35, Williams Papers.

[119]Memo of Conversation, President Diem and Gen Williams, 5 Mar 58, Williams Papers.

[120]Msgs, ALUSNA to CNO, 051134z Dec 58, 190807z Oct 58, and 301019z Dec 58, copies of all in records of ACSI.

[121]Duiker, *The Communist Road to Power*, ch. 7; Thayer, "Southern Vietnamese Revolutionary Organizations," p. 42.

ing difficulty and increasing weakness, the party bases, although not completely destroyed, were significantly weakened and in some areas quite seriously."[122] In Gia Dinh Province party membership declined from more than 1,000 in mid-1954, to 385 in mid-1957, to about 6 in mid-1959.[123]

By the end of 1958 surviving party cadres in many parts of South Vietnam had apparently decided, on their own initiative, to escalate the struggle beyond armed propaganda and assassinations even though this violated the party line. Armed units were formed into companies or battalions usually numbering less than one hundred men, armed with rifles, grenades, light machine guns, and sometimes merely pikes.[124]

The renewed Viet Cong activity was most intense in War Zone D, a heavily forested region about fifty kilometers northeast of Saigon. Here Viet Cong units no longer always retreated from South Vietnamese Army forces of equal or inferior strength. During March 1959 there were at least ten firefights between army troops and the Viet Cong in which thirteen government soldiers were killed, wounded, or reported missing; five rifles, two automatic weapons, and a jeep were destroyed.[125] In May 1959 a Viet Cong force occupying high ground in War Zone D, northeast of the town of Bien Hoa, successfully stood off attacks by an entire army battalion, then disengaged before the government troops could bring up artillery.[126]

The Party Central Committee had meanwhile convened its fifteenth plenum in January 1959. At the urging of Le Duan, who had just completed an inspection tour of the South, and of other southern Communist leaders the Central Committee adopted a resolution endorsing the use of armed force to overthrow the Diem regime.[127] By May 1959 new directives were on their way from Hanoi to party leaders in the South. Insurgents, specially trained in the North, were infiltrated back into South Vietnam. A new Central Committee Directorate for South Vietnam was established, and communication routes into the South through Laos were improved and expanded.[128] A new stage in the long struggle for South Vietnam had begun.

[122]*Tinh Hinh Nam Bo Tu San Hoa Binh Lap La Den Hien Nay* ("The Situation in Nam Bo From the Restoration of Peace to the Present"), p. 32, cited in Thayer, "Southern Vietnamese Revolutionary Organizations," p. 42; Experiences of the South Vietnam Revolutionary Movement During the Past Several Years, p. 9.

[123]Thayer, "Southern Vietnamese Revolutionary Organizations," p. 42.

[124]Ibid.; ARVN Intel Rpts, 10 Apr 57, and 3 Apr 59, Attachments to OARMA to ACSI, 25 May 59, records of ACSI.

[125]ARVN Monthly Intel Summary, Mar 59, Incl to OARMA to ACSI, 9 Jul 59, R511−59, records of ACSI.

[126]Memo of Conversation, Williams with President Diem, 11 May 59, Williams Papers.

[127]*An Outline History of the Vietnam Worker's Party* (Hanoi: Foreign Languages Publishing House, 1970), pp. 108−09.

[128]Duiker, *The Communist Road to Power*, pp. 187−90.

17

Things Fall Apart, July 1959—June 1960

In the early evening of 8 July 1959, a Viet Cong squad attacked the quarters of the American detachment advising the South Vietnamese 7th Infantry Division at Bien Hoa, about seventeen kilometers north of Saigon. The quarters were located about a hundred yards from a river in a grassy field surrounded by a two-strand barbed-wire fence which had no alarm devices attached. Two South Vietnamese Army guards were posted in front of the quarters, facing a road on the side away from the river. The members of the detachment watched a movie each night at seven o'clock, a practice apparently well known in the division area. Two young women from the nearby town had occasionally attended the movie as guests. (It was later alleged that the two were Viet Cong agents.) The Vietnamese guards also frequently watched the movie through the windows of the dining hall.[1] It was thus relatively easy for a Viet Cong squad of 6 men to slip through the barbed-wire fence on the river side without detection. Three men took station at the windows and raked the mess hall with automatic weapons fire. In the brief but bloody action the 13-man detachment lost 1 man wounded and 2 killed, the first advisers to die by enemy action (Maj. Dale R. Buis and M. Sgt. Chester M. Ovnand).[2] The attack exemplified the transition from the serious, yet scattered and sporadic, Viet Cong activities of 1958 and early 1959 to a sustained campaign of terrorism and military action which was to increase steadily in size and intensity through the early 1960s.

A New Viet Cong Strategy

Although the Viet Cong had been rebuilding their armed units and incorporating armed sect elements since early 1957, they had usually kept

[1]Interv, author with Lasche, 30 Aug 79.
[2]USARPAC Weekly Intel Summary, 13 Jul 59, pp. 8–9; CIA Current Weekly Intel Summary, 16 Jul 59. Copies in CMH.

well out of the path of government forces and attacked only occasionally to achieve some special purpose. A number of armed propaganda units did operate in the lowlands of central Vietnam and the delta, but they were no match for the well-armed South Vietnamese troops. Meanwhile the scattered full-time armed units in the swamps and jungles, according to a Communist history, "became idle and during these inactive periods their main elements could not develop but deteriorated spiritually as well as organizationally."[3] The increasing dissatisfaction of southern cadres with this situation had probably contributed to the January 1959 resolution of the 15th Party Congress which sanctioned armed struggle to overthrow the Diem government.[4]

Following the passage of that resolution the Nam Bo Regional Committee, the Viet Cong high command for South Vietnam headed by Le Duan and Pham Heng, devised a number of new policies. Political agitation was to continue, but armed activities were to be stepped up. These activities would not, as in the past, be limited mainly to propaganda conducted by armed units but would also include "motivating the people to take up arms and fight so as to lower the enemy's prestige, overthrow the enemy administration [and] resist the enemy."[5] Bases were also to be consolidated and control expanded. The committee established three classifications for areas of South Vietnam. The first was "cities and weak rural areas," where party presence was slight or the geographical situation was unfavorable. In those regions the party's program would still emphasize political agitation and subversion, with armed activities playing a supporting role. However, in "strong rural areas" where party influence was great and in "base areas," inaccessible jungle or swamp, cadres were to make the transition to armed resistance.[6] About this same time highly trained southern Communists who had regrouped in the North in 1954 began to slip back into the South. Traveling in groups of forty or fifty they made their way by truck through Laos and then on foot into South Vietnam.[7]

By late 1959 the results of the new Viet Cong strategy were everywhere apparent. During the last six months of 1959 assassinations of government officials, police, and village notables, which had averaged eleven a month during late 1958 and early 1959, more than doubled. Kidnappings reached an all-time high of 343 in that period compared to 236 during all of 1958. During November 1959 alone, eighty-nine people were kidnapped, almost as many as had been kidnapped during the entire first half of that year.[8] In parts of the lower Mekong Delta and the Central Highlands the Communists arranged "spontaneous uprisings" in contested hamlets and villages. Riots and mass

[3]The Situation in Nam Bo Since the Restoration of Peace to the Present (document, apparently written in 1961, seized by U.S. forces in Phuoc Long Province, Apr 69), copy in CMH, pp. 58 – 59.
[4]See ch. 16.
[5]The Situation in Nam Bo Since the Restoration of Peace, p. 57.
[6]Ibid., *The Communist Road to Power*, p. 40.
[7]Duiker, *The Communist Road to Power*, p. 40.
[8]Country Team Study Group Report on Internal Security Situation in Vietnam, Incl to Ltr No. 1, Joint U.S. Army-Navy Attache, 12 Feb 60, records of ACSI.

demonstrations organized by the Viet Cong spread disorder and often pro-voked harsh government suppression. At the same time, small units of guerrillas would attack isolated government posts and watchtowers, driving out the government security forces and arming themselves from captured weapons.[9] During the last half of 1959 Viet Cong–initiated ambushes and attacks on government posts averaged well over 100 a month.[10]

In this intensified campaign the South Vietnamese Army suffered a num-ber of reverses. In September, six army companies totaling over 360 men plus a company of Civil Guard troops began operations against a Viet Cong battalion in a heavily wooded sector of flooded marshland in Kien Phong Province close to the Cambodian border. Traveling in sampans and large launches, the lead company was rounding a bend in a stream when about 100 insurgents concealed on a patch of high ground opened fire. Most of the men jumped overboard in panic; an eventual tally showed 12 men killed, 14 wounded, and 9 missing or captured. The South Vietnamese battalion com-mander was subsequently court-martialed.[11] Two weeks later, in the same province, a group of forty-five South Vietnamese troops, when attacked by a small group of Viet Cong, surrendered en masse.[12]

In other parts of Military Region V, the southern and southeastern prov-inces of Vietnam, government troops during October and November twice attempted to conduct sweeps, only to be ambushed and forced to retreat. In one engagement the Viet Cong surrounded and captured an entire company. After disarming the survivors, the insurgent leaders boasted that they could defeat the South Vietnamese Army at will, then forced the soldiers to watch while they ambushed a second company coming to the rescue of the first. Only one of the captive army soldiers tried to escape or warn his comrades, and his attempts were unavailing because his fellow captives hesitated to make any try at resistance.[13] In November in Quang Ngia Province, a detach-ment of 25 to 50 Viet Cong, which had been destroying bridges and sabotag-ing communications, attacked and captured a squad of army engineers. Bands of Communists sometimes boldly entered district towns and remained for several hours, haranguing the population before departing unmolested. In October a group of 80 to 100 Viet Cong entered the town of Kien An in Kien Phong Province, attacked the district office, killed the district chief and 6 members of the Civil Guard, released 70 prisoners, and made off with twenty-three rifles.[14]

Diem's brother, Ngo Dinh Can, who ran the northern provinces of South

---

[9]Duiker, *The Communist Road to Power*, pp. 191–93.

[10]CIA Current Weekly Intel Summary, 17 Mar 60, pt. II, p. 9, copy in CMH.

[11]Msg, CHMAAG to CINCPAC, 7 Oct 59, Williams Papers; USARPAC Intel Bulletin, Oct–Nov 59, p. 32, copy in CMH; Col James O. Kent for Gen Williams, 2 Oct 59, sub: Ambush of Elements of 43d Regiment, Folder 69, Williams Papers.

[12]Country Team Study Group Report on Internal Security Situation in Vietnam, p. 17.

[13]Memo, Col James O. Kent for Williams, 12 Oct 59, sub: Conference of General Officers, Folder 69, Williams Papers.

[14]Ibid.; USARPAC Intel Bulletin, Oct–Nov 59, p. 8; Country Team Study Group Report on Internal Security Situation in Vietnam, p. 4.

Vietnam, told a group of provincial administrators that the internal security situation in the Mekong Delta was "worse than in 1954," and Diem himself told the National Assembly that the southern provinces were in a "state of siege."[15] The CIA reported that in the marshy Ca Mau region at the southern tip of the country the Communists had "achieved virtual control over whole villages and districts."[16]

Disturbed by the disappointing performance of the South Vietnamese forces, General Williams proposed to revoke a long-standing practice whereby American advisers were forbidden to accompany South Vietnamese units into combat. Williams considered that the army's marginal achievements were attributable to poor planning and lack of aggressiveness, both of which he believed could be at least partially corrected by the presence of American advisers.[17] Up to this time MAAG advisers had been assigned principally to South Vietnamese Army corps and division headquarters, training commands, and logistic agencies. Advisers posted to regiments and separate battalions had remained at the division headquarters whenever their units were assigned a combat mission or one likely to result in combat. On 25 May 1959, the Commander in Chief, Pacific, Admiral Harry D. Felt, informed General Williams that American advisers assigned to Vietnamese Army regiments and separate battalions could go along on operational missions "provided they do not become involved in actual combat."[18]

The Diem regime responded to the increased insurgency with a variety of expedients. The National Assembly passed a stringent new internal security law, generally referred to as Law 10 – 59; it empowered the government to try suspected terrorists through special roving military tribunals which had authority to impose the death penalty. The provinces of An Giang, Kien Giang, and An Xuyen in the western part of the Mekong Delta, traditionally a Viet Cong stronghold, were placed under the direct control of the chief of Military Region V, who was given emergency powers including command of all military units in the area and indirect authority over civil functions.[19] Yet within a month the commander was complaining of his inability to govern the provinces. He estimated that it would require a field division plus a territorial regiment to restore some semblance of government control.[20]

In May Diem and his brother Nhu announced that they were planning to regroup isolated peasant households into fortified villages that could be protected more easily. Under that program, begun in late 1959, the widely scattered rural population was to be relocated in "prosperity and density centers"—soon called agrovilles—situated along major roads and canals, where they could more easily be reached by security forces and protected (and watched) by the government. The intent was to separate the population

[15]USARPAC Intel Bulletin, Oct – Nov 59, p. 27.
[16]CIA Current Weekly Intel Summary, 9 Apr 59, pt. II, p. 5, copy in CMH.
[17]Ltr, Williams to CINCPAC, 31 Mar 59, Williams Papers.
[18]Ltr, CINCPAC to Williams, 25 May 59, and Memo of Conversation, Williams with President Diem, 4 Jun 59, both in Williams Papers.
[19]USACGSC, Staff Study on Army Aspects of Military Assistance, p. 6.
[20]Memo of Conversation, Williams with President Diem, 5 Jun 59, Williams Papers.

Agroville Under Construction *at Vi Thanh, Phong Dinh Province.*

from the Viet Cong, thereby eliminating the insurgents' source of supplies, recruits, and intelligence. To make the new centers more attractive to those forced to relocate, they were to have such amenities as schools, electricity, and medical clinics.[21]

Various factors combined to foredoom the agroville program, chief among them the Vietnamese peasants' traditional attachment to their ancestral homes and family tombs. The peasants resented the uprooting, particularly the move to undeveloped locations sometimes far from their rice paddies and gardens. They were also incensed at having to provide the labor to construct communal facilities. Although the president's technical advisers assured him that the government had the resources to pay for the labor, Diem refused to authorize compensation. The peasants also had to build their own houses, and the 300 piasters provided by the government were rarely sufficient to cover costs. The resentment occasioned by the disruption facilitated Viet Cong support and recruiting. Far from improving security, the agrovilles produced such an increased tempo of Viet Cong countermeasures that by early 1961 the program had virtually ground to a halt.

The sudden upsurge of Viet Cong activity came as a surprise to Americans

[21]For a detailed account, see Joseph J. Zasloff, *Rural Resettlement in Vietnam: An Agroville in Development*, Michigan State University Advisory Group, (Saigon, 1961).

both in Saigon and Washington. In April 1959, Maj. Gen. Samuel L. Myers, General Williams' deputy during 1957 and 1958, had expressed the view of the Military Assistance Advisory Group that "the Viet Minh guerrillas [have] ceased to be a major menace to the government."[22] In July General Williams had remarked that "although the internal security situation in South Vietnam continues decidedly unstable, there has been no alarming deterioration so far as assassinations and kidnappings are concerned." He agreed with President Diem's observation that "the security situation in the [Mekong] Delta has greatly improved."[23] A conference of U.S. Army intelligence officers in Hawaii in September concluded that the Viet Cong posed no serious threat and that "the general security situation in the South Vietnam countryside shows a steady improvement in comparison with the position twelve months ago."[24] As late as January 1960, General Williams noted that "the internal security situation here now, although at times delicate, is better than it has been at any time in the last two or three years."[25]

Based on those assessments, many Americans viewed the upswing of insurgent activity as evidence that the government's programs and security measures were proving effective and that the increased assassinations and raids were simply the last desperate expedients of an insurgent organization that had failed in all its attempts to subvert the Diem regime and found itself on the brink of defeat. As Diem explained to General Williams, "the strategic battle against the VC [Viet Cong] has been won; now remains the tactical battle, which means the complete cleaning out of the many small centers of Viet Cong activity."[26] That was essentially the interpretation Ambassador Durbrow and other members of the country team presented to the Senate Foreign Relations Committee in July 1959.

The "last gasp" interpretation soon gained wide currency around Washington. "Vietnam's Gains Spur Red Terror" read the headline of an article in *Business Week* in July 1959.[27] Ernest K. Lindley explained to readers of *Newsweek* that "Viet Minh infiltrators have just launched a new campaign of terrorism and sabotage— probably because economically South Vietnam has far outstripped the 'workers paradise' to the North."[28] There was much evidence for that viewpoint. The Viet Cong were indeed suffering considerably from the counterinsurgency measures of the South Vietnamese government. Wholesale arrests under Law 10–59 and continuing counterinsurgency operations served to deplete the ranks of the hard-core Communist faithful and their sympathizers. The 1959 decision of the Central Committee to initiate armed insurrection was a tacit admission by the Communists of their inability to overthrow the Diem government through propaganda, sabotage, agitation,

---

[22]Senate, Committee on Foreign Relations, Subcommittee on State Department Organization and Public Affairs, *Situation in Vietnam, Hearings, Jul 59*, p. 27.
[23]Ltr, Williams to CINCPAC, 13 Jul 59, Folder 52, Williams Papers.
[24]Min, USARPAC-FARELF Intel Conference, 1 – 4 Sep 59, records of ACSI.
[25]Brucker Briefing Papers, 7 Jan 60, Williams Papers.
[26]Memo of Conversation, President Diem with Gen Williams, 30 Sep 59, Williams Papers.
[27]*Business Week*, 18 July 1959, p. 2.
[28]Ernest K. Lindley, "An Ally Worth Having," *Newsweek*, 25 June 1959.

and subversion. Indeed Diem's strong countermeasures threatened the very existence of the party in the South. Viet Cong documents speak frankly of "encountering difficulties, obstacles and losses . . . under the enemy's cruel terrorism."[29] A Viet Cong history asserts, "By mid-1959 the party's structures had severely disintegrated. There were only a few party chapters left in each province. . . . The majority of party members were known, and being illegal lived in the jungle or in underground tunnels all year long."[30]

Yet both Diem and his American advisers failed to recognize the extent to which the measures aimed at suppressing the Viet Cong increased antigovernment sentiment in the countryside and created a reservoir of potential recruits for the Viet Cong.[31] To Diem Communist insurgency was primarily a military and administrative problem to be solved by more roads, more and better agrovilles, more security forces. Noting that he had begun a program to train village militia in guerrilla and antiguerrilla tactics, he said that recently captured prisoners were already reporting that "the Communists have now given up hope of controlling the countryside because of the presence of young men trained in guerrilla tactics."[32]

General Williams agreed that security forces were the key. "I believe the task facing the government of Vietnam," he said, "is primarily one of achieving greater efficiency in the Army, Civil Guard and Self-Defense Force through centralized direction, coordination and motivation." American advisers saw "no evidence of rumored peasant discontent with the government of Vietnam." When officials of the American embassy proposed assigning an officer who spoke Vietnamese to try to ascertain conditions in rural areas, Williams predicted that the project would produce "only marginal results."[33]

Williams discounted views that the insurgency was caused by fundamental economic and social conditions in Vietnamese rural society. The Diem government, he believed, was faced with a "hard core [of] Viet Cong agents left in the south at the armistice, augmented from time to time by new blood shipped in from the north."[34] Those agents coerced the peasants into cooperating by threats, sabotage, and terrorism. According to Williams,

The Vietnamese farmer . . . if secure from threat, would live as he has for thousands of years in the past, content with his lot on his rice paddy. . . . The truth is that the population of South Vietnam, like any other, is more responsive to fear and force than to an improved standard of living. The conclusion is clear: The paramount consideration is to gain and maintain a superiority of force in all parts of the country. This is done by developing the

[29]Experiences of the South Vietnam Revolutionary Movement, p. 10.
[30]The Situation in Nam Bo Since the Restoration of Peace, pp. 56–57, passim. See also Race, *War Comes to Long An*, pp. 97–104, 183–84.
[31]John C. Donnell, *Viet Cong Recruitment: Why and How Men Join*, Rand Memorandum, RM–5486–ISA/ARPA (December 1967), pp. 41–44; W. P. Davison and J. J. Zasloff, *A Profile of Viet Cong Cadres*, Rand Memorandum, RM–4983–ISA/ARPA (June 1966), pp. 8–11.
[32]Memo of Conversation, President Diem with Adm Radford, 4 Jan 60, Williams Papers.
[33]Msg, Williams to CINCPAC, 131227z Jul 59, Williams Papers.
[34]Ibid.; Ltr, Williams to Senator Mike Mansfield, 20 May 60, Folder 73, Williams Papers.

military and police potential as the most urgent objective of our national program in Vietnam.[35]

What both General Williams and the proponents of economic development failed to realize was that South Vietnam was no longer a traditional society.[36] The long war against the French and the various programs and "reforms" of the Diem regime had fundamentally disrupted the traditional social and economic structure of the Vietnamese village.[37] During the long struggle against France thousands of people in the Ca Mau peninsula, in the central provinces of Thua Thien, Quang Nam, and Quang Ngai, and in the heavily wooded areas northwest of Saigon had lived for years under the rule of the Viet Minh. In those areas land was redistributed and traditional authority figures, such as large landowners and village notables, were displaced and positions of prestige and responsibility reallocated. "The peasantry had *seen* . . . the village councils forced to sleep in outposts and to move in the countryside with armed escorts. . . . The Viet Minh . . . had destroyed the sense of inevitability which had kept the 'contented peasants' quietly farming the fields."[38]

The Diem government merely added to the social dislocation of the war years. The most powerful organized non-Communist groups, the Hoa Hao and Cao Dai, had been destroyed. The large landowners and village notables had returned but felt threatened by the sweeping, albeit ineffective, land reforms of the Diem regime.[39] Of even greater consequence, Diem abolished the elected village councils and replaced many local officials with outsiders, either Catholic refugees from the North or supporters of the regime from the country's northern provinces. The new officials were as arrogant, corrupt, and venal as their predecessors and carried the additional onus of being strangers with alien accents and no local ties.

All of these factors combined to create an unusually fertile environment for the Viet Cong. Contrary to General Williams' analysis, "stay behind" agents and "new blood shipped from the north" constituted only a portion of the Viet Cong. By late 1959 the insurgents included large numbers of former Viet Minh—some of them non-Communists—who had ceased to be active politically until Viet Cong persuasion and the real or imagined injustices of the Diem regime brought them back into the resistance. There were also many young recruits, who had never been connected with the Viet Minh.[40]

---

[35]Memo, Williams for Ambassador Durbrow, 25 Feb 60, sub: Balance Between Security and Development in Newly Emerging Countries, Folder 77, Williams Papers.

[36]The following summary is based primarily on the work of Paul Mus and John T. McAlister. Their analysis in its main points is now generally accepted by students of Vietnam. John T. McAlister, Jr., and Paul Mus, *The Vietnamese and Their Revolution* (New York: Harper and Row, 1970); see especially Mus, "Vietnam: A Nation Off Balance," pp. 524 – 38.

[37]Paul Berman, *Revolutionary Organization: Institution Building Within the People's Liberation Armed Forces* (Lexington, Mass.: D. C. Heath, 1974), p. 44.

[38]Race, *War Comes to Long An*, pp. 39 – 40.

[39]Robert L. Sansom, *The Economics of Insurgency in the Mekong Delta in Vietnam* (Cambridge: MIT Press, 1970), p. 58.

[40]Donnell, *Viet Cong Recruitment*, pp. v – vi; Zasloff, *Origins of the Insurgency in South Vietnam*, pp. 1 – 6, passim.

As in the earlier insurrections against the French, the Viet Cong leadership placed strong, indeed overwhelming, emphasis on gaining the acceptance and support of the local population. Viet Cong cadres often spoke of the "Three Togethers" that were part of their rules of conduct: eating together, living together, and working together with the people. Viet Cong soldiers or civilian functionaries were severely disciplined for stealing from or otherwise molesting villagers or even for being rowdy or disorderly.[41] In contrast, a report prepared for the assistant secretary of defense described Vietnamese government officials as displaying "arrogance, capriciousness, dishonesty and cruelty."[42]

Proselytizing and recruiting for the Viet Cong armed forces were carried on incessantly in any area where the party could gain a foothold by cadres who were thoroughly familiar with the locality and its people. "If a man was experiencing family problems, had gone badly into debt, was in trouble with the law, was about to be drafted into the Army or had been mistreated by the government officials," he could expect a visit from Viet Cong recruiters who would commiserate with him, direct his anger or anxiety at the Saigon government, and persuade him to join their movement.[43] Other likely recruits were men who had served in the Viet Minh resistance against the French or were relatives of those who had. When necessary the Viet Cong did not hesitate to employ coercion, most often blackmail or kidnapping, and these methods were to become more common after 1961 as the level of conflict in South Vietnam escalated rapidly. In the earlier period, however, persuasion and propaganda predominated.[44]

The Viet Cong Take the Offensive

Both the Americans and the South Vietnamese were slow to grasp the significance of these developments. Although U.S. intelligence analysts were aware that the Viet Cong were actively proselytizing, organizing, and carrying on terrorist activities in certain provinces, it was difficult to appreciate how broad and deep the sources of support for the Viet Cong were and how quickly the Viet Cong might shift from propaganda, intimidation, and assassination to effective military action.[45]

[41]Davison, *Some Observations on Viet Cong Operations in the Villages*, pp. 39–41; John C. Donnell, Guy J. Pauker, and Joseph J. Zasloff, *Viet Cong Motivation and Morale*, Rand Memorandum, RM–4507–ISA (March 1965), pp. 38–39.

[42]Davison, *Some Observations on Viet Cong Operations in the Villages*, p. 41.

[43]Ibid., p. 2.

[44]Berman, *Revolutionary Organization*, pp. 50–76; Donnell, Pauker, and Zasloff, *Viet Cong Motivation and Morale*, p. 18.

[45]By the fall of 1960 the Vietnamese Army intelligence staff had a file containing the names of over 100,000 known Viet Cong or Viet Cong sympathizers; Msg, CINCUSARPAC to ACSI, 230242z Nov 60, records of ACSI. Scholars are still uncertain as to how the Viet Cong attained their extraordinary success in the 1960–63 period. Two major schools of interpretation exist, one of which tends to stress the dominant role of organization, indoctrination, and technique in the

The event which signaled that shift occurred on 26 January 1960 in Tay Ninh Province in the town of Trang Sup, northeast of Saigon. In the early morning four Viet Cong companies, totaling about 200 men, attacked the headquarters of the South Vietnamese Army's 32d Regiment. Quickly over-running outlying sentry posts before the alarm could be given, they pene-trated the bivouac area, destroyed two large barracks and the battalion head-quarters building with shaped charges, damaged four other buildings, and killed or wounded sixty-six South Vietnamese troops. Having thoroughly reconnoitered the area in advance, the Viet Cong made off with about 350 rifles, 30 Browning automatic rifles, 150 carbines, 40 pistols, 2 machine guns, 2 mortars, and quantities of ammunition.[46] A member of the Viet Cong Tay Ninh Province Committee, Vo Van An, later revealed that "the purpose of the attack was to launch the new phase of the conflict with a resounding victory and to show that the military defeat of [the South Vietnamese Army] was easy, not difficult."[47]

If that was the enemy's intention he succeeded admirably. The attack at Trang Sup shocked the Diem government and its American advisers. It was, said General Williams, a "severe blow to the prestige of the Vietnamese Army and [an] indication of the VC ability to stage large-size well-planned attacks."[48] It "really put the Vietnamese in a tizzy."[49]

Many Americans were "in a tizzy" as well. Reports of the Tay Ninh fight brought requests from the State Department for a detailed assessment of the internal security situation in South Vietnam.[50] Completed by a study group of the country team in early February 1960, the assessment concluded that the South Vietnamese government was "actively engaged in an internal war which is constantly debilitating its armed forces at all levels"; vigorous action

growth of the Viet Cong insurgency while the other emphasizes economic, political, and social grievances and disruption. Examples of the first school are Douglas Pike, *Viet Cong: The Organiza-tion and Techniques of the National Liberation Front* (Cambridge, Mass.: MIT Press, 1966); Charles Wolf, Jr., "Insurgency and Counter-Insurgency: New Myths and Old Realities," *Yale Review* 50 (Winter 1967): 225 – 41; and Berman, *Revolutionary Organization.* Representative of the second school are Sansom, *The Economics of Insurgency in the Mekong Delta of Vietnam;* and Bernard Fall, "Viet Nam in the Balance," *Foreign Affairs* 45 (October 1966). The numerous Rand studies of the Viet Cong reflect both viewpoints. Neither school would altogether deny the existence of genuine social and economic grievances or discount the Viet Cong's superb organizational techniques. No writer of either school has suggested, as General Williams did, that the Viet Cong could be dealt with by "gaining and maintaining a superiority of force in all parts of the country"; Ltr, Williams to Mansfield, 20 May 60.

[46]Msg, Chief, MAAG, to CINCPAC, 29 Jan 60; Ltr, Williams to Maj Gen Samuel L. Myers, 20 Mar 60. Both in Folder 75, Williams Papers.

[47]Race, *War Comes to Long An,* p. 107. In a letter to the Chief of Military History, General Williams has suggested that at the time of the raid the bulk of the battalion was attending a civil affairs function in a nearby town; Ltr, Lt Gen Samuel T. Williams to Chief of Military History, 17 May 79, Historians files, CMH. However, the chief of the Combined Arms Training Organization clearly stated that the attack occurred *"after* [italics added] members of the regiment returned from 21st Div memorial service"; Memo, Chief, CATO, for Chief, MAAG, sub: Final Rpt, 32d Regiment Incident, 26 Jan 60, file 250/15, records of MAAG VN, RG 334.

[48]Msg, Williams to CINCPAC, 261015z Jan 60, Williams Papers.

[49]Ltr, Williams to Myers, 20 Mar 60.

[50]Ltr, ARMA to ACSI, 25 Apr 60, sub: Conversations Regarding Vietnamese Army Programs, S – 14 – 60 OUSARMA, records of ACSI.

was imperative to cope with the deteriorating security situation. Paying scant attention to economic, social, and psychological factors, the country team report stressed administrative and organizational changes. A clear-cut chain of command was necessary to direct the operations of government forces against the Viet Cong, and the group recommended establishing a strong centralized military command in threatened areas without regard to province boundaries. The commanders of those areas should be provided up to two full army divisions to assist in reestablishing control.

While recognizing that the use of army divisions would interfere with conventional training, the study group believed that total commitment of two full divisions to internal security operations was better than piecemeal commitment of individual battalions and regiments, which had been the procedure during the preceding year. The two divisions committed to "the internal security command could and should be trained for the role they are designed to play, i.e., guerrilla warfare, and also relieved of current conventional unit training programs."[51] The study group also emphasized that the South Vietnamese government should recognize "ability rather than political loyalty" as the criterion for appointment of government officials in order to develop a "hard core" of dedicated public servants.[52]

General Williams generally concurred with the country team's report. Soon after the attack at Trang Sup, Williams had "a very frank conference" with President Diem and strongly urged that he adopt a number of long-overdue corrective measures.[53] He stressed strict adherence to the chain of command, an end to political interference in the assignment of commanders, centralized control of the various intelligence agencies, and establishment of an inspector general's division in the general staff modeled on that of the U.S. Army.[54] Williams nevertheless took exception to the view that the situation was out of control, and he strongly opposed the study group's recommendation that more army units be diverted to internal security. Even in the wake of the Trang Sup attack, Williams considered the number of troops assigned to "pacification duties . . . beyond all reason." About a third of the infantry battalions, he noted, had been on continuous internal security duty during 1959 and had received no formal training of any kind. In concert with the Civil Guard and Self-Defense Corps, the troops already assigned to security operations were more than ample to handle the Viet Cong. The problem lay in rectifying the chain of command and in improving methods used by the Civil Guard.[55]

Through at least the first half of 1960, General Williams continued to believe that there was nothing fundamentally wrong with the South Vietnamese Army that reform and elimination of favoritism could not cure.

[51]Country Team Study Group Report on Internal Security Situation in Vietnam.
[52]Ibid.
[53]Msg, CHMAAG to CINCPAC, 040931z Feb 60, Williams Papers.
[54]Ibid.; Memo of Conversation, Gen Williams with President Diem, 1 Feb 60, Williams Papers.
[55]Memo, Gen Williams for U.S. Ambassador, 2 Feb 60, sub: Conference With Mr. Thuan, Folder 78, Williams Papers.

Despite the burst of Viet Cong activities, he thought South Vietnamese commanders should be capable of "regaining control in due time . . . if let alone and given proper help by civilians." He pointed out that while the Viet Cong appeared able to "hit Civil Guard Posts and grab off officials with apparent ease," they usually "give the Army and Marines a wide berth."[56] In May he reassured Senator Mike Mansfield that it would probably be possible to begin scaling down the size of the Military Assistance Advisory Group by about 15 percent in 1961 and by an additional 20 percent in 1962.[57]

Although Williams was correct in observing that the Viet Cong more often attacked Civil Guard and Self-Defense Corps posts, their clashes with army troops sometimes proved disturbing. In Kien Giang Province in the Mekong Delta, for example, a portion of a battalion, while engaged on a sweep, was attacked by about 200 Viet Cong. Two officers, including the battalion commander, were captured; 24 men were killed or wounded, and the unit lost fifteen rifles and its radio. Not far away on 2 March an estimated 100 Viet Cong ambushed a South Vietnamese company, and when two other companies tried to move forward to assist, a force of about 300 Viet Cong ambushed them. Total South Vietnamese casualties were 4 killed, 9 wounded, and over 30 missing. Three days later, in neighboring Kien Phong Province, a Viet Cong battalion ambushed another company, and in a matter of minutes 5 South Vietnamese troops were wounded and 8 killed.[58]

In their new war against the government the Viet Cong employed many of the methods and tactics that had served the Viet Minh so well against the French. Viet Cong tactics stressed speed—rapid concentration and quick dispersal of forces—and mass—numerical superiority in the immediate area of action—combined with thorough preparation, surprise, and deception. The most common large-scale Viet Cong action was the ambush, normally laid at carefully selected points along well-traveled roads or trails. Frequently a platoon would dig pits in a semicircle on one side of the road. After two or three men entered the pit, a fourth would cover it with bamboo wattle and grass and remove all traces of digging. He then would take a concealed position with an automatic weapon to cover a charge or withdrawal. At the attack signal the men would leap from their pits to assault the surprised enemy on the road.

When conditions were favorable the Viet Cong also staged surprise attacks against small South Vietnamese Army military posts. These were usually thoroughly reconnoitered, often with the aid of civilian sympathizers. Occasionally the Viet Cong were able to subvert or intimidate individual soldiers or more frequently Civil Guardsmen and Self-Defense Corpsmen, who would help the Viet Cong to infiltrate a post before an attack, sabotage a radio, or fail to give the alarm when the attack began.

---

[56]Ltr, Williams to Myers, 20 Mar 60; ibid. to Lt Col Robert B. Jaccard, 25 May 60, Williams Papers.

[57]Ltr, Williams to Mansfield, 20 May 60.

[58]CIA Field Intel Rpt, CS 3/437,025, 12 May 60, sub: Vietnamese Communist Activities in South Vietnam, copy in CMH.

Vietnamese Navy Patrol Boats *on the Song Be River.*

In their guerrilla warfare the Viet Cong employed an array of mines and booby traps, ranging from grenades rigged to trip wires, to concealed trenches filled with sharpened bamboo stakes, to large mines capable of wrecking a truck. The Viet Cong often used mines as the first stage of guerrilla action in areas where they had recently established their presence. Only a short period of instruction was required to familiarize new recruits and part-time partisans with simple mines, and the devices could later be used in raids and ambushes as the guerrillas gained strength and experience.[59]

Some of the more serious guerrilla incidents occurred along the roads, rivers, and canals, control of which President Diem considered so vital to defeating the insurgency. On 25 March 1960, a South Vietnamese company patrolling the Cai Nuoc River in An Xuyen Province about two kilometers from the town of Cai Ngay was ambushed by several companies of Viet Cong concealed on the riverbanks. Over fifty soldiers were killed or wounded; twenty-five were reported missing. The company lost 27 rifles, 6 submachine guns, 7 Browning automatic rifles, and a 60-mm. mortar.[60] A few days later

---

[59]MAAG Translation, ARVN Monthly Review, "Know Your Enemy," Issue Nos. 1, 2, and 6, copies in Williams Papers.

[60]CIA Field Intel Rpt CS 3/438,613, 19 May 60, sub: Communist Attacks in the Southern Provinces of South Vietnam, copy in CMH.

South Vietnamese troops traveling in junks on the Vam Xang Canal in Ba Xuyen Province spotted other soldiers in South Vietnamese uniforms moving along the sides of the canal. The troops on the banks suddenly opened fire with rifles and automatic weapons. Two junks were sunk and over a hundred South Vietnamese soldiers killed.[61]

The South Vietnamese often performed poorly even when surprise was absent. In an operation in War Zone D, South Vietnamese forces completely surrounded a Viet Cong force guarding a large supply of rice, but during the night "practically the entire VC force was able to slip through the cordon carrying the rice on their backs."[62] A more revealing episode occurred in Kien Giang Province. A Vietnamese Army company commander received advance warning that the Viet Cong were planning to attack his unit at a small hamlet in Kien An district. He immediately ordered his troops to dig in and prepared fields of fire and sandbag emplacements for his machine guns. That night a Viet Cong band surrounded the post and fired a few bursts of automatic weapons fire into the company positions, followed by megaphone appeals to surrender. The Viet Cong force was inferior to the army company in both numbers and weapons but was accompanied by about 100 unarmed civilians, who rushed the post with the Viet Cong shouting "Forward! Forward!" This tactic completely unnerved the government troops, many of whom "fled in disorder and did not fire a single shot."[63] The South Vietnamese Army company sustained twenty-eight casualties; the Viet Cong, who leisurely searched the post collecting weapons, clothing, ammunition, and signal equipment, came away with at least two-dozen rifles and two submachine guns.[64]

Few reports of army setbacks ever reached Saigon through normal channels. Despite the deteriorating security situation, South Vietnamese commanders continued to report increasing success against the Viet Cong. At a conference of senior American advisers to South Vietnamese divisions in April 1960, all but one officer rated the morale of his division as high, excellent, or very high, its responsiveness to American advice as good or very responsive.[65] A few weeks later, General Williams told an American news correspondent that the South Vietnamese Army was doing "quite well" in operations against the insurgents. "Do you think the forces in being are capable of handling the Viet Cong?" asked the reporter. "The armed forces in being are whipping them right now," Williams replied.[66]

The South Vietnamese high command reported 931 Viet Cong killed and almost 1,300 captured from mid-January to mid-April 1960. Yet the govern-

---

[61]Ibid.

[62]CIA Field Intel Rpt, CS 3/402,599, 22 Jan 59, sub: Additional Information on NVA Action in War Zone D, copy in CMH; MAAG Translation, ARVN Monthly Review, "Know Your Enemy," Issue No. 3, copy in Williams Papers.

[63]MAAG Translation, ARVN Monthly Review, "Know Your Enemy," Issue No. 8, copy in Williams Papers.

[64]Ibid.

[65]Senior Advisers Conference Notes, 27–29 Apr 60, with Attachments, in Folder 80, Williams Papers.

[66]MFR, Interv of Gen Williams by *Time-Life*, 2 Jun 60, Williams Papers.

ment forces reported only 150 weapons captured.[67] At the same time, weapons lost by South Vietnamese troops exceeded 1,000: 660 M1 rifles, 400 other rifles, 82 pistols, 90 submachine guns, 8 mortars, and various other weapons. To General Williams it appeared that the Viet Cong were "arming themselves from captured weapons."[68] A Ministry of Defense official estimated that in a single month the South Vietnamese troops lost enough weapons to arm a battalion.[69]

"Too often," General Williams pointed out, "reports of engagements show large losses of weapons without corresponding personnel losses."[70] When he brought that fact to the attention of the president, Diem explained blandly that "the arms were usally lost when the soldiers went to retrieve the bodies of dead comrades."[71] Williams found it difficult to "understand how a well-trained and properly indoctrinated soldier feels it necessary to throw his weapons away."[72]

The Breakdown of the Army

The answer, as was becoming increasingly plain, was that South Vietnamese forces were in no way well trained and indoctrinated. Reports of successes were deliberately manufactured to satisfy the demands of President Diem and to protect the reputation of the commanders involved. A field grade officer assigned to the general staff told a representative of the American embassy that reports from the provinces were routinely doctored "to make it appear that they were continually conducting successful anti-communist operations." One report claimed that South Vietnamese forces in Phuong Dinh Province had captured sixty members of the Viet Cong Tay Do Battalion; investigation revealed that the prisoners were all civilians and that the Tay Do Battalion did not exist.[73] "Concealment of the existing situation has become so ingrained in some officials," noted a CIA report, "that they tend to reject any facts which do not fit their optimistic evaluations."[74]

As two senior officials of the Ministry of Defense explained to their American advisers, Diem "refuses to listen to unpleasant facts and . . . becomes furious with individuals who tell him such things." His brother,

[67]Six Minute Reports, Senior Advisers Conference Notes, 27–29 Apr 60, Incl to Memo, Col Sam J. Rasor for Chief, CATO Div, 18 Apr 60, sub: Senior Advisers Conference Special Report, copy in Folder 80, Williams Papers.

[68]Memo, Williams for Cols Rasor and Barrett, 23 May 60, sub: Loss of Weapons, Folder 80, Williams Papers.

[69]Memo of Conversation, Col C. P. Kent with Mr. Chieu, 8 Aug 60, Folder 90, Williams Papers.

[70]Memo, Williams for Rasor and Barrett, 23 May 60, sub: Loss of Weapons.

[71]Memo of Conversation, Williams with Diem, 23 May 60, Williams Papers.

[72]Memo, Williams for Rasor and Barrett, 23 May 60, sub: Loss of Weapons.

[73]CIA Field Intel Rpt, CS 3/450,291, 22 Sep 60, sub: Attitude of High Command Toward VNA Field Reports, copy in CMH.

[74]CIA Field Intel Rpt, 15 Apr 60, sub: Causes of Deterioration of Security in Southwest Provinces, copy in CMH.

Ngo Dinh Nhu, the only individual to whom Diem might have listened, was as isolated as the president and "never leaves his office to learn by first hand observation what the situation is."[75] Instead, both Nhu and Diem relied on a network of informants from the Can Lao Party, who, like the field commanders, told them mainly what they wanted to hear.

A story making the rounds of the Saigon bureaucracy told of an army captain who, upon being appointed province chief, made a thorough inspection of his province and concluded that the security situation was very serious and that he had insufficient means and authority to accomplish anything. When he reported his findings to Diem, the president summarily reduced him to the rank of private and returned him to his unit.[76] Whether or not the story was apocryphal, it accurately reflected the hazards of honest reporting.

The deliberate falsification of operational reports plus the lack of any reliable and precise method for advisers to assess the effectiveness of their units may account for the failure of Americans in the advisory group to recognize the progressive breakdown of South Vietnamese units. More difficult to explain is the breakdown itself. Why, after more than three years of training and operations, should the army prove incapable of coping with relatively small bodies of generally less well armed and equipped Viet Cong forces?

One reason for the disparity between the impressive appearance of South Vietnamese troops in training schools and on parade and their mediocre performance in combat was simply that the well turned out troops on the parade ground were not the soldiers who normally did battle with the Viet Cong. After a short period of basic training, most new recruits or draftees were sent directly to tactical units while more experienced enlisted men, noncommissioned officers, and officers served in rear area headquarters or in agencies of the Ministry of Defense.[77] Combat units were seriously short of officers and noncommissioned officers and had as many as 50 percent new men in the ranks. In the 43d Infantry Regiment, for example, sixteen of sixty-two officers were on detached duty outside the regiment; only 60 percent of authorized strength in noncommissioned officers was assigned, a third of whom were on detached duty. "A combat rifle company," General Williams pointed out, "cannot be successful . . . with only 50 or 60 percent or less of its NCOs present for duty."[78]

The most frequent explanation for army failures heard in Saigon was that the troops were receiving improper or inappropriate training.[79] General Williams and his officers usually responded that the problem was not improper

---

[75]Memos, Col Ernest P. Lasche for CHMAAG, 26 Jul 60, sub: Summary of Conversation at DOD, and 14 Mar 60, sub: Conversation With Dr. Diem. Both in Williams Papers, Folders 89 and 60, respectively.

[76]Ibid.

[77]Ltr, ARMA to ACSI, 25 Apr 60, sub: Conversations Regarding Vietnamese Army Programs.

[78]Ltr, Williams to Than Thuat Diem, 9 Apr 60, Williams Papers.

[79]Memo, Williams for Senior Advisers, 26 Feb 60, sub: Activities, Folder 80, Williams Papers.

training but rather lack of training. Throughout 1959 an average of 25 battalions was constantly assigned to security operations; by 1960 the number had risen to 34, with an additional 20 battalions assigned to static defensive duties.[80] Individual training was frequently superficial or incomplete. The basic training cycle at the Quang Trung Training Center was only eight weeks long, and "the hours devoted to various subjects were not sufficient for the draftee to properly absorb the instruction." That was particularly true of marksmanship. In theory, the recruit was to receive additional basic training after he joined his unit, but the pressure of operational requirements usually precluded such training.[81] In fact, some soldiers were assigned to operations without any training whatever.

The three-phase unit training program was also seriously retarded. Phase one, basic unit training for platoons, companies, and battalions, was an eleven-week cycle emphasizing movement exercises over various types of terrain. Phase two consisted essentially of command post exercises. Phase three included actual field maneuvers, but many units failed to progress that far.[82] One adviser rated the state of training of many units as so poor that "I wouldn't have trusted most platoon leaders to go out on their own with their platoon. . . . They'd be lucky to be able to march down a straight road!"[83] Furthermore, many Vietnamese officers failed to appreciate the value of training. Peacetime training, said the director of the Command and General Staff School, General Pham Xuan Chieu, was unimportant and lacked "realism." In a combat situation the troops could in effect teach themselves because they would be "motivated and learn fast."[84]

Few South Vietnamese officers shared, or even understood, the American officers' belief in coordination, teamwork, loyalty to superiors and subordinates, skill, and delegation of authority. Yet these ideas were fundamental to the U.S. style of military operations. Nor did the Vietnamese officers see their government or the army as an entity; they viewed each in terms of their own particular bureau, agency, or battalion, independent of, and usually in competition with, other agencies and units. As one American adviser noted, "Coordination among agencies to achieve unity of effort and effect for the common good is almost unknown: more than this, it is zealously avoided as an undesirable encroachment on individual agency prerogatives. . . . There is much to lead one to believe that, given freedom to do so, the [South] Vietnamese would quickly scrap the military organization so carefully developed by [the advisory group] and revert quite happily to what they were familiar with in the past."[85] Another adviser reported that South Vietnamese

[80]Ltr, Williams to Ambassador Durbrow, 19 Apr 60, Folder 77, Williams Papers.
[81]Memo, Col Charles A. Symroski, 9 Oct 59, sub: Training Matters; Ltr, Williams to President Diem, 12 Aug 60. Both in Williams Papers, Folders 76 and 74, respectively.
[82]Lt. Gen. Dong Van Khuyen, *The RVNAF*, Indochina Monograph Series (Washington: U.S. Army Center of Military History, 1980), p. 189.
[83]Interv, author with Lasche, 30 Aug 79.
[84]Memo, Col James R. Kent for CHMAAG, 19 May 60, sub: Training, Williams Papers.
[85]Ltr, Col E. P. Lasche to Gen Williams, 27 Jul 60, sub: Lessons Learned in Vietnam, Williams Papers.

officers were uninterested in training above the battalion level because they had no notion of ever operating with larger units.[86]

The communications gap between U.S. advisers and their counterparts also posed problems. Not only were most American military advisers unfamiliar with the society, culture, and language of South Vietnam, but the advisory role itself was unfamiliar. A senior American adviser described that role as "entirely new and challenging to most American soldiers. They have spent most of their lives giving and executing orders. As advisers to South Vietnamese counterparts, they neither give nor take orders; they have a much less positive role—that of giving advice, providing guidance and exerting influence."[87] Separated by a wide gulf of culture and language, the American adviser could have only the vaguest idea of the effect his guidance and suggestions were having on the unit he advised. Advisers found their counterparts affable, highly accessible, and always willing to listen to advice. But that advice seldom produced significant results, for even when South Vietnamese commanders issued new orders or directives, they were reluctant to compel their subordinates to comply with them.[88]

One American adviser set himself the seemingly modest goal of discouraging the soldiers in his regiment from carrying their boots and even an occasional chicken slung from their rifles, a practice common in Vietnam. After much preaching and expostulating, the adviser had nearly eliminated the practice by the time of his departure. On his final day of duty he was pleased to observe not a single boot or fowl suspended from any soldier's weapon. Delayed a few days at the airport, the triumphant adviser decided to return surreptitiously to view his unit on the march. Much to his chagrin he found that the boots and chickens had already resumed their time-honored places.[89]

Even had the Vietnamese commanders wanted to follow the suggestions of their American advisers, it is doubtful whether they could have done so. The Americans routinely referred to the officers they advised as their "counterparts." In fact, they were in no way the counterpart of the American captains, majors, and colonels assigned to the advisory detachments. "It may not be exaggerating at all to observe," a senior adviser remarked, "that almost every American junior officer has a better understanding of method, procedure and initiative, than does the average senior Vietnamese official, civilian or military."[90]

Politicization of the army was rampant. Politically approved officers or those with relatives in high places rose quickly to command while others languished. CIA informants reported that in some units command was actu-

---

[86]Memo, Kent for CHMAAG, 19 May 60, sub: Training.

[87]Reports, Senior Adviser, 2d Inf Div, 11 Apr 60, and Senior Adviser to Corps and 2d Inf Regt, 27 Apr 60, Incl 2 to Senior Advisers Conference Notes, 27–29 April 60, Folder 80, Williams Papers.

[88]Ltr, Lasche to Williams, 27 Jul 60, sub: Lessons Learned in Vietnam.

[89]Interv, author with Symroski, 16 Aug 79.

[90]Memo, Col Ernest Lasche for CHMAAG, 3 Mar 60, sub: Conversation With Mr. Dung, Folder 89, Williams Papers.

ally exercised not by the nominal commanders but by "political officers" of the Can Lao Party.[91] A common joke among Vietnamese officers was that promotion was based on the "Three Ds," which stood for the Vietnamese *Dang* ("party," that is, the Can Lao), *Dao* ("religion"—Catholicism), and *Du*, a vulgar expression for Diem's native region of central Vietnam.[92] Viet Cong leaders presented a striking contrast to the officers of the Vietnamese Army. Unlike Communist functionaries in Europe, who were usually regarded as ruthless opportunists out to enjoy the benefits of party membership, Viet Cong officers had few privileges and much responsibility. Former South Vietnamese Army soldiers who deserted to, or were captured by, the Viet Cong were "impressed by the lack of insignia on the officers' and non-commissioned uniforms and the fact that the officers lived under the same hardships in the field as do the men."[93]

It was also apparent that the army was heavily infiltrated by agents and sympathizers of the Viet Cong. The precise extent of the penetration will probably never be known, but that it was extensive there can be little doubt. During the first half of 1960, for example, the army conducted five major operations in five separate areas of the Mekong Delta: in each case "there was every evidence that the Viet Cong knew in advance" the tactical plan, route, and timing of the operation.[94] The Central Intelligence Agency believed that as early as the spring of 1958 the Viet Cong had penetrated the South Vietnamese general staff, and in June 1959 the *Surete* arrested Cpl. Nguyen Van Sau, who had been the personal bodyguard to the assistant chief of staff for more than three years, as a Viet Cong agent. It was also estimated that the Viet Cong had agents in the engineers, the Center for Aerial Photography, the First Military District Recruiting Bureau, and the Ministry of Defense.[95] At the end of 1959 a captain commanding a communications company in the Saigon area and one of his officers were arrested for espionage; as company commander, the captain had had access to all classified messages as well as to cipher books and equipment. Even Diem's Can Lao Party was thoroughly penetrated by the Viet Cong, and in January 1960 two officers in the operations section of the general staff, both members of the party, were discovered to be Viet Cong agents.[96]

Whether due to espionage, poor leadership, lack of communication, or inadequate training, in the early months of 1960 the South Vietnamese Army

[91]Corruption in the Diem regime is discussed in Dispatch 267, Durbrow to State Dept, 16 Mar 60, sub: Internal Security and Corruption, 751G.00/3–1660, records of Dept of State.
[92]Khuyen, *The RVNAF*, pp. 53–54. CIA Field Intel Rpts, CS 3/372,690, 7 Oct 58, sub: Discontent Among Senior Officers, and CS 3/363,933, 28 Jul 59, sub: South Vietnamese Deserters.
[93]Donnell, Pauker, and Zasloff, *Viet Cong Motivation and Morale*, p. 61.
[94]CIA Field Intel Rpt, CS/433,419, 14 Apr 60, sub: Speculation on Existence of High Level VC Agent.
[95]CIA Field Intel Rpts, CSOB 3/636,057, 29 May 58, sub: Information Available to VN Communists Through Penetration of VNA General Staff, and CS 3/357,777, 10 Jun 58, sub: Organization of VN Communist Military Espionage Committee in Saigon-Cholon Area.
[96]CIA Field Intel Rpt CS 3/424,172, 14 Jan 60, sub: Further Information on Communist Net in VNA.

had shown itself clearly unequal to the task of coping with the steadily growing insurgency. A search for some new solution had already begun.

18

"Something Extra and Special"

As the seriousness of the insurgency became more apparent during the early weeks of 1960, American and South Vietnamese leaders began to consider what new measures might be adopted to deal with the deteriorating security situation. President Diem had his own ideas. On 15 February 1960, without consulting General Williams or any other American, the president began a new program by ordering commanders of divisions and military regions to form ranger companies composed of volunteers from the army, the reserves, retired army personnel, and the Civil Guard. Trained in antiguerrilla warfare, each company was to have 131 men—an 11-man headquarters and three 40-man platoons. The military regions and divisions were expected to organize 50 companies by early March. Of these, 32 would be attached to the various military regions and 18 to the divisions.[1]

The Counterinsurgency Controversy

General Williams first learned of the project on 20 February from Nguyen Dinh Thuan, Under Secretary of State for National Defense, who explained that the new units were to train at Nha Trang during March, April, and May. Thuan requested that the Military Assistance Advisory Group arrange for U.S. Army Special Forces teams to be assigned to Vietnam to assist in training.[2] The idea of forming ranger or commando units was not new to the advisory group. As early as 1958 the Vietnamese general staff had proposed setting up special units variously called scout, commando, or ranger

---

[1]DOD Temporary Instruction No. 760 – QP/BB/j/M, 16 Feb 60; RVNAF Instruction, 24 Feb 60, sub; Commandos. Copies in Williams Papers.
[2]Memo, Williams for Ambassador, 20 Feb 60, sub: Conversations With Mr. Thuan; Msg, Williams to CINCPAC, 220317z Feb 60. Both in Williams Papers.

companies, but General Williams had always firmly opposed such a course.[3] His deputy for training, General Myers, recalled that the small Commando School at Nha Trang "had been started by the French. The French Army has commandos and the American Army doesn't have commandos; it never has had commandos and he [Williams] didn't think very much of having that school and that's probably . . . the reason it was so small and its efforts never got expanded."[4]

Williams and his staff saw the president's newest project as "hasty, ill-considered, and destructive to overall instruments of power," and argued that it would be necessary to cannibalize three or four existing army companies to provide the personnel for a single commando company. They questioned how the program could be legally supported under the current manpower ceiling for the military assistance program, and added that it would prove a serious drain on already limited supplies of such critical items of equipment as radios. What was needed to conquer the Viet Cong, Williams believed, was not specialized units but a reorganized, well-equipped, and revitalized Civil Guard; intensive training for units between operations; an improved counterintelligence system; and a clear chain of command.[5]

Williams also questioned how the companies, once created, could be employed. Recent experience in the delta had shown that it was risky to employ units smaller than a battalion in counterinsurgency operations. Consequently, the commando companies would have to be attached to some larger unit. "A young ARVN battalion commander has his hands full with his [regular] companies. . . . To plan for and control one or two additional and attached ranger companies complicates his planning and control and any mission given his command to execute."[6]

Diem was unimpressed with these objections. To the visiting commander of the U.S. Army, Pacific, General I. D. White, he explained that since the guerrilla threat to internal security had been added to the long-standing external threat posed by North Vietnam, 20,000 rangers were needed above and beyond the regular army to deal with the new threat. If funds were not available to support 20,000, he would propose starting with half that number.[7]

General White was as unenthusiastic as Williams about the ranger companies. Even a 10,000-man force was unnecessary, he believed, and would represent an unwarranted financial burden on the government of Vietnam, one which it would eventually try to pass on to the United States. White believed that regular army forces operating as small units would be adequate to cope with the Viet Cong. Although recognizing that such small-unit operations would interfere with the normal training program, he believed that

[3]Memo, Williams for Chief, CATO, 15 Sep 58, sub: Mobile Operations, Folder 42, Williams Papers.
[4]Interv, author with Myers, 22 – 23 Feb 77.
[5]Attachment to Ltr, Williams to Ambassador Durbrow, 11 Mar 60, sub: Commandos, Folder 77, Williams Papers.
[6]Memo, Williams for U.S. Ambassador, 1 Jun 60, sub: Training of the RVNAF, Folder 77, Williams Papers.
[7]MFR, 23 Feb 60, sub: Visit of Gen I. D. White to President Diem, Folder 73, Williams Papers.

the South Vietnamese government was unable to afford "an army to be organized, trained, and located primarily to resist external attack and also raise a special security force—especially when the guerrillas are by far the greater threat."[8] The Commander in Chief, Pacific, Admiral Felt, agreed that commando units were unnecessary and pointed out that while antiguerrilla training for army units was essential, "equal attention must be given to economic, political and social aspects of the problem."[9]

Although General Williams had long opposed withdrawing army units from training to conduct antiguerrilla operations, he apparently now concluded that to do so would be far less disturbing than to create the ranger force. The new standard South Vietnamese division, he noted, had been specifically designed for two missions, not one, so that divisions could be easily broken down into regiments, battalions, or even company-size units.[10] In the face of President Diem's continuing refusal to abandon his plan for ranger companies, however, Williams decided that "the best we can do is to try and get the figure of 10,000 reduced." In that he succeeded, for Diem finally agreed to start with 5,000 men on a "trial and error basis."[11]

To many American observers in Saigon and Washington, the ranger project appeared to be simply a device to enable Diem to add more troops to the army beyond the 150,000-man ceiling that the United States had agreed to support.[12] Some also wondered whether the demand for ranger units was not evidence of serious shortcomings in the American training program, particularly of a failure adequately to train and prepare the South Vietnamese Army for antiguerrilla warfare.[13] Civilian officials in the Defense Department's Advanced Research Projects Agency argued that the fact that South Vietnamese forces, far superior numerically to some 3,000 to 5,000 Viet Cong, had been unable to control the insurgency demonstrated that "conventionally trained, conventionally organized and conventionally equipped military organizations are incapable of employment in anti-guerrilla operations."[14]

General Williams vigorously contested such reasoning. As early as September 1958, he pointed out, the Military Assistance Advisory Group had prepared a paper on "basic principles of anti-guerrilla operations" based on U.S. doctrine and had distributed it to senior South Vietnamese commanders and their advisers. All relevant U.S. Army field manuals had also been translated into Vietnamese and made available by early 1957. In addition, a limited amount of instruction in antiguerrilla tactics had been given to

[8]Ltr, White to Williams, 5 Mar 60, Folder 73, Williams Papers.
[9]Msg, CINCPAC to CHMAAG, 4 Mar 60, Williams Papers.
[10]Ltr, Williams to I. D. White, 14 Mar 60, Folder 73, Williams Papers.
[11]Memo, Williams for Ambassador Durbrow, 10 Mar 60, sub: Commando Force, Folder 77, Williams Papers.
[12]Ltr, Williams to Maj Gen Samuel L. Myers, 20 Mar 60, Folder 75, Williams Papers; Ltr, Durbrow to Secy of State, 10 Mar 60, 751G.00/3–1060, records of Dept of State.
[13]Memo, Ambassador Durbrow for Gen Williams, 19 Apr 60, sub: Antiguerrilla Training, Folder 77, Williams Papers.
[14]Memo, Director, Policy and Planning Div, ARPA (W. H. Godel), for Asst Secy of Defense, ISA, 15 Sep 60, sub: Vietnam, ISA 092VN, RG 330.

students at the Vietnamese Staff College and at noncommissioned officer schools.[15]

In answer to this line of argument the Advanced Research Projects Agency observed that the United States would ultimately have to "recognize the similarity between [the Viet Cong insurgency] and that of its own French and Indian, revolutionary and banana wars of history. Despite the statement . . . that the tactics and training for this kind of warfare can be derived from a field manual, it is suggested that this particular field manual has long been out of print in U.S. and French military circles." The agency preferred to see the formation of lightly equipped, self-sustaining paramilitary organizations at the village level. "These forces should be provided not with conventional arms and equipment requiring third and fourth level maintenance but with a capability to be farmers, or taxi drivers during the day and anti-guerrilla forces at night."[16]

General Williams rejected the contention that the advisory group had created a conventional army built around divisions too large and unwieldy to be effective against guerrillas. The new standard division, he argued, had been designed to conduct combat operations against either conventional or guerrilla forces. The South Vietnamese soldier had the same mobility as the Viet Cong guerrilla, and his equipment was lighter and better.[17] Antiguerrilla training, said Williams, was a supplement to and not a substitute for individual and small-unit combat training. Only when soldiers mastered the latter fundamentals could they effectively go on to learn the more open and fluid style of warfare characteristic of counterguerrilla operations.

As an example, if two fire teams of a squad have not learned to advance each other by extremely well-coordinated fire and movement, with each man doing his job . . . they cannot be expected to perform effectively in attempting the same task with the extremely limited observation, the obstacles, and the far greater control problems that characterize jungle or swamp operations against a guerrilla enemy.[18]

The entire question of antiguerrilla or, as it was coming to be called, counterinsurgency warfare was complicated by the fact that the U.S. Army had paid little attention to the need to develop counterinsurgency training and doctrine during the 1950s.[19] If the field manuals on antiguerrilla warfare made available by General Williams to the South Vietnamese Army were inadequate, as the Advanced Research Projects Agency contended, this inadequacy reflected an Army-wide deficiency rather than one peculiar to the advisory group. The counterinsurgency controversy, morever, was another instance in which personal and bureaucratic rivalries within the country team

---

[15]Memo, Williams for All MAAG Advisers, 4 Apr 60, sub: Notes on Antiguerrilla Operations, Williams Papers.

[16]Memo, Director, Policy and Planning Div, ARPA, for Asst Secy of Defense, ISA, 15 Sep 60, sub: Vietnam.

[17]Memo, Williams for U.S. Ambassador, 1 Jun 60, sub: Training of the RVNAF.

[18]Ibid.

[19]See ch. 14, p. 273.

complicated what should have been a technical question. General Williams had long been at odds, both personally and professionally, with the ambassador, the military attaches, and the U.S. Operations Mission, and it is hard to escape the impression that these individuals derived a certain amount of bitter satisfaction from the fact that the general's training methods were now being called into question.[20]

Yet both Williams and his critics missed the central fact that the ineffectiveness of the Vietnamese Army was not something that could have been dealt with simply through finding a more effective training program. Much more basic were the problems of corruption, incompetence, low morale, poor leadership, and lack of security. These intrinsic weaknesses, in turn, were merely reflections of the weaknesses of the Diem regime and its manifest inability to cope with what was by now a growing social revolution. But since weapons and training were far more amenable to influence than political and social problems, American leaders continued to concentrate on the former and neglect the latter.

The belief that the military had to be concerned with the political and social aspects of combating insurgency was held by few U.S. officers before the early 1960s. It was only in 1961 that the Army's Special Warfare School at Fort Bragg introduced a course of lectures, largely at the insistence of the State Department, on "the economic, social and political and psychological factors which create revolutionary conditions in a country."[21] As the Army's chief of research and development observed, the traditional "wall of separation between politics and the military . . . does not work against communist-supported guerrillas where political and military actions are one."[22] Within the country team the problems went even deeper than the "wall of separation" between the military and politics, for by consistently and vigorously discouraging serious criticism of the Vietnamese government, as General Williams had done since 1957, the advisory group had exerted a negative influence on efforts by other elements of the U.S. mission to come to grips with the underlying social and economic conditions fueling the Viet Cong insurgency.

While Diem experimented with commando units, Washington for the first time since the sect crisis of 1955 was becoming seriously concerned about developments in Vietnam. This concern was fueled by reports from the American embassy in Saigon. These reports stressed the growing discontent with the Diem regime in the countryside; the arbitrary, apathetic, corrupt, or

[20]Both General Williams and Ambassador Durbrow spoke quite frankly about their personality conflicts in their interviews with CMH historians. See also Interv with Mr. Leland Barrows, 12 Jul 76, Historians files, CMH. On attache-MAAG relations, see Msgs, ARMA to ACSI, 11 Sep 57, S−31−57, OARMA 350.09, and 25 Apr 60, S−14−60, OARMA, both in records of ACSI.
[21]Memo for Walt W. Rostow, 23 Jan 61, sub: Adequacy of Proposed U.S. Army Program of Instruction at Fort Bragg and Fort Gulick on Counterguerrilla Operations, National Security files: Meetings and Memos, Box 325, John F. Kennedy Library.
[22]Memo, Lt Gen Arthur G. Trudeau for Director's Office and Division Chiefs, Office, Chief of R&D, 20 Mar 61, sub: Guerrilla Warfare, National Security files: Meetings and Memos, Box 325, John F. Kennedy Library.

inefficient manner in which many government officials carried out their duties; and the stepped-up guerrilla activities of the Viet Cong. Communist guerrillas no longer operated in squads of 3 to 12 but in bands of 30, 50, or 100 men. Total insurgent armed strength by March 1960 was estimated at more than 3,000 men. Ambassador Durbrow could only offer the hope that Diem now realized the gravity of the situation and was prepared to eliminate corruption, select capable administrators, and take other steps to win the confidence of the local population.[23]

In Washington Army Chief of Staff Lyman L. Lemnitzer was reading Durbrow's reports and becoming impatient with what he considered the "routine way" in which the State and Defense Departments were dealing with the deteriorating situation in Vietnam. General Lemnitzer directed the Army staff to recommend actions which might be taken both to focus attention on the situation and to provide increased help to Vietnam.[24]

One obvious measure would be to make available the Army's specialists in guerrilla warfare, the Special Forces, to help develop Diem's commando forces. General Williams favored such a plan but worried that the introduction of Special Forces personnel would cause the total advisory strength in the country to rise above the allowable maximum. This difficulty was met by assigning them to Vietnam on temporary duty.[25] In May, at the invitation of President Diem, 3 U.S. Army Special Forces training teams of 10 men each from the 77th Special Forces Group on Okinawa arrived in Vietnam, along with 13 U.S. Army intelligence specialists and 3 psychological warfare specialists.

Although Special Forces representatives had recommended to General Williams a minimum training period of 7 weeks (9 weeks was the norm for U.S. troops), the Vietnamese ranger course was restricted to 4 weeks. Emphasis was placed on training officers and noncommissioned officers of commando and rifle companies.[26] The teams established courses at Nha Trang and at the headquarters of the 5th Division at Song Mao. After two or three four-week courses had been completed, the Americans were to revert to the status of advisers, and South Vietnamese graduates of the course were to become the instructors.[27]

Williams continued to hope that the Vietnamese ranger project could be phased out after a time, but Diem was determined to continue. In June the South Vietnamese general staff unanimously recommended that the new ranger companies be incorporated into the TO/E strength of the regular army. Accepting the inevitable, the advisory group began plans to eliminate a rifle

---

[23]Am Embassy, Saigon, to Dept of State, 2 Mar 60, 751k.00/3–260, 10 Mar 60, 751k.00/3–1060, and 7 Mar 60, 751k.00/3–760. Copies in Historians files, CMH.

[24]Memo, CofSA for DCSOPS, 12 Mar 60, sub: Antiguerrilla Training for Vietnam, CS 091 Vietnam.

[25]Memo, Col Edwin F. Black, 11 Mar 60, sub: Special Forces Personnel for South Vietnam; Fact Sheet, 19 May 60, sub: Counterguerrilla Training Assistance for South Vietnam. Both in CS 091 Vietnam.

[26]Ibid.; Ltr, Williams to Tran Van Don, 1 May 60, Folder 73, Williams Papers.

[27]Ibid.; Durbrow to State Dept, 19 Apr 60, 751G.00/4–1960, records of Dept of State.

company from each battalion of the standard division, leaving three companies per battalion; the spaces thus made available would then be used to
absorb the ranger companies within the divisional force structure.[28]

Although the ranger program continued, like other activities of the South
Vietnamese Army it was rendered largely ineffective by inefficiency, corruption, and apathy. Of 311 officers and enlisted men who attended the first
course, 218 graduated; in the second class of 364, 63 students dropped out
within the first two weeks. The high attrition rate was attributed to absences
without leave, desertion, malingering, sickness, and simple resignations.[29]
Adding to these difficulties were the usual problems of poor leadership
and lack of attention by higher command. MAAG advisers complained that
instructions by the Vietnamese general staff setting forth the criteria for
selection of officers for the ranger units were being ignored by field commanders and that, beyond issuing follow-up instructions, the chief of staff felt
unable to take any further action. The officer selected as chief of rangers, with
responsibility for organizing and administering the new units, was in fact
fully occupied with an operational command in Military Region V and had
little time for other matters.[30]

All the while the situation in South Vietnam worsened. As the Viet Cong
routinely attacked installations and routed government security patrols, a
senior South Vietnamese government official confided to a member of the
American embassy that the security situation in the southwestern provinces
was so bad that unless drastic action were taken, the government would
probably lose control of Kien Tuong and Kien Phong Provinces and the entire
Ca Mau peninsula.[31] Also disturbing were reports that Viet Cong activity in
the heretofore relatively quiet north central provinces had begun to increase.
In September, for example, a band of 60 to 100 Viet Cong attacked a district
headquarters in the town of Dong An in Quang Nam Province. The district
office, the Civil Guard posts, and the *Surete* offices were burned to the
ground, and most of the guardsmen were killed or wounded. When a survivor managed to call for help by radio, an army unit arrived on the scene and
made contact with the Viet Cong at the nearby village of Phuoc Son, but the
Viet Cong quickly brushed aside the government troops and escaped. Casualties among the government forces were nine killed and fourteen wounded.
Although Diem described the action to Durbrow as "a striking victory" and
claimed that the Viet Cong had incurred at least equal casualties, American
observers were less sure.[32]

Given the increased emphasis on counterinsurgency, attention inevitably
turned to the recent example of British success in suppressing Communist

[28]Ltr, Williams to Adm Felt, 18 Jun 60, Folder 74, Williams Papers.
[29]Maj Albert Robichaud, Memo of Conversations with Gen Williams, 24 Jul 60, Williams
Papers.
[30]Memo, Maj Gen John F. Ruggles for CHMAAG, 8 May 60, sub: Conversation With Gen
Chiem.
[31]CIA Field Intel Rpt, CS 31439,186, 3 Jun 60, sub: Deterioration of Security Situation and
Strength of Communist Guerrillas; Current Intel Weekly Summary, 17 Mar 60, pp. 9–10.
[32]Am Embassy to State Dept, 10 Oct 60, 751k–MSP/10–1060, records of Dept of State.

insurgency in Malaya.[33] Many Americans hoped that the lessons, tactics, and techniques learned in Malaya could be applied to Vietnam. During a visit to Malaya in 1960 President Diem received a briefing on counterguerrilla operations there, and he subsequently invited a British officer to visit Saigon and make suggestions for improving the Vietnamese counterinsurgency effort.[34] When the British government invited the South Vietnamese to send officers to attend their course at the Malayan Jungle School, however, the experience proved to be short and unhappy. The first class of Vietnamese officers, "poorly selected" in General Williams' view, made a marginal showing and returned to complain that the British "treated them like colonials." General Ty subsequently visited the school and announced that it had little to offer that was not available in South Vietnam.[35]

The U.S. Defense Department's principal expert on guerrilla warfare, Brig. Gen. Edward Lansdale, also doubted the usefulness of the British experience. The Malayan insurgency was "sharply different, in many areas," he said, from the problems in South Vietnam. The Malayan Communist rebels were ethnic Chinese who were easily identified. The British and Malayans had been fighting the Communists for eight years at a cost which the Vietnamese government could hardly afford. "There can be a subtle sapping of the American character in this trend toward reliance upon others," Lansdale believed. The American experience in dealing with the Huks in the Philippines had demonstrated that U.S. advisers were perfectly capable of helping Asians to achieve success in a guerrilla war. "All we have to do is remember the lessons we learned in the recent past."[36]

Lansdale's views on how to deal with developments in Vietnam were set out in a memorandum for Deputy Assistant Secretary of Defense for International Security Affairs James H. Douglas. The memorandum called attention to many of the problems which had been troubling officers of the advisory group: overlapping lines of authority and the lack of a clear-cut chain of command; the serious interruptions to South Vietnamese Army training caused by the commitment of inexperienced units to active operations; the continuing stalemate on jurisdiction over, and support for, the Civil Guard; and the complications raised by the formation of the new ranger companies. Lansdale also went beyond these questions to stress the fundamental importance of constructing "a sound political basis first" to give meaning to the

[33]On the Malayan insurgency, see Lucien Pye, *Guerrilla Communism in Malaya* (Princeton: Princeton University Press, 1956); Richard Clutterbuck, *The Long Long War* (New York: Frederick A. Praeger, 1966); Noel Barber, *The War of the Running Dogs* (New York: Weybright and Tolley, 1971); and Robert Taber, *The War of the Flea* (Charleston: The Citadel Press, 1970).
[34]Memo, Brig Gen Edward Lansdale for Gen Bonesteel, 25 Apr 60, sub: Third Country Doctrine, Internal Security, CS 091 Vietnam, RG 319, and Folder 74, Williams Papers.
[35]Ltr, Williams to Adm Felt, 6 Aug 60, Folder 74, Williams Papers.
[36]Memo, Lansdale for Hayden Williams, 14 Apr 60, sub: Counterguerrilla Training; ibid. for Gen Bonesteel, 19 May 60, sub: Third Country Doctrine, Internal Security. Copies in Folder 74, Williams Papers.

other required actions. Accomplishing this task "will require something *extra* and *special* by both Vietnam and the United States."[37]

Lansdale's ideas received a favorable reception at an interdepartmental conference on Vietnam held in Washington in March 1960. Although the problems relating to training, command and control, and the Civil Guard would have to be dealt with, the conference concluded, "military operations without a sound political basis will be only a temporary solution." The United States by its advice and support to the Diem regime had helped to create and perpetuate the unsatisfactory political and administrative character-istics of that regime; the United States therefore was obligated to advise the Vietnamese regarding solutions to their present problems. The most expedi-tious means of assisting the Vietnamese government would be to establish a corps of U.S. advisers at the provincial as well as the national level to alert the Saigon government to deficiencies and to advise local government person-nel on means to overcome those shortcomings.[38]

Crisis Planning

Although the conference proposals presaged many of the viewpoints and measures of the mid-1960s, they had little immediate impact. The path of U.S. policy during the last months of the Eisenhower and the first months of the Kennedy administrations was more clearly foreshadowed in April 1960 when senior officers of the Military Assistance Advisory Group and its equiva-lent in Laos, the Programs Evaluation Office, met with the CINCPAC staff at a Pacific Commanders Conference.

In addition to considering the deteriorating security of Vietnam, the com-manders gathered on Okinawa also confronted the situation in neighboring Laos. Most American commanders believed that Laos was critically important to the defense of Vietnam and all mainland Southeast Asia. Its rugged mountain terrain and heavy jungle offered ideal concealment for infiltration routes into South Vietnam and Thailand; the best known of these was the so-called Ho Chi Minh Trail, which leads down the Annamite mountain chain into the Central Highlands of South Vietnam.[39] The Mekong valley between Laos and Thailand had long been considered another likely invasion route for Communist forces striking at Saigon or Bangkok.[40]

The independence of the small mountain kingdom had been confirmed by the Geneva Agreements, and the Laotian government, led by Souvanna

[37]Ibid. for Deputy Secy of Defense James H. Douglas, 17 Mar 60, sub: Security Situation in Vietnam, CS 091 Vietnam, RG 319.

[38]MFR, Lt Col Joseph M. Flesch, Asst to Dir, Far East Region, OASD/ISA, 25 Mar 60, sub: Conference on Internal Security in Vietnam and Related Problems of Civil Administration, March 18, 1960, I – 13187/W ISA 092, records of ISA, RG 330.

[39]Memo, CHMAAG, Vietnam, for CINCPAC, 1 Sep 61, sub: First Twelve-Month Report of Chief MAAG, Vietnam, copy in CMH.

[40]Msg, CINCPAC to OSO, 282258z Mar 56; HQ, Far East Command, Rpt of Joint Intelligence Conference, 1/ – 10 Apr 56. Both in records of ACSI.

Phouma, had pledged to refrain from joining any military alliances or accepting military aid "except for the purpose of its effective territorial defence."[41] Under that broad exception the Laotian government agreed to allow the United States to finance and equip the 25,000-man Royal Laotian Army and to establish a disguised military advisory group, the Programs Evaluation Office, to train and advise it. At the same time, Prime Minister Souvanna Phouma had pursued a tortuous policy of negotiation, maneuver, and accommodation in regard to the Communist- and North Vietnamese–dominated Pathet Lao. In 1958, following national elections, a coalition government had been established, and the Pathet Lao had agreed to integrate their troops into the Royal Laotian Army.

When Souvanna's government fell in July 1958, it was replaced by one headed by Phoui Sananikone, an advocate of "pro-Western neutrality" who had the wholehearted backing of the United States. Phoui took a hard line against the Pathet Lao, demanding that the remaining Pathet Lao battalions immediately integrate into the Royal Army. When one of the battalions slipped through the surrounding government troops and fled across the border to North Vietnam, Phoui retaliated by arresting the Pathet Lao representatives in Vientiane. By mid-summer 1959 the Pathet Lao and government forces were again at war, with North Vietnam providing arms, equipment, and cadres to the Pathet Lao and the United States stepping up its aid to the Phoui government and helping to expand the Royal Army from 25,000 to 29,000 men. In August Phoui's government proclaimed a state of emergency in five provinces and complained to the United Nations that North Vietnamese soldiers were fighting in Laos. Fighting had died down somewhat by early 1960, but there was little ground for optimism about the future.

The conferees on Okinawa were well aware that contingency planning for Indochina had long been sketchy and confined mainly to the problem of countering a large-scale North Vietnamese or combined Chinese and North Vietnamese invasion. Until early 1959 Pacific Command Operations Plan 46 had formed the basis for planning in regard to Indochina. This plan, with its emphasis on primary dependence on indigenous ground forces backed by U.S. air and naval support possibly using atomic weapons, had always been heartily disliked by Army strategists.[42] Under Plan 46 the Army's combat contribution to the defense of Vietnam would be limited to elements of a single division plus support forces, a missile unit, and a helicopter company.[43] In 1957, General White had pointed out that the plan was unrealistic in that it failed to pay sufficient attention to guerrilla warfare, which he believed undoubtedly would be employed by enemy forces. Since the enemy in a guerrilla war could be expected to disperse, infiltrate friendly forces, and present no conventional front, there would be few lucrative targets for the air and naval bombardment emphasized in Operations Plan 46.

---

[41]Department of State, *Foreign Relations of the United States, 1952–1954*, vol. 16, *The Geneva Conference* (Washington, 1981), p. 1544.

[42]See ch. 14, p. 272.

[43]Annual History, USARPAC, 1st Half FY 59, Jul-Dec 58, pp. 78–79, copy in CMH.

The Army was also unhappy about the relatively small role assigned to its ground forces in the plan. As early as 1955 Army planners had complained that the other services, in stressing U.S. air and naval action in any intervention in Southeast Asia, were ignoring the fact that "once battle is joined by the Communists and indigenous armies on the periphery of Communist China unless stabilizing elements of U.S. infantry, artillery and armor are present the U.S. Navy and Air Force will be unable to distinguish between friend and foe in the resulting confusion."[44]

These Army misgivings had not been resolved by the new general contingency plan for the defense of mainland Southeast Asia introduced in 1959. Operations Plan 32, developed at Headquarters, Pacific Command, was intended to counter the entire span of Communist activity from subversion through overt aggression. The plan was divided into phases. Phase I was an alert phase. Phase II extended from the time the United States decided to take military action against a Communist insurgency until the friendly government regained control or the conflict escalated into a full-scale local war. Phase III dealt with an external attack by North Vietnam, while Phase IV dealt with an attack by the People's Republic of China.[45]

Pacific Command had intended to develop detailed and separate plans for action in both Laos and Vietnam. Given the sense of urgency, however, the Laos plan received far greater attention, and was developed far earlier, than the Vietnam plan, and it was the Laos portion of Operations Plan 32 which bothered Army commanders most. The plan called for airlifting a joint task force composed of a Marine division, a Marine air wing, an Army logistics command, and elements of the 25th Infantry Division to Laos in Phase II operations. The Army took strong exception to the fact that the projected joint task force was to be under Marine Corps command. General White argued that since Laos was a landlocked country, operations there should primarily be the mission of the Army rather than the Marines.[46] The Army also objected to having to supply logistical support for units of another service, a situation that potentially could lead to administrative and budgetary problems.

Admiral Felt replied to Army objections in 1959 by announcing that if and when he was convinced that the Army had "the capability to move into SE Asia as fast as required he will reconsider the use of Marine Forces and command relations."[47] General White was well aware that the presence of a complete, readily deployable Marine division and air wing on Okinawa provided Felt with a ready source of ground combat units which the Army,

[44]Tab A to Summary Sheet, Acting ACofS G–3, 27 Apr 55, sub: Pattern of Service Opposition to the Army, CS 320TS, RG 319.

[45]CINCPAC Command History, 1961, pp. 20–21; Annual History, USARPAC, Jan-Jun 59, p. 87. Copies in CMH.

[46]Memo, CINCUSARPAC for CINCPAC, 18 Jul 59, sub: Draft CINCPAC OPlan 32–59, copy in CMH; Ltr, Gen I. D. White to Gen Lyman Lemnitzer, 6 Jun 59, DCSOPS TS–59–325, DCSOPS records.

[47]Msg, CINCUSARPAC to Dept of Army for CSUSA, 212324z Jul 59, DCSOPS TS 1901042, DCSOPS records.

whose nearest available forces were in Hawaii and the continental ·United States, would find hard to match. White therefore recommended that deployable Army forces be permanently stationed on Okinawa as soon as possible.[48] An Army airborne battle group was subsequently deployed to Okinawa in 1960, and planning began for upgrading logistical facilities in the Western Pacific and Southeast Asia to support the forward deployment of other Army combat forces.[49] These small steps marked the beginning of an Army buildup in the Western Pacific that would rapidly gain momentum during the first years of the Kennedy administration.

Logistical facilities in South Vietnam itself were also inadequate to support any significant deployment of U.S. troops. Planners in the Military Assistance Advisory Group estimated, for example, that because of the state of South Vietnam's airfields, it would take thirty to forty days to bring in a large number of troops by air.[50] Although the advisory group had developed plans to enlarge and improve airfield facilities at strategic locations, so long as the United States continued to abide by the Geneva Agreements no construction, other than to improve existing airfields at Saigon and Da Nang under the guise of meeting the needs of commercial aviation, could be accomplished.[51]

The restrictions of the Geneva Agreements also had continued to limit the number of American officers and men in the advisory group. The strategem of reinforcing the advisory group through the Temporary Equipment Recovery Mission had begun to wear thin with members of the International Control Commission. As early as 1957 the ICC, under the pressure of continued protests from North Vietnam, was "seriously questioning the status and the work done by the TERM."[52]

The commission began to insist on receiving periodic reports on the mission's activities and on inspecting its installations. During 1957 and 1958 General Williams repeatedly warned that the mission's cover as an equipment retrieval operation could hardly be maintained indefinitely. Although he urged the ambassador and other members of the country team to take steps to legitimize the equipment recovery mission's status to protect its important training function, the State Department considered that recommendation to be "politically unfeasible."[53]

By December 1958, when the ICC asked that the Temporary Equipment Recovery Mission be closed out by mid-1959, something clearly had to be done to avoid a crippling decrease in the advisory group. Pointing out that the total number of American and French advisers in Vietnam at the time of

---

[48]Ltr, White to Lemnitzer, 6 Jun 59.
[49]Summary Sheet with Incls, DCSOPS, 1 Sep 59, sub: Additional Battle Group for Pacific Command, DCSOPS TS 1901042, and Msg, CINCUSARPAC to CSUSA, 220920z Aug 59, both in DCSOPS records; Ltr, I. D. White to CofSA, 3 Aug 60, CS 334 SEATO, RG 319; Summary Sheet, Brig Gen L. J. Lincoln, 17 Sep 60, sub: Establishment of Forward Stockage Points in Support of Contingency Plans, DCSLOG TS 0263–60, DCSOPS records.
[50]Memo of Conversations, Williams with President Diem, 19 Mar 60, Williams Papers.
[51]Memo for Record, prepared by Gen Williams as a commentary on and guide to documents concerning the problem of air base construction, Mar 71, Williams Papers.
[52]Ambassador Durbrow to State Dept, 22 Jan 58, copy in Folder 30, Williams Papers.
[53]Ltr, Williams to Mansfield, 20 May 60.

the agreements was 888, the State Department intimated to the control commission that the United States might increase the advisory group to that figure. It then requested an increase only to 685, 7 spaces less than the combined total of the advisory group and TERM. This reduced figure, noted General Williams, was intended "as a sop for the [ICC] to make it easier to convince the Indians that we are not violating the Geneva Accords."[54] The International Control Commission on 19 April 1960 approved the increase.

The Counterinsurgency Plan

While Laos, command arrangements, deployments, and logistical problems thus had occupied much attention in the late 1950s, the problem of what might be done in Vietnam short of military intervention remained. Out of the discussions of this problem in Okinawa in 1960 emerged a study on counterinsurgency operations in Laos and South Vietnam. The authors of the study believed that "the majority of the population in South Vietnam and Laos live in rural areas and have little or no interest in political ideologies. They are neither extreme nationalists nor dedicated Communists but rather they are apathetic toward each, willing to support whichever side is in momentary local control but only to the degree necessary to avoid inciting the wrath of the other side toward them."[55] This view of the people of Vietnam as apathetic, pliable, and willing to obey any authority which held superior power could have been written by an American consular officer in Indochina during the 1920s and 1930s or by a French colonial administrator. It totally overlooked the political and social upheavals in Vietnam since World War II and the revolutionary nature of the Communist insurgency.

Yet these ideas about Vietnam were not confined to Pacific commanders. General Lansdale, an acknowledged expert in Washington on the subject of Indochina, wrote a few months later that "damn few" Vietnamese farmers could be "talked into believing that Diem is no good and that the Vietcong is the wave of the future." Most farmers, he believed, helped the Viet Cong either because of anger at the government—mostly attributable to the misbehavior of troops on counterinsurgency operations—or because of fear of Viet Cong terrorism. Misbehavior by the troops could be countered by "an alert commander and constant supervision to ensure the proper behavior of troops under the vexing conditions of counter-guerrilla operations. The VN Army has been by and large, rather good at this in the past."[56]

Given such views it is scarcely surprising that the Okinawa study regarded the Communist threat in South Vietnam as a problem to be dealt with

[54]Memo, Williams for Ambassador Durbrow, 14 May 60, sub: Official U.S. Personnel in Vietnam, records of MAAG Vietnam. See also Ltr, Williams to Mansfield, 20 May 60, and Interv, author with Durbrow, 9 Dec 76.

[55]Memo, CINCPAC for JCS, 27 Apr 60, sub: Counterinsurgency Operations in South Vietnam and Laos, I – 13796/60 ISA 092, RG 330.

[56]Memo, Lansdale for Lt Gen Lionel C. McGarr, 11 Aug 60, sub: Vietnam, copy in CMH.

through military and administrative remedies. The study did note the need for a program "to win the peoples' confidence and cooperation for their government and security forces," but, as outlined, this program consisted mainly of such measures as trial and punishment of terrorists, indoctrination of the people and security forces, low-cost self-help projects, and relocation and resettlement of former Communists. The main thrust was placed on "gaining control of the population on a continuing basis."

To attain this object, the study, drawing heavily on what the authors believed to be the lessons learned in Malaya and the Philippines, emphasized measures to ensure centralized control of the counterinsurgency effort; improved intelligence collection and identification and apprehension of terrorists; better training of the self-defense forces; and the reestablishment of governmental authority at all levels of society. Specifically, the study recommended reorganizing the South Vietnamese government at the national level to improve command and control. This effort might include the establishment of a national security council with various subcouncils at the regional, district, and village levels; the appointment of a director of security operations; and other measures. The study also incorporated the long-standing recommendation of the Military Assistance Advisory Group that the Civil Guard and all other internal security forces be transferred from the Ministry of the Interior to the Ministry of Defense, and declared that the South Vietnamese government should establish operational control systems to integrate its civil, military, and police efforts in accordance with a coordinated national plan. The United States, for its part, should be prepared to support such a plan through reorganizing the advisory group and providing more funds.[57]

There is no evidence that anyone at CINCPAC headquarters was aware that the situation bore an ominous resemblance to that of late 1953 and early 1954. Once again America's ally in Indochina seemed in danger, again the situation was perceived as "an emergency," and again the solution offered was a plan—not the Letourneau-Allard plan or the Navarre plan this time, but what came to be called the counterinsurgency plan. As before, far more attention was focused on the details of the plan than on the likelihood that it could be carried out successfully.

Admiral Felt forwarded the Okinawa study to the Joint Chiefs of Staff with a recommendation that it be used as a basis for future actions and that it be submitted to the country team for further development, including cost estimates.[58] The Joint Chiefs and the secretary of defense concurred in Admiral Felt's recommendation and forwarded the study to the State Department with the suggestion that the State and Defense Departments work together in developing appropriate implementing instructions for the country team.[59]

By this time leaders in Washington had ceased to treat Indochina in

[57]Counterinsurgency Operations in South Vietnam and Laos, Incl to Ltr, CINCPAC (Adm Felt) to JCS, 27 Apr 60, sub: CINCPAC Study to Combat Insurgency, JCS records.
[58]Ltr, CINCPAC to JCS, 27 Apr 60, sub: CINCPAC Study to Combat Insurgency; Note by Secretaries to Holders of JCS 1992/82: Counterinsurgency Operations in South Vietnam, 20 Jul 60, JFM 9060/3360 (27 Apr 60), JCS records.
[59]Memo, JCS for Secy of Defense, 6 Jun 60, sub: Counterinsurgency Operations in South

the "routine manner" that had bothered General Lemnitzer a few months before. The National Security Council reviewed the situation in Laos and Vietnam at its meeting of 24 May 1960, and Secretary of State Christian A. Herter warned that the United States should be prepared for the possibility of new aggression by the People's Republic of China as well as stepped-up Communist guerrilla efforts in Southeast Asia. In a letter to Secretary of Defense Thomas S. Gates, Jr., he asked whether additional measures could be taken to improve the counterguerrilla capabilities of the governments of Laos and Vietnam.[60]

The Defense Department replied that the current military assistance program for Vietnam was adequate but that we "should be sure that the country team is exerting appropriate efforts to aid the administration in effecting needed political reforms," an interesting comment in light of the fact that the Military Assistance Advisory Group had usually opposed as impolitic and unwise efforts to bring about political reform in the Diem regime. The Defense Department also emphasized the need for better coordination between the United States and Vietnamese agencies in training, equipping, and advising the South Vietnamese Army and paramilitary forces—thus obliquely calling attention to the long-standing opinion of the military that the Ministry of Defense should coordinate and control all internal security forces.[61]

Through the summer of 1960 State and Defense Department representatives at various levels discussed the venerable question of the Civil Guard. By early 1960 the guard consisted of some 53,000 men still organized, after the French fashion, into stationary, mobile, and border companies. These units were scattered throughout South Vietnam, with the national headquarters in Saigon exercising no effective control. Within each province, command of Civil Guard units was assigned to the province chiefs, who in some cases had no military experience.[62] Since 1959 the guard had been the responsibility of the Public Safety Division of the U.S. Operations Mission in Saigon. The Operations Mission had agreed with the Vietnamese government to support 32,000 men, who were to be trained by civilian contract employees; however, by late 1960 the details were still being negotiated, and most Civil Guard units had received little or no training. Members of the Military Assistance Advisory Group argued that the Public Safety Division plan, even if implemented in a timely fashion, would still fail to provide the guard with the type of organization and equipment necessary to enable it to conduct sustained combat operations against the Viet Cong. The Civil Guard companies would still lack control headquarters in the field as well as the required logistical

Vietnam and Laos, JCSM – 232 – 60, JFM 9060/3360 (27 Apr 60); Note by Secretaries to Holders of JCS 1992/82: Counterinsurgency Operations in South Vietnam, 20 Jul 60; Ltr, James H. Douglas (Acting Secy of Defense) to Christian Herter, 16 Sep 60, JFM 9060/3360 (27 Apr 60). All in JCS records.

[60]Ltr, Herter to Secy of Defense, 11 Jun 60, I – 14397/60, ISA 381, RG 330.

[61]Ltr, Acting Secy of Defense to Secy of State, 9 Sep 60, I – 14397/60, ISA 381, RG 330.

[62]Ltr, HQ, MAAGV, to CINCPAC, 20 Sep 60, sub: Status Rpt on Ranger Companies, Civil Guard, and Self Defense Corps, file 250/6, records of MAAG Vietnam, RG 334.

support units. Whatever plan was adopted, moreover, the problem of assembling the units for training would remain formidable since guard units on operational missions would first have to be relieved by Vietnamese Army formations, and then training areas and equipment, of which there was very little, would have to be found for them.[63] The Joint Chiefs of Staff and the Defense Department strongly supported the advisory group's recommendation that the operational control of the Civil Guard and its training be assigned to the Vietnamese Ministry of Defense for the duration of the emergency.[64] Yet State and Defense representatives in Saigon were unable to reach a final agreement on the question.[65]

Meanwhile, the situation in Vietnam continued to deteriorate. A Special National Intelligence Estimate on South Vietnam published in August 1960 noted that Viet Cong activities were becoming more widespread and intense, that support for insurgents from North Vietnam appeared to be increasing, and that senior North Vietnamese cadres and military supplies such as communications equipment were moving south through Laos and Cambodia and by junk along the eastern coastline. The estimate rejected the earlier contention that the increase in Viet Cong activity was a desperate last-ditch effort prompted by the success of the Diem government's programs; instead, it suggested that "indications of increasing dissatisfaction with the Diem government" in the countryside had probably encouraged the North Vietnamese to step up their support for the Viet Cong guerrillas.[66]

The estimate also took into account growing hostility to the Diem regime among non-Communist urban groups such as intellectuals, businessmen, and civil servants. "Criticism by these elements focuses on Ngo family rule, especially the roles of the President's brother, Ngo Dinh Nhu, and Madame Nhu, the pervasive influence of the Can Lao . . ., Diem's virtual one man rule; and the growing evidence of corruption in high places." The estimate concluded that if "these adverse trends . . . remain unchecked, they will almost certainly in time cause the collapse of Diem's regime."[67]

In September 1960 the Third National Congress of the Vietnam Workers Party, the first since 1951, convened in Hanoi to discuss the decision of the Central Committee to support an armed insurgency in South Vietnam. In a report to the congress, Le Duan called for the formation of a broad National United Front in the South. The number of southern-born members of the Politburo was increased to four, and the congress adopted a resolution calling for the liberation of the South "from the rule of the American imperialists and their henchmen" and for national reunification.[68] Although the congress still

---

[63]Ibid.

[64]Memo, Rear Adm E. J. O'Donnell for Mr. Irwin, 6 Jun 60, sub: Training of Civil Guard in Vietnam, I – 14269/60, ISA 092, RG 330.

[65]Ibid. for Asst Secy of State (ISA), 4 Oct 60, sub: Actions, Civil Guard Vietnam, I – 1606/60, ISA 324 – 5VN, RG 330.

[66]SNIE 63.1 – 60, 23 Aug 60, *U.S.-Vietnam Relations*, 10:1298 – 1301.

[67]Ibid., 10:1298 – 99 and 1301.

[68]Thayer, "Southern Vietnamese Revolutionary Organizations," pp. 44 – 45; Duiker, *Communist Road to Power*, pp. 193 – 95.

accorded top priority to the socialist revolution in North Vietnam, the meeting marked a significant shift toward greater emphasis on the struggle for the South.

With these developments in mind, Secretary Herter readily concurred in the dispatch of a joint State-Defense message directing the country team in Saigon to develop an overall plan to support the Diem government in a "national emergency effort" to defeat the Viet Cong and restore order and stability to the country. When worked out in detail, the plan was to be submitted to Washington for coordination and approval.[69] These instructions simply transferred back to the country team the long-standing State and Defense debate about the best means for dealing with the Vietnam situation. The debate was further complicated at the end of August when General Williams was succeeded by Lt. Gen. Lionel C. McGarr.

General McGarr had carefully prepared for his assignment while commandant of the U.S. Army Command and General Staff College. Like General Williams, McGarr recognized the importance of basic individual and small-unit combat training. He acknowledged the South Vietnamese Army's need to be able to repel a North Vietnamese attack, yet it seemed to McGarr that insurgency was the most immediate danger. To deal with that danger, McGarr believed that it would be necessary to increase the size of the South Vietnamese Army sufficiently to permit rotating units between combat operations and training, to straighten out the Vietnamese chain of command, and to "redirect . . . training and operations emphasis towards a greatly improved counter-guerrilla posture."[70]

To a much greater extent than Williams, McGarr viewed counterinsurgency as a distinct species of warfare requiring development of special doctrine and techniques. The contrast could be seen in McGarr's reaction to the ranger companies. As General Williams had predicted, these hybrid units were making a poor showing in operations against the Viet Cong, yet General McGarr's approach was not to question the need for the ranger units but to advocate more effective training for them and an increase in their number.[71]

As commandant of the Command and General Staff College, McGarr had overseen studies of counterinsurgency, and after assuming command of the Military Assistance Advisory Group he directed preparation of "Tactics and Techniques of Counter-Insurgent Operations," a comprehensive study intended as the tactical military section of the country team's overall counterinsurgency plan. The advisory group planners called for such measures as reorganizing and strengthening the South Vietnamese Army's chain of command (a measure which all American officials had urged since 1957); improving its intelligence capability; increasing its authorized force levels by 20,000 men, to include additional ranger companies; transferring the Civil Guard to

---

[69]Joint State-DOD Msg, Secy of State to Saigon, 19 Oct 60, 751.5MSP/10–1960, records of Dept of State.

[70]First Twelve-Month Report of Chief MAAG, Vietnam, Sep 61, copy in Lionel McGarr Folder, Historians files, CMH.

[71]Ibid.

General McGarr *(right) inspects Vietnamese honor guard with Generals Williams and Ty.*

the Ministry of Defense; improving the army's civil affairs and civic action programs; and increasing border and coastal surveillance operations.

Ambassador Durbrow agreed with some of the advisory group's recommendations but emphasized that combating the Viet Cong guerrillas was only part of the problem facing the Diem regime. The ambassador believed that the Vietnamese government was confronting "two separate but related dangers": the threat of a coup originating with non-Communist opponents of the regime in Saigon, and the gradually expanding Viet Cong threat in rural areas. Military and security measures would be important in meeting the Viet Cong threat, although they would not, in themselves, be sufficient. "Political, psychological and economic measures" would also be necessary to meet the "Saigon danger."[72]

Durbrow felt that Diem would have to take drastic and far-reaching action. The State Department agreed with Durbrow's analysis, and on 14 October 1960 the ambassador met alone with Diem to read him a formal memorandum suggesting measures to "broaden and increase his popular support." These measures included appointing a full-time minister of defense, adding one or two members of the non-Communist opposition to the cabinet, restrict-

[72]Durbrow to Secy of State, 16 Sep 60, 751k.00/9 – 1660, records of Dept of State.

ing or abolishing the secret Can Lao Party, empowering the National Assembly to introduce bills on the initiative of the deputies and to investigate any department or agency of the government through public hearings, relaxing controls over the press, conducting elections for village officials, increasing the legal price of rice, paying a modest sum for compulsory labor in the agrovilles and on other government public works, and initiating a system of limited subsidies to the residents of the agrovilles during the initial period of readjustment.

Durbrow's suggestions were no more than what reform-minded South Vietnamese, such as Vice President Tho, had been urging for some time.[73] Yet Diem could not broaden the base of his support for the simple reason that except for his relatives, some elements of the Catholic community, and a handful of bureaucrats and officers, mostly tied to him by kinship, support for his regime did not exist. He felt he could not bring additional men into power or give responsibility to new organizations unless they could be controlled and therefore trusted.

President Diem did not, and perhaps could not, explain this situation to Durbrow. Instead, he responded, as usual, that although most of the measures were desirable, the "stepped up activities of the Viet Cong made [their implementation] difficult." Durbrow replied that it was precisely for that reason that he had urged that the measures be carried out. Referring discretely to growing criticism of the president's brother, Ngo Dinh Nhu, and his wife, the ambassador suggested that perhaps they might be sent abroad temporarily on some important mission; Diem replied that unfavorable rumors about the Nhus were the work of the Communists.[74]

These problems with Diem influenced Durbrow's approach to the preparation of the counterinsurgency plan. He believed that some of the measures proposed by the advisory group and the Commander in Chief, Pacific, were unnecessary and that others ought to be used as bargaining chips to induce Diem to make the necessary changes in his government and administration. His main points of difference with the MAAG draft plan concerned raising the Vietnam force levels by 20,000 men, increasing support to Vietnam's military budget, and shifting control of the Civil Guard to the Ministry of Defense. More troops could be found to man counterinsurgency operations and to facilitate rotating units between operations and training, Durbrow believed, simply by drawing on some of the divisions assigned to guarding the northern border. Although recognizing that doing so would be a calculated risk, Durbrow pointed out that "any threat of external aggression seems fairly remote, particularly in view of the moral deterrent represented by the International Control Commission and physical deterrent represented by SEATO." He believed that to increase the Vietnamese force level "would

[73]Durbrow to State Dept, 10 Oct 60, 751k.00/10−1060; Ltr, Dang Van Sung to J. William Fulbright, Incl to Ltr, Carl Marcy to J. Graham Parsons, 7 Oct 60, 751k.00/10−760. Both in records of Dept of State.
[74]State Dept to Am Embassy, 7 Oct 60, 751k.00/10−760; Durbrow to Secy of State, 15 Oct 60, 751k.00/10−1560. Both in records of Dept of State.

be to play to Diem's proclivity for thinking in terms only of security and survival and . . . increase his tendency to neglect adequate political and psychological measures."[75]

Although Durbrow and his staff no longer questioned the need for the advisory group to train the Civil Guard—in view of the level of insurgency, the United States Operations Mission and the advisers from Michigan State University were clearly unequal to that task—the ambassador still objected to transferring the Civil Guard from the Ministry of the Interior to the Ministry of Defense. If that were done, Durbrow said, the guard would soon be virtually amalgamated with the army and "eventually [all] hope that [it] will serve as a provincial police force will be lost." The ambassador also believed that the South Vietnamese government could fairly be asked to carry more of the financial burden of a stepped-up security program.[76]

General McGarr, to the contrary, believed that the insurgency had reached such a level that an enlarged military force was vital, as well as better coordination within the South Vietnamese government. Under current conditions, he believed, social and political reforms were of secondary importance, and pressuring Diem to undertake them might undermine Diem's confidence and trust in the United States. The Commander in Chief, Pacific, and the Department of Defense held a similar view. Speaking for John N. Irwin II, the Assistant Secretary of Defense for International Security Affairs, General Lansdale noted that "while criticism of Diem's government in metropolitan areas adds to his problems and interacts with Viet Cong plans, the Viet Cong remains the primary threat to security."[77]

In a sense both Durbrow and Lansdale were "right." Durbrow was correct in pointing out that if Diem did not undertake energetic measures of political and economic reform, his government was headed for disaster. Yet Lansdale was equally correct in pointing out, in a later report, that to treat Diem "as an opponent to be beaten to his knees" would be fruitless and counterproductive. The unhappy fact was that, pressure or no pressure, Diem was not likely to change. Nevertheless, Lansdale argued, Diem remained the only chance for stability in South Vietnam. While he should be "informed as soon as possible through appropriate channels of the gravity with which the US government views the internal security situation," he should also be assured "of our intent to provide material assistance and of our unswerving support to him in this time of crisis."[78]

---

[75]Durbrow to Secy of State, 5 Sep 60, 751k.5MSP/9–560, records of Dept of State.

[76]Ibid. See also Ltr, Williams to Adm Felt, 8 Jun 59, Folder 54, Williams Papers; Memo of Conversations, President Diem, Nguyen Dinh Thuan, Frank E. Walton, Donald Q. Coster, 24 Jun 60, Incl to USARMA to ACSI, 14 Jul 60, records of ACSI.

[77]Msg, CINCPAC to CHMAAG, Vietnam, Oct 60, JMF 9155.3/3410 (18 Jan 61), JCS records; Memo, Lansdale for Adm E. J. O'Donnell, 13 Sep 60, sub: Possible Courses of Action in Vietnam, *U.S.-Vietnam Relations*, vol. 2, pt. IV.A.5, Tab 4, p. 52.

[78]Memo, Lansdale for Regional Director, Far East, ISA, 13 Sep 60, sub: Possible Courses of Action in Vietnam, *U.S.-Vietnam Relations*, 10:1308.

General McGarr *visits Montagnard village near Dalat.*

The Coup Attempt

Just how unswerving American support of Diem was came into question a few weeks later. At 0300 on 11 November 1960 three battalions of the South Vietnamese Army's elite paratrooper group surrounded the presidential palace and issued a manifesto calling for political reforms, the formation of a new government, and more effective prosecution of the war against the Communist insurgents.[79] Although there had been persistent reports of disaffection within the armed forces—Lt. Col. Nguyen Chanh Thi, commander of the elite army airborne brigade, had openly boasted of his ability to achieve a coup—the rebellion nevertheless came as a surprise to most Americans, civil and military.[80] As recently as the previous March General Williams had declared that "a coup is no nearer now than it was in 1955" and that Diem's opponents had "no following in the country at large."[81] The leaders of the coup, Col. Nguyen Chanh Thi and Lt. Col. Vuong Van Dong, had been numbered among Diem's most loyal supporters (Thi had helped Diem defeat

---

[79]For a good account of the incident, see Stanley Karnow, "Diem Defeats His Own Best Generals," *The Reporter*, 19 January 1961, pp. 24–29.

[80]Ltr, ARMA, Col B. B. Cheston, to ACSI, 22 Oct 60, S–34–60, records of ACSI; USARPAC Intel Summary, Oct 60, records of USARPAC.

[81]Ltr, Williams to Brig Gen Edgar C. Doleman, 4 Mar 60, Folder 73, Williams Papers.

the Binh Xuyen in 1955), and the paratroopers were considered to be the most effective and well-disciplined force in the army.

Diem, his brother Nhu, and Madame Nhu barricaded themselves in the wine cellar of the palace and began sending calls for help over Diem's private radio net to loyal army units in the countryside. To gain time, the president pretended to parley with the rebels, agreeing to a long list of reforms including a coalition government, free elections, freedom of the press, and a more effective campaign against the Viet Cong.

During those uncertain hours, General McGarr and Ambassador Durbrow attempted to remain neutral. This stance differed considerably from the American position in 1954 during the crisis with General Hinh, when Washington had made it unequivocally clear that the United States stood firmly behind Diem. In 1960, Durbrow's actions indicated that the State Department, if not actually welcoming a change, was prepared to accept one. As the ambassador described it, "we did all in our power to prevent bloodshed and urge [the] rebels when they had power to oust Diem that he should be given [an] active role in any government established."[82] Durbrow urged Diem to negotiate with the rebels, an action which General Lansdale later criticized as "badly-timed and demoralizing meddling in Vietnam's affairs."[83]

From the beginning, the uprising was amateurish and disorganized. The leaders had failed to set up roadblocks, seize the radio stations, or take over the communications network.[84] During the early stages the palace was defended by only thirty men. The rebels easily could have killed or captured Diem, but they preferred to parley and thus played into the president's hands.[85] When loyal troops arrived, the paratroopers surrendered, and the leaders fled to Cambodia.

Despite the comic opera qualities of the attempted coup, it had serious and far-reaching repercussions. As J. Graham Parsons, Assistant Secretary of State for Far Eastern Affairs, noted, the attempt had "proven that there is a serious lack of support among the military and other elements for many aspects of the government's policies."[86] It also demonstrated that the army was far from being the highly professional, nonpolitical body that O'Daniel, Williams, and later McGarr hoped it would become.

To Diem, there were lessons to be learned from the attempted coup, but he still did not see among them any necessity for far-reaching social and political reform. Instead, the incident reinforced the president's already well-

---

[82]Telg, Durbrow to Secy of State, 4 Dec 60, *U.S.-Vietnam Relations,* 10:1334–36.

[83]See J. Graham Parsons for Herter to Am Embassy, Saigon, 11 Nov 60, and Memo, Lansdale for Dep Secy of Defense, 15 Nov 60, sub: Vietnam, both in *U.S.-Vietnam Relations,* 10:1327 and 1330–31, respectively. The author later asked Ambassador Durbrow if it was true that "some members of the American mission believed it would not be a bad thing for Diem to step down at that point." Durbrow replied that that was a view held mainly by "liberals" who "did not understand the situation in Vietnam or how the Communists operate." Interv, author with Durbrow, 9 Dec 76.

[84]Karnow, "Diem Defeats His Own Best Generals," p. 26.

[85]Telg, Durbrow to Secy of State, 4 Dec 60, *U.S.-Vietnam Relations,* 10:1336.

[86]State Dept to Saigon, 12 Nov 60, 751k.00/11–1260, records of Dept of State.

developed paranoia. Since he felt his disregard for the chain of command and his insistence on personal command of army troops had been a major element in his salvation, he was now less inclined than ever to agree to any conventional military command arrangement, to delegate authority, or to appoint "outsiders" to positions of authority. At the same time, urban opponents of Diem, such as the Saigon professional and business classes, were disappointed by his failure to implement the reforms he had promised during the crisis, and senior army officers concluded that Diem and Nhu could not be bargained with. Next time, there would be no compromises.

The attempted coup failed to produce any noticeable change in American planning or policy in regard to South Vietnam except that Ambassador Durbrow withdrew his opposition to the proposed 20,000-man increase in the strength of the South Vietnamese Army.[87] He did so under pressure from General McGarr and the Defense Department and in the face of obvious escalation of insurgency by Communists in Laos as well as South Vietnam. A few days later, at the beginning of January 1961, Durbrow cabled the completed draft of the counterinsurgency plan to Washington.

The plan was based on the assumptions that "at the present time the Diem government offers the best hope" for defeating the Viet Cong, that the Diem government had "the basic potential to cope with the Viet Cong threat if necessary corrective measures were taken," and that the most vital task for the United States in Vietnam was to aid in the eradication of the Communist insurgency.[88] The plan provided for a 20,000-man increase in the South Vietnamese Army, financed by the United States at a cost of about $28 million. The Civil Guard was to be expanded to 68,000 men, with slightly less than half trained, equipped, and supplied at American expense. In return for this increased assistance, the South Vietnamese government was expected to implement a large number of measures designed to achieve and maintain political and economic stability and bring about the defeat of the Viet Cong. These measures included organizational and administrative reforms such as the establishment of a National Emergency Council and the appointment of a director of operations for counterinsurgency, transfer of the Civil Guard to the Ministry of Defense, and implementation of a coordinated intelligence and counterintelligence program and an effective program of psychological warfare and civic action. At the end of January, ten days after his inauguration, President John F. Kennedy approved the counterinsurgency plan and authorized the necessary funds to implement it.

While the counterinsurgency plan was being discussed, the Defense Department had done what it could unilaterally to aid the Vietnamese government in combating the insurgency. In April 1960 Diem had requested and had received more modern portable radio communicators (AN/PRC – 10s) to replace World War II–era signal equipment in the Vietnamese Army inven-

[87]Durbrow to State Dept, 29 Dec 60, 751k.00/12 – 2960, records of Dept of State.
[88]U.S. Plan for Counterinsurgency in South Vietnam, p. 4, Incl to Am Embassy, Saigon, to State Dept, 4 Jan 61. A copy of the plan is in Historians files, CMH. All quotations are from the plan and its annexes.

tory.[89] At the same time, the Vietnamese, with General Williams' endorsement, had requested eleven H – 34 helicopters to provide the means for rapid movement of army forces to points under attack by the Viet Cong. Since the H – 34 was the standard U.S. Army helicopter and the eleven aircraft would have to be taken from operational inventories, the request was at first refused by Washington. Some months later, under repeated urging from both McGarr and Durbrow, the Defense Department dispatched the helicopters to Vietnam.[90] Neither this additional material nor the counterinsurgency plan itself had much lasting impact.

The counterinsurgency plan would never be fully implemented, yet it represented a significant milestone in the long evolution of American policy in regard to South Vietnam. It was a tacit recognition that the American effort, begun by General O'Daniel and carried on primarily by General Williams, to create an army that could provide stability and internal security as well as defense against external aggression had failed and that new measures would be required if insurgency was to be suppressed.

But the counterinsurgency plan, while doubtlessly viewed as innovative by its authors, was really not a new departure. On the whole, the plan represented a culmination of the traditional American approach to Vietnamese problems. Its provisions for an expanded force structure, a better trained and better armed Civil Guard under the Defense Ministry, a clear, simplified, and rationalized chain of command, and an improved intelligence network were an amalgam of the major reforms which Americans in the advisory group had been urging since 1956. With the drastic deterioration of the security situation, American military leaders fell back on organizational, technical, and bureaucratic measures as the most appropriate devices to combat the Viet Cong.

Once again American leaders decided that added increments of military aid and organizational reforms were the proper solution and disregarded the advice of those who, like General Ridgway in 1955 and Ambassador Durbrow in 1960, had warned that the fundamental problem was primarily political and psychological. Most American leaders continued to believe that corruption and incompetence in the Vietnamese government and army, the rigidity and oppressiveness of the Diem regime, and the lack of effective social and economic reforms were problems that could be resolved simply by persuading or pressuring our ally into adopting the appropriate "programs" or administrative remedies. It was a pattern that was to be repeated on a greater and more tragic scale in the 1960s.

From the viewpoint of the new American president, the crisis in South Vietnam came at a critical time for the United States in international affairs.

---

[89]Memo, William T. McCormick for Secy of Army, 29 Apr 60, sub: Signal Equipment for Emergency Situation in Vietnam, I – 13735/60, ISA 413.44, RG 330.
[90]CINCPAC Command History, 1960, pp. 142 – 43; Msg, CHMAAG, Saigon, to CINCPAC, 01128 Nov 60, and Saigon to Secy of State, No. 956, 4 Nov 60, both in records of MAAG Vietnam, RG 334; Memo, Lt Col John S. D. Eisenhower for ASD, 12 Dec 60, I – 17621/60, ISA 452.1 Vietnam, RG 330.

By mid-1961 the Soviet Union was putting pressure on Berlin; an American-supported invasion force at the Bay of Pigs in Cuba had surrendered; and the United States and the Soviet Union had agreed in principle to a cease-fire in Laos and a neutral coalition government, an agreement that conceivably could lead to a Communist takeover. Lest what was happening in Laos cause the South Vietnamese to lose heart, Kennedy directed a sweeping reappraisal of the American position in South Vietnam. A new era in America's relations with Southeast Asia was beginning.

19

Assessment

Many people have come to regard the French Indochina War (1946–1954) as a rehearsal for the Vietnam War (1965–1973). Similarly, the early advisory period (1955–1960) to a degree foreshadows the period of Vietnamization during the Nixon and Ford administrations. True, there were important differences. The Military Assistance Advisory Group under Generals O'Daniel and Williams labored under advantages and disadvantages unknown to its successors in the 1960s and 1970s. The advantages were relative peace and calm in the countryside, especially from 1956 to 1958, and a relatively strong, stable civil government in Saigon. The disadvantages were the restrictions imposed by the Geneva Agreements on the size and activities of the military advisory effort, the strong budgetary constraints of the Eisenhower era, and the lack of attention and interest on the part of Washington leaders to the problems of Vietnam between 1956 and 1960. Another important difference was that in the Vietnamization years the United States was phasing down its military and civilian involvement.[1] During the late 1950s, the degree of American involvement was relatively stable.

Yet despite the differences the two periods share a common overriding theme. In both the early advisory stage and the later period of Vietnamization, American leaders were attempting to help the Vietnamese armed forces attain an ability to hold their own against their enemies without the assistance of large numbers of U.S. or other allied ground forces. In the 1950s this policy was precipitated by the rapid withdrawal of French combat forces from Vietnam and the inability of American forces to replace them because of limitations imposed by the Geneva Agreements and the New Look defense policy of the Eisenhower administration.

---

[1]Vietnamization had a wide number of definitions, but generally was taken to mean the assumption by the government and armed forces of the Republic of Vietnam of all aspects of the war effort, together with the policies and techniques employed to expedite this assumption of responsibility. For a fuller discussion of Vietnamization, see DF, Col Howard W. Keller, MAC J–3, 9 Nov 69, sub: Definition and Meaning of Vietnamization, copy in CMH.

Senior Advisers' Conference Participants, January 1960

1. Col. P. T. Boleyn
2. Brig. Gen. J. B. Lampert
   Deputy Chief, MAAG, Logistics
3. Lt. Col. Lu Lan
4. Brig. Gen. Pham Xuan Chieu
   Chief of Staff, ARVN
5. Col. E. J. Ingmire
6. Lt. Gen. S. T. Williams
   Chief, MAAG, Vietnam
7. Col. C. A. Symroski
8. Col. S. G. Brown, Jr.
9. Maj. Gen. J. F. Ruggles
10. Col. J. T. Barrett
    Deputy Chief, MAAG, Training
11. Col. N. P. Ward III
12. Col. A. P. Rollins
    Chief of Staff
13. Capt. J. J. Flachsenhar
14. Lt. Col. Tran Ngoc Nhan
15. Col. R. R. Patterson
16. Col. E. P. Lasche
17. Col. E. J. Stann
18. Col. R. M. Miner
19. Col. R. E. Daehler
20. Col. J. E. Robb
21. Col. S. J. Razor
22. Col. L. E. Wellendorf
23. Col. J. J. Butler
24. Col. A. L. Leonard
25. Col. L. D. Fargo
26. Col. W. W. Stromberg
27. Lt. Col. B. B. Caulder
28. Col. M. C. Taylor
29. Col. D. M. Witt
30. Col. J. C. Speedie
31. Col. J. A. Ulrich
32. Maj. Dang Van Khuyen
33. Lt. Col. F. R. Wilkinson
34. Lt. Col. W. W. Roberts
35. Lt. Col. D. C. Wade
36. Comdr. J. P. Wicks
37. Lt. Col. W. F. Tucker
38. Lt. Col. T. J. Farrell, Jr.
39. Lt. Col. E. C. Davis
40. Lt. Col. C. P. Sirles
41. Lt. Col. A. G. Johnson
42. Col. G. R. True
43. Lt. Col. J. P. Sheffey III
44. Lt. Col. M. Kusiv
45. Lt. Col. E. H. Thomas
46. Maj. R. H. Bolan
47. Lt. Col. J. E. Olson
48. Col. J. R. Kent
49. Lt. Col. W. L. Willey
50. Lt. Col. E. D. Fitzpatrick
51. Lt. Col. C. H. Cole, Jr.
52. Lt. Col. M. P. Stockton
53. Maj. T. P. Carroll
54. Lt. Col. D. R. Rose
55. Maj. C. W. Thomas
56. Lt. Col. J. R. Michael
57. Maj. J. C. Marschhausen
58. Maj. M. Barszcz
59. Lt. Col. W. T. Drake
60. Maj. F. H. Serafini
61. Maj. K. J. Miller
62. Maj. J. H. Selden
63. Maj. L. A. Brown
64. Maj. W. Mule
65. Maj. Nguyen Phu Sanh
66. Lt. Col. D. E. MacDonald
67. Maj. Nguyen Vinh Nghi
68. Lt. Col. N. Dunlap
69. Maj. R. H. Oestreich
70. Maj. F. A. Mulroney
71. Lt. Col. R. Kinnes
72. Lt. Col. W. R. Bond
73. Lt. Col. C. E. Burner

Senior Advisers' Conference Participants, January 1960

In both cases the Vietnamization effort ended in failure. The reasons for the failure of the second Vietnamization are still being assessed; the reasons for the failure of the first are easier to delineate. In the 1950s American military aims in Vietnam were never clearly defined. Although many Washington leaders believed that Communist subversion was a greater threat to South Vietnam than an overt, large-scale invasion, U.S. contingency planning tended to emphasize the latter. The chiefs of the Military Assistance Advisory Group therefore understandably tended to concentrate on building an army geared to resist attack from the North. In doing so they were merely following contemporary thinking, for in the 1950s, in contrast to the 1960s, there was little interest in, or knowledge of, counterinsurgency warfare within the U.S. armed forces.

The need for a capable security force to deal with the threat of internal subversion was not ignored. Yet responsibility for the training and equipping of paramilitary forces such as the Civil Guard and the Self-Defense Corps was vested not in the advisory group but in other agencies of the U.S. country team, agencies which differed radically in their view of the proper mission, composition, and employment of these forces. This disagreement was further complicated by delays, bureaucratic infighting, and personality clashes. The result was that when insurgency once again became a serious threat in 1959, the paramilitary forces were still unprepared, untrained, and unequipped to cope with it.

Consequently, the Vietnamese Army had to be directly committed against the Communist insurgents. Its indifferent performance in combat against the Viet Cong even after four years of U.S. support and training can be attributed to two sets of factors. The first involved weaknesses inherent in the Vietnamese Army as an institution. The rampant politicization in the higher ranks of the officer corps had enabled incompetent but politically reliable officers to attain and retain positions of responsibility and high command. An absence of unifying national spirit, motivation, or patriotism on the part of most Vietnamese soldiers reflected the lack of any widespread popular support for the Diem regime. Another factor was the poor security system of the army and its penetration at all levels by Viet Cong agents. Still another important element was the system of divided authority, routine insubordination, and overlapping responsibility deliberately fostered by Diem within the army's command system to ensure that no military leader became too powerful. Added to this pattern was the inadequate technical competence of the Vietnamese combat soldier, who was often a recent conscript whose training had been interrupted or never started. Contemporary critics also pointed to the lack of specific training for guerrilla warfare, yet the Vietnamese Army's level of proficiency in basic combat skills was often so low as to make the question of specialized training irrelevant.

At the same time, the very organization, composition, and outlook of the Military Assistance Advisory Group ensured that the American advisers would remain either unaware of these inherent deficiencies or powerless to change them. The so-called short tour limited most U.S. advisers to less than eleven months in which to win the confidence of their Vietnamese counter- parts and influence them to take needed measures to increase the effective- ness of their units. A wide gap in customs and culture also separated the advisers from their counterparts, a gap made wider by the small number of American officers able to communicate in any language other than English.

The limited ability of U.S. advisers to influence their counterparts holds true even for General Williams. He enjoyed President Diem's trust and confi- dence to an extent probably equaled by few other Americans, yet Williams' remark that "I can't remember one time that President Diem ever did any- thing of importance concerning the military that I recommended against" is surely an exaggeration.[2] General Williams was unable to induce Diem to abandon favoritism in the appointment of officers, to rationalize the chain of command, or to abandon the project to create ranger battalions out of existing army formations. Moreover, Williams' closeness to Diem inclined him, in the view of some observers, to identify so closely with the president that he resisted and attempted to blunt all criticism of Diem, whether well founded or otherwise.

The success of an adviser was measured by his ability to influence his Vietnamese counterpart. Few were willing to report forthrightly that they had been unable to bring about needed reforms and improvements in the units to which they were assigned. Since the whole system of rating the performance of the Vietnamese Army was built upon the subjective, nonstandardized evaluations made by the advisers and their superiors, Saigon and Washington were guaranteed a superficial assessment. The dogged "Can Do" attitude of most officers and noncommissioned officers who tended to see all faults in the army as correctable, all failures as temporary, only further contributed to overoptimistic reports.

Considering the small size of the Military Assistance Advisory Group and the many limitations imposed upon its activities, its accomplishments with the weak, demoralized, divided, and disorganized army it inherited in 1955 represent a remarkable achievement. The complete reorganization of the Vietnamese Army, the establishment of a well-conceived and comprehensive school and training system, and the introduction, at least on paper, of a rationalized chain of command were only a few of the advisory group's solid contributions. Yet the subsequent failure of the South Vietnamese Army as an effective fighting force can only underline the warning which the Joint Chiefs of Staff gave to Secretary of State Dulles in 1954: that strong and stable governments and societies are necessary to support the creation of strong armies. That the reverse is seldom true would be clearly and tragically demon- strated in the years to follow.

---

[2]"Why U.S. is Losing in Vietnam," *U.S. News and World Report*, 9 November 1964.

Bibliographical Note

Official Records

Official records used in the preparation of this work fall into two broad categories: those that have been accessioned by the National Archives and are identifiable by record group (RG) number, and those still in the custody of various government agencies that have not been evaluated or processed by an archivist. The latter only occasionally have identifying numbers; since these numbers will lose their identifying function once the records have been processed by the Archives, they have not been included in citations. Copies of many of the documents cited in the footnotes have been collected and are on file in the U.S. Army Center of Military History (CMH), from which they will be retired for permanent retention.

Of fundamental importance for this volume are the records, in the National Archives, of the War Department general and special staffs (RG 165) and the succeeding records of the Army staff (RG 319), particularly the files of the Office of the Assistant Chief of Staff for Operations (ACofS G – 3) and the Office of the Deputy Chief of Staff for Military Operations (DCSOPS). Also of special interest are the files of the Office of the Chief of Psychological Warfare (PSYWAR), a subordinate agency of G – 3. Records (RG 334) of the Military Assistance Advisory Group (MAAG), Indochina (later Military Assistance Advisory Group, Vietnam), are spotty for most of the 1950s. They are supplemented by the excellent and extensive records of the Office of the Assistant Chief of Staff for Intelligence (ACSI), which contain reports and messages by attaches in Southeast Asia and intelligence material passed to the United States by the French and Vietnamese governments. Of particular value are the so-called G – 2 ID files (RG 165), a reference collection incorporating not only intelligence documents originated by the Army but information received from foreign governments, the State Department, and other U.S. intelligence agencies.

The files of the Department of State frequently provide the best record of American activities and policies in regard to Indochina, particularly for the period prior to the 1954 Geneva Conference. The most important are the 851G and 751G decimal files, which contain State Department messages and memorandums and also messages and reports by the Military Assistance Advisory Group that have not been preserved elsewhere. Also significant are the files of the Office of Philippine and Southeast Asian Affairs, which contain valuable material on policy discussions within the State Department and between the department and other agencies. The State Department Historical Division's Documentary History of U.S. Policy Toward Indochina, prepared in 1954, also contains many useful items not easily found elsewhere in the records.

The records of the Joint Chiefs of Staff (RG 218) are another valuable source for the study of high-level policymaking. In addition, the JCS Historical Division has prepared two manuscript histories—History of the Indochina Incident, 1940 – 1954, and The Joint Chiefs of Staff and the War in Vietnam, 1954 – 1959—which are excellent guides to the JCS records. Files of other agencies of the Defense Department relating to Indochina are thin for most of the 1950s. However, some materials may be found in the records of the Office of the Assistant Secretary of Defense for International Security Affairs (ASD, ISA) and the Office of Military Assistance (OMA), both in RG 330, National Archives.

The Dwight D. Eisenhower Library in Abilene, Kansas, holds the minutes of National Security Council (NSC) meetings during 1953 – 60 and other significant documents relating to the policy of the Eisenhower administration toward Indochina. The Central Intelligence Agency (CIA) made available records relating to OSS (Office of Strategic Services) activities in Southeast Asia during and immediately after World War II and unevaluated field intelligence reports, mostly relating to the political situation in South Vietnam and internal security problems there during the late 1950s.

Finally, the records of two important field commands are of significant value in tracing the evolution of U.S. policy and action during World War II: the records of the China theater (RG 332, National Archives), particularly General Albert C. Wedemeyer's personal files, and the records of Southeast Asia Command (WO 203, Public Records Office, London). British Foreign Office records regarding Indochina in FO 371 were also consulted. Also of interest is the History of U.S. Forces in the China Theater, a manuscript in the Center of Military History.

Personal Collections

By far the most important collection of personal papers for this volume were the files generously made available by Lt. Gen. Samuel T. Williams. Comprising the personal and official correspondence, message files, and memorandums of General Williams during his tour of duty as chief of the Military Assistance Advisory Group in Vietnam, they constitute almost a documentary history of that organization. Also of primary significance are the papers of former Army Chief of Staff J. Lawton Collins pertaining to his special mission to Vietnam, 1954 – 55, and the papers of Lt. Gen. John W. O'Daniel concerning his several visits to Vietnam and duty as chief of the Military Assistance Advisory Group. The Collins Papers have been deposited in the National Archives; the O'Daniel Papers are in the Center of Military History.

Through the kindness of Madame la Marechale de Lattre de Tassigny, the author was permitted to examine a portion of the papers of Marshal de Lattre relating to Indochina, a valuable source for the French view of the conflict. The papers of Maj. Gen. Philip E. Gallagher in the Center of Military History are important for an understanding of the U.S. Army role in Vietnam during the period of the August Revolution. Other papers examined include the Matthew B. Ridgway Papers, U.S. Army Military History Institute, Carlisle Barracks, Pennsylvania, and the Arthur W. Radford and Milton E. Miles Papers at the U.S. Naval Historical Center, Washington, D.C.

Interviews

Many individuals with firsthand experience of the events described in the volume generously agreed to provide oral history interviews. Many also read and commented on the manuscript in draft form. These individuals include Maj. Gen. Philip E. Gallagher, Kenneth P. Landon, Maj. Gen. Robert B. McClure, Abbot Low Moffat, Archimedes L. A. Patti, Reginald Ungern, Col. R. F. C. Vance, General Albert C. Wedemeyer, Frank White, and James R. Withrow, who discussed the World War II period. Col. Donald Dunn, Lt. Gen. James M. Gavin, Ambassador Edmund Gullion, Lt. Gen. John W. O'Daniel, Charlton Ogburn, General Matthew B. Ridgway, and His Excellency M. Jean Sainteny discussed the period of the Franco–Viet Minh War. Lt. Col. Edward M. Dannemiller, Lt. Gen. George Forsythe, Col. James Muir, Lt. Gen. Samuel L. Myers, Col. John E. Robb, Maj. Gen. John F. Ruggles, Col. Eugene Stann, Brig. Gen. Charles A. Symroski, and Col. Nathaniel P. Ward, all former officers in the Military Assistance Advisory Group, contributed their recollections as did General Williams himself. Ambassador Leland Barrows, Christian A. Chapman, Col. Richard H. Comstock, Ambassador Elbridge Durbrow, Gerald C. Hickey, and Rufus Phillips provided other perspectives from within the U.S. mission.

Generals Williams and O'Daniel were interviewed by Charles B. MacDonald and Charles V. P. von Luttichau of the Center of Military History. All other interviews, as well as a second one with O'Daniel, were conducted by the author. Transcripts of most of these interviews are on file at the Center of Military History. The author also consulted summaries of interviews conducted by the JCS Historical Division in 1954 with former officers of the Military Assistance Advisory Group, Indochina.

The Dulles Oral History Collection at Princeton University contains a number of interviews which shed light on the Eisenhower policies toward Indochina, especially the Dien Bien Phu crisis. However, their value is limited by the fact that the interviewers apparently had little or no specialized knowledge of this subject. The interviews therefore need to be carefully checked against the documentary records now becoming available. Other oral history interviews of value are those of General Graves B. Erskine and Col. Victor J. Croizat in the U.S. Marine Corps Oral History Collection, Marine Corps Historical Center.

Memoirs

A number of individuals who figured prominently in this work have written their own account of events. The most important are Dean Acheson, *Present at the Creation: My Years in the State Department* (New York: W. W. Norton, 1969); J. Lawton Collins, *Lightning Joe: An Autobiography* (Baton Rouge: Louisiana State University Press, 1979); Tran Van Don, *Our Endless War: Inside Vietnam* (San Rafael, Calif.: Presidio, 1978); Edward G. Lansdale, *In the Midst of Wars* (New York: Harper & Row, 1972); Paul Ely, *L'Indochine dans la Tourmente* (Paris: Librairie Plon, 1964); Henri Navarre, *L'Agonie de L'Indochine* (Paris: Librairie Plon, 1956); Matthew Ridgway, *Soldier: The Memoirs of Matthew B. Ridgway* (New York: Harper & Bros., 1956); and Jean Sainteny, *Histoire d'une Paix Manquee* (Paris: Fayard, 1967).

The memoirs of Admiral Arthur Radford, *From Pearl Harbor to Vietnam: The Memoirs of Admiral Arthur W. Radford*, ed. Stephen Jurika, Jr. (Stanford, Calif.: Hoover Institution Press, 1980), and Archimedes L. Patti, *Why Vietnam: Prelude to America's Albatross* (Berkeley: University of California Press, 1981), appeared too late to be used in this work. However, Mr. Patti generously called the attention of the author to the documents on which his account is based. Likewise the Radford memoirs are based, in large part, on the JCS records to which the author had access.

Printed Works

In addition to the diplomatic documents published in the Department of State *Foreign Relations of the United States* series, now available through 1954, two other documentary collections are of special value. The first is the famous Pentagon Papers, a documentary history of the war up to 1967 prepared by the Department of Defense. Of the various editions, that published by the U.S. Government Printing Office *(United States – Vietnam Relations, 1945 – 1967: A Study Prepared by the Department of Defense*, 12 vols. [Washington, 1971]) is by far the most extensive. However several documents which do not appear there may be found in *The Senator Gravel Edition of the Pentagon Papers*, 4 vols. (Boston: Beacon Press, 1971). The second collection of note is Gareth Porter, ed., *Vietnam: The Definitive Documentation of Human Decisions*, 2 vols. (Stanfordville, N.Y.: Coleman Enterprises, 1979) which, while far from definitive, contains a large number of hard-to-locate and not previously published items.

Some Significant Secondary Works

On the rise of nationalism and communism in Vietnam two works are indispensable: John T. McAlister and Paul Mus, *The Vietnamese and Their Revolution* (New York: Harper & Row, 1970), and John T. McAlister, *Vietnam: The Origins of Revolution* (Garden City, N.Y.: Doubleday, 1971). Of equal importance are studies by two scholars familiar with Vietnamese sources: Alexander B. Woodside, *Community and Revolution in Modern Vietnam* (Boston: Houghton Mifflin, 1976) and William J. Duiker, *The Rise of Nationalism in Vietnam: 1900–1941* (Ithaca: Cornell University Press, 1976). Also useful is David G. Marr, *Vietnamese Anticolonialism, 1885–1925* (Berkeley: University of

California Press, 1971). Of the older works, Joseph Buttinger's *Vietnam: A Dragon Embattled*, 2 vols. (New York: Praeger, 1967), remains a mine of information, especially on French policy. The various works by Bernard B. Fall—*The Two Vietnams: A Political and Military Analysis*, 2d ed. rev. (New York: Praeger, 1967), *Last Reflections on a War* (Garden City, N.Y.: Doubleday, 1967), and *Viet-Nam Witness: 1953–55* (New York: Praeger, 1966)—must be used with caution because of their strong pro-French bias. ⅄

On the military aspects of the First Indochina War, Bernard Fall, *Street Without Joy*, 4th ed. (Harrisburg, Pa.: Stackpole Co., 1967) and Edgar O'Ballance, *The Indochina War, 1945 – 54: A Study in Guerrilla Warfare* (London: Faber & Faber, 1964) remain the only general works in English, although they are inadequate and sometimes inaccurate as to details. Ronald E. Irving, *The First Indochina War: French and American Policy, 1945–54* (London: C. Helm, 1975) is very good on French domestic politics and policymaking. There is no general history of U.S. policy toward Indochina during the 1940s and 1950s. George C. Herring's *America's Longest War: The United States and Vietnam, 1950–1975* (New York: Wiley, 1979) is the most recent narrative based on primary sources, but it is brief and superficial concerning these years.

Communist policies and actions for this period are even more poorly documented. Most of the serious studies of Viet Cong organization and operations between 1954 – 60 rely on the same handful of captured documents, most of them of unknown reliability. The best guides through this maze are Jeffrey Race, *War Comes to Long An* (Berkeley: University of California Press, 1972), Robert L. Sansom, *The Economics of Insurgency in the Mekong Delta of Vietnam* (Cambridge, Mass.: MIT Press, 1970), Carlyle A. Thayer, "South Vietnamese Revolutionary Organizations and the Vietnamese Workers Party" in Joseph J. Zasloff and McAlister Brown, ed., *Communism in Indochina* (Lexington, Mass.: Lexington Books, 1971), and William J. Duiker, *The Communist Road to Power in Vietnam* (Boulder, Colo.: Westview Press, 1981). Professor Duiker kindly made available to the author portions of his draft manuscript, which are cited in this work.

Index